THE STR...

WITH
THE V...

D1492562

Tr...
Le...
Co...
Editor: Tania Biswas

SHIKKAKUMON NO SAIKYOKENJA Volume 1
©Shinkoshoto / SB Creative Corp.
Original Character Designs: ©Huuka Kazabana
©Friendly Land/SQUARE ENIX CO., LTD.
First published in Japan in 2017 by SQUARE ENIX CO., LTD.
English translation rights arranged with SQUARE ENIX
CO., LTD. and SQUARE ENIX, INC.
English translation © 2020 by SQUARE ENIX CO., LTD.

ISBN: 978-1-64609-040-2

Library of Congress Cataloging-in-Publication
Data is on file with the publisher.

Printed in the U.S.A.
First printing, August 2020
10 9 8 7 6 5 4 3 2 1

SQUARE ENIX
MANGA & BOOKS
www.square-enix-books.com

THE STRONGEST SAGE GOES CAMPING

by **Shinkoshoto**

A few days had passed since the announcement of our exam results. As newly admitted students to the academy, we were sent into the woods near the capital for the time-honored "Camping Training."

"I hope you were all listening this morning..." barked the headmaster, "...since I won't be repeating the rules again. And I take it you remember your assigned parties?"

The training saw us split into groups of three, and my partners just happened to be some familiar faces.

"Good to have ya on the team, Li'l Matty," said Alma.

"P-pleasure to be working with you!" added Lurie.

"Sure thing. We'll get it done!" I replied.

In terms of Crest distribution, we were well-balanced.

Greetings exchanged, the headmaster started afresh.

"First, the hunting trial! As explained earlier, you'll be hunting monsters and competing to bag the most valuable prizes! Any questions?" he said, surveying the group.

Nobody made a peep.

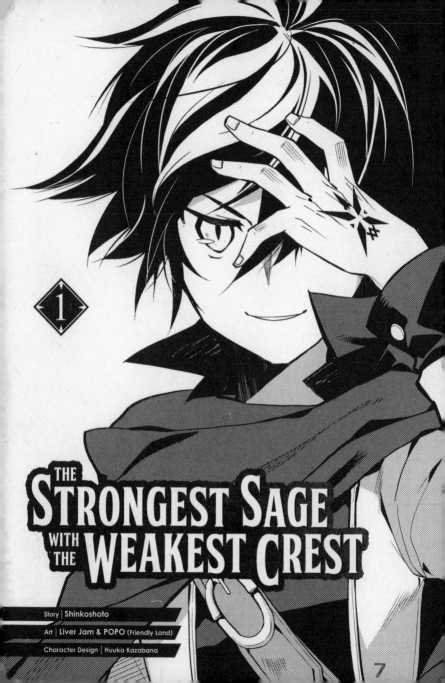

THE
STRONGEST SAGE
WITH
THE WEAKEST CREST

Story | Shinkoshoto

Art | Liver Jam & POPO (Friendly Land)

Character Design | Huuka Kazabana

Contents

THE STRONGEST SAGE WITH THE WEAKEST CREST

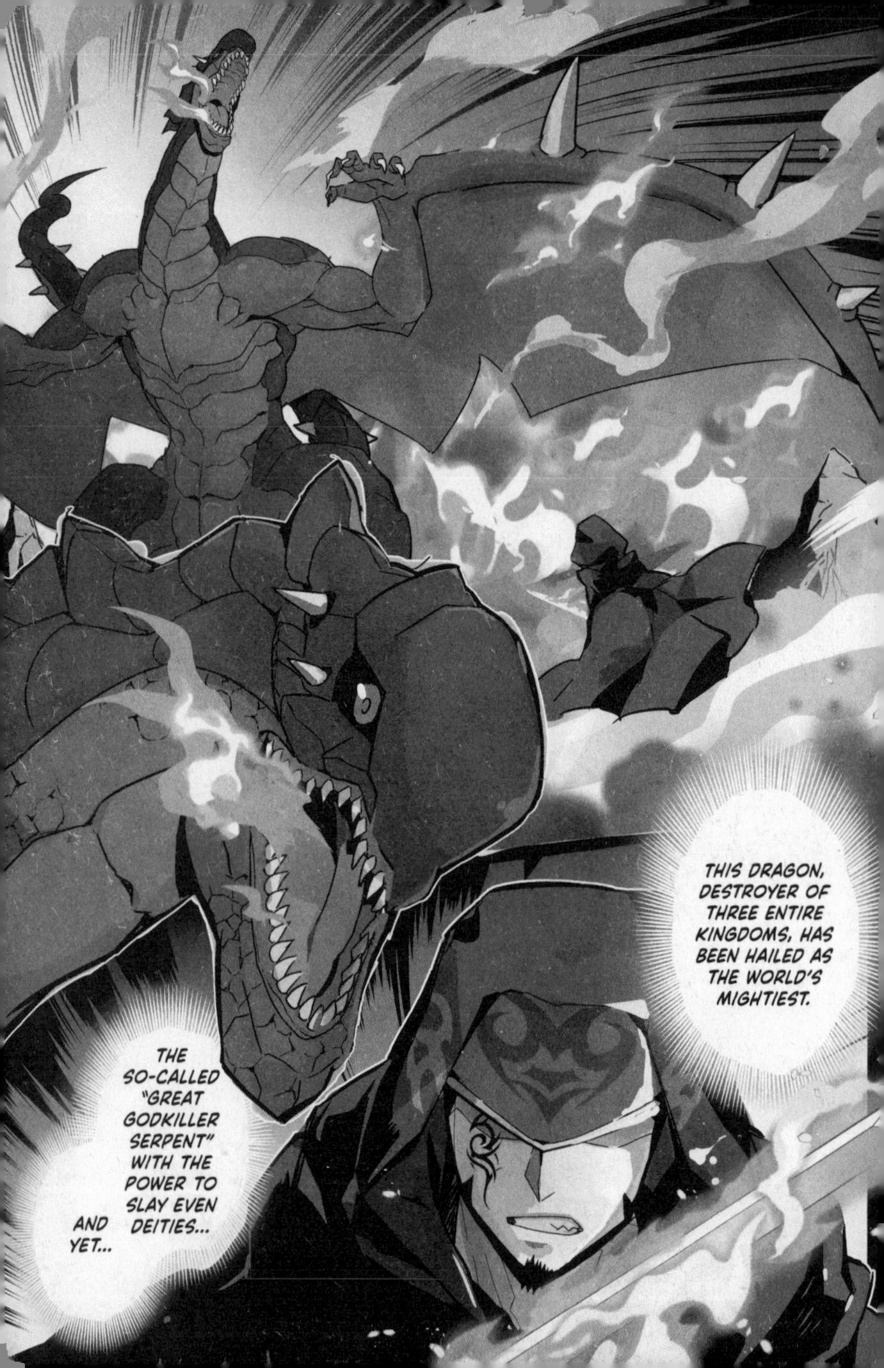
THIS DRAGON, DESTROYER OF THREE ENTIRE KINGDOMS, HAS BEEN HAILED AS THE WORLD'S MIGHTIEST.
THE SO-CALLED "GREAT GODKILLER SERPENT" WITH THE POWER TO SLAY EVEN DEITIES...
AND YET...

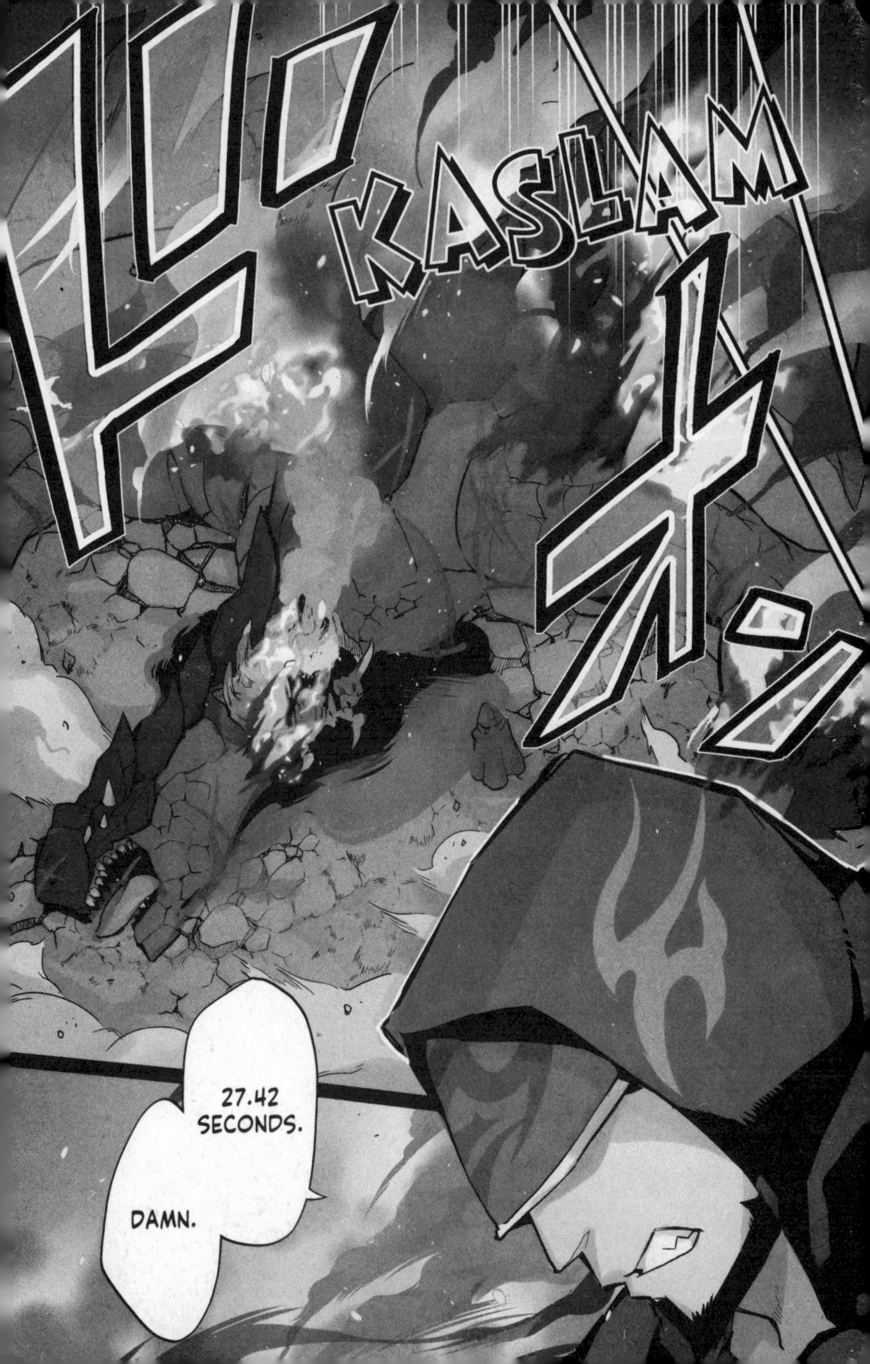
KASLAM
27.42 SECONDS.
DAMN.

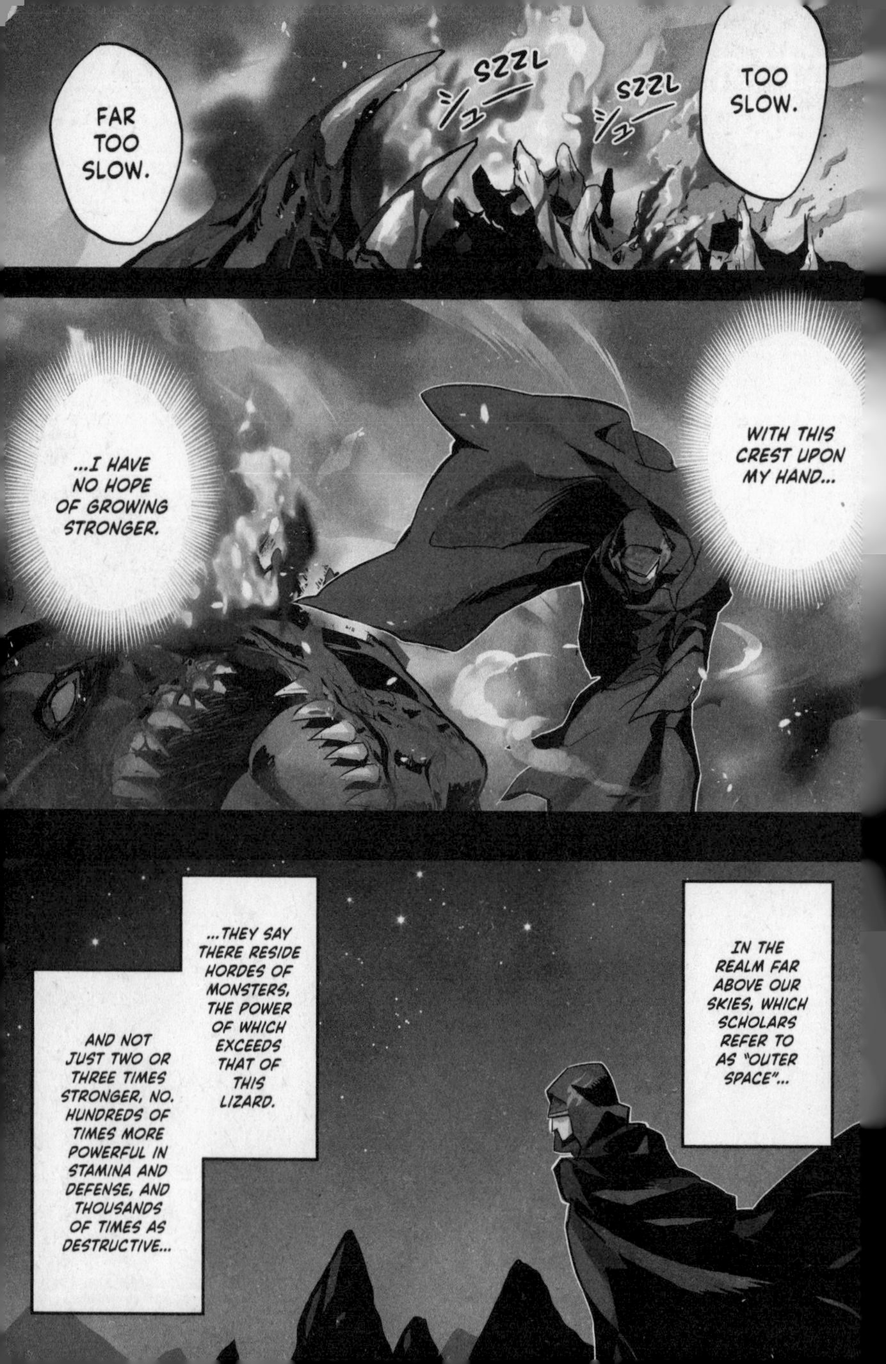
TOO SLOW.
SZZL シュー
SZZL シュー
FAR TOO SLOW.
WITH THIS CREST UPON MY HAND...
...I HAVE NO HOPE OF GROWING STRONGER.
IN THE REALM FAR ABOVE OUR SKIES, WHICH SCHOLARS REFER TO AS "OUTER SPACE"...
...THEY SAY THERE RESIDE HORDES OF MONSTERS, THE POWER OF WHICH EXCEEDS THAT OF THIS LIZARD.
AND NOT JUST TWO OR THREE TIMES STRONGER, NO. HUNDREDS OF TIMES MORE POWERFUL IN STAMINA AND DEFENSE, AND THOUSANDS OF TIMES AS DESTRUCTIVE...

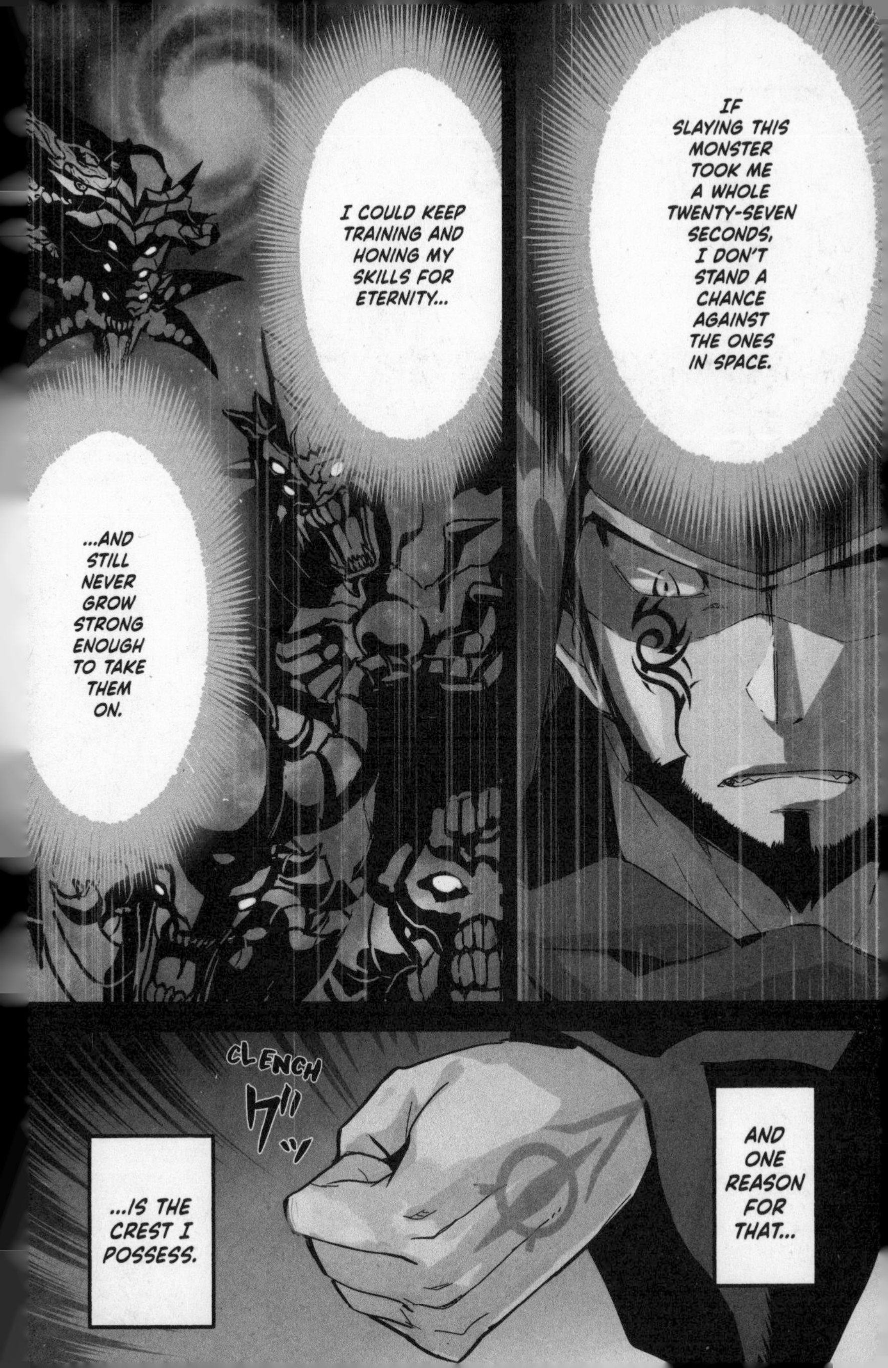
IF SLAYING THIS MONSTER TOOK ME A WHOLE TWENTY-SEVEN SECONDS, I DON'T STAND A CHANCE AGAINST THE ONES IN SPACE.
I COULD KEEP TRAINING AND HONING MY SKILLS FOR ETERNITY...
...AND STILL NEVER GROW STRONG ENOUGH TO TAKE THEM ON.
AND ONE REASON FOR THAT...
CLENCH
グッ
...IS THE CREST I POSSESS.

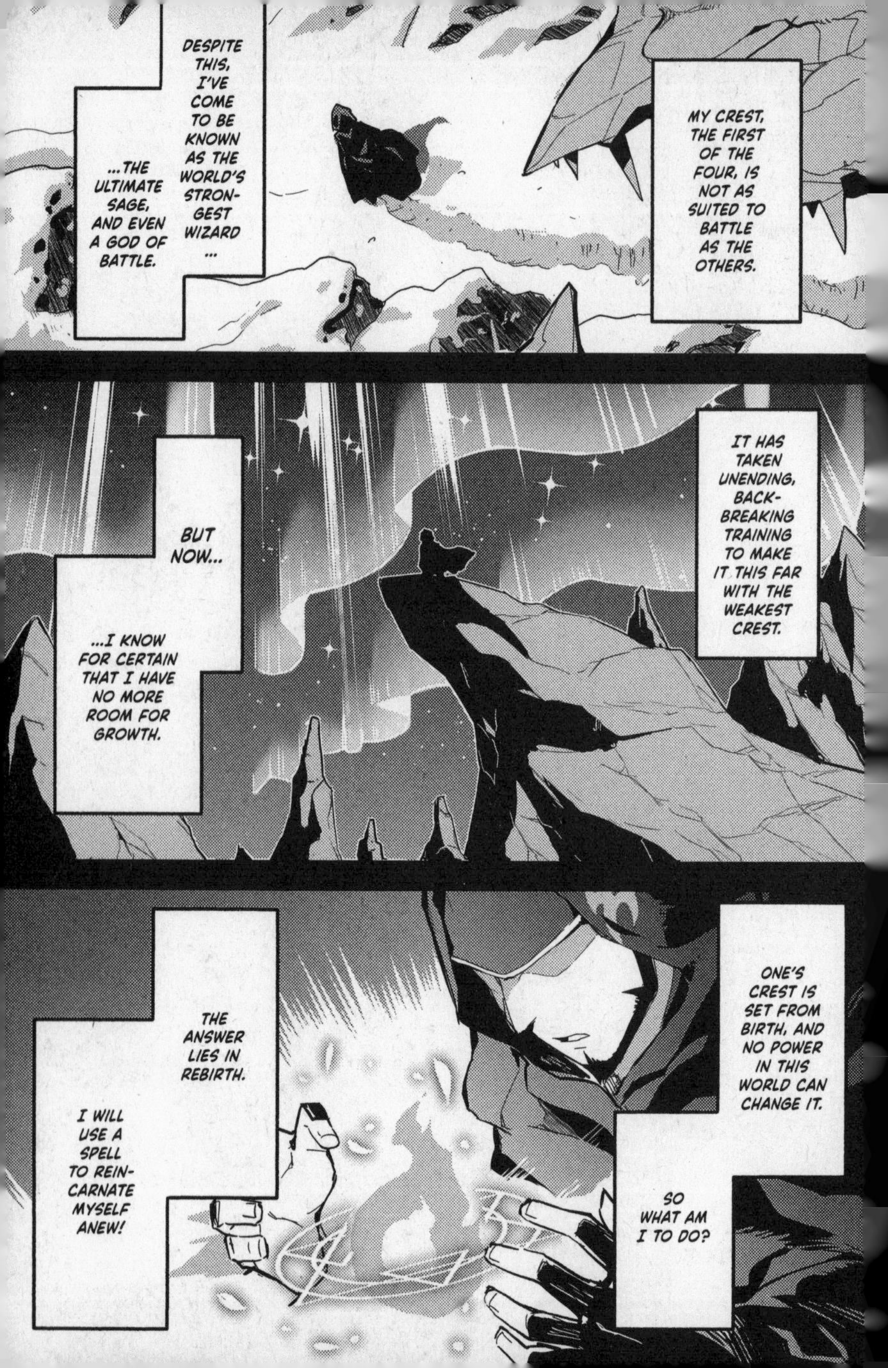
MY CREST, THE FIRST OF THE FOUR, IS NOT AS SUITED TO BATTLE AS THE OTHERS.
DESPITE THIS, I'VE COME TO BE KNOWN AS THE WORLD'S STRONGEST WIZARD...
...THE ULTIMATE SAGE, AND EVEN A GOD OF BATTLE.
IT HAS TAKEN UNENDING, BACK-BREAKING TRAINING TO MAKE IT THIS FAR WITH THE WEAKEST CREST.
BUT NOW...
...I KNOW FOR CERTAIN THAT I HAVE NO MORE ROOM FOR GROWTH.
ONE'S CREST IS SET FROM BIRTH, AND NO POWER IN THIS WORLD CAN CHANGE IT.
SO WHAT AM I TO DO?
THE ANSWER LIES IN REBIRTH.
I WILL USE A SPELL TO REINCARNATE MYSELF ANEW!

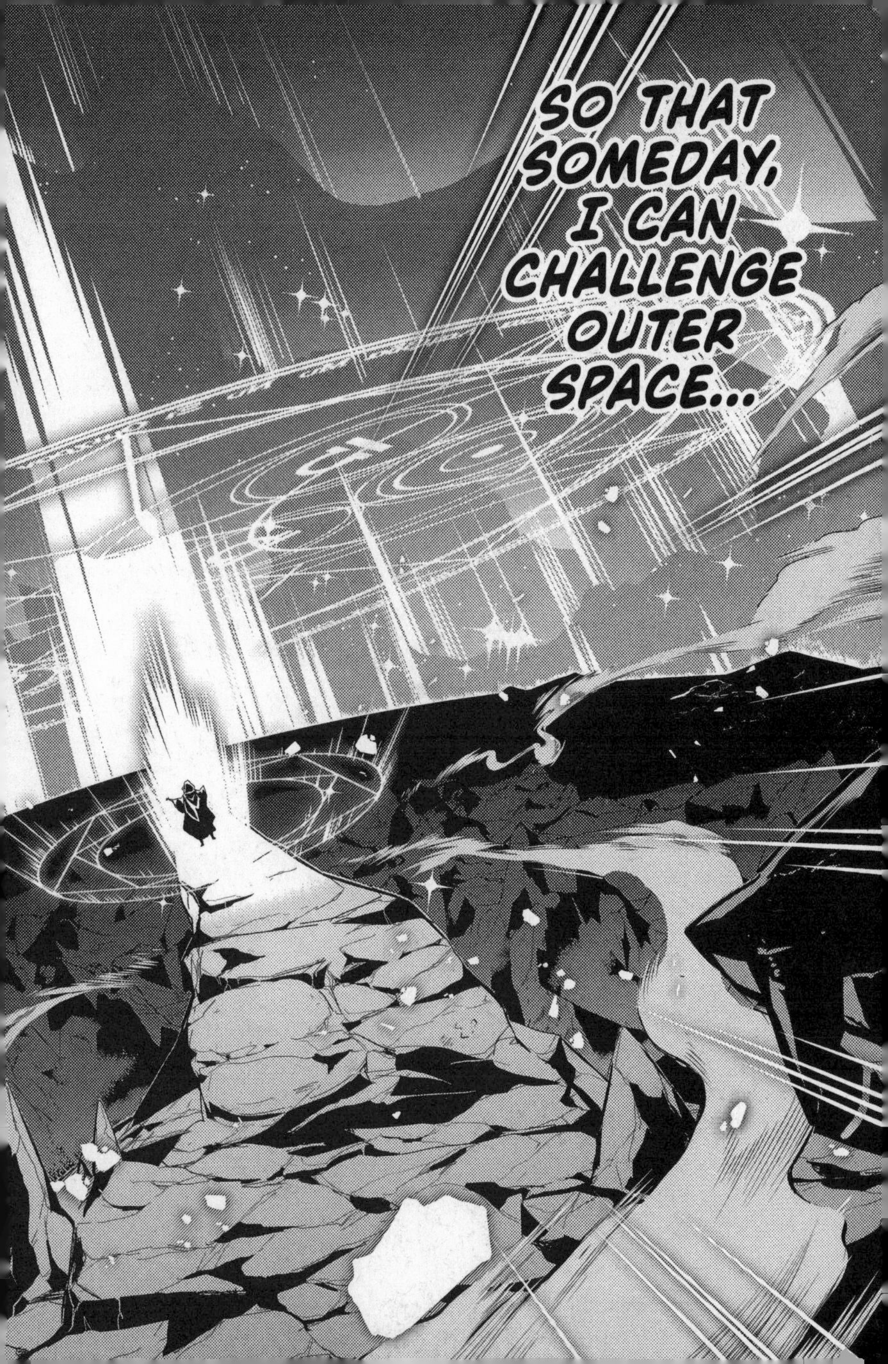
SO THAT SOMEDAY, I CAN CHALLENGE OUTER SPACE...

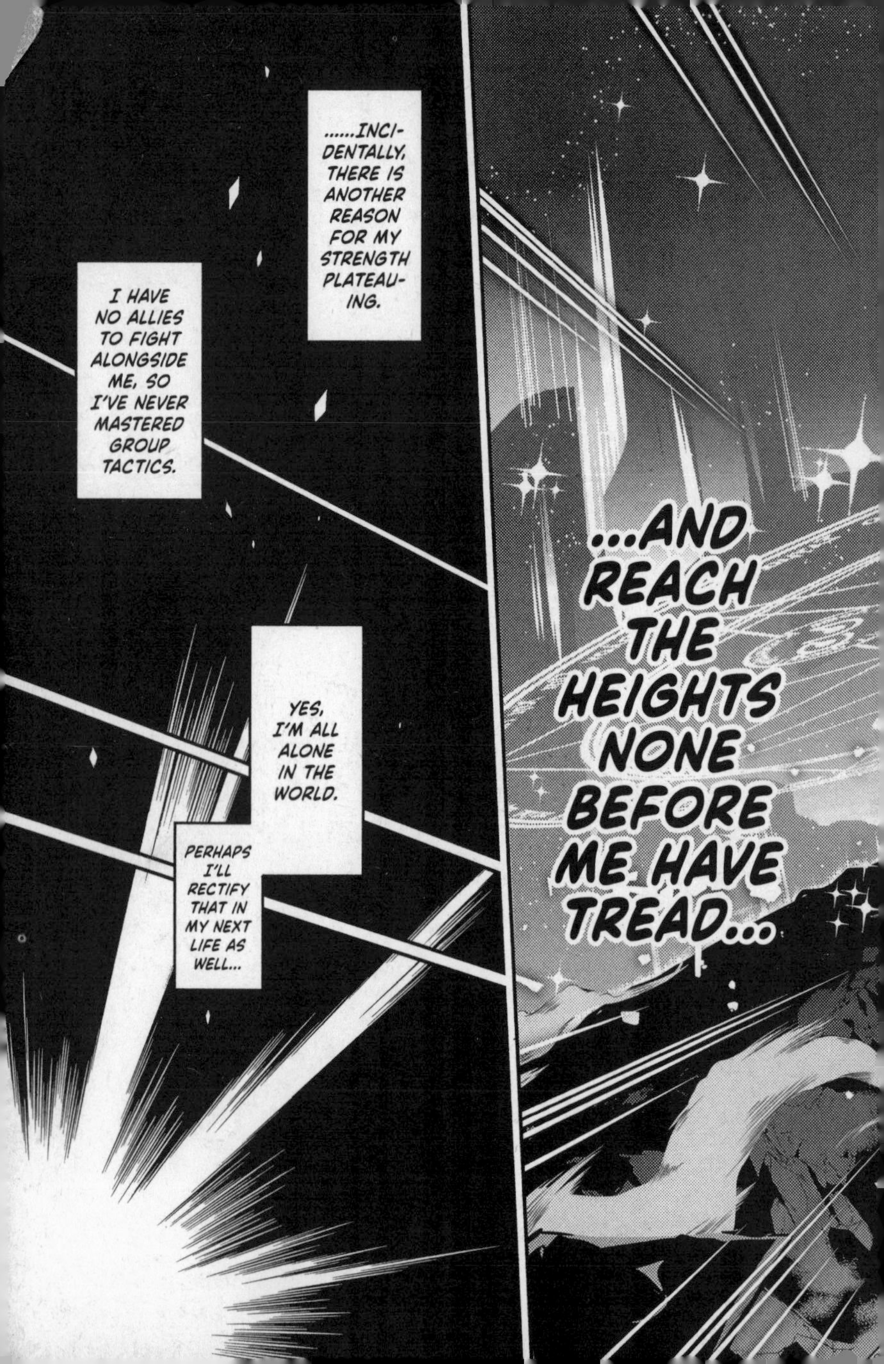
...AND REACH THE HEIGHTS NONE BEFORE ME HAVE TREAD...
......INCIDENTALLY, THERE IS ANOTHER REASON FOR MY STRENGTH PLATEAUING.
I HAVE NO ALLIES TO FIGHT ALONGSIDE ME, SO I'VE NEVER MASTERED GROUP TACTICS.
YES, I'M ALL ALONE IN THE WORLD.
PERHAPS I'LL RECTIFY THAT IN MY NEXT LIFE AS WELL...

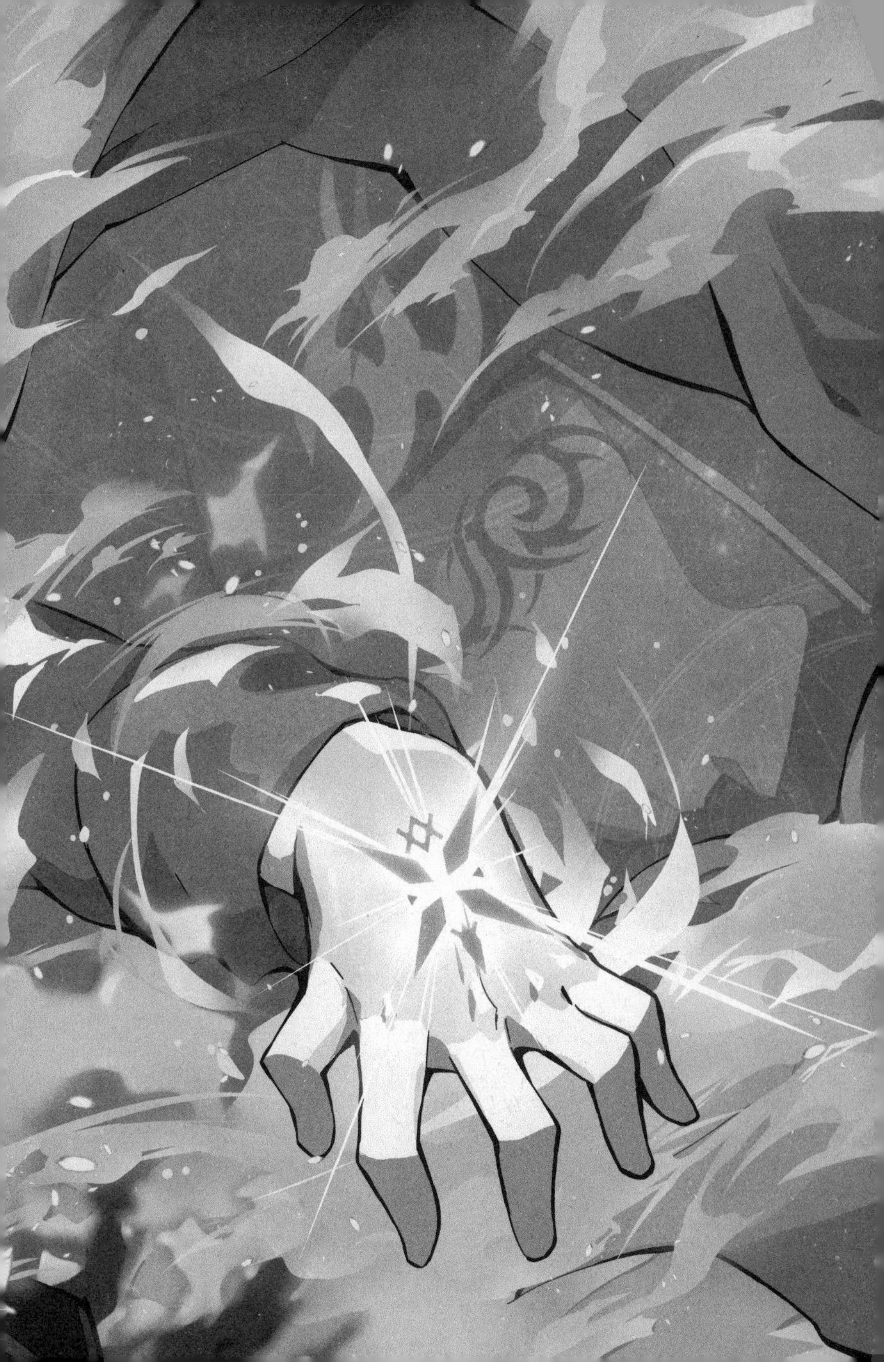

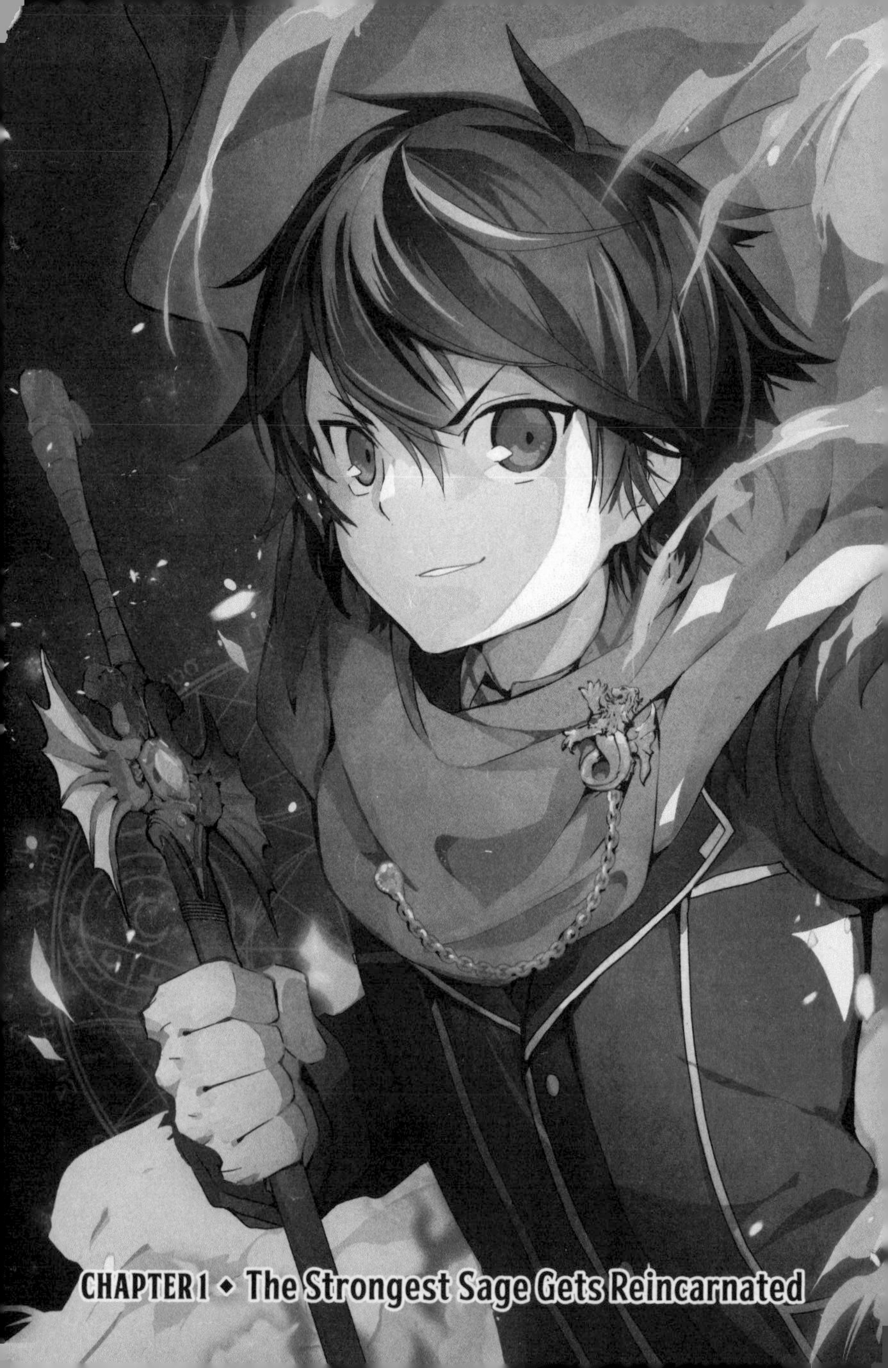

CHAPTER 1 ◆ The Strongest Sage Gets Reincarnated

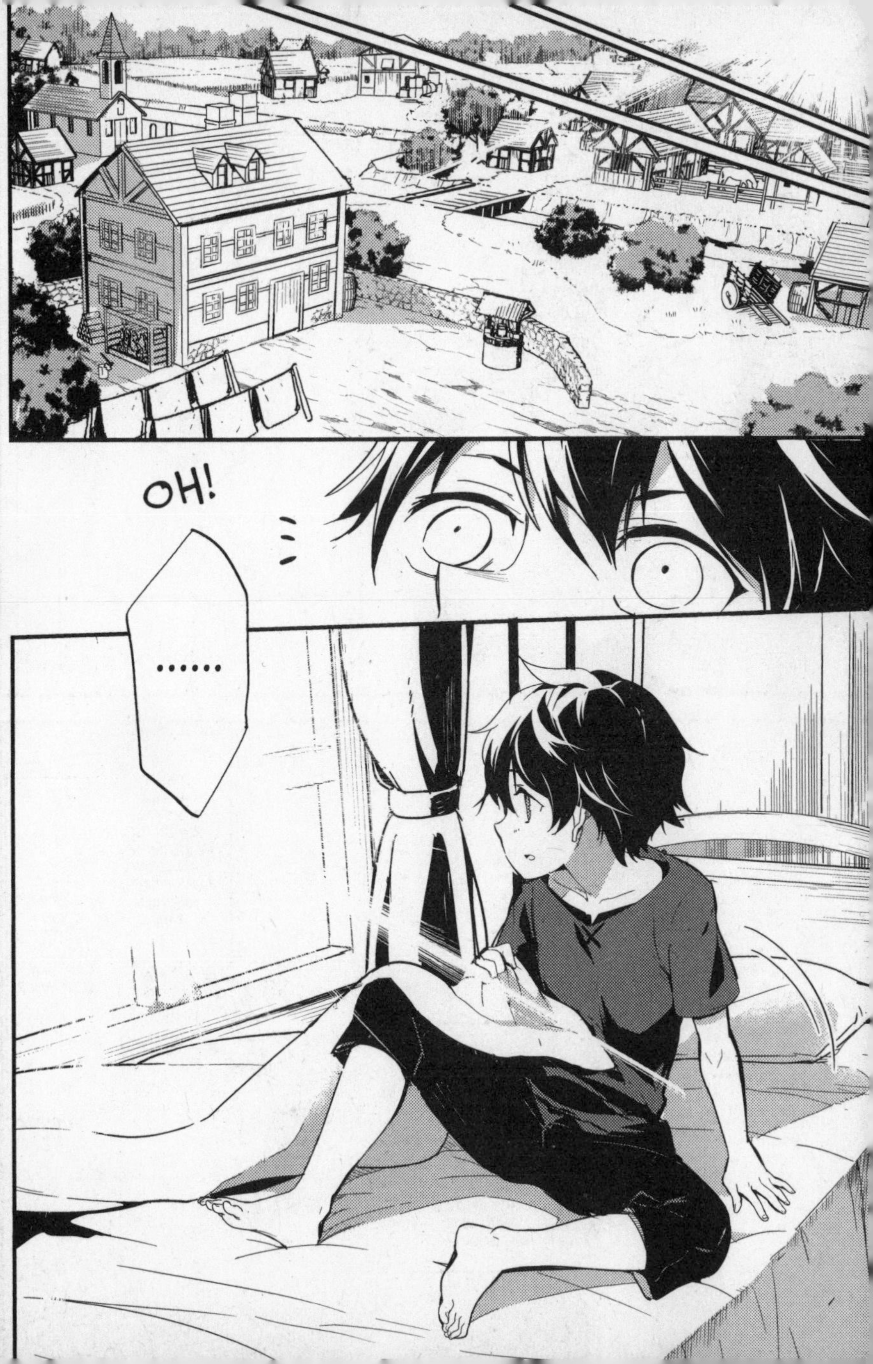
OH!
......

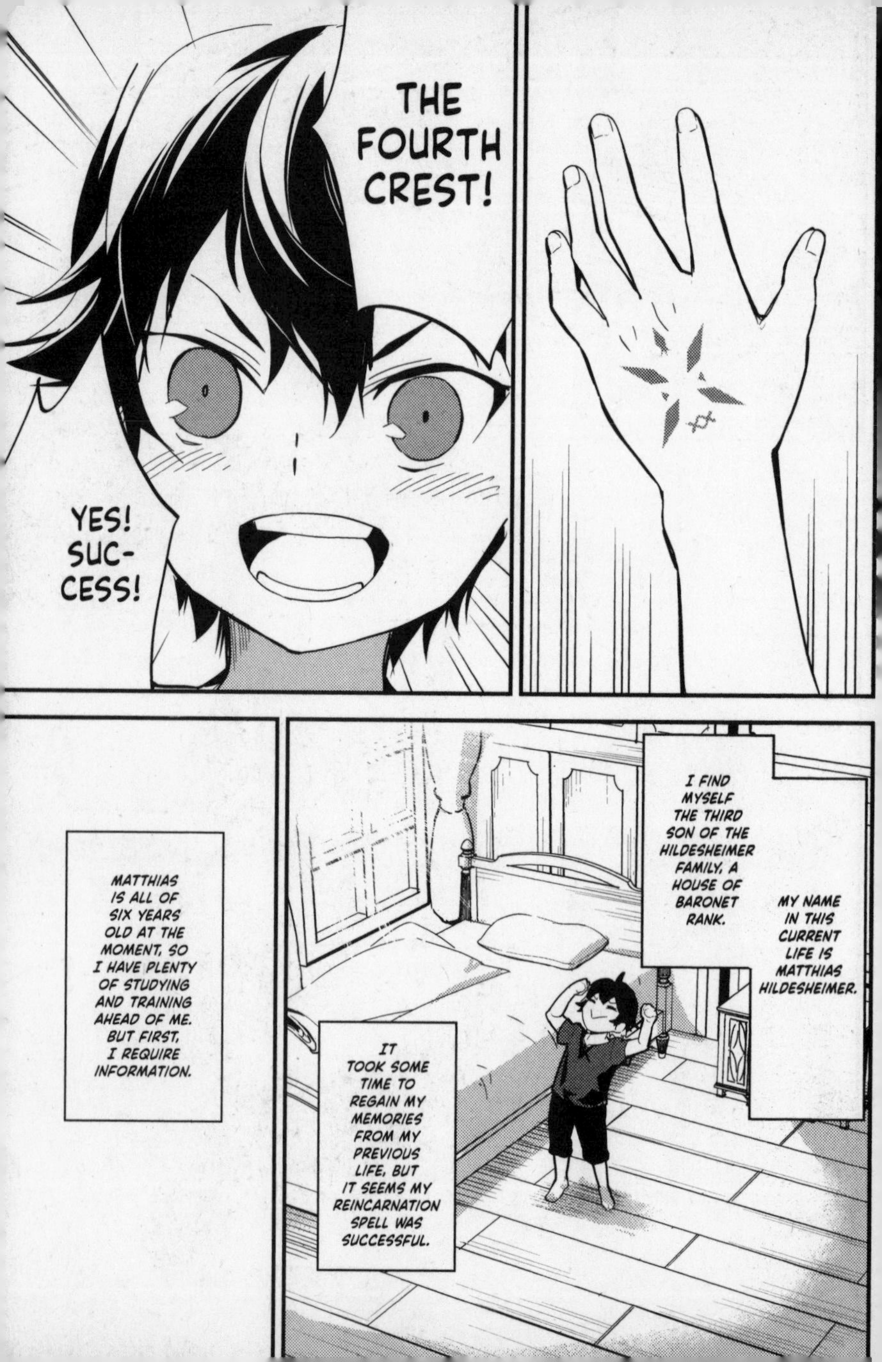
THE FOURTH CREST!
YES! SUC-CESS!
MY NAME IN THIS CURRENT LIFE IS MATTHIAS HILDESHEIMER.
I FIND MYSELF THE THIRD SON OF THE HILDESHEIMER FAMILY, A HOUSE OF BARONET RANK.
IT TOOK SOME TIME TO REGAIN MY MEMORIES FROM MY PREVIOUS LIFE, BUT IT SEEMS MY REINCARNATION SPELL WAS SUCCESSFUL.
MATTHIAS IS ALL OF SIX YEARS OLD AT THE MOMENT, SO I HAVE PLENTY OF STUDYING AND TRAINING AHEAD OF ME. BUT FIRST, I REQUIRE INFORMATION.

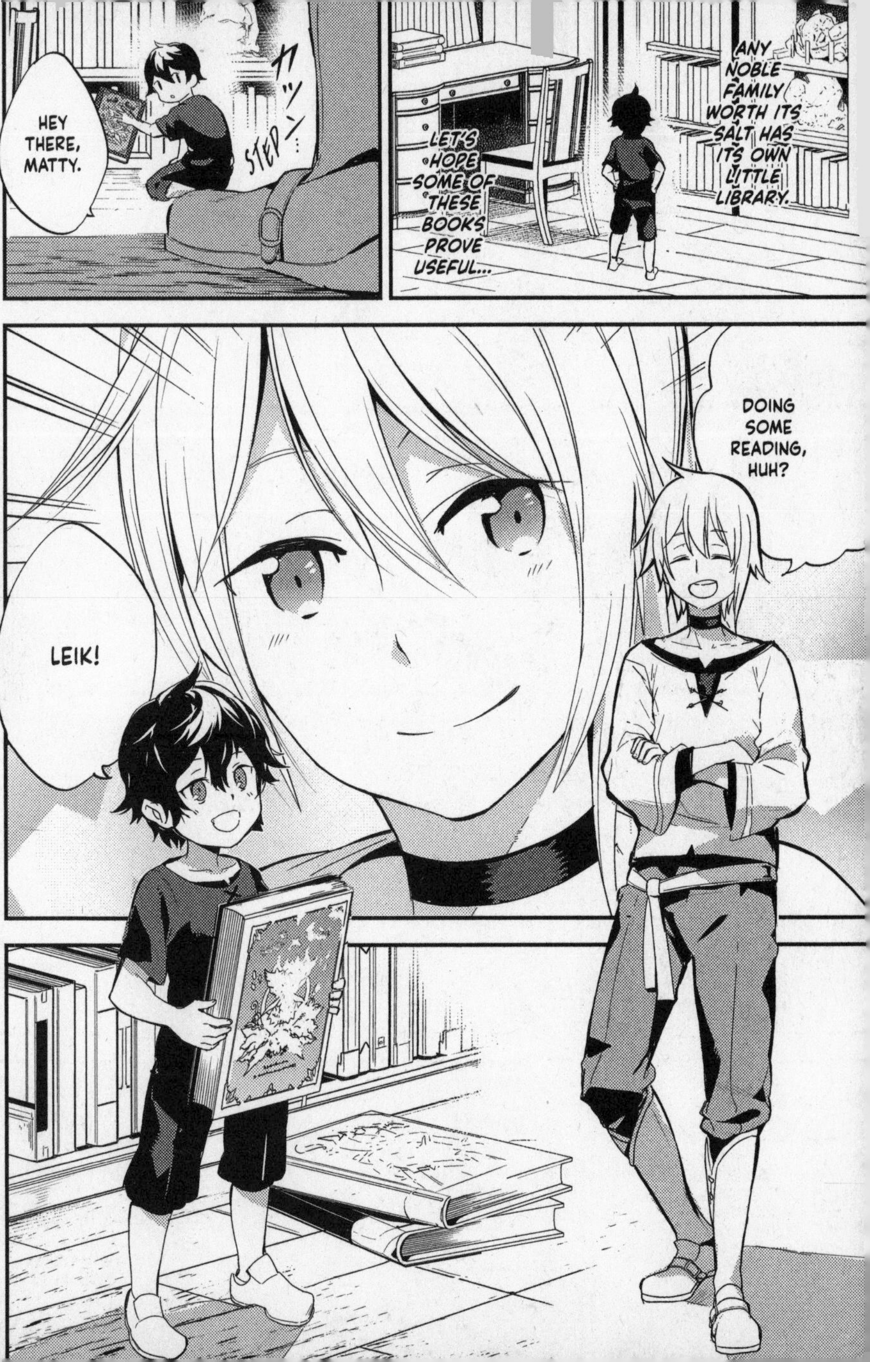
ANY NOBLE FAMILY WORTH ITS SALT HAS ITS OWN LITTLE LIBRARY.
LET'S HOPE SOME OF THESE BOOKS PROVE USEFUL...
カツン…
STEP
HEY THERE, MATTY.
DOING SOME READING, HUH?
LEIK!

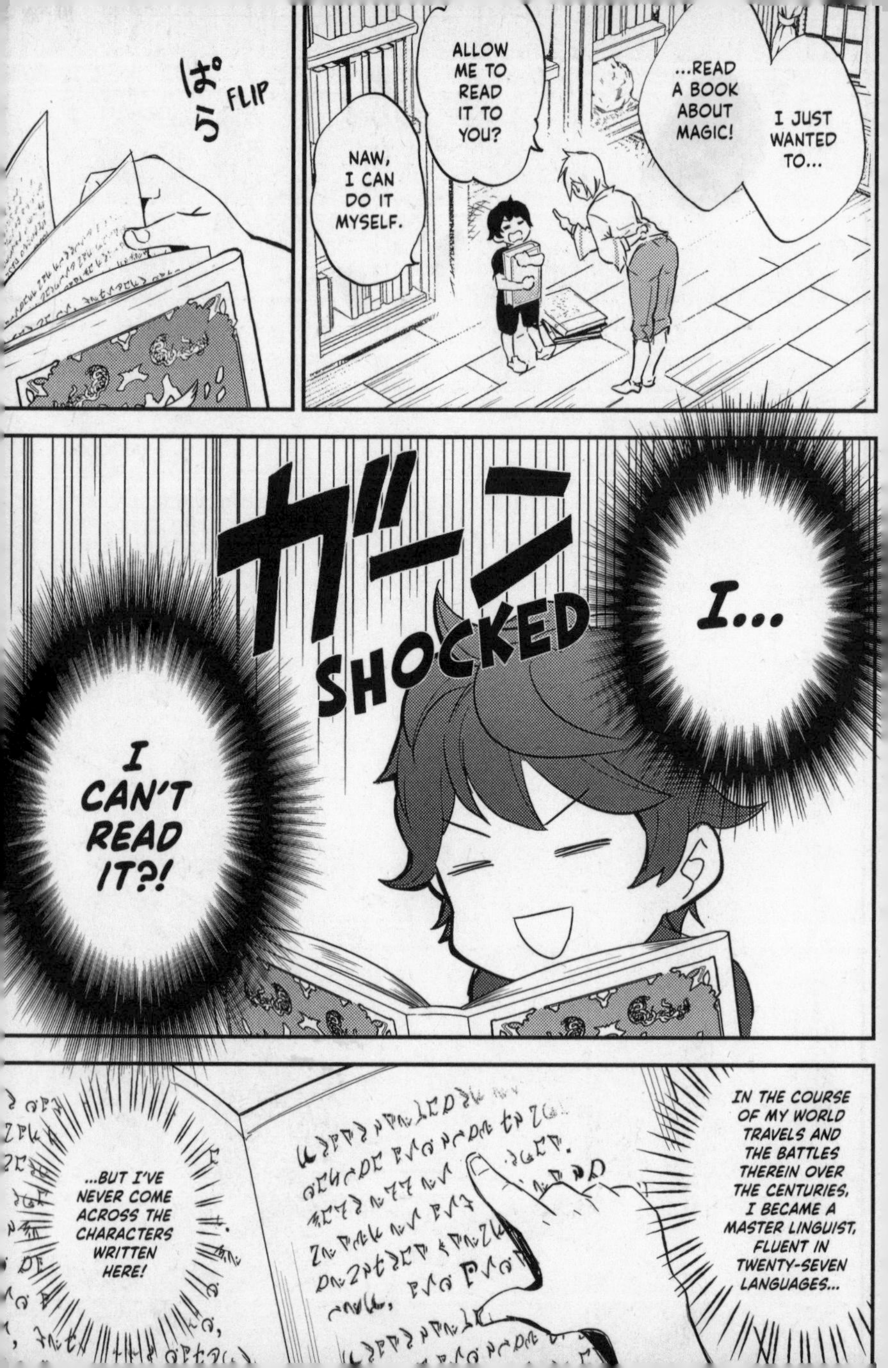
I JUST WANTED TO...
...READ A BOOK ABOUT MAGIC!
ALLOW ME TO READ IT TO YOU?
NAW, I CAN DO IT MYSELF.
ぱら FLIP
I...
ガーン SHOCKED
I CAN'T READ IT?!
IN THE COURSE OF MY WORLD TRAVELS AND THE BATTLES THEREIN OVER THE CENTURIES, I BECAME A MASTER LINGUIST, FLUENT IN TWENTY-SEVEN LANGUAGES...
...BUT I'VE NEVER COME ACROSS THE CHARACTERS WRITTEN HERE!

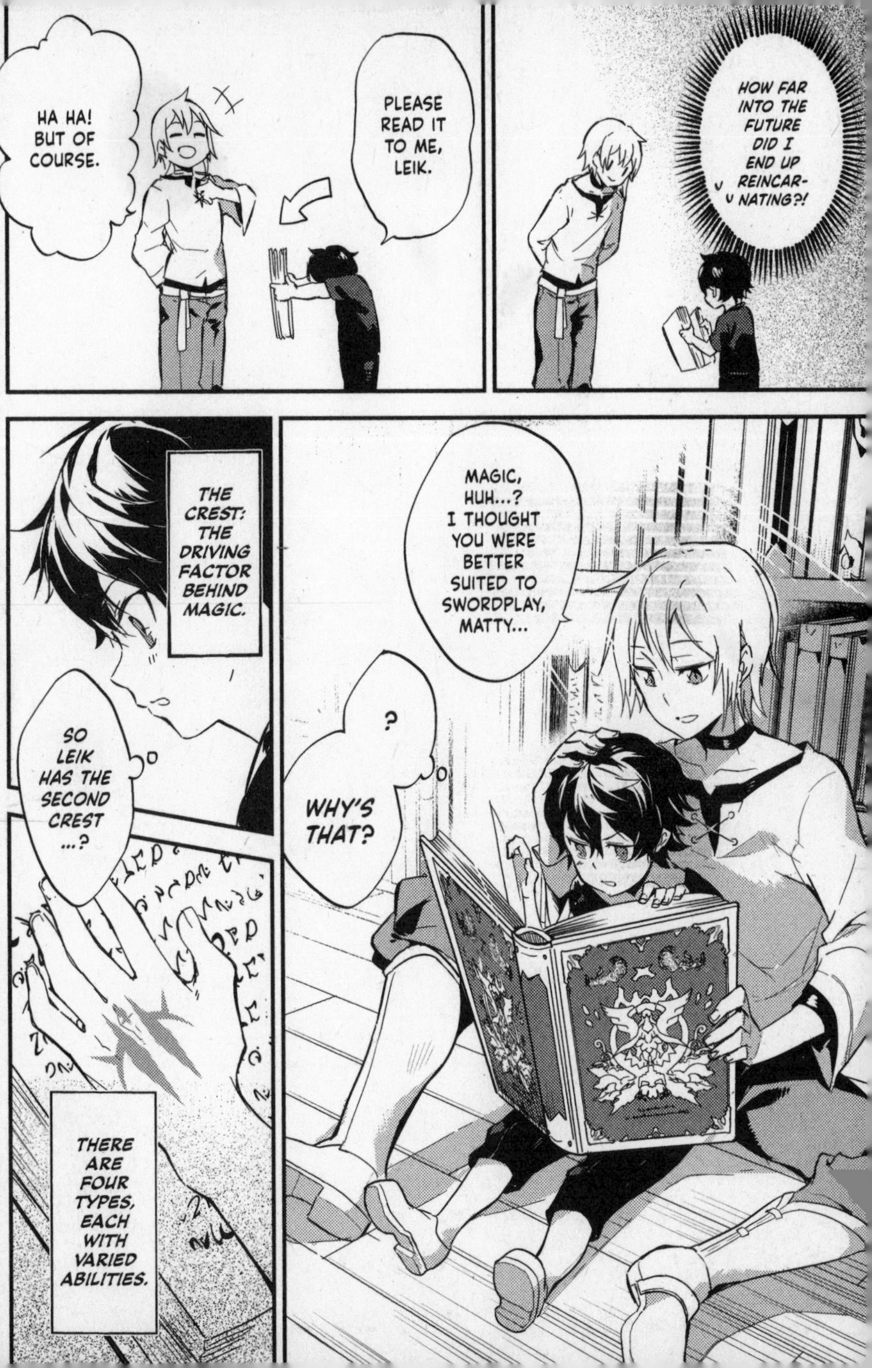
HOW FAR INTO THE FUTURE DID I END UP REINCARNATING?!
PLEASE READ IT TO ME, LEIK.
HA HA! BUT OF COURSE.
MAGIC, HUH...? I THOUGHT YOU WERE BETTER SUITED TO SWORDPLAY, MATTY...
?
WHY'S THAT?
THE CREST: THE DRIVING FACTOR BEHIND MAGIC.
SO LEIK HAS THE SECOND CREST...?
THERE ARE FOUR TYPES, EACH WITH VARIED ABILITIES.

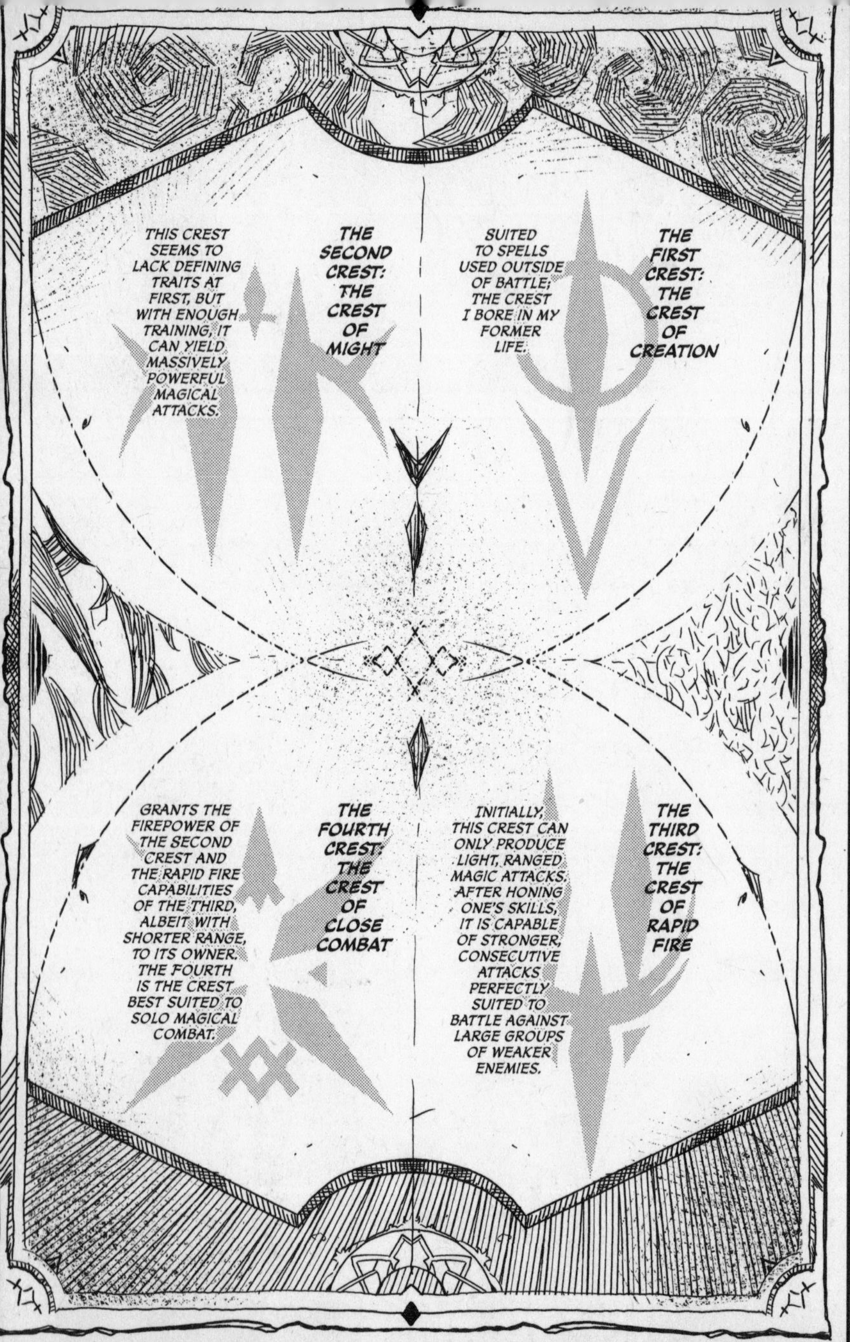
THE FIRST CREST: THE CREST OF CREATION
SUITED TO SPELLS USED OUTSIDE OF BATTLE; THE CREST I BORE IN MY FORMER LIFE.
THE SECOND CREST: THE CREST OF MIGHT
THIS CREST SEEMS TO LACK DEFINING TRAITS AT FIRST, BUT WITH ENOUGH TRAINING, IT CAN YIELD MASSIVELY POWERFUL MAGICAL ATTACKS.
THE THIRD CREST: THE CREST OF RAPID FIRE
INITIALLY, THIS CREST CAN ONLY PRODUCE LIGHT, RANGED MAGIC ATTACKS. AFTER HONING ONE'S SKILLS, IT IS CAPABLE OF STRONGER, CONSECUTIVE ATTACKS PERFECTLY SUITED TO BATTLE AGAINST LARGE GROUPS OF WEAKER ENEMIES.
THE FOURTH CREST: THE CREST OF CLOSE COMBAT
GRANTS THE FIREPOWER OF THE SECOND CREST AND THE RAPID FIRE CAPABILITIES OF THE THIRD, ALBEIT WITH SHORTER RANGE, TO ITS OWNER. THE FOURTH IS THE CREST BEST SUITED TO SOLO MAGICAL COMBAT.

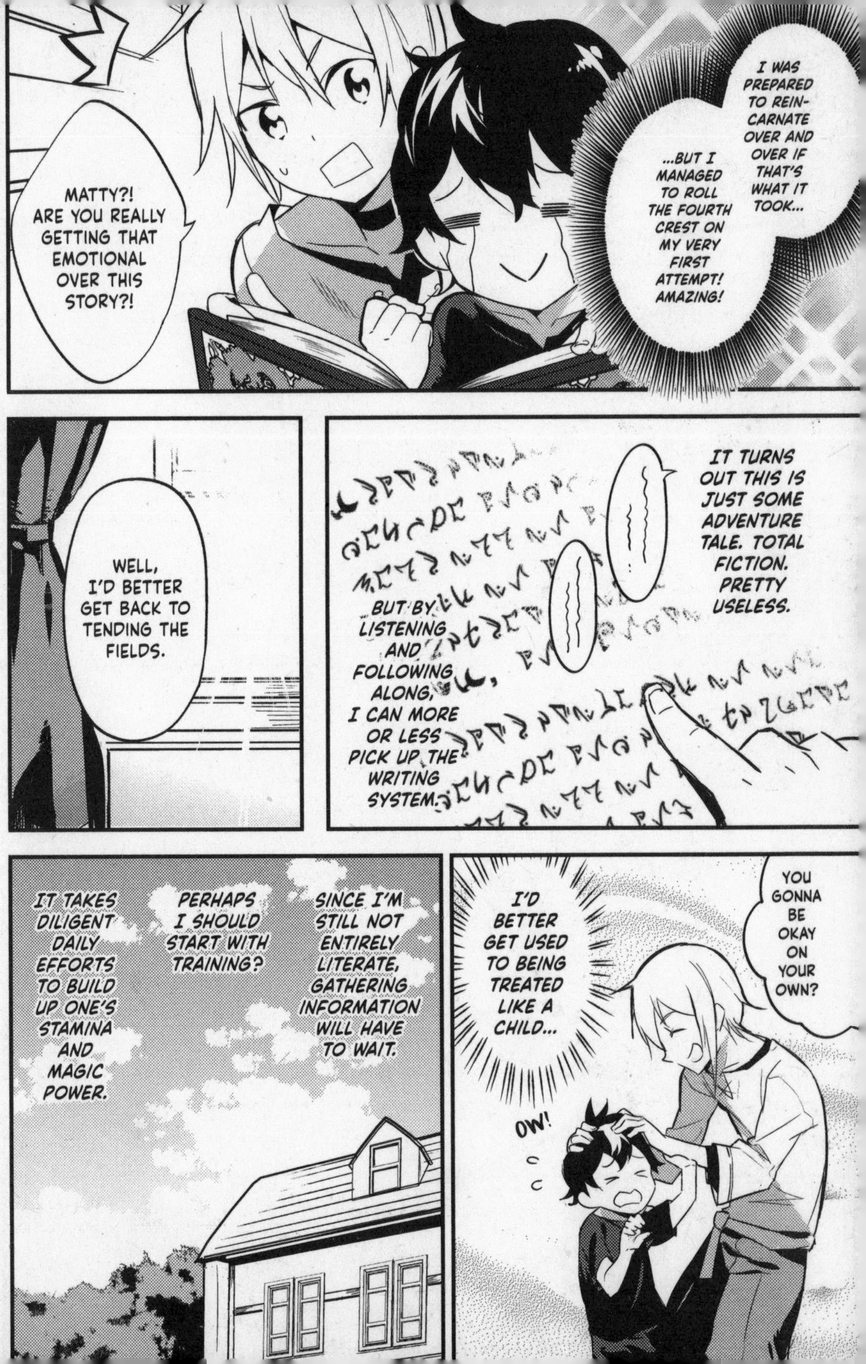
I WAS PREPARED TO REINCARNATE OVER AND OVER IF THAT'S WHAT IT TOOK...
...BUT I MANAGED TO ROLL THE FOURTH CREST ON MY VERY FIRST ATTEMPT! AMAZING!
MATTY?! ARE YOU REALLY GETTING THAT EMOTIONAL OVER THIS STORY?!
IT TURNS OUT THIS IS JUST SOME ADVENTURE TALE. TOTAL FICTION. PRETTY USELESS.
BUT BY LISTENING AND FOLLOWING ALONG, I CAN MORE OR LESS PICK UP THE WRITING SYSTEM.
WELL, I'D BETTER GET BACK TO TENDING THE FIELDS.
YOU GONNA BE OKAY ON YOUR OWN?
I'D BETTER GET USED TO BEING TREATED LIKE A CHILD...
OW!
SINCE I'M STILL NOT ENTIRELY LITERATE, GATHERING INFORMATION WILL HAVE TO WAIT.
PERHAPS I SHOULD START WITH TRAINING?
IT TAKES DILIGENT DAILY EFFORTS TO BUILD UP ONE'S STAMINA AND MAGIC POWER.

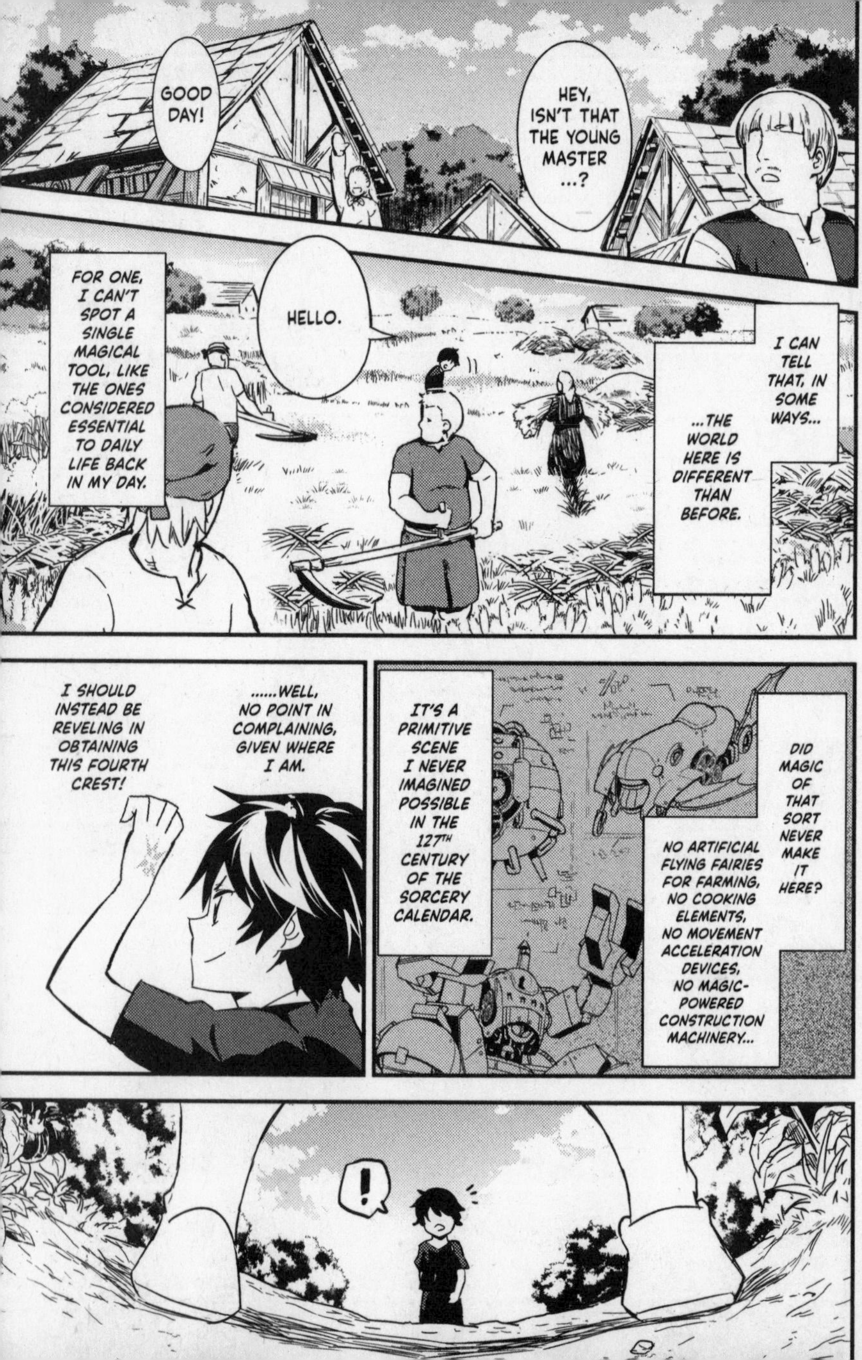
HEY, ISN'T THAT THE YOUNG MASTER ...?
GOOD DAY!
I CAN TELL THAT, IN SOME WAYS...
...THE WORLD HERE IS DIFFERENT THAN BEFORE.
HELLO.
FOR ONE, I CAN'T SPOT A SINGLE MAGICAL TOOL, LIKE THE ONES CONSIDERED ESSENTIAL TO DAILY LIFE BACK IN MY DAY.
DID MAGIC OF THAT SORT NEVER MAKE IT HERE?
NO ARTIFICIAL FLYING FAIRIES FOR FARMING, NO COOKING ELEMENTS, NO MOVEMENT ACCELERATION DEVICES, NO MAGIC-POWERED CONSTRUCTION MACHINERY...
IT'S A PRIMITIVE SCENE I NEVER IMAGINED POSSIBLE IN THE 127TH CENTURY OF THE SORCERY CALENDAR.
......WELL, NO POINT IN COMPLAINING, GIVEN WHERE I AM.
I SHOULD INSTEAD BE REVELING IN OBTAINING THIS FOURTH CREST!
!

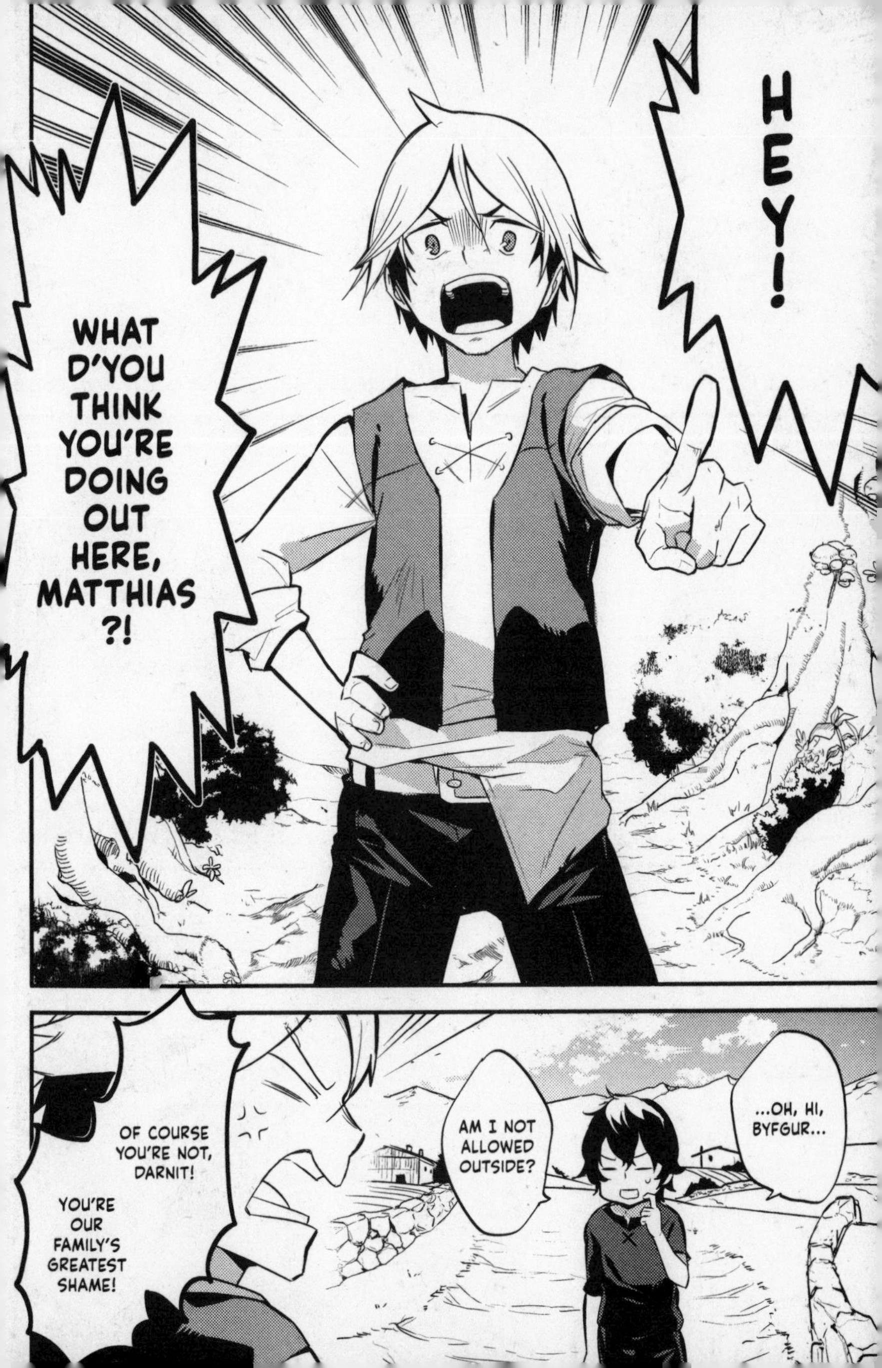
HEY!
WHAT D'YOU THINK YOU'RE DOING OUT HERE, MATTHIAS?!
...OH, HI, BYFGUR...
AM I NOT ALLOWED OUTSIDE?
OF COURSE YOU'RE NOT, DARNIT!
YOU'RE OUR FAMILY'S GREATEST SHAME!

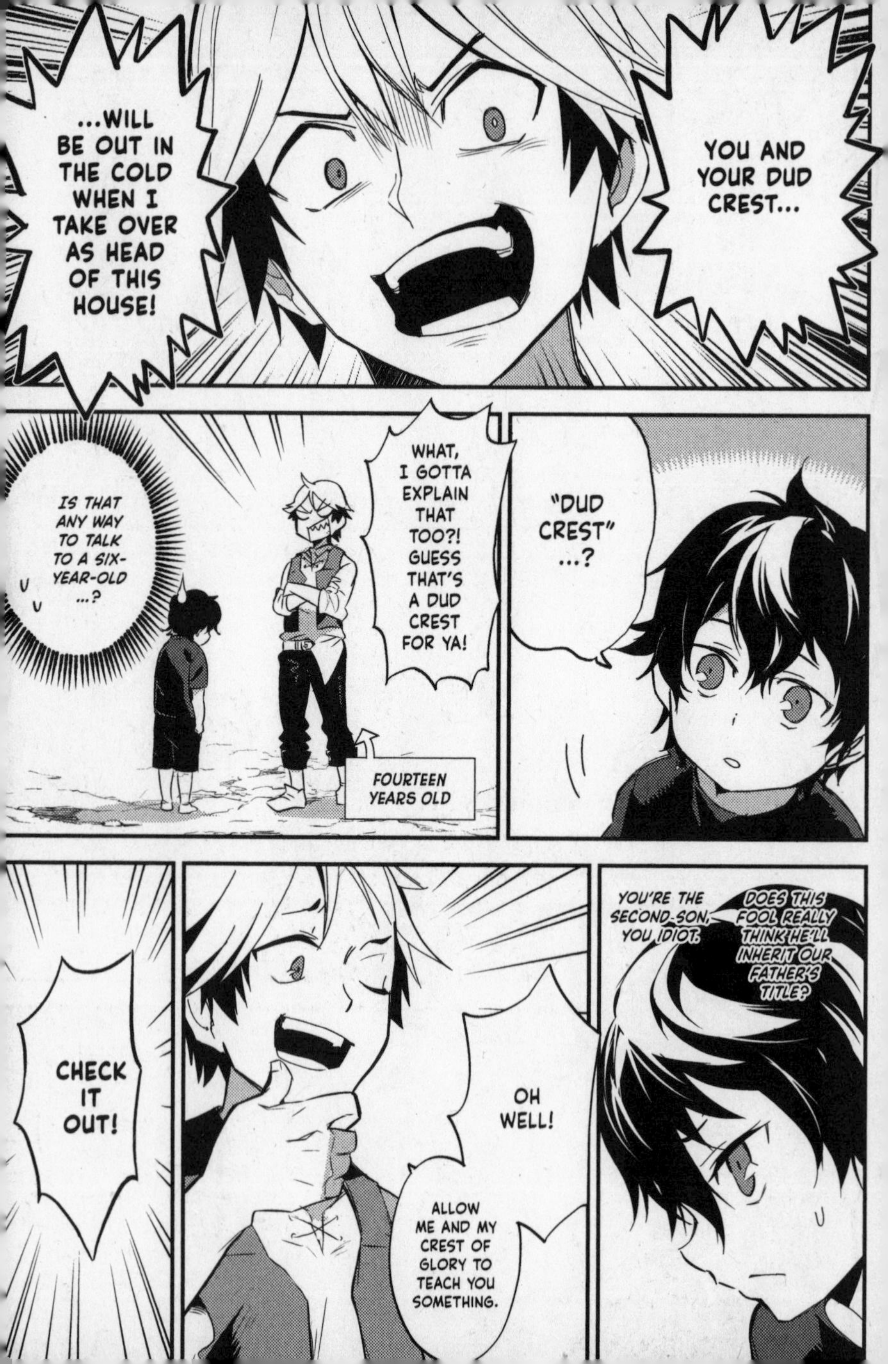
YOU AND YOUR DUD CREST...
...WILL BE OUT IN THE COLD WHEN I TAKE OVER AS HEAD OF THIS HOUSE!
"DUD CREST" ...?
WHAT, I GOTTA EXPLAIN THAT TOO?! GUESS THAT'S A DUD CREST FOR YA!
IS THAT ANY WAY TO TALK TO A SIX-YEAR-OLD ...?
FOURTEEN YEARS OLD
DOES THIS FOOL REALLY THINK HE'LL INHERIT OUR FATHER'S TITLE?
YOU'RE THE SECOND-SON, YOU IDIOT.
OH WELL!
ALLOW ME AND MY CREST OF GLORY TO TEACH YOU SOMETHING.
CHECK IT OUT!

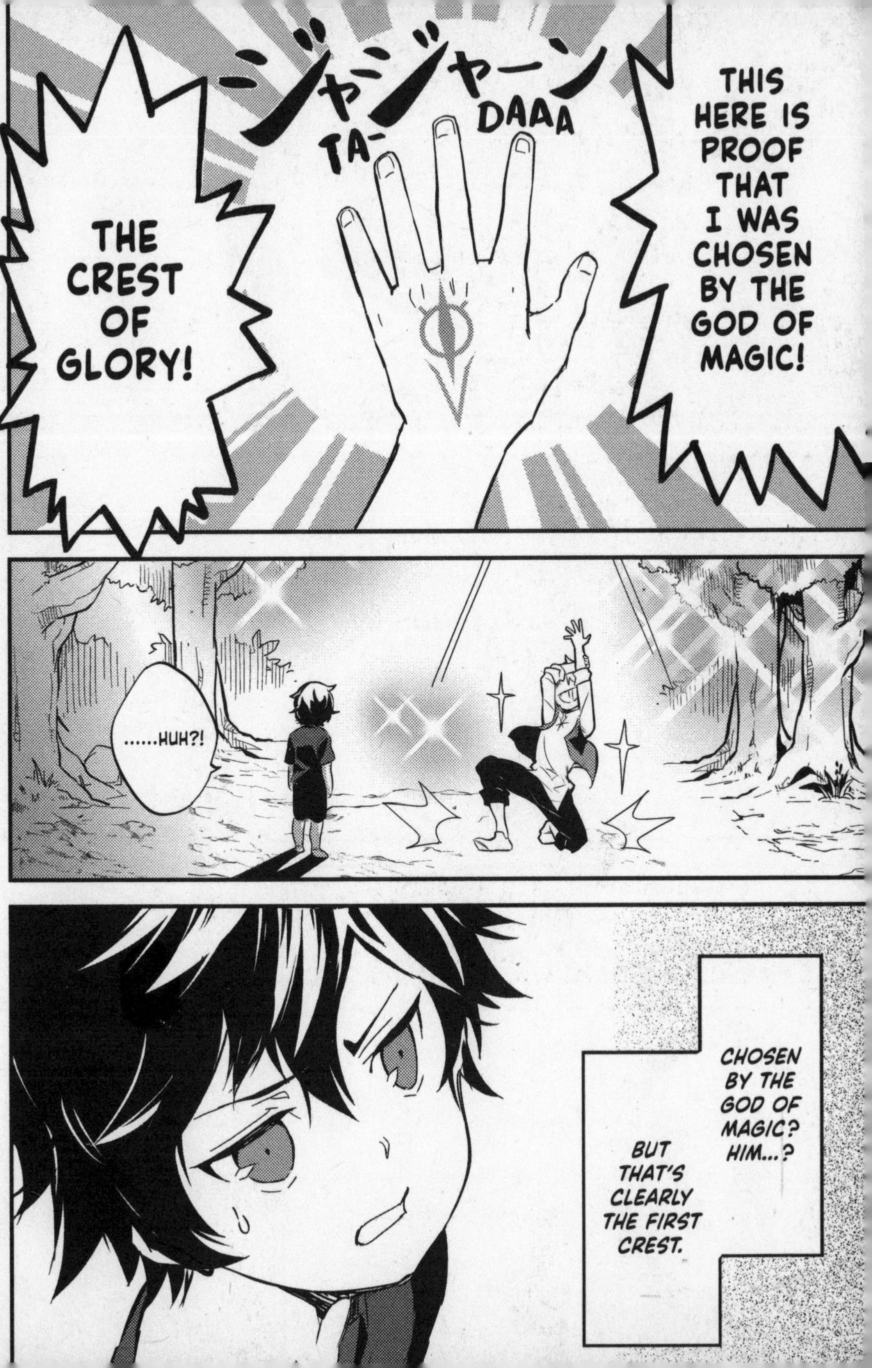
ジャジャーン
TA-DAAA
THIS HERE IS PROOF THAT I WAS CHOSEN BY THE GOD OF MAGIC!
THE CREST OF GLORY!
......HUH?!
CHOSEN BY THE GOD OF MAGIC? HIM...?
BUT THAT'S CLEARLY THE FIRST CREST.

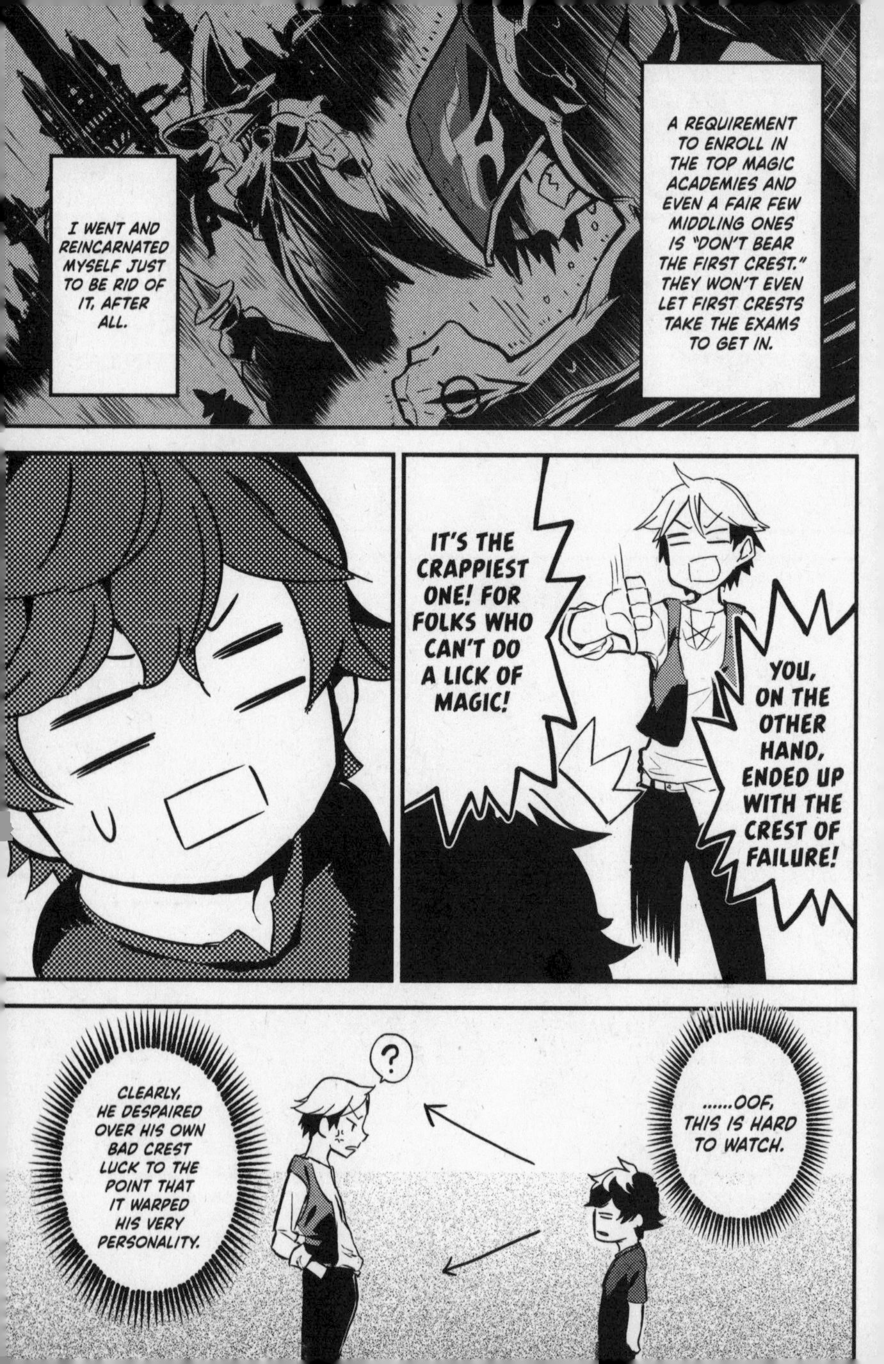
A REQUIREMENT TO ENROLL IN THE TOP MAGIC ACADEMIES AND EVEN A FAIR FEW MIDDLING ONES IS "DON'T BEAR THE FIRST CREST." THEY WON'T EVEN LET FIRST CRESTS TAKE THE EXAMS TO GET IN.
I WENT AND REINCARNATED MYSELF JUST TO BE RID OF IT, AFTER ALL.
IT'S THE CRAPPIEST ONE! FOR FOLKS WHO CAN'T DO A LICK OF MAGIC!
YOU, ON THE OTHER HAND, ENDED UP WITH THE CREST OF FAILURE!
......OOF, THIS IS HARD TO WATCH.
?
CLEARLY, HE DESPAIRED OVER HIS OWN BAD CREST LUCK TO THE POINT THAT IT WARPED HIS VERY PERSONALITY.

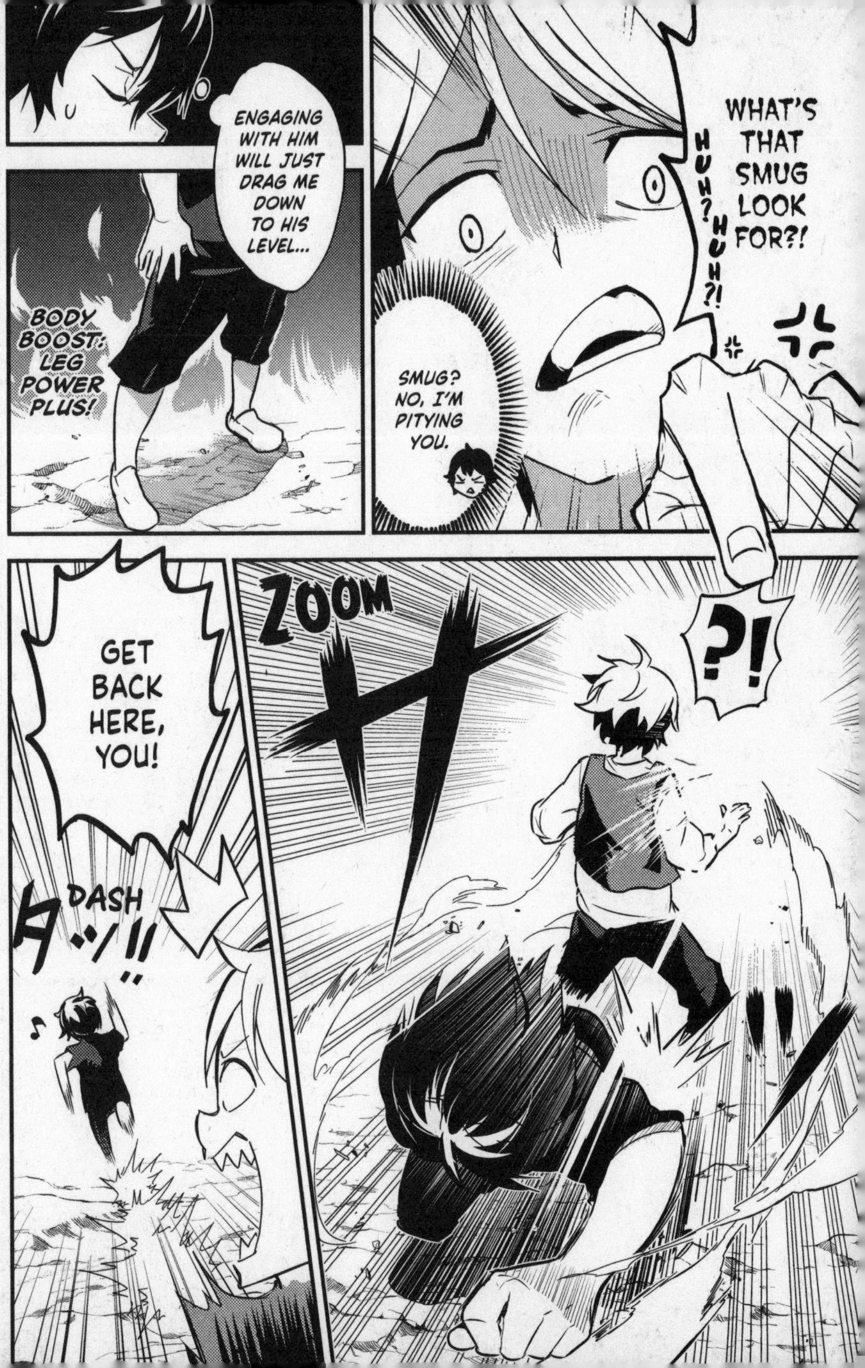
WHAT'S THAT SMUG LOOK FOR?!
HUH? HUH?!
SMUG? NO, I'M PITYING YOU.
ENGAGING WITH HIM WILL JUST DRAG ME DOWN TO HIS LEVEL...
BODY BOOST: LEG POWER PLUS!
?!
ZOOM
GET BACK HERE, YOU!
DASH
ダッ!!

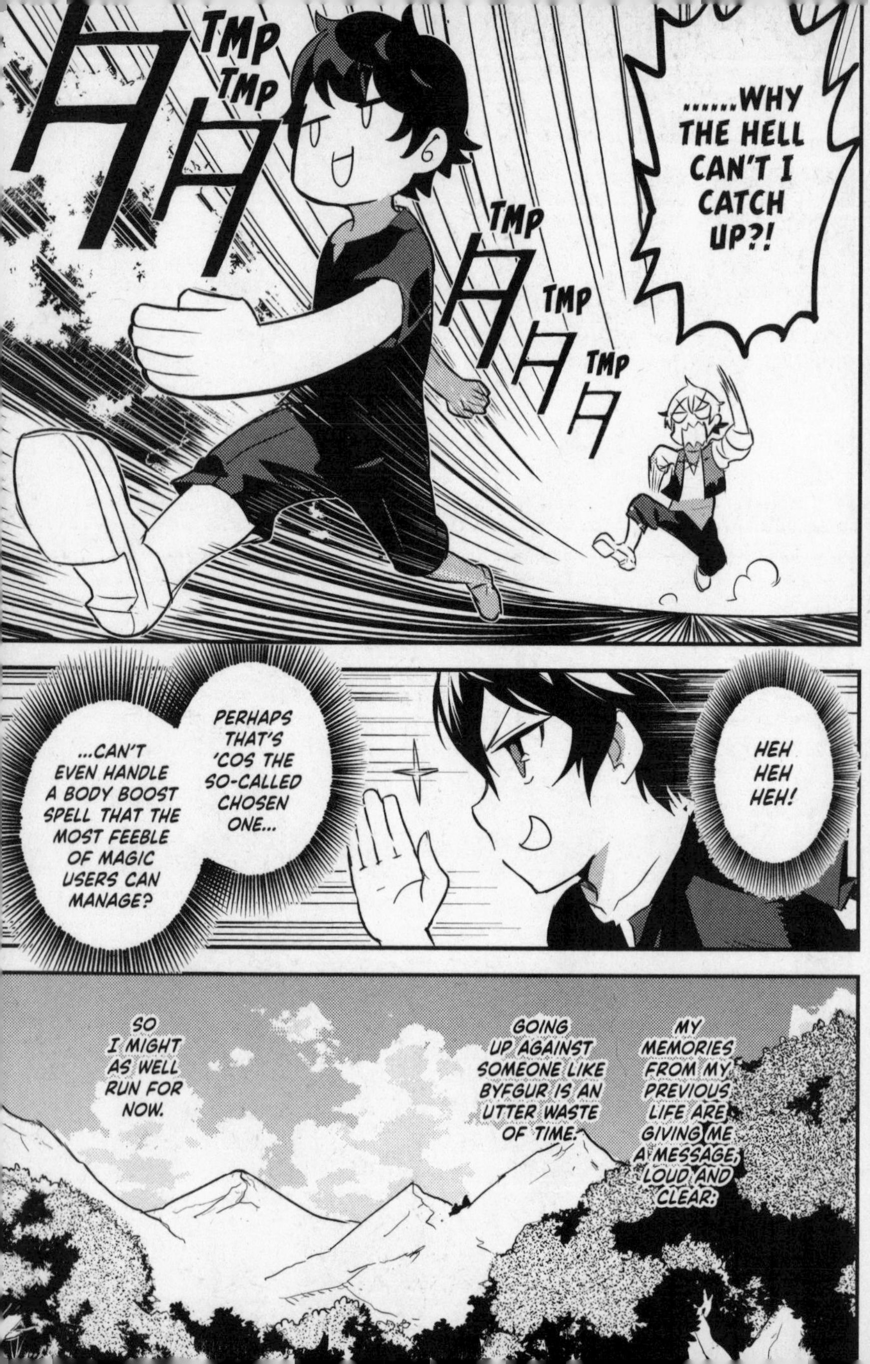
......WHY THE HELL CAN'T I CATCH UP?!
TMP TMP
TMP
TMP
TMP
HEH HEH HEH!
PERHAPS THAT'S 'COS THE SO-CALLED CHOSEN ONE...
...CAN'T EVEN HANDLE A BODY BOOST SPELL THAT THE MOST FEEBLE OF MAGIC USERS CAN MANAGE?
MY MEMORIES FROM MY PREVIOUS LIFE ARE GIVING ME A MESSAGE, LOUD AND CLEAR:
GOING UP AGAINST SOMEONE LIKE BYFGUR IS AN UTTER WASTE OF TIME.
SO I MIGHT AS WELL RUN FOR NOW.

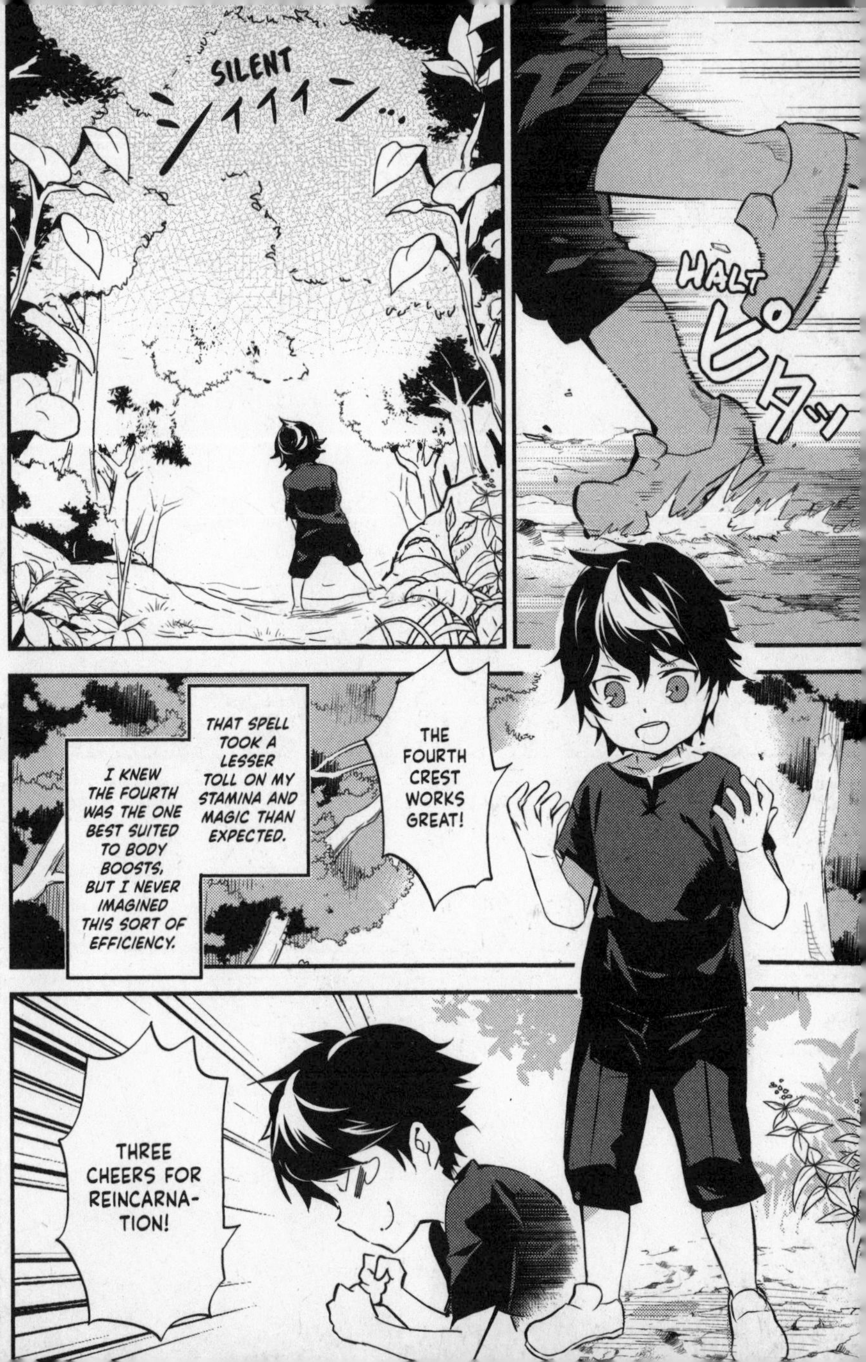
HALT
ピタッ
SILENT
シィイイン…
THE FOURTH CREST WORKS GREAT!
THAT SPELL TOOK A LESSER TOLL ON MY STAMINA AND MAGIC THAN EXPECTED.
I KNEW THE FOURTH WAS THE ONE BEST SUITED TO BODY BOOSTS, BUT I NEVER IMAGINED THIS SORT OF EFFICIENCY.
THREE CHEERS FOR REINCARNATION!

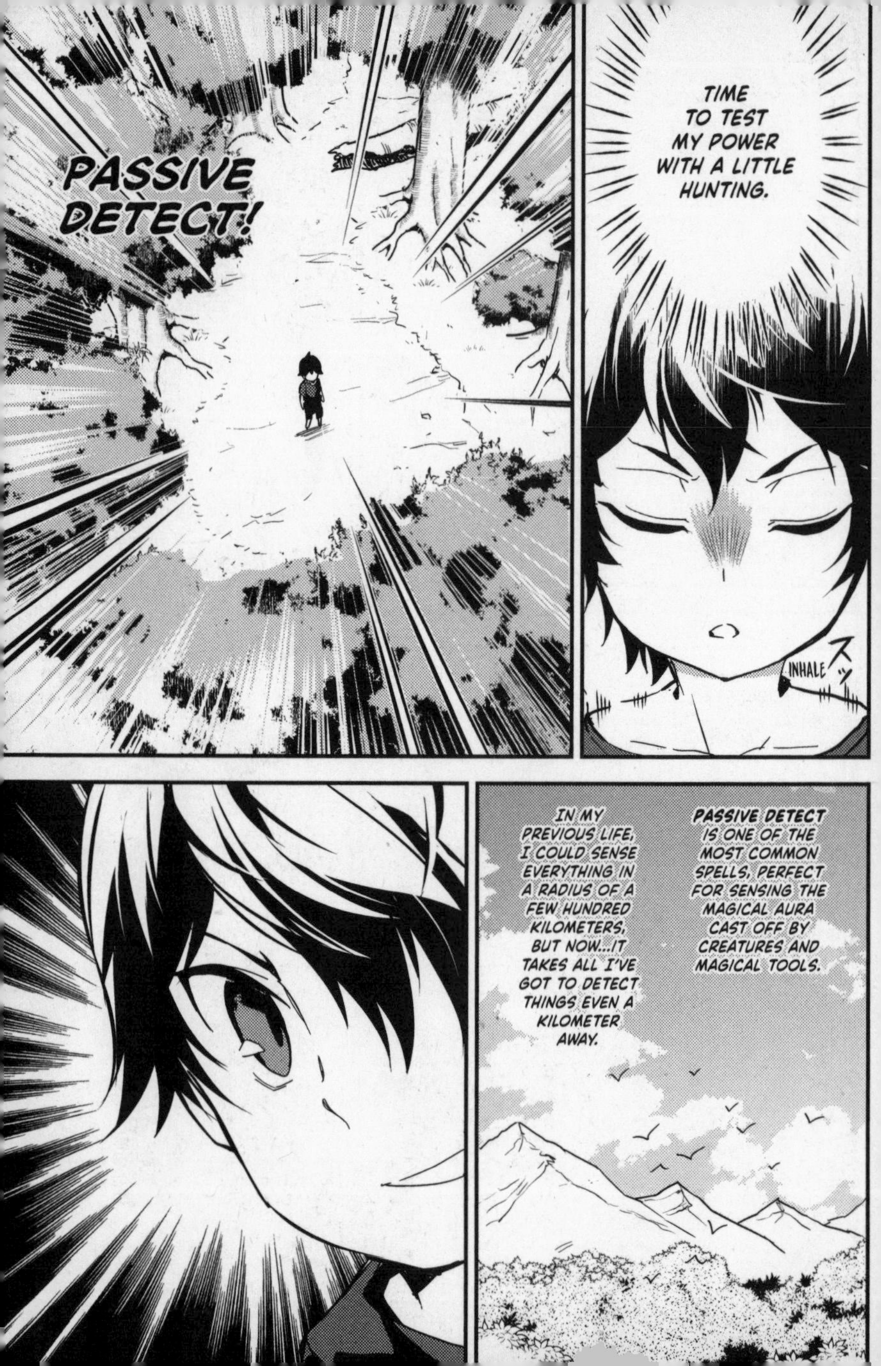
TIME TO TEST MY POWER WITH A LITTLE HUNTING.
INHALE
スッ
PASSIVE DETECT!
PASSIVE DETECT IS ONE OF THE MOST COMMON SPELLS, PERFECT FOR SENSING THE MAGICAL AURA CAST OFF BY CREATURES AND MAGICAL TOOLS.
IN MY PREVIOUS LIFE, I COULD SENSE EVERYTHING IN A RADIUS OF A FEW HUNDRED KILOMETERS, BUT NOW...IT TAKES ALL I'VE GOT TO DETECT THINGS EVEN A KILOMETER AWAY.

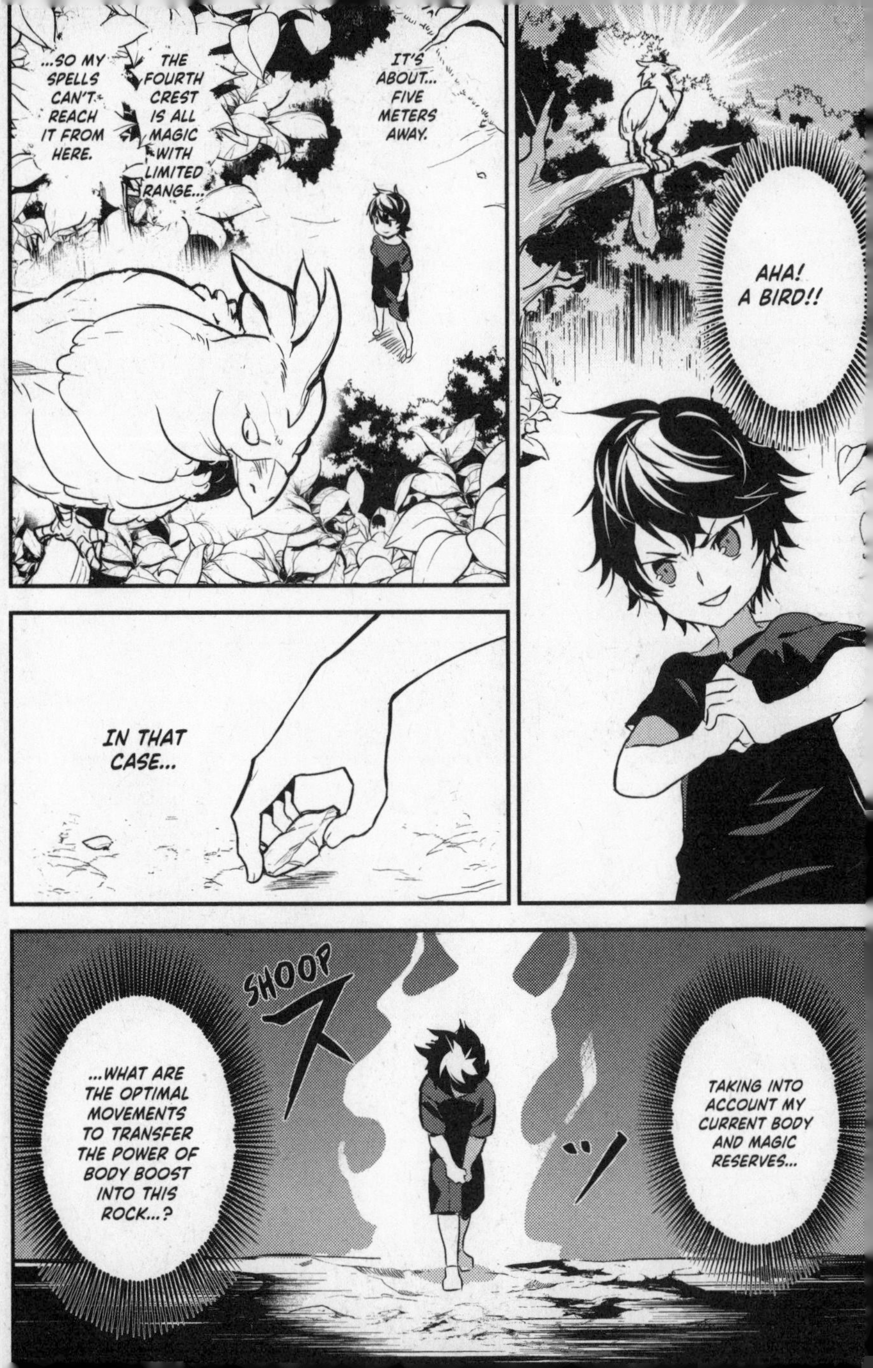
AHA! A BIRD!!
IT'S ABOUT... FIVE METERS AWAY.
THE FOURTH CREST IS ALL MAGIC WITH LIMITED RANGE...
...SO MY SPELLS CAN'T REACH IT FROM HERE.
IN THAT CASE...
SHOOP
TAKING INTO ACCOUNT MY CURRENT BODY AND MAGIC RESERVES...
...WHAT ARE THE OPTIMAL MOVEMENTS TO TRANSFER THE POWER OF BODY BOOST INTO THIS ROCK...?

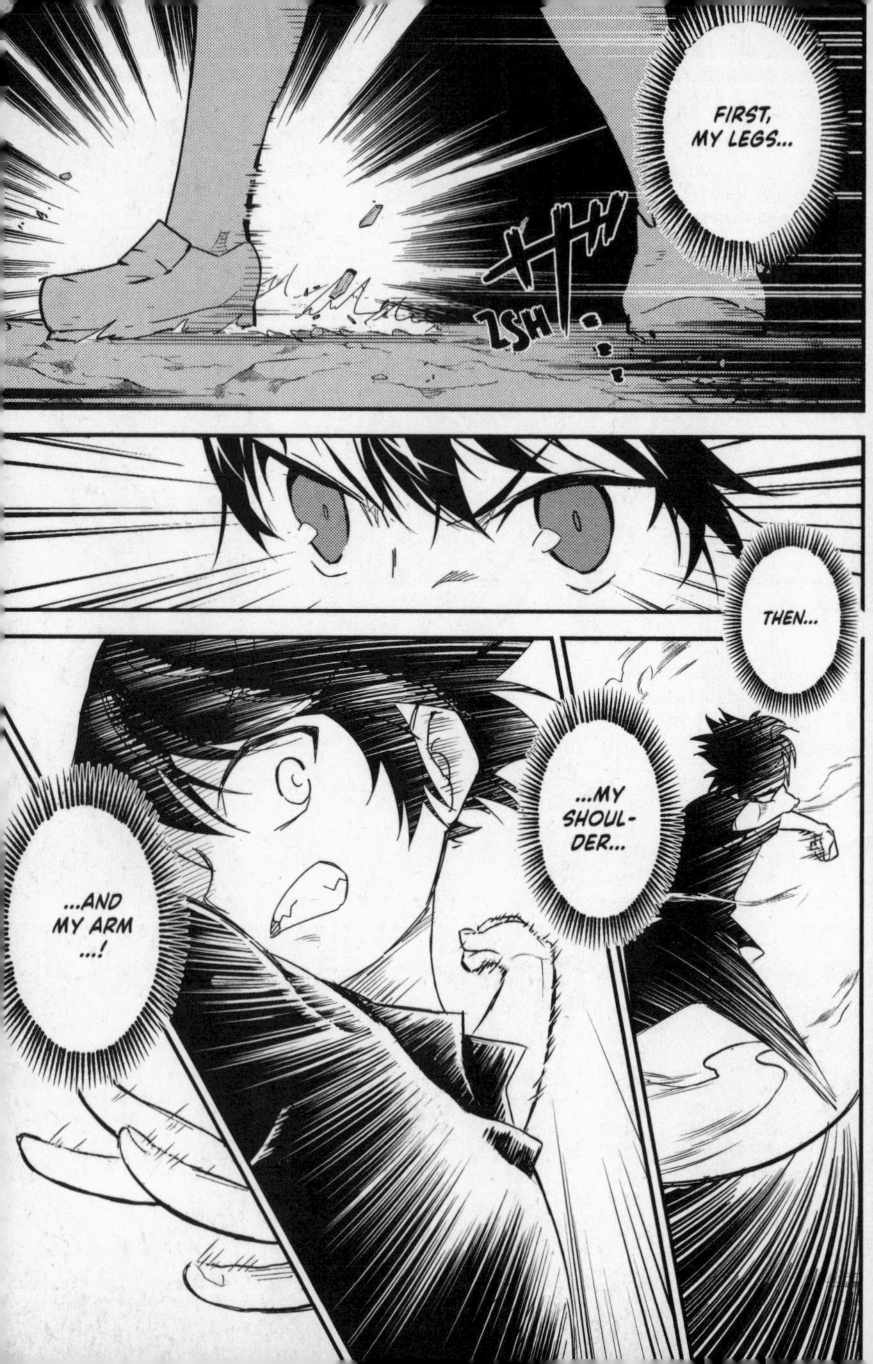
FIRST, MY LEGS...
ZSH
THEN...
...MY SHOUL-DER...
...AND MY ARM ...!

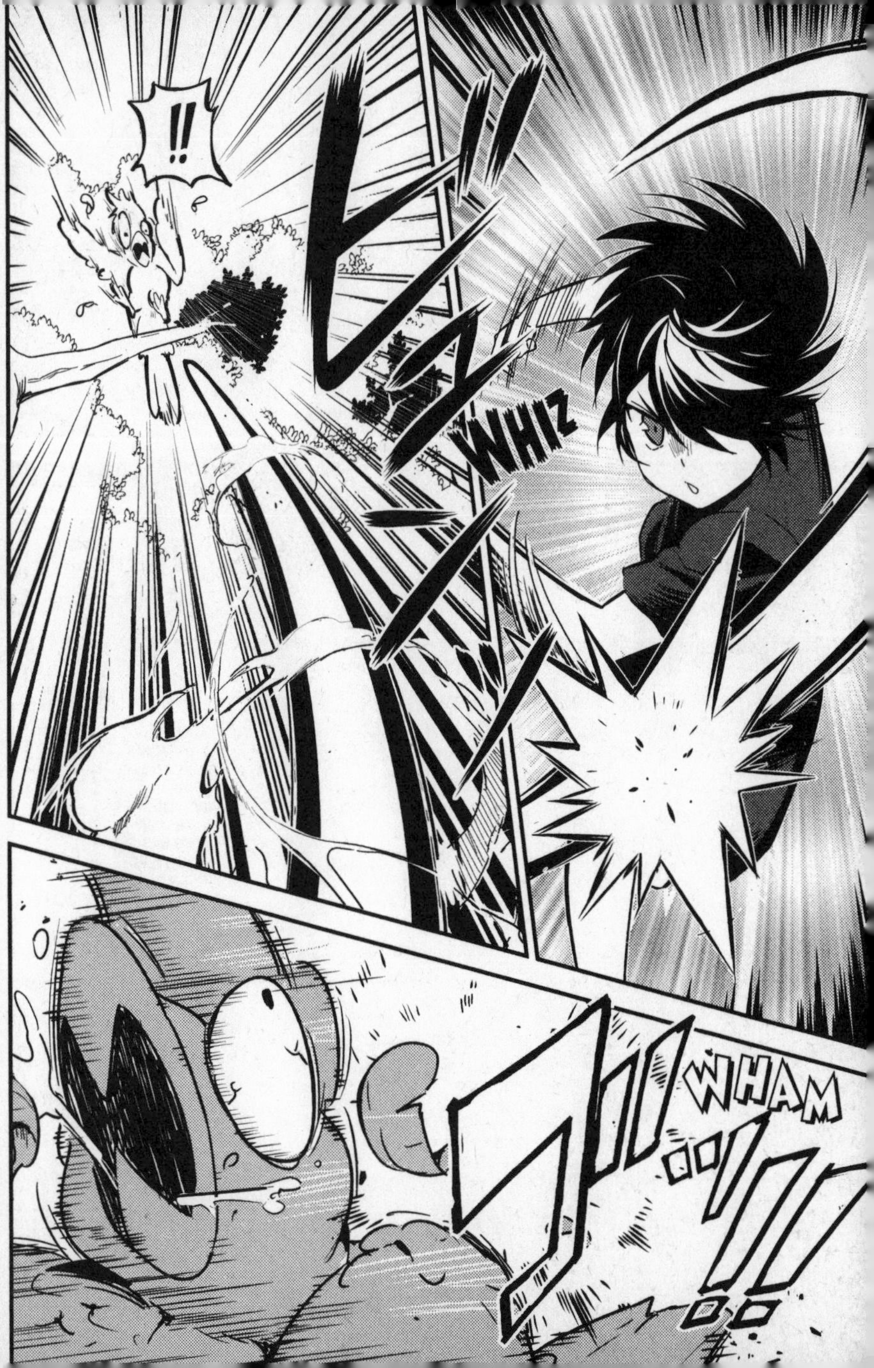
!!
WHIZ
WHAM

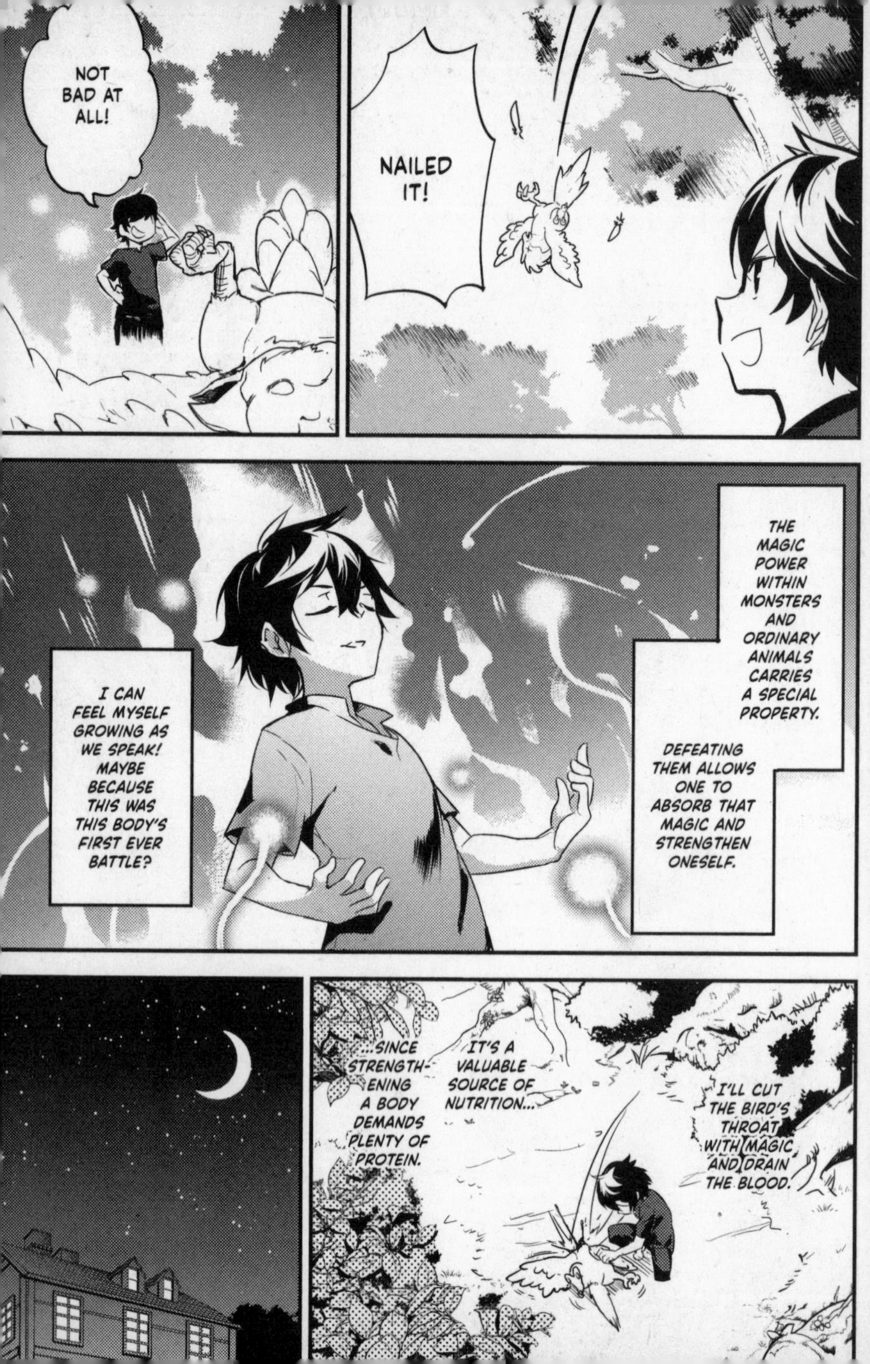
NAILED IT!
NOT BAD AT ALL!
THE MAGIC POWER WITHIN MONSTERS AND ORDINARY ANIMALS CARRIES A SPECIAL PROPERTY.
DEFEATING THEM ALLOWS ONE TO ABSORB THAT MAGIC AND STRENGTHEN ONESELF.
I CAN FEEL MYSELF GROWING AS WE SPEAK! MAYBE BECAUSE THIS WAS THIS BODY'S FIRST EVER BATTLE?
I'LL CUT THE BIRD'S THROAT WITH MAGIC AND DRAIN THE BLOOD.
IT'S A VALUABLE SOURCE OF NUTRITION...
...SINCE STRENGTH-ENING A BODY DEMANDS PLENTY OF PROTEIN.

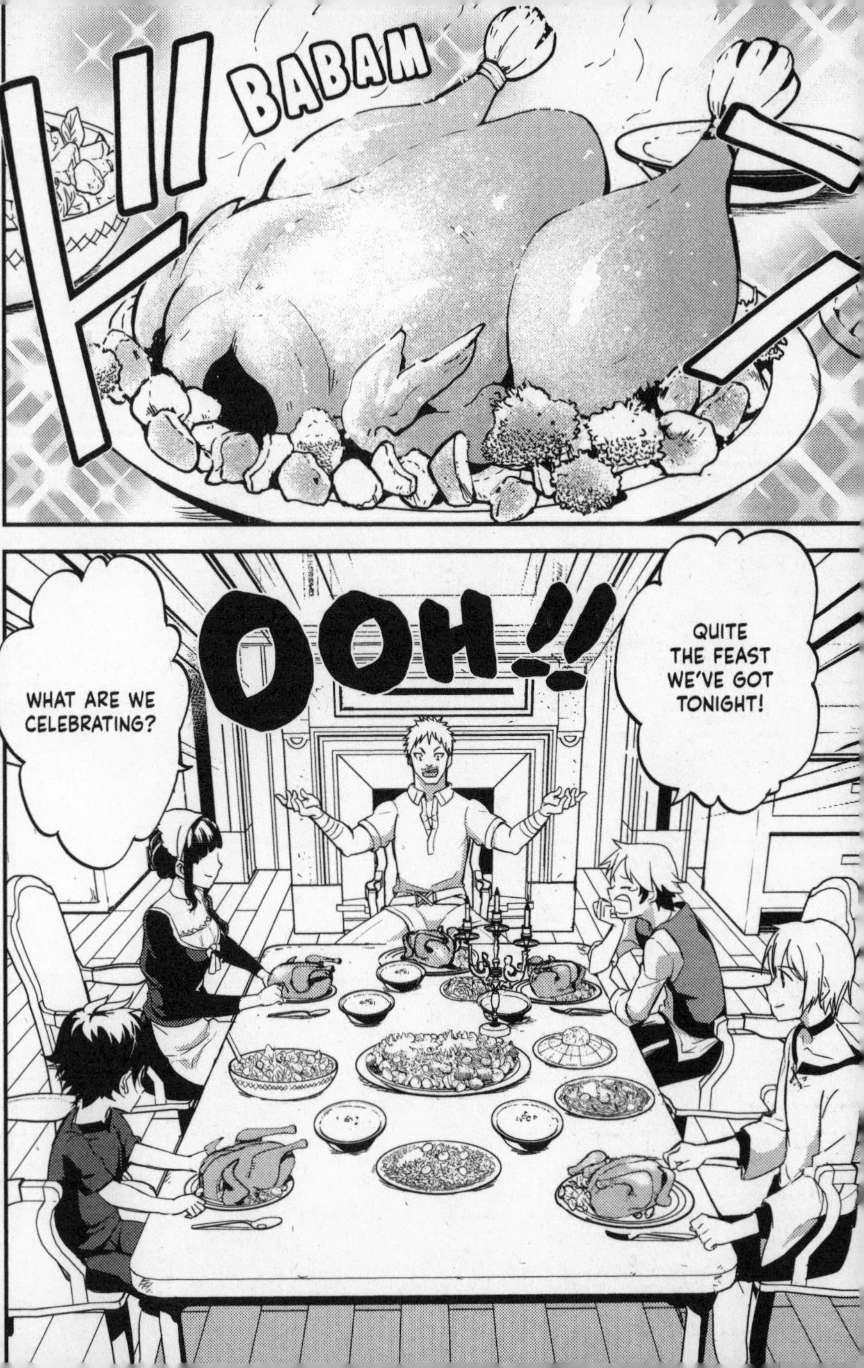
BABAM
QUITE THE FEAST WE'VE GOT TONIGHT!
OOH!!
WHAT ARE WE CELEBRATING?

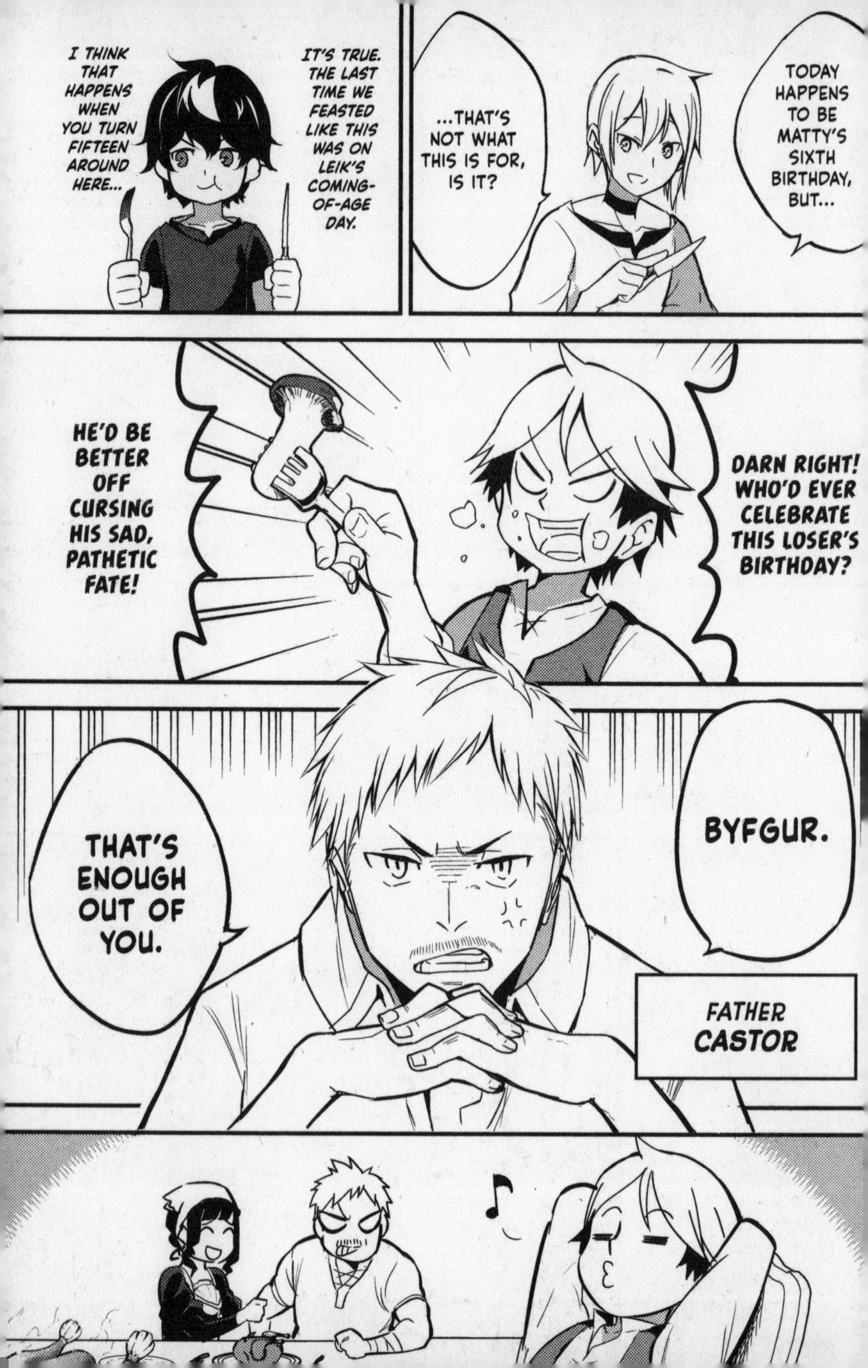

TODAY HAPPENS TO BE MATTY'S SIXTH BIRTHDAY, BUT...
...THAT'S NOT WHAT THIS IS FOR, IS IT?
IT'S TRUE. THE LAST TIME WE FEASTED LIKE THIS WAS ON LEIK'S COMING-OF-AGE DAY.
I THINK THAT HAPPENS WHEN YOU TURN FIFTEEN AROUND HERE...
DARN RIGHT! WHO'D EVER CELEBRATE THIS LOSER'S BIRTHDAY?
HE'D BE BETTER OFF CURSING HIS SAD, PATHETIC FATE!
BYFGUR.
FATHER CASTOR
THAT'S ENOUGH OUT OF YOU.

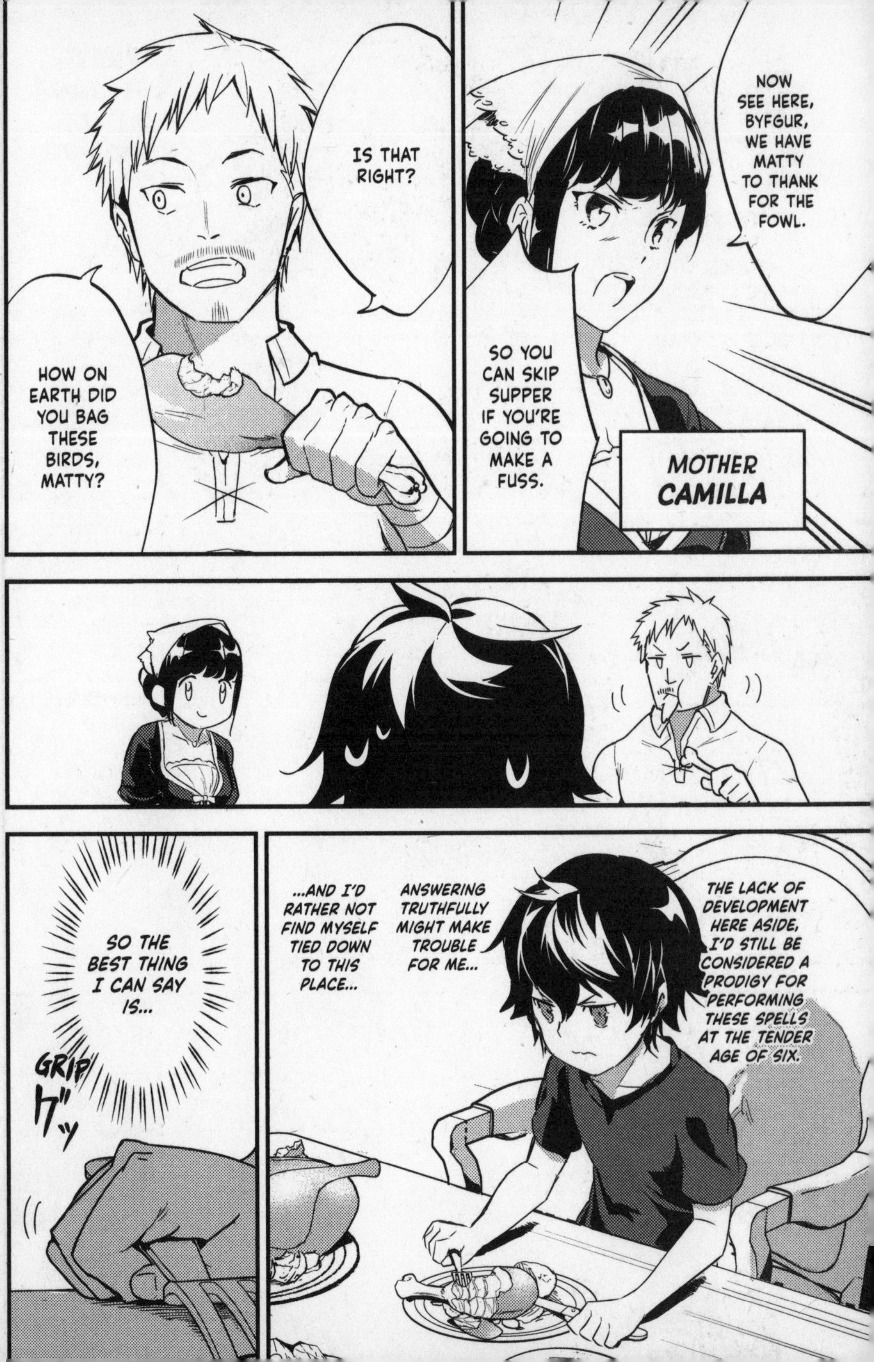
NOW SEE HERE, BYFGUR, WE HAVE MATTY TO THANK FOR THE FOWL.
SO YOU CAN SKIP SUPPER IF YOU'RE GOING TO MAKE A FUSS.
MOTHER CAMILLA
IS THAT RIGHT?
HOW ON EARTH DID YOU BAG THESE BIRDS, MATTY?
THE LACK OF DEVELOPMENT HERE ASIDE, I'D STILL BE CONSIDERED A PRODIGY FOR PERFORMING THESE SPELLS AT THE TENDER AGE OF SIX.
ANSWERING TRUTHFULLY MIGHT MAKE TROUBLE FOR ME...
...AND I'D RATHER NOT FIND MYSELF TIED DOWN TO THIS PLACE...
SO THE BEST THING I CAN SAY IS...
GRIP

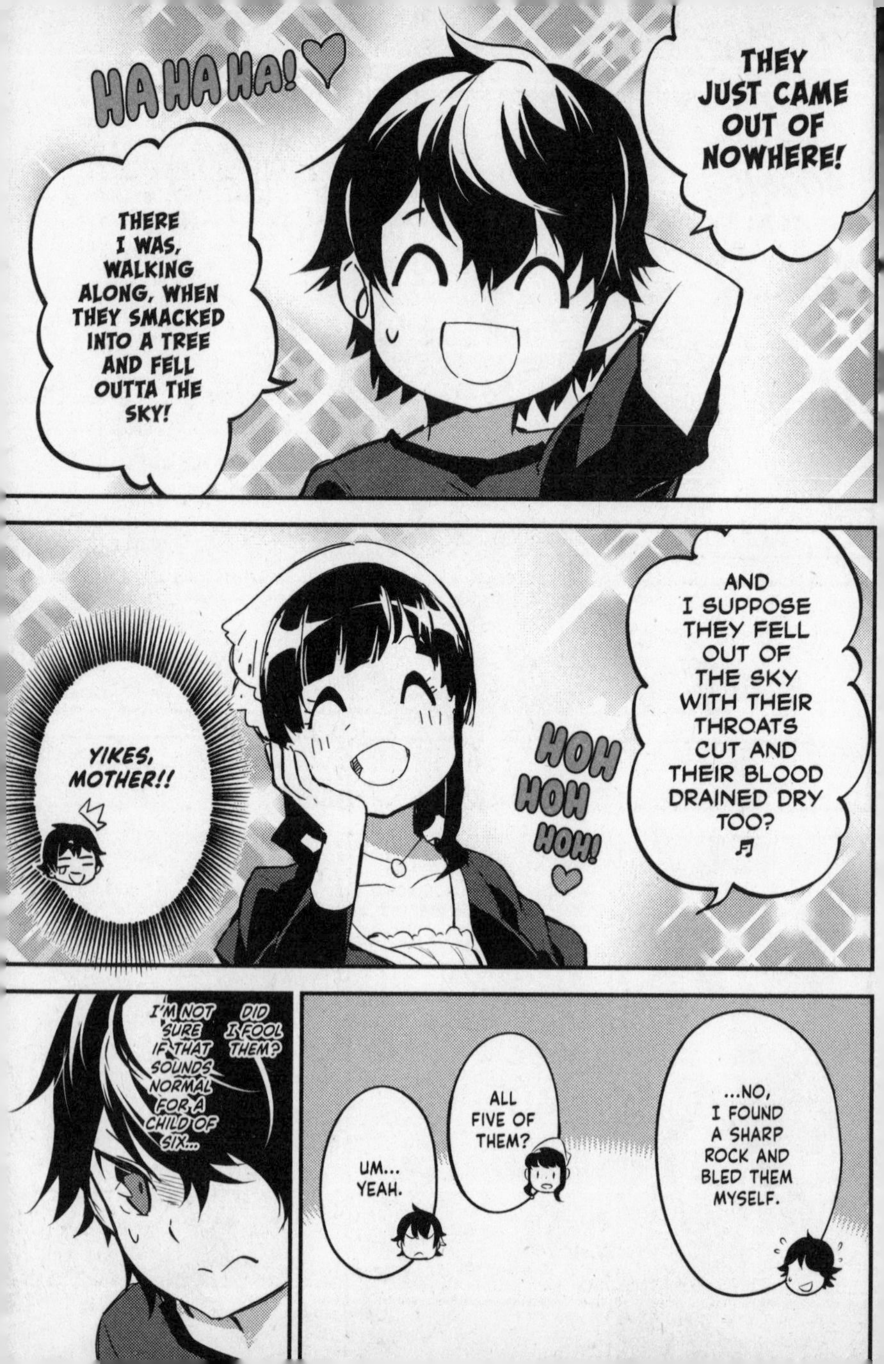
THEY JUST CAME OUT OF NOWHERE!
HAHAHA! ♥
THERE I WAS, WALKING ALONG, WHEN THEY SMACKED INTO A TREE AND FELL OUTTA THE SKY!
AND I SUPPOSE THEY FELL OUT OF THE SKY WITH THEIR THROATS CUT AND THEIR BLOOD DRAINED DRY TOO? ♫
HOH HOH HOH! ♥
YIKES, MOTHER!!
...NO, I FOUND A SHARP ROCK AND BLED THEM MYSELF.
ALL FIVE OF THEM?
UM... YEAH.
DID I FOOL THEM?
I'M NOT SURE IF THAT SOUNDS NORMAL FOR A CHILD OF SIX...

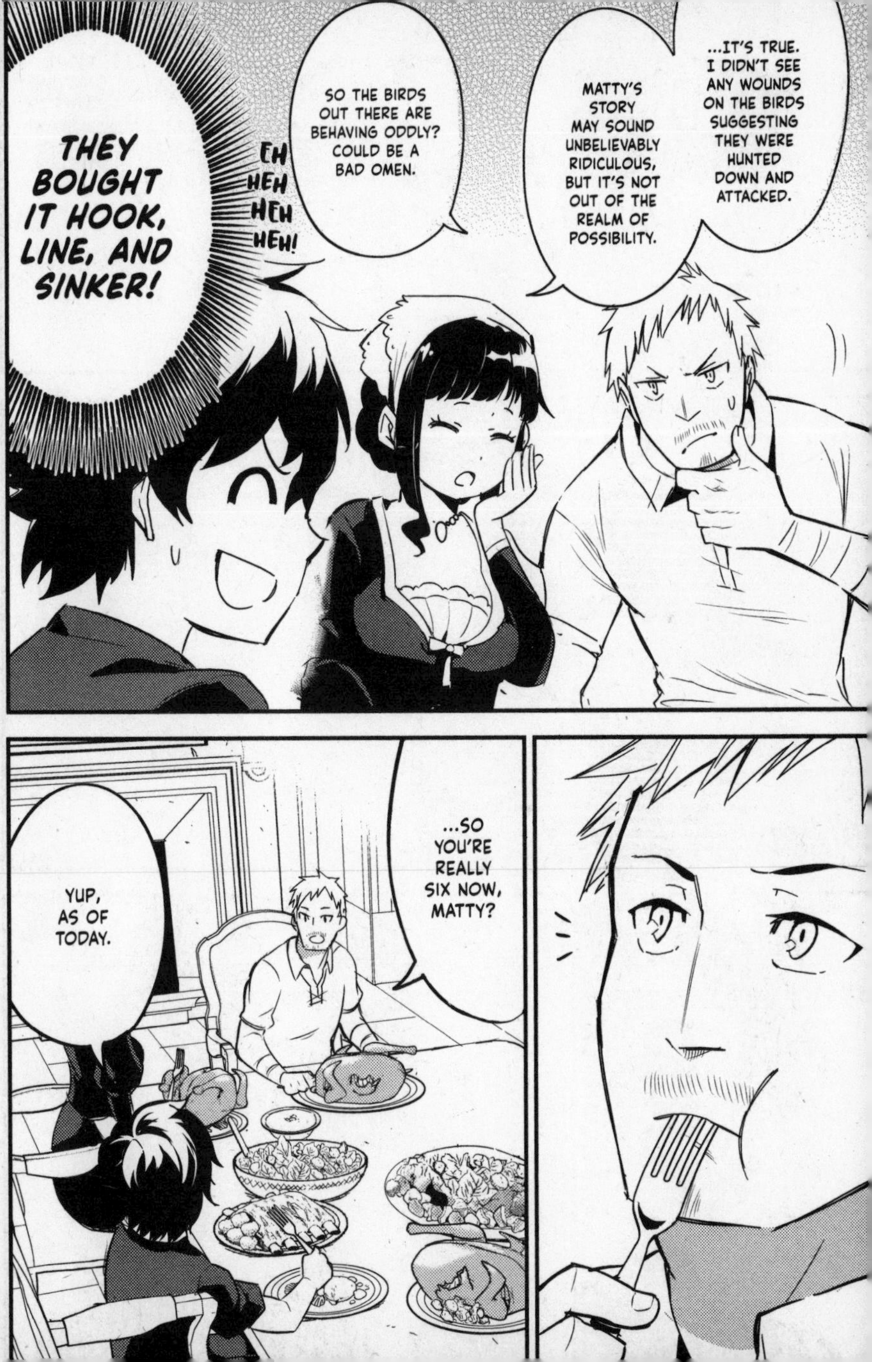
...IT'S TRUE. I DIDN'T SEE ANY WOUNDS ON THE BIRDS SUGGESTING THEY WERE HUNTED DOWN AND ATTACKED.
MATTY'S STORY MAY SOUND UNBELIEVABLY RIDICULOUS, BUT IT'S NOT OUT OF THE REALM OF POSSIBILITY.
SO THE BIRDS OUT THERE ARE BEHAVING ODDLY? COULD BE A BAD OMEN.
EH HEH HEH HEH!
THEY BOUGHT IT HOOK, LINE, AND SINKER!
...SO YOU'RE REALLY SIX NOW, MATTY?
YUP, AS OF TODAY.

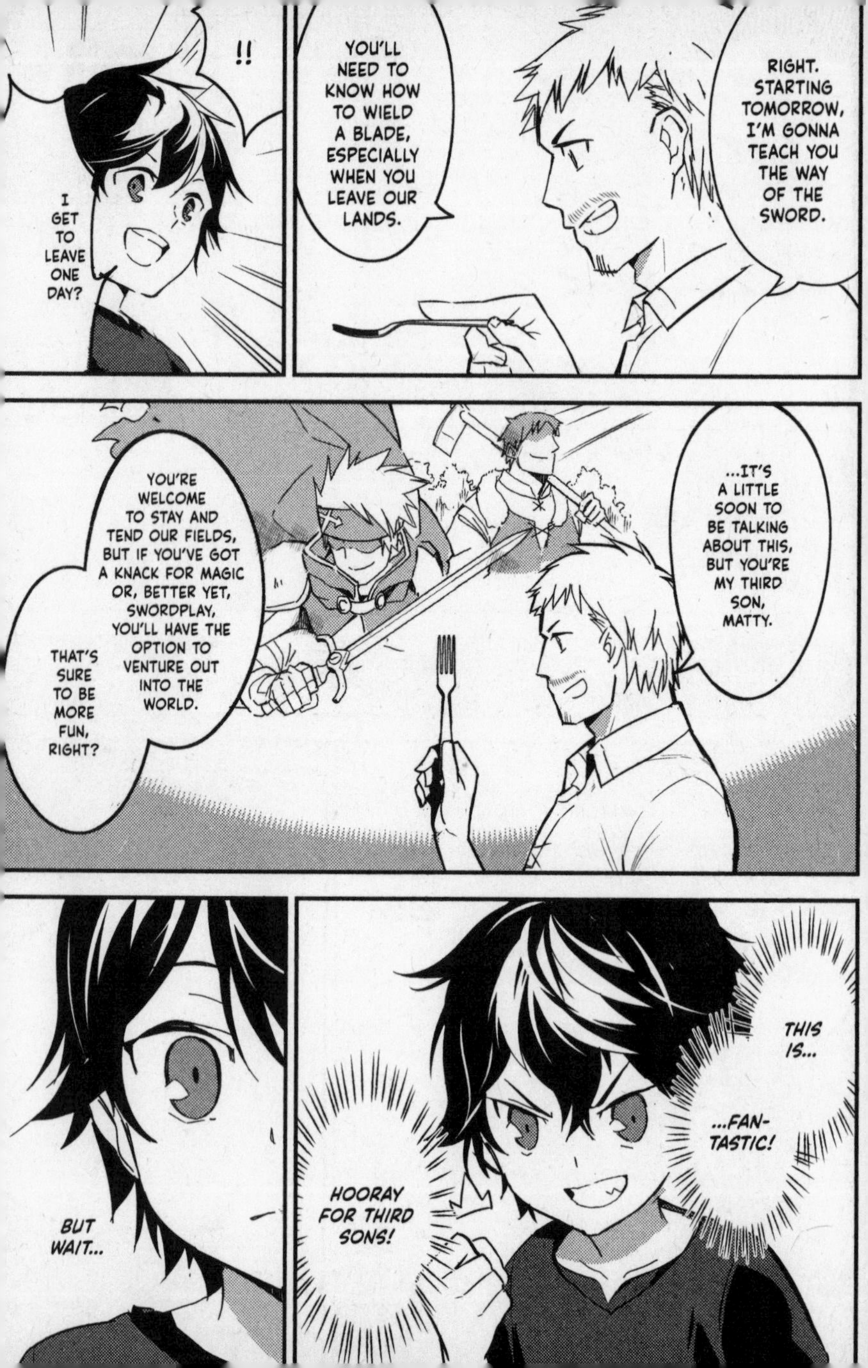
RIGHT. STARTING TOMORROW, I'M GONNA TEACH YOU THE WAY OF THE SWORD.
YOU'LL NEED TO KNOW HOW TO WIELD A BLADE, ESPECIALLY WHEN YOU LEAVE OUR LANDS.
!!
I GET TO LEAVE ONE DAY?
...IT'S A LITTLE SOON TO BE TALKING ABOUT THIS, BUT YOU'RE MY THIRD SON, MATTY.
YOU'RE WELCOME TO STAY AND TEND OUR FIELDS, BUT IF YOU'VE GOT A KNACK FOR MAGIC OR, BETTER YET, SWORDPLAY, YOU'LL HAVE THE OPTION TO VENTURE OUT INTO THE WORLD.
THAT'S SURE TO BE MORE FUN, RIGHT?
THIS IS...
...FAN-TASTIC!
HOORAY FOR THIRD SONS!
BUT WAIT...

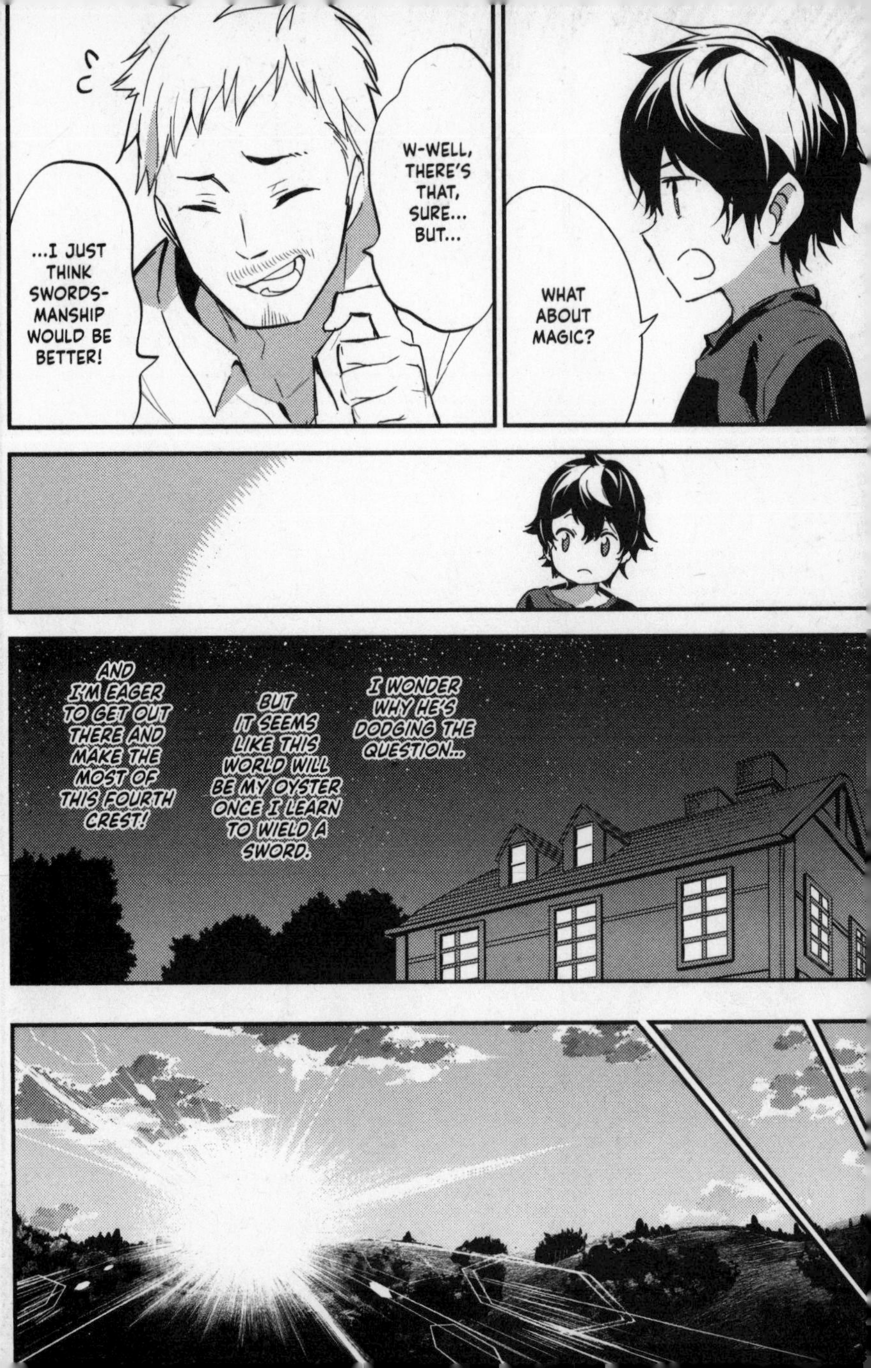
WHAT ABOUT MAGIC?
W-WELL, THERE'S THAT, SURE... BUT...
...I JUST THINK SWORDSMANSHIP WOULD BE BETTER!
I WONDER WHY HE'S DODGING THE QUESTION...
BUT IT SEEMS LIKE THIS WORLD WILL BE MY OYSTER ONCE I LEARN TO WIELD A SWORD.
AND I'M EAGER TO GET OUT THERE AND MAKE THE MOST OF THIS FOURTH CREST!

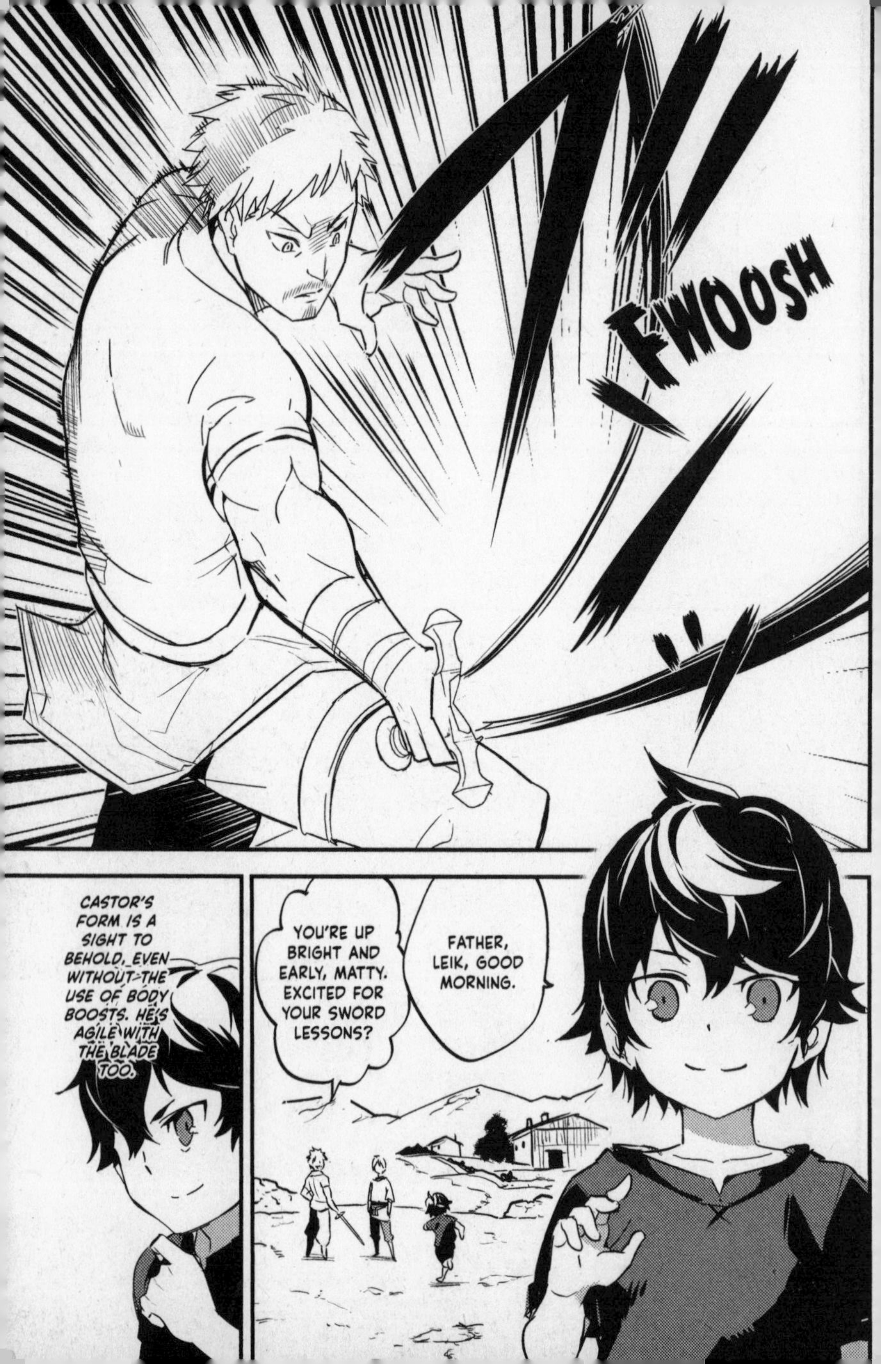
FWOOSH
FATHER, LEIK, GOOD MORNING.
YOU'RE UP BRIGHT AND EARLY, MATTY. EXCITED FOR YOUR SWORD LESSONS?
CASTOR'S FORM IS A SIGHT TO BEHOLD, EVEN WITHOUT THE USE OF BODY BOOSTS. HE'S AGILE WITH THE BLADE TOO.

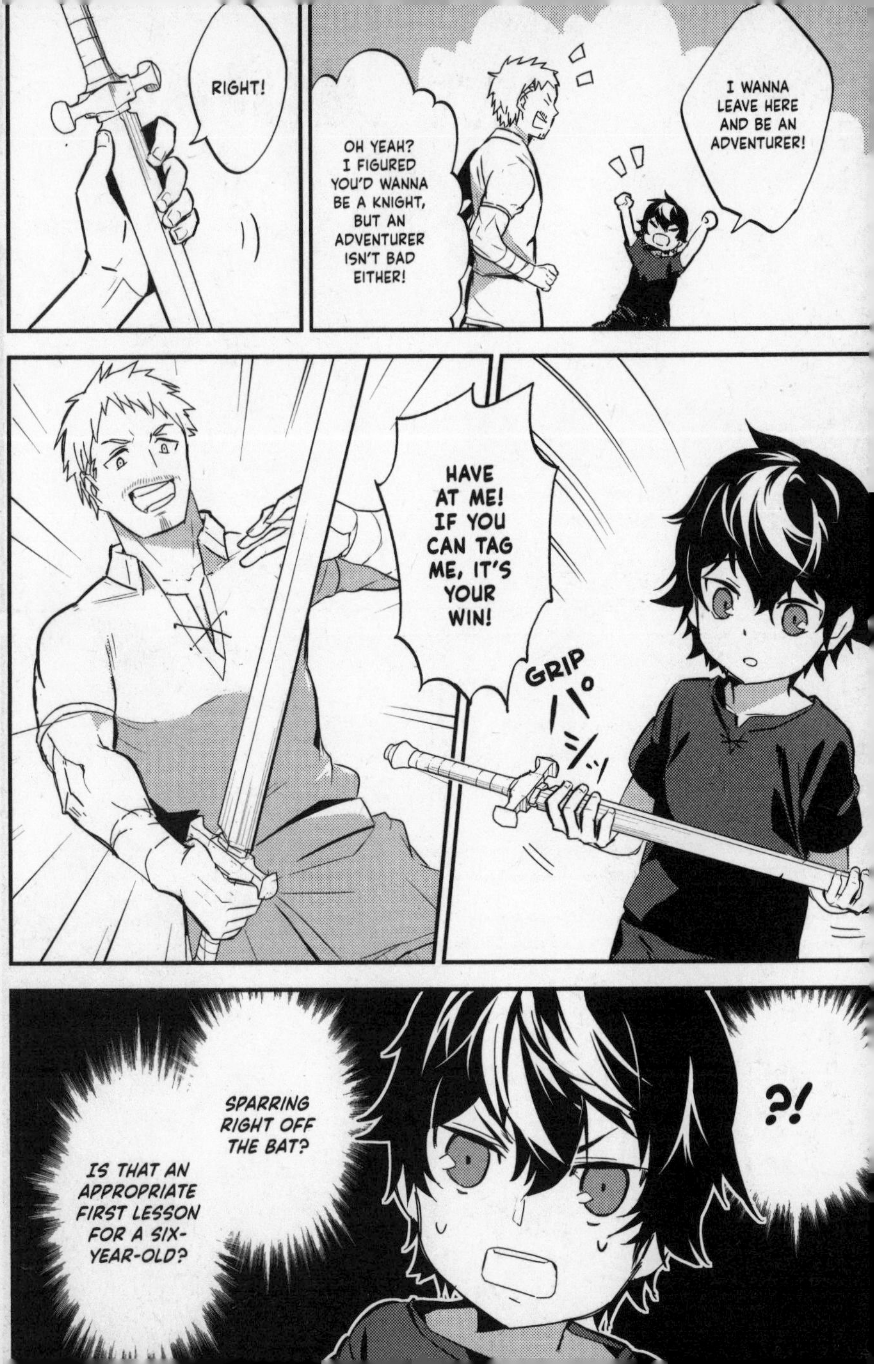
I WANNA LEAVE HERE AND BE AN ADVENTURER!
OH YEAH? I FIGURED YOU'D WANNA BE A KNIGHT, BUT AN ADVENTURER ISN'T BAD EITHER!
RIGHT!
HAVE AT ME! IF YOU CAN TAG ME, IT'S YOUR WIN!
GRIP
パシッ
?!
SPARRING RIGHT OFF THE BAT?
IS THAT AN APPROPRIATE FIRST LESSON FOR A SIX-YEAR-OLD?

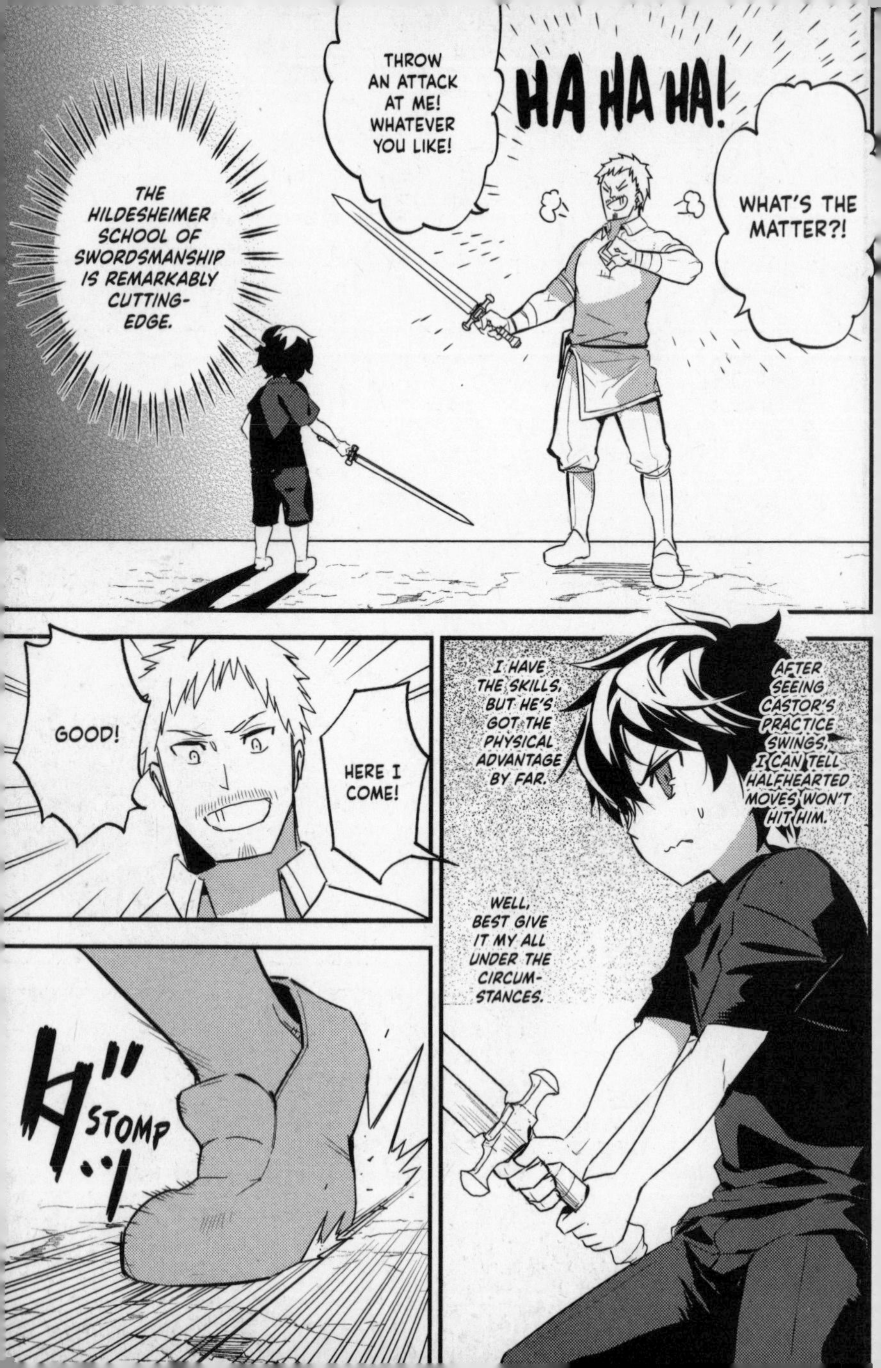
HA HA HA!
WHAT'S THE MATTER?!
THROW AN ATTACK AT ME! WHATEVER YOU LIKE!
THE HILDESHEIMER SCHOOL OF SWORDSMANSHIP IS REMARKABLY CUTTING-EDGE.
AFTER SEEING CASTOR'S PRACTICE SWINGS, I CAN TELL HALFHEARTED MOVES WON'T HIT HIM.
I HAVE THE SKILLS, BUT HE'S GOT THE PHYSICAL ADVANTAGE BY FAR.
WELL, BEST GIVE IT MY ALL UNDER THE CIRCUM-STANCES.
HERE I COME!
GOOD!
ドッ
STOMP

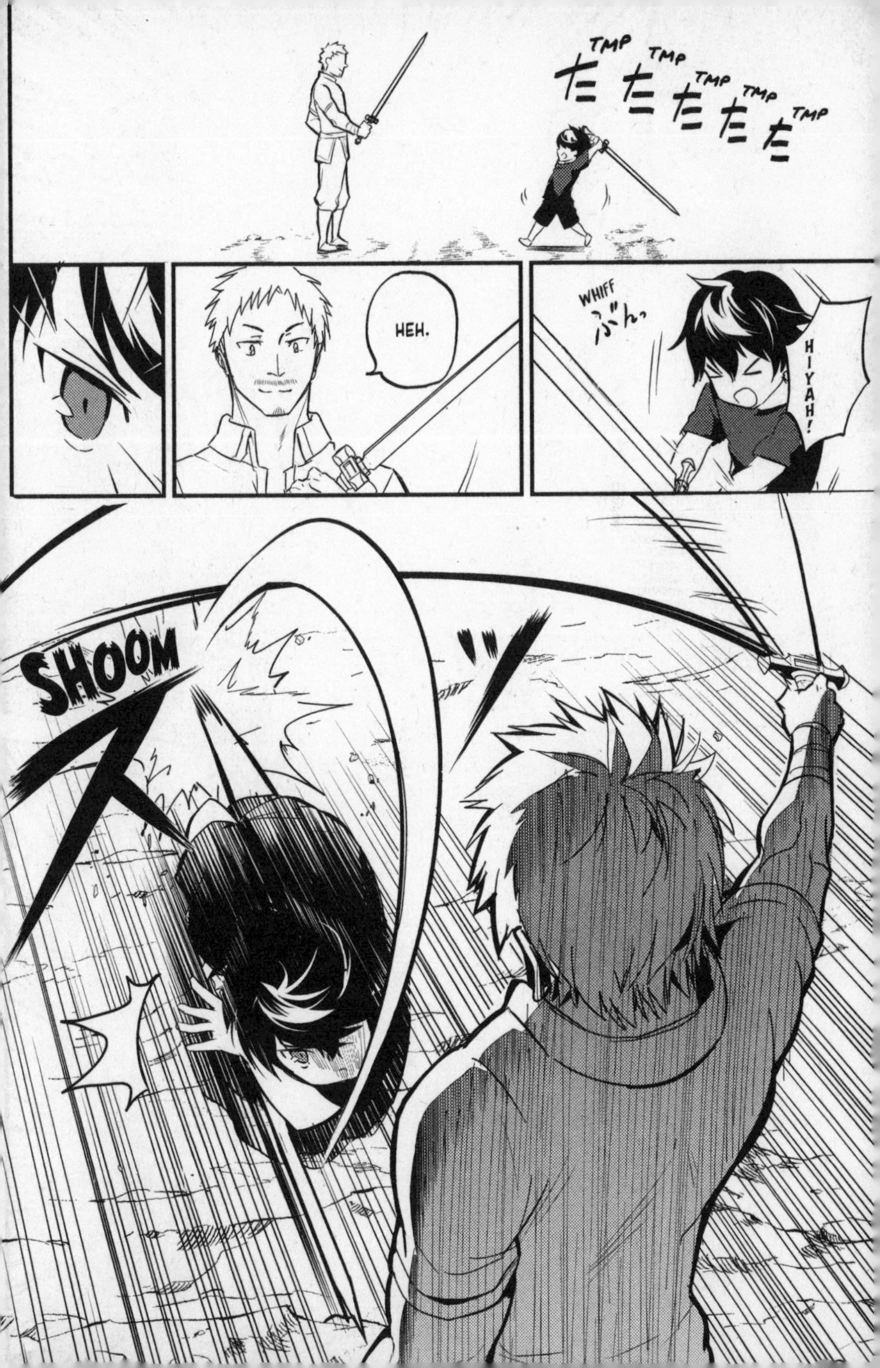
TMP TMP TMP TMP TMP
たたたたた
WHIFF
ぶんっ
HIYAH!
HEH.
SHOOM

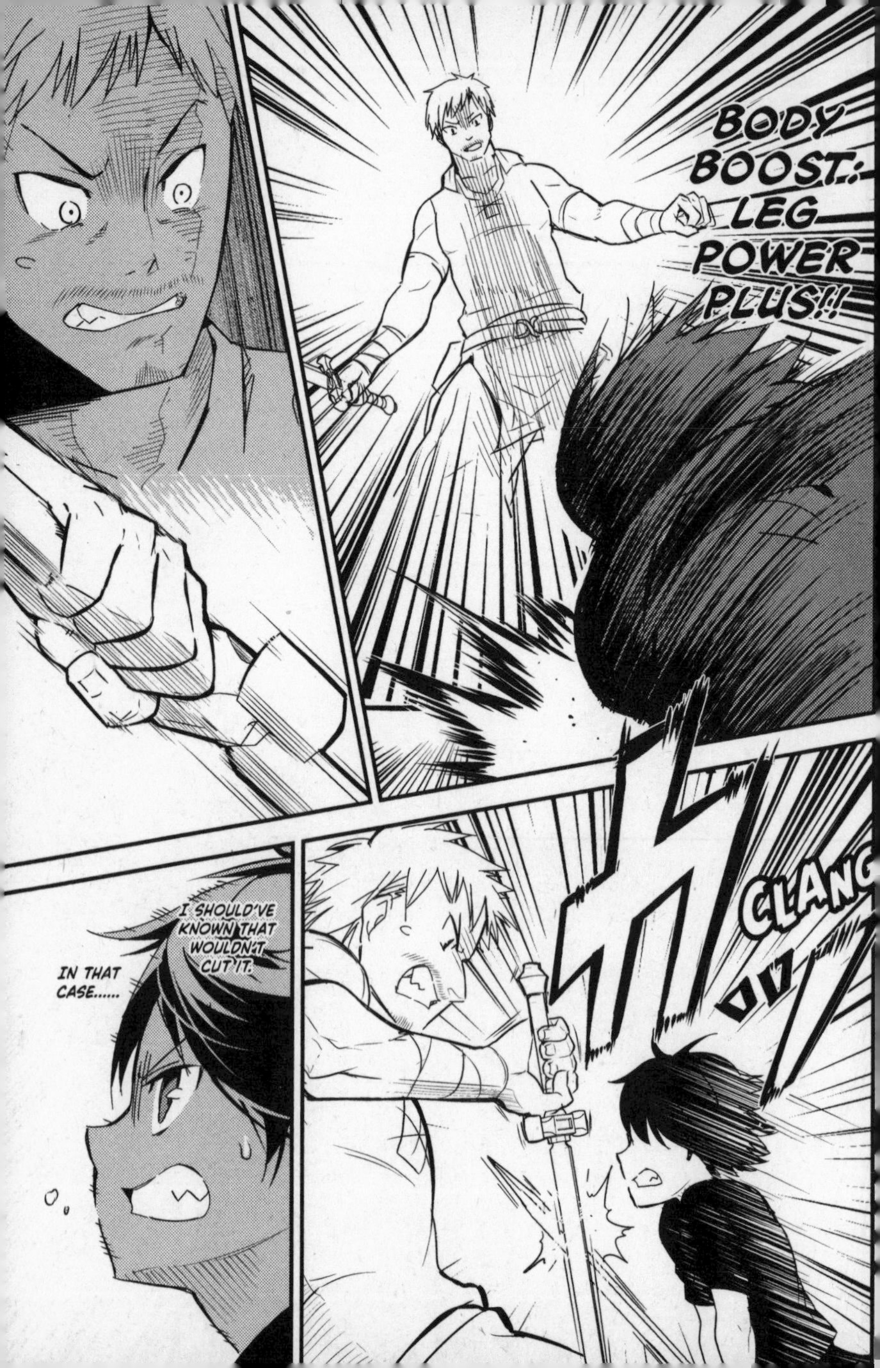
BODY BOOST: LEG POWER PLUS!!
CLANG
I SHOULD'VE KNOWN THAT WOULDN'T CUT IT.
IN THAT CASE......

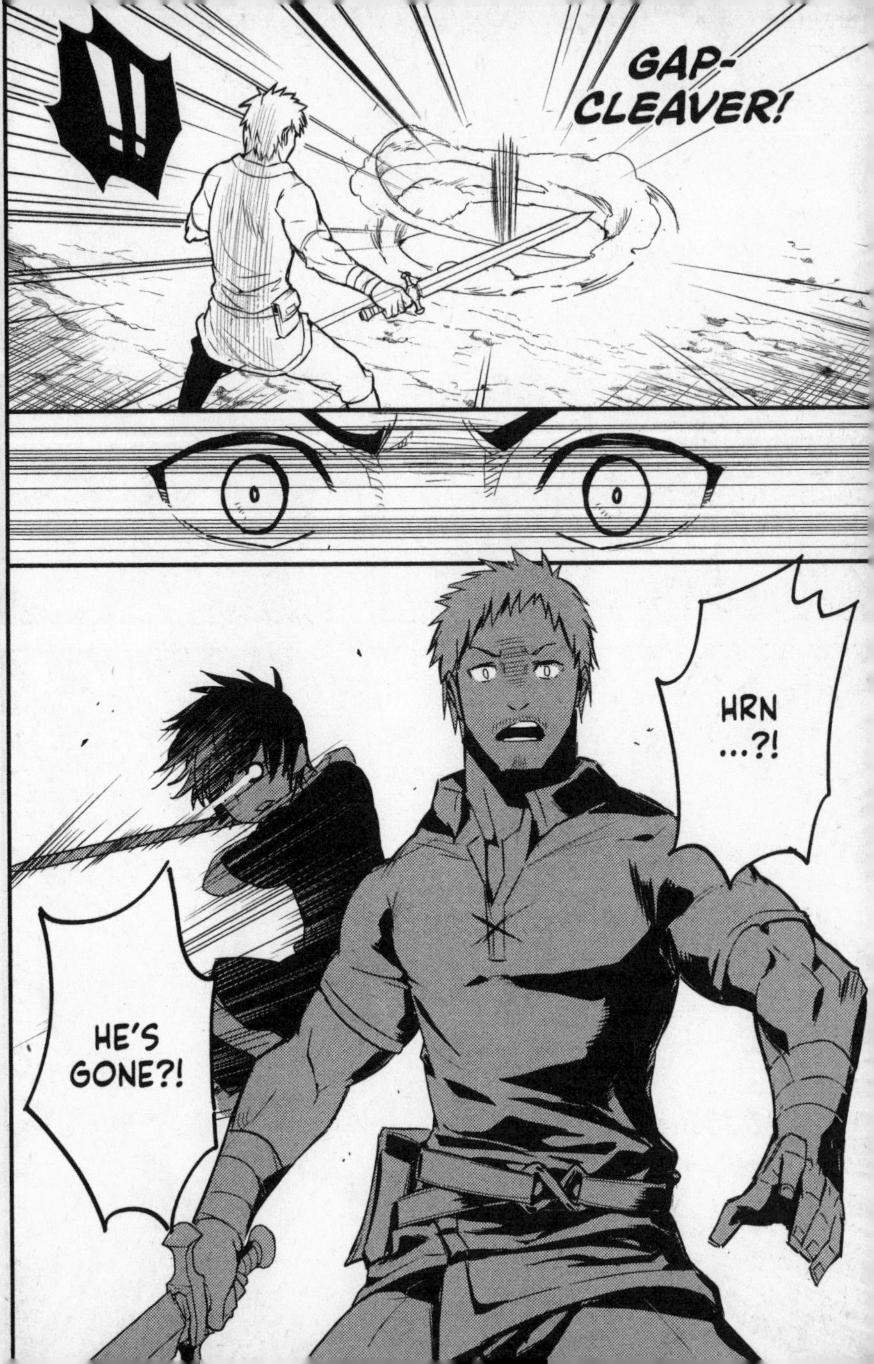
GAP-CLEAVER!
!!
HRN ...?!
HE'S GONE?!

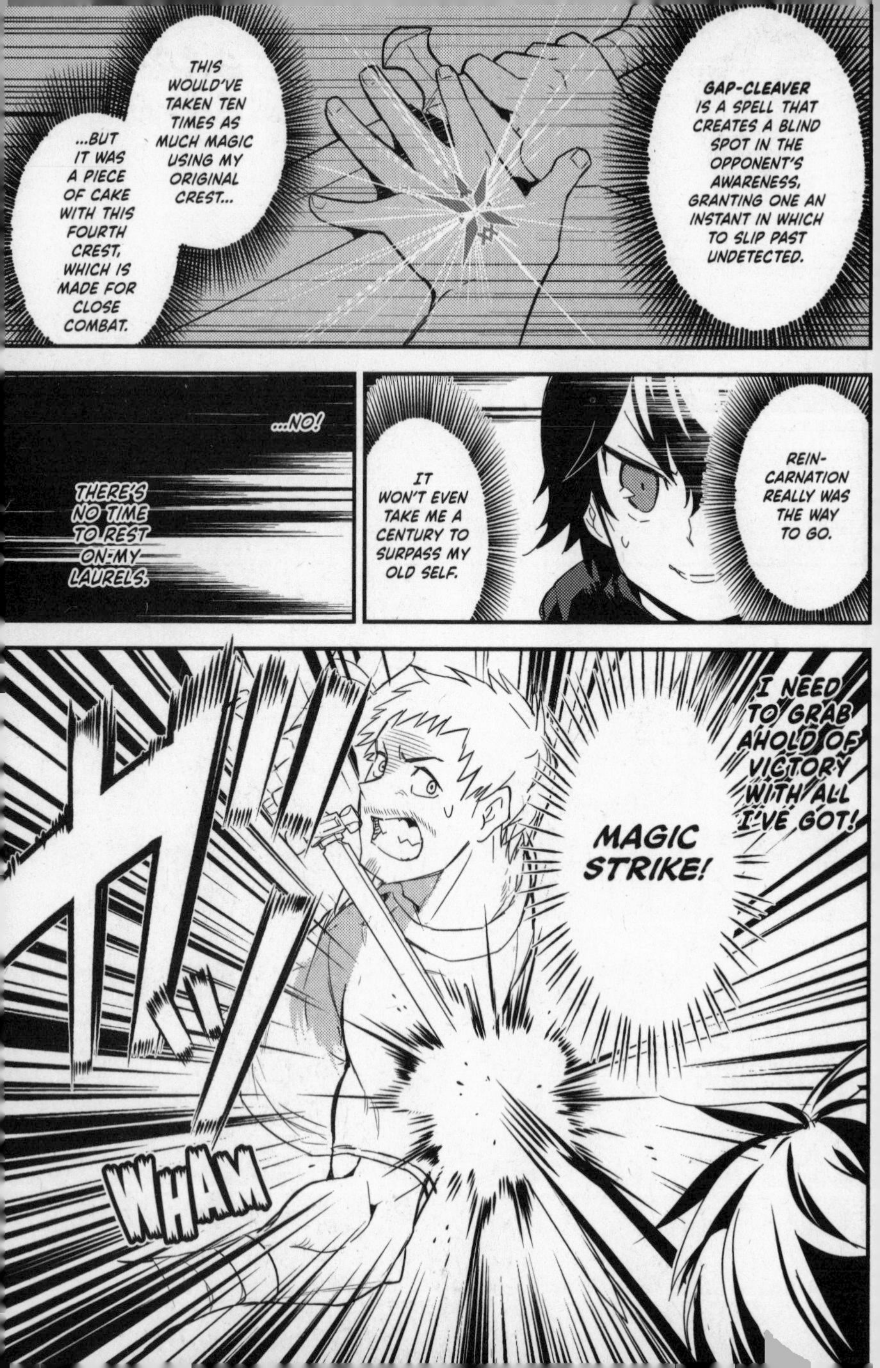
GAP-CLEAVER IS A SPELL THAT CREATES A BLIND SPOT IN THE OPPONENT'S AWARENESS, GRANTING ONE AN INSTANT IN WHICH TO SLIP PAST UNDETECTED.
THIS WOULD'VE TAKEN TEN TIMES AS MUCH MAGIC USING MY ORIGINAL CREST...
...BUT IT WAS A PIECE OF CAKE WITH THIS FOURTH CREST, WHICH IS MADE FOR CLOSE COMBAT.
REIN-CARNATION REALLY WAS THE WAY TO GO.
IT WON'T EVEN TAKE ME A CENTURY TO SURPASS MY OLD SELF.
...NO!
THERE'S NO TIME TO REST ON MY LAURELS.
I NEED TO GRAB AHOLD OF VICTORY WITH ALL I'VE GOT!
MAGIC STRIKE!
WHAM

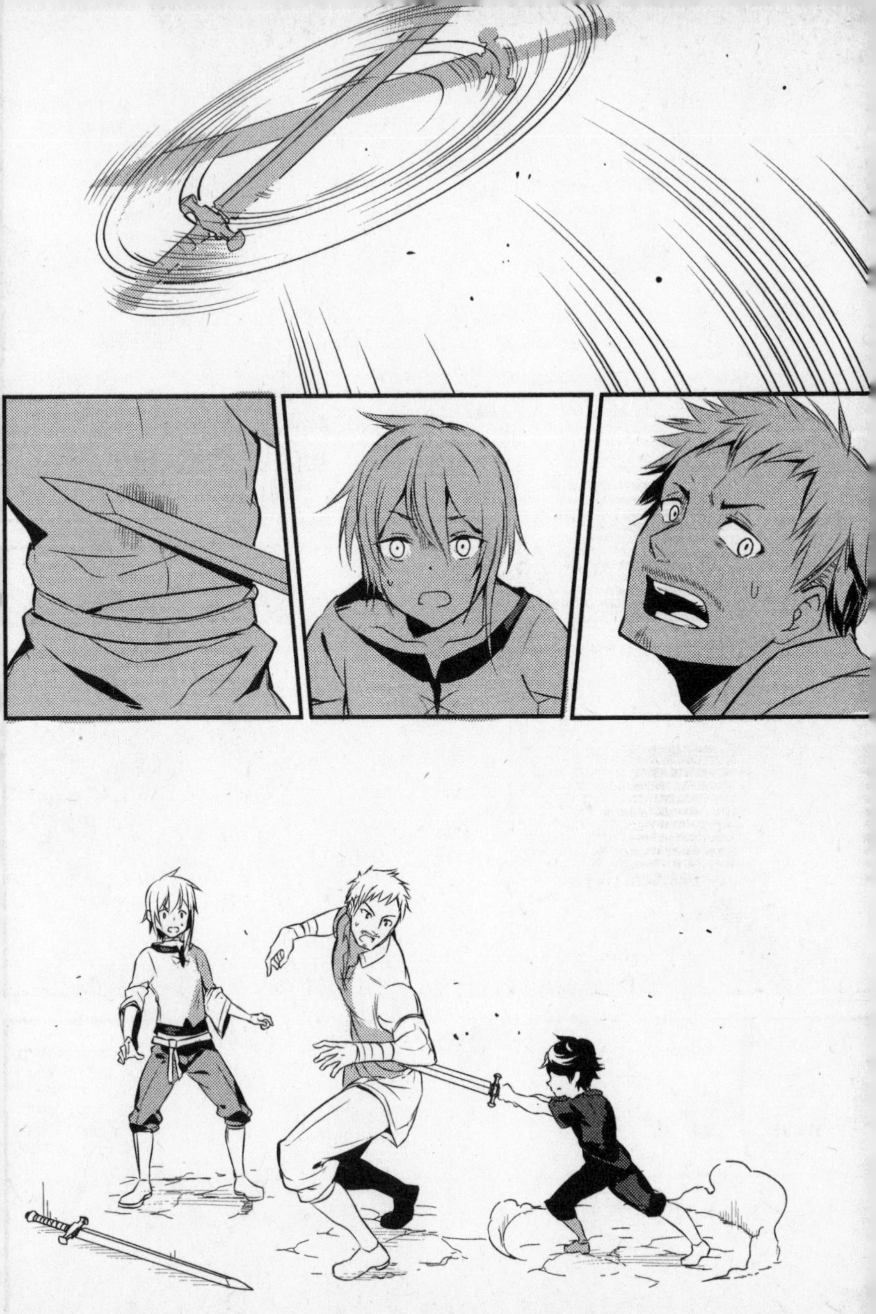

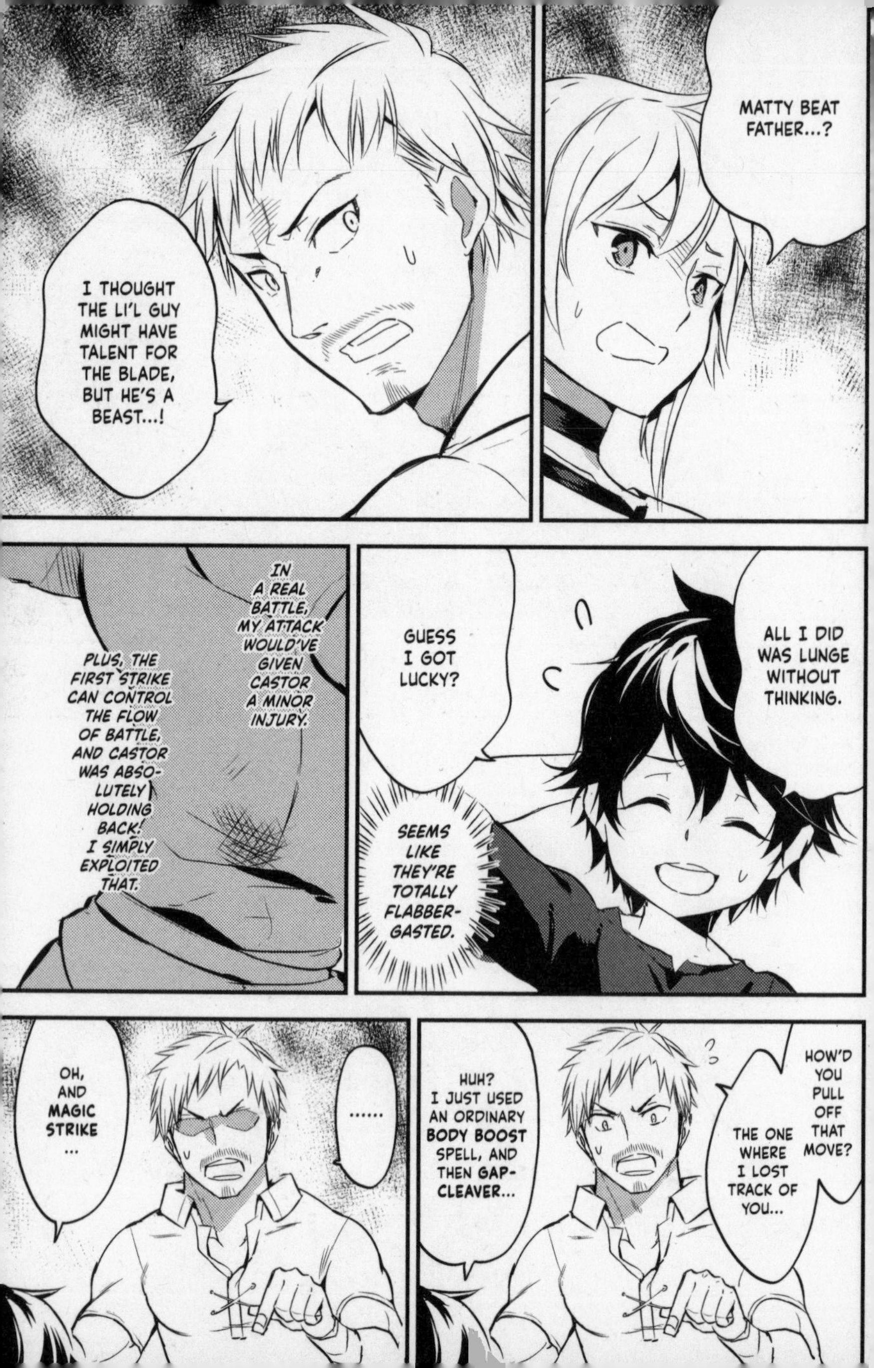
MATTY BEAT FATHER...?
I THOUGHT THE LI'L GUY MIGHT HAVE TALENT FOR THE BLADE, BUT HE'S A BEAST...!
ALL I DID WAS LUNGE WITHOUT THINKING.
GUESS I GOT LUCKY?
SEEMS LIKE THEY'RE TOTALLY FLABBER-GASTED.
IN A REAL BATTLE, MY ATTACK WOULD'VE GIVEN CASTOR A MINOR INJURY.
PLUS, THE FIRST STRIKE CAN CONTROL THE FLOW OF BATTLE, AND CASTOR WAS ABSO-LUTELY HOLDING BACK! I SIMPLY EXPLOITED THAT.
HOW'D YOU PULL OFF THAT MOVE?
THE ONE WHERE I LOST TRACK OF YOU...
HUH? I JUST USED AN ORDINARY **BODY BOOST** SPELL, AND THEN GAP-CLEAVER...
......
OH, AND MAGIC STRIKE ...

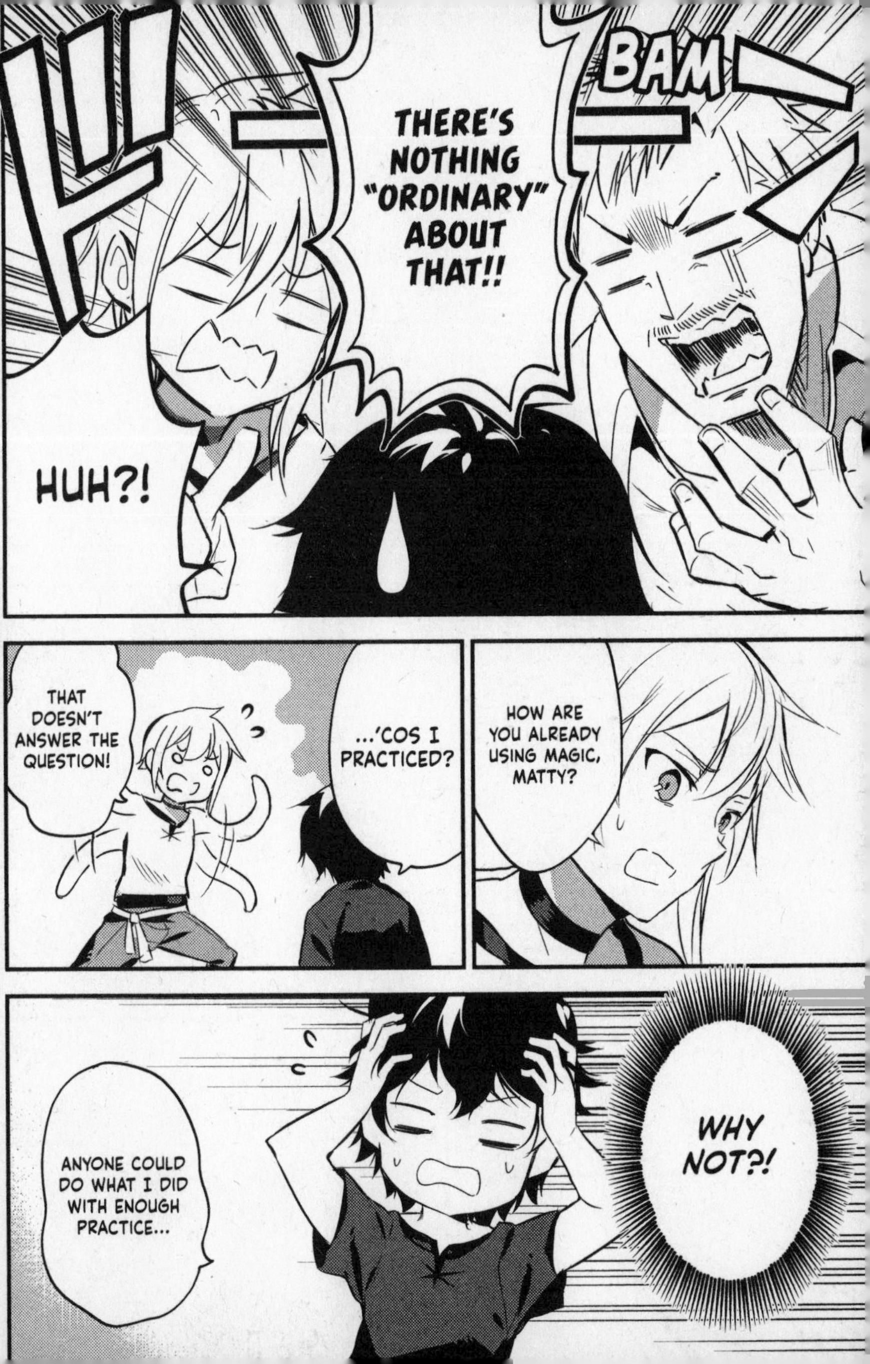
BAM
THERE'S NOTHING "ORDINARY" ABOUT THAT!!
HUH?!
HOW ARE YOU ALREADY USING MAGIC, MATTY?
...'COS I PRACTICED?
THAT DOESN'T ANSWER THE QUESTION!
WHY NOT?!
ANYONE COULD DO WHAT I DID WITH ENOUGH PRACTICE...

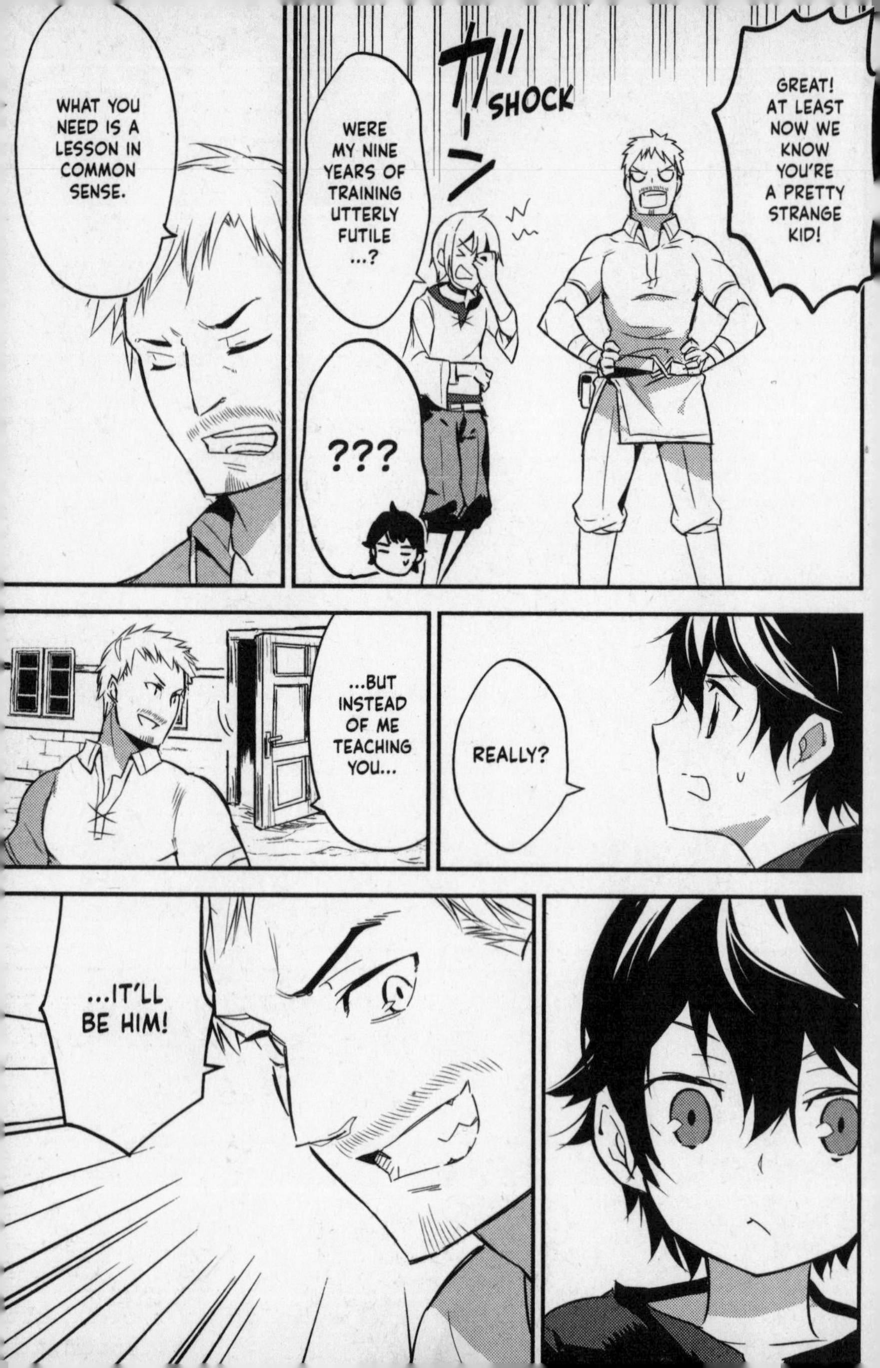
GREAT! AT LEAST NOW WE KNOW YOU'RE A PRETTY STRANGE KID!
SHOCK
WERE MY NINE YEARS OF TRAINING UTTERLY FUTILE ...?
???
WHAT YOU NEED IS A LESSON IN COMMON SENSE.
REALLY?
...BUT INSTEAD OF ME TEACHING YOU...
...IT'LL BE HIM!

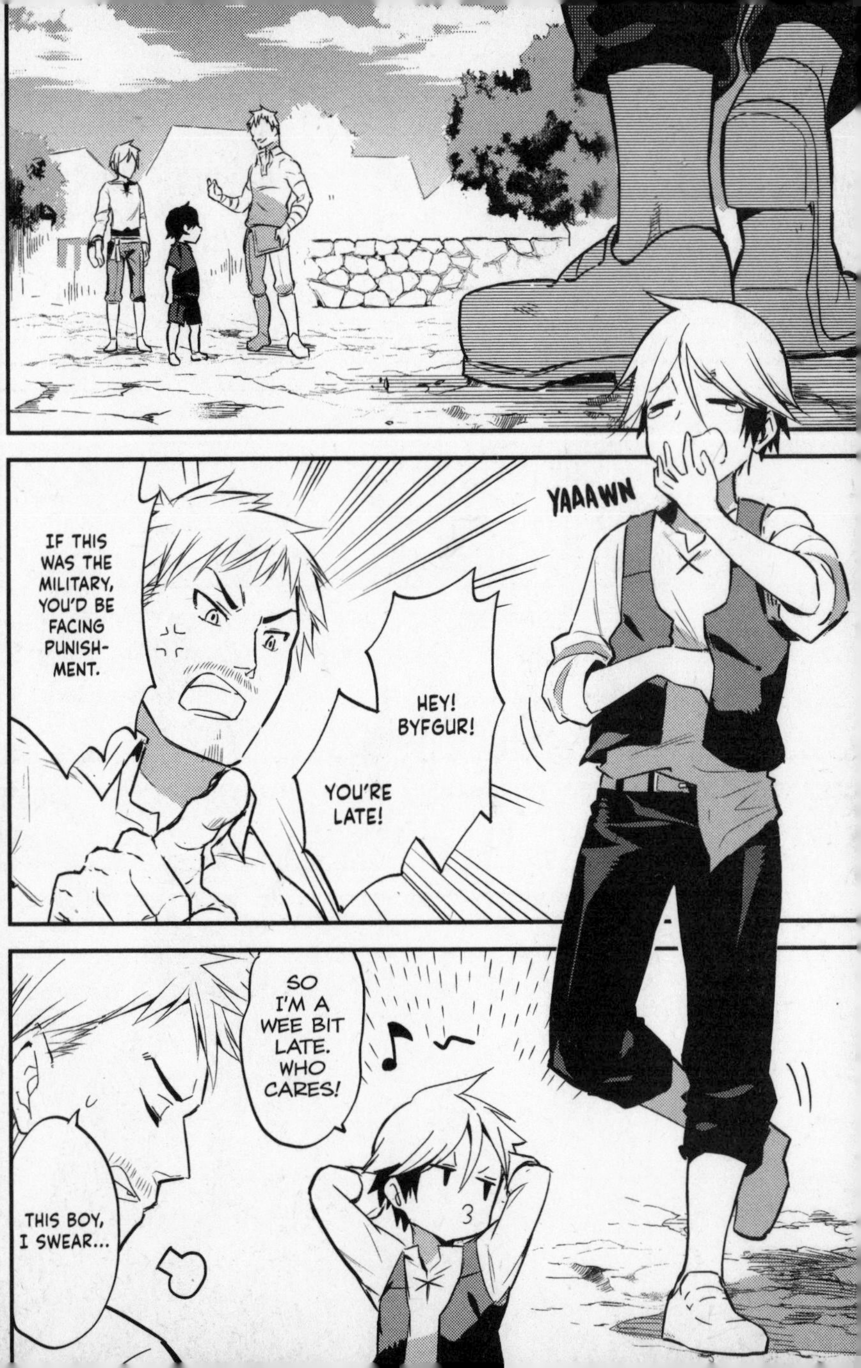
YAAAWN
HEY! BYFGUR!
YOU'RE LATE!
IF THIS WAS THE MILITARY, YOU'D BE FACING PUNISHMENT.
SO I'M A WEE BIT LATE. WHO CARES!
♪~
THIS BOY, I SWEAR...

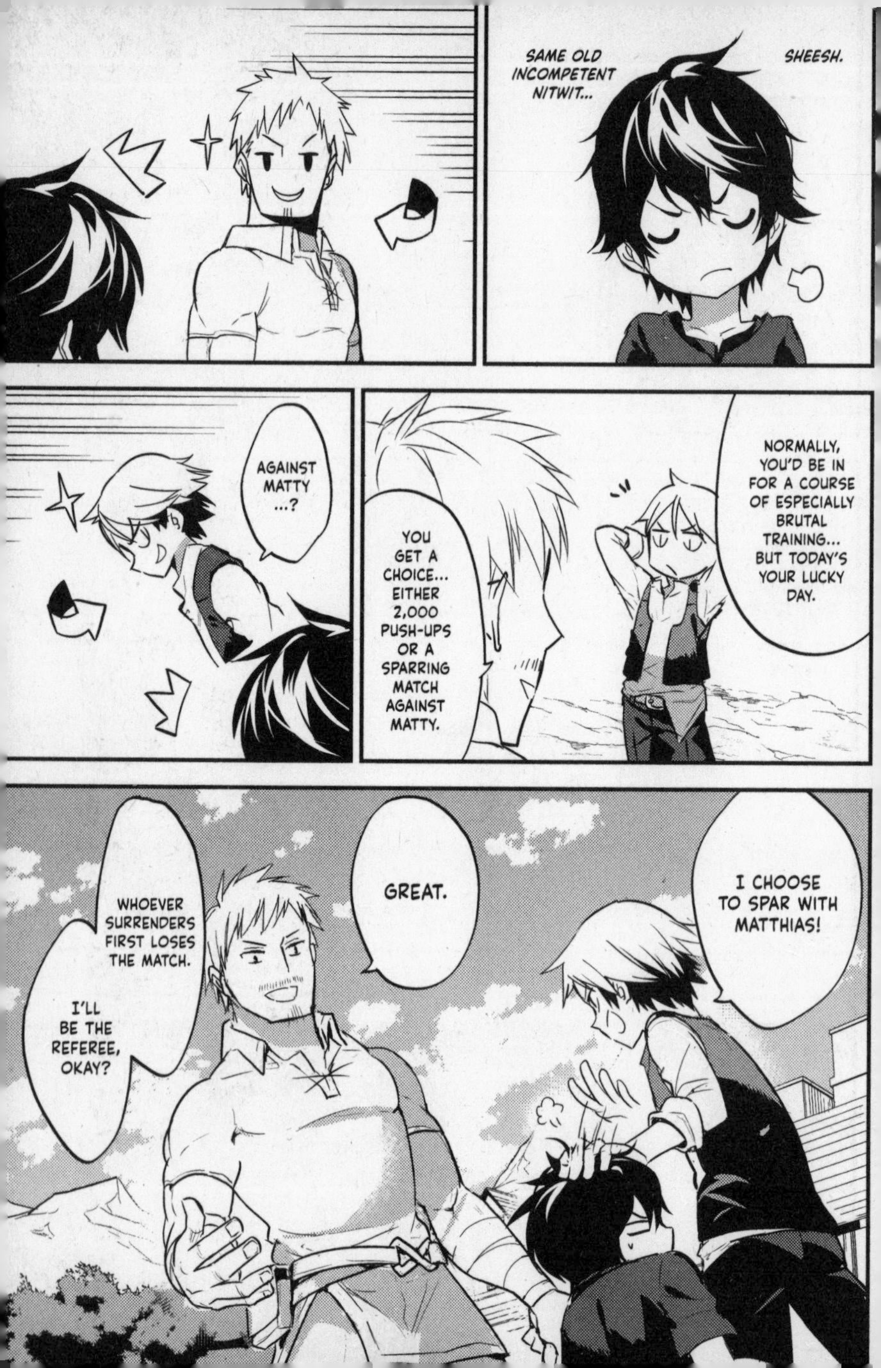
SHEESH.
SAME OLD INCOMPETENT NITWIT...
NORMALLY, YOU'D BE IN FOR A COURSE OF ESPECIALLY BRUTAL TRAINING... BUT TODAY'S YOUR LUCKY DAY.
YOU GET A CHOICE... EITHER 2,000 PUSH-UPS OR A SPARRING MATCH AGAINST MATTY.
AGAINST MATTY ...?
I CHOOSE TO SPAR WITH MATTHIAS!
GREAT.
WHOEVER SURRENDERS FIRST LOSES THE MATCH.
I'LL BE THE REFEREE, OKAY?

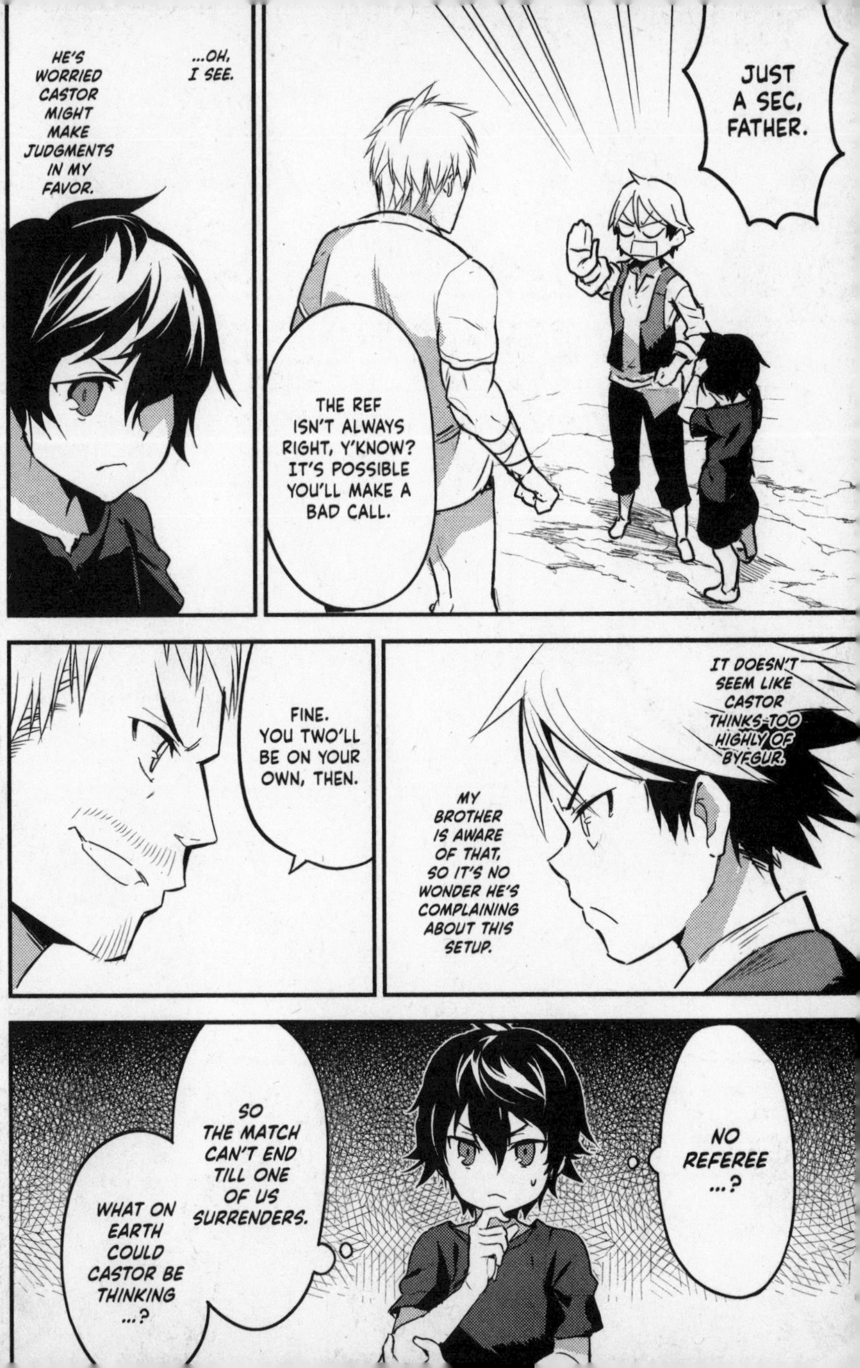
JUST A SEC, FATHER.
THE REF ISN'T ALWAYS RIGHT, Y'KNOW? IT'S POSSIBLE YOU'LL MAKE A BAD CALL.
...OH, I SEE.
HE'S WORRIED CASTOR MIGHT MAKE JUDGMENTS IN MY FAVOR.
IT DOESN'T SEEM LIKE CASTOR THINKS TOO HIGHLY OF BYFGUR.
MY BROTHER IS AWARE OF THAT, SO IT'S NO WONDER HE'S COMPLAINING ABOUT THIS SETUP.
FINE. YOU TWO'LL BE ON YOUR OWN, THEN.
NO REFEREE ...?
SO THE MATCH CAN'T END TILL ONE OF US SURRENDERS.
WHAT ON EARTH COULD CASTOR BE THINKING ...?

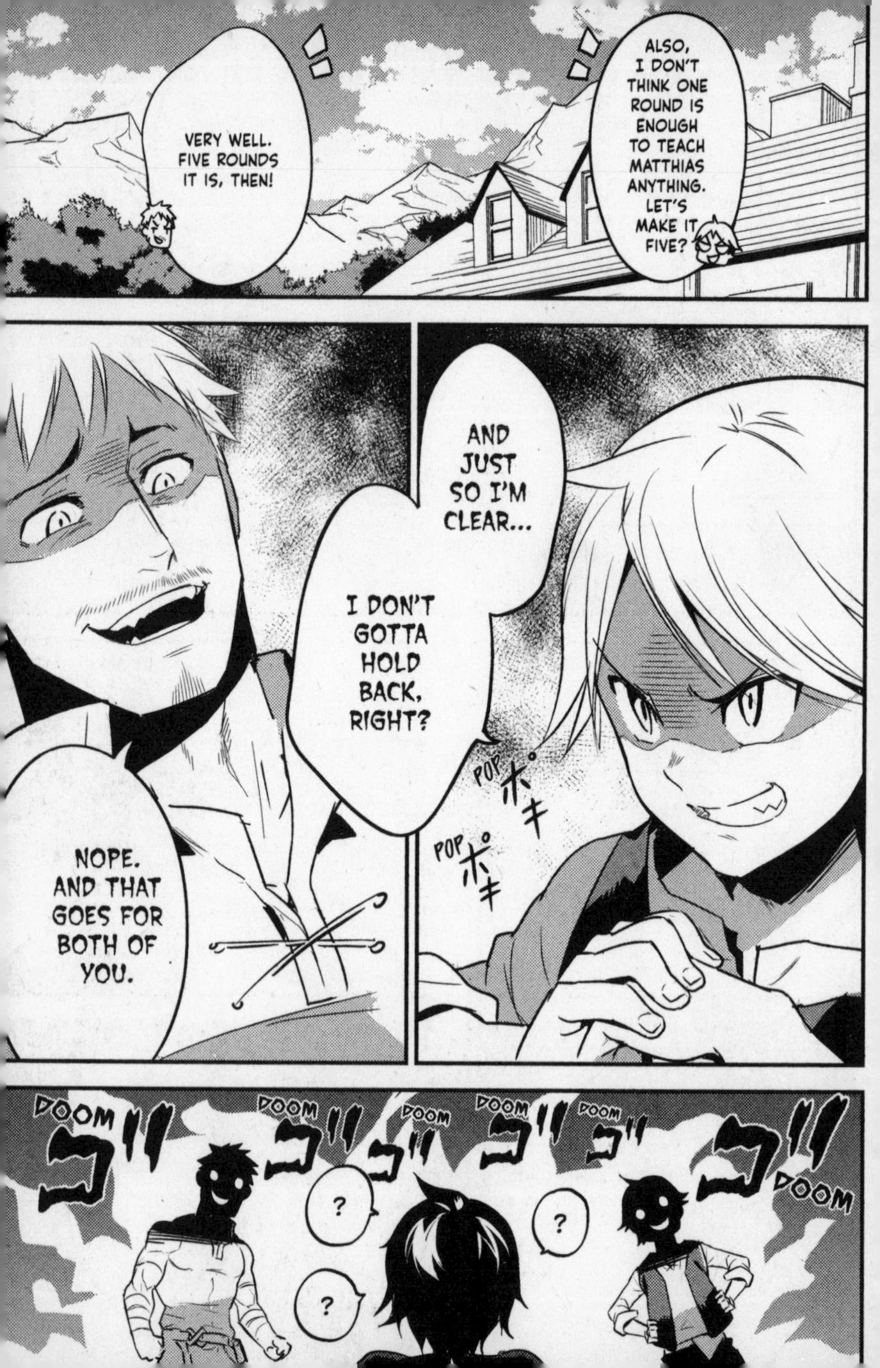
ALSO, I DON'T THINK ONE ROUND IS ENOUGH TO TEACH MATTHIAS ANYTHING. LET'S MAKE IT FIVE?
VERY WELL. FIVE ROUNDS IT IS, THEN!
AND JUST SO I'M CLEAR...
I DON'T GOTTA HOLD BACK, RIGHT?
POP
POP
NOPE. AND THAT GOES FOR BOTH OF YOU.
DOOM
DOOM
DOOM
DOOM
DOOM
DOOM
?
?
?

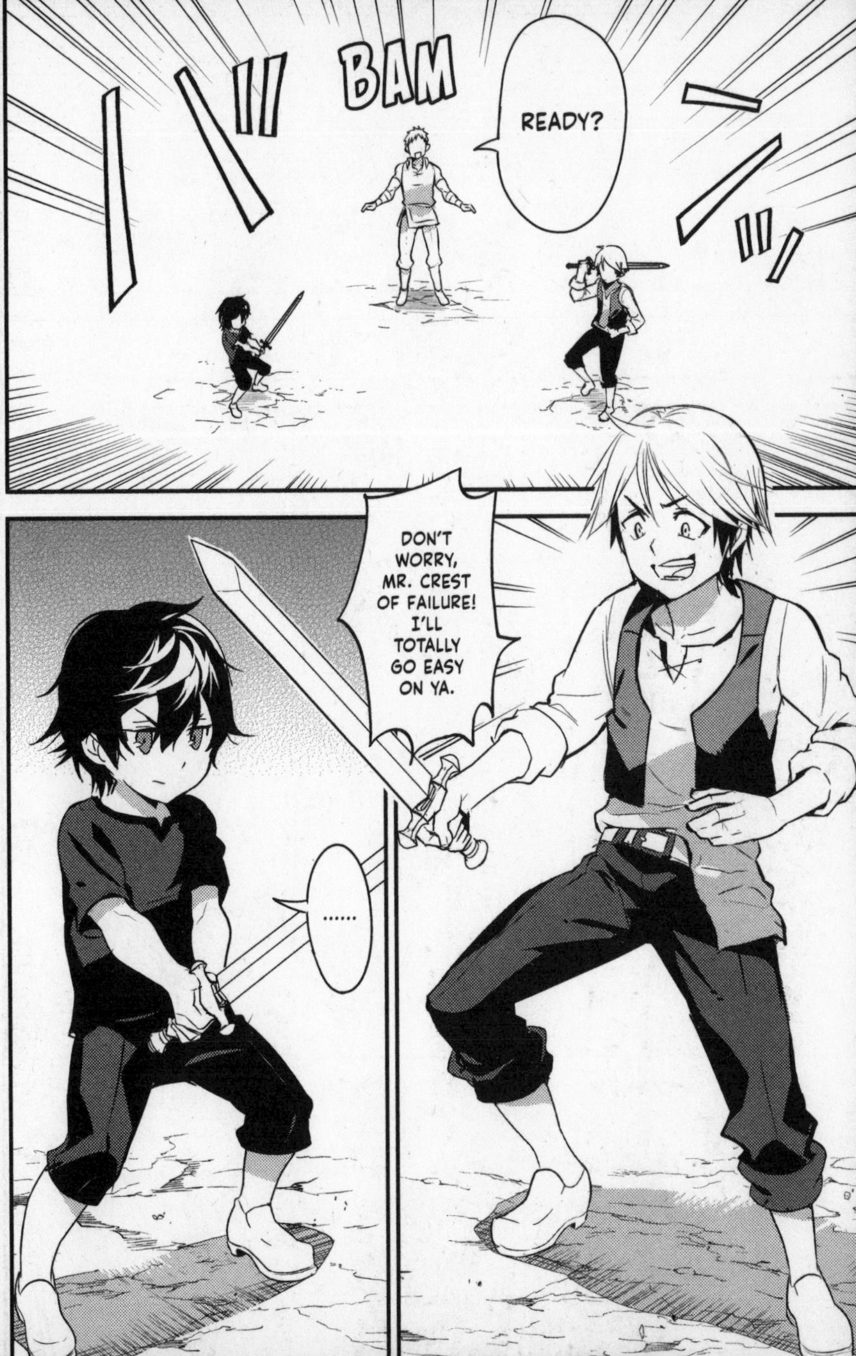
READY?
BAM
DON'T WORRY, MR. CREST OF FAILURE! I'LL TOTALLY GO EASY ON YA.
......

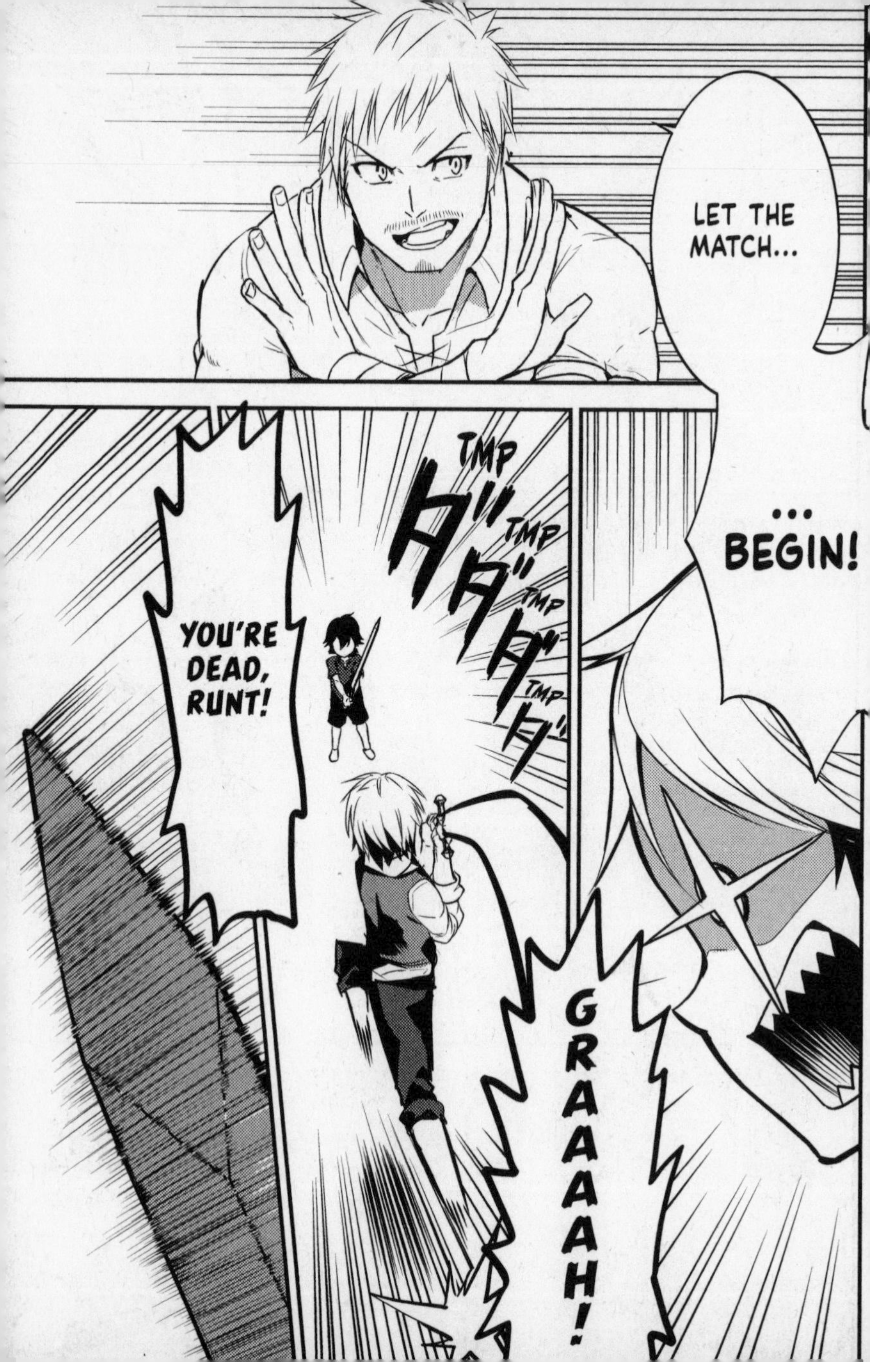
LET THE MATCH...
...BEGIN!
TMP
TMP
TMP
TMP
ダダダダ
YOU'RE DEAD, RUNT!
GRAAAAAH!

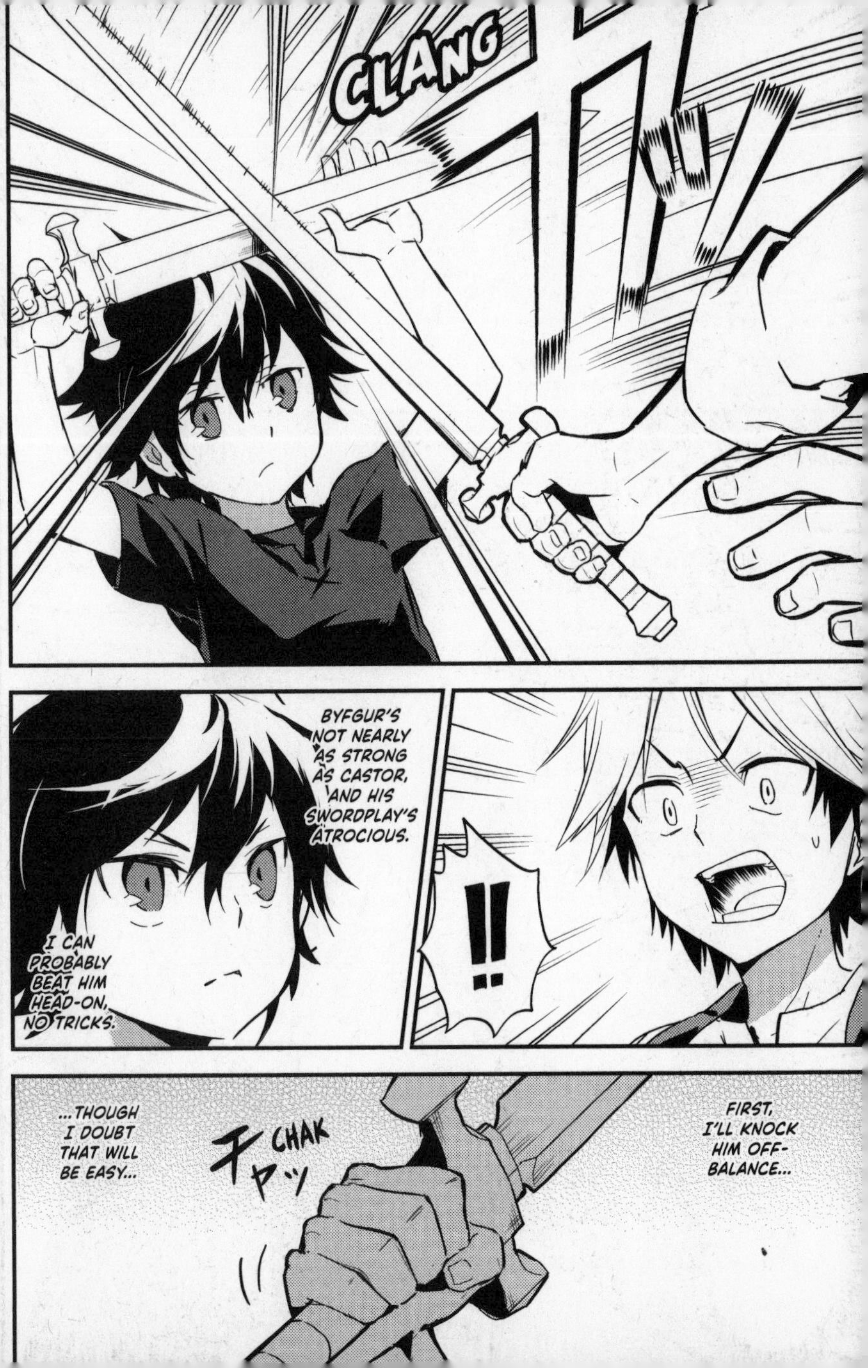
CLANG
!!
BYFGUR'S NOT NEARLY AS STRONG AS CASTOR, AND HIS SWORDPLAY'S ATROCIOUS.
I CAN PROBABLY BEAT HIM HEAD-ON, NO TRICKS.
FIRST, I'LL KNOCK HIM OFF-BALANCE...
チャッ
CHAK
...THOUGH I DOUBT THAT WILL BE EASY...

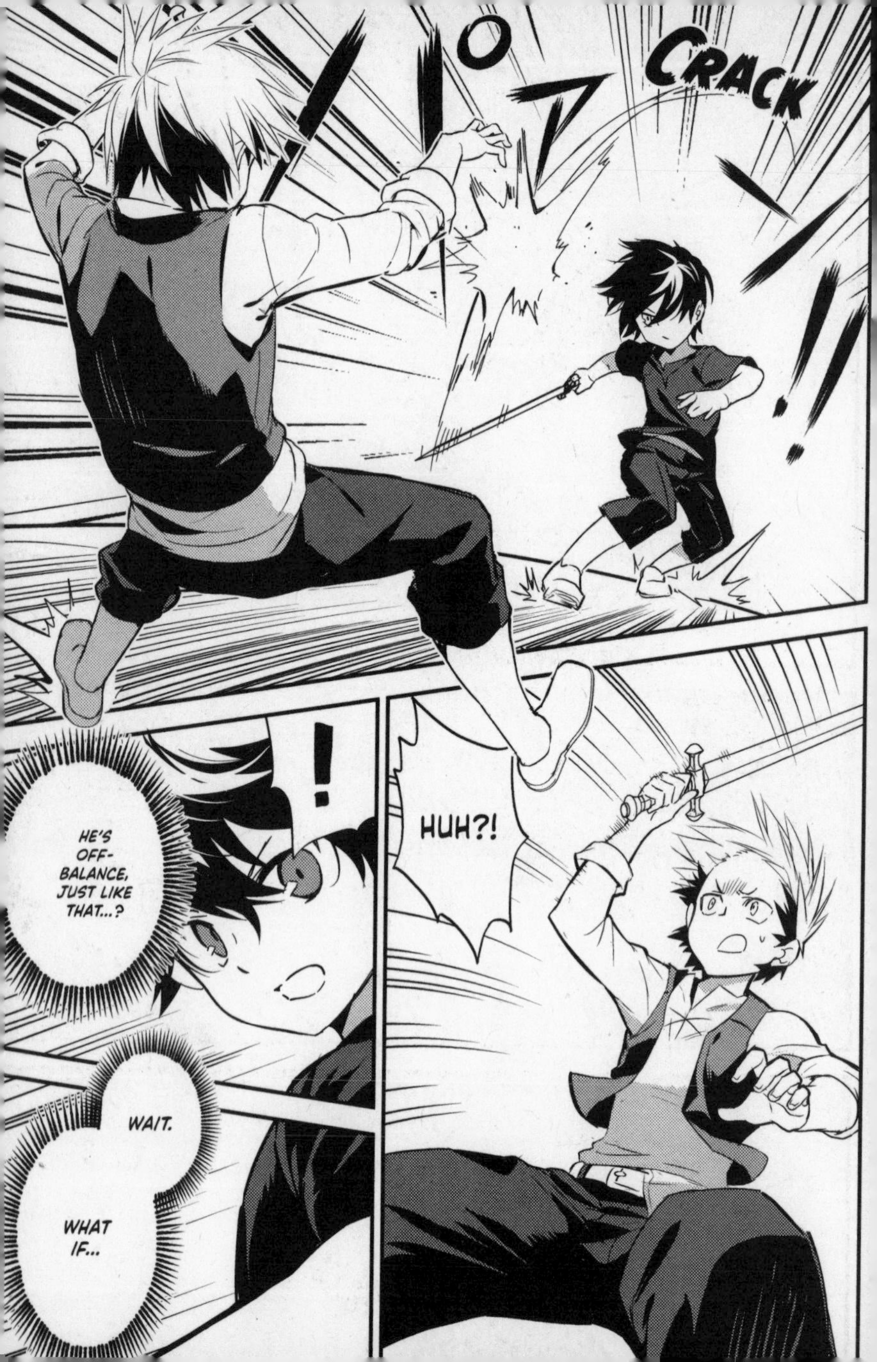
CRACK
HUH?!
!
HE'S OFF-BALANCE, JUST LIKE THAT...?
WAIT.
WHAT IF...

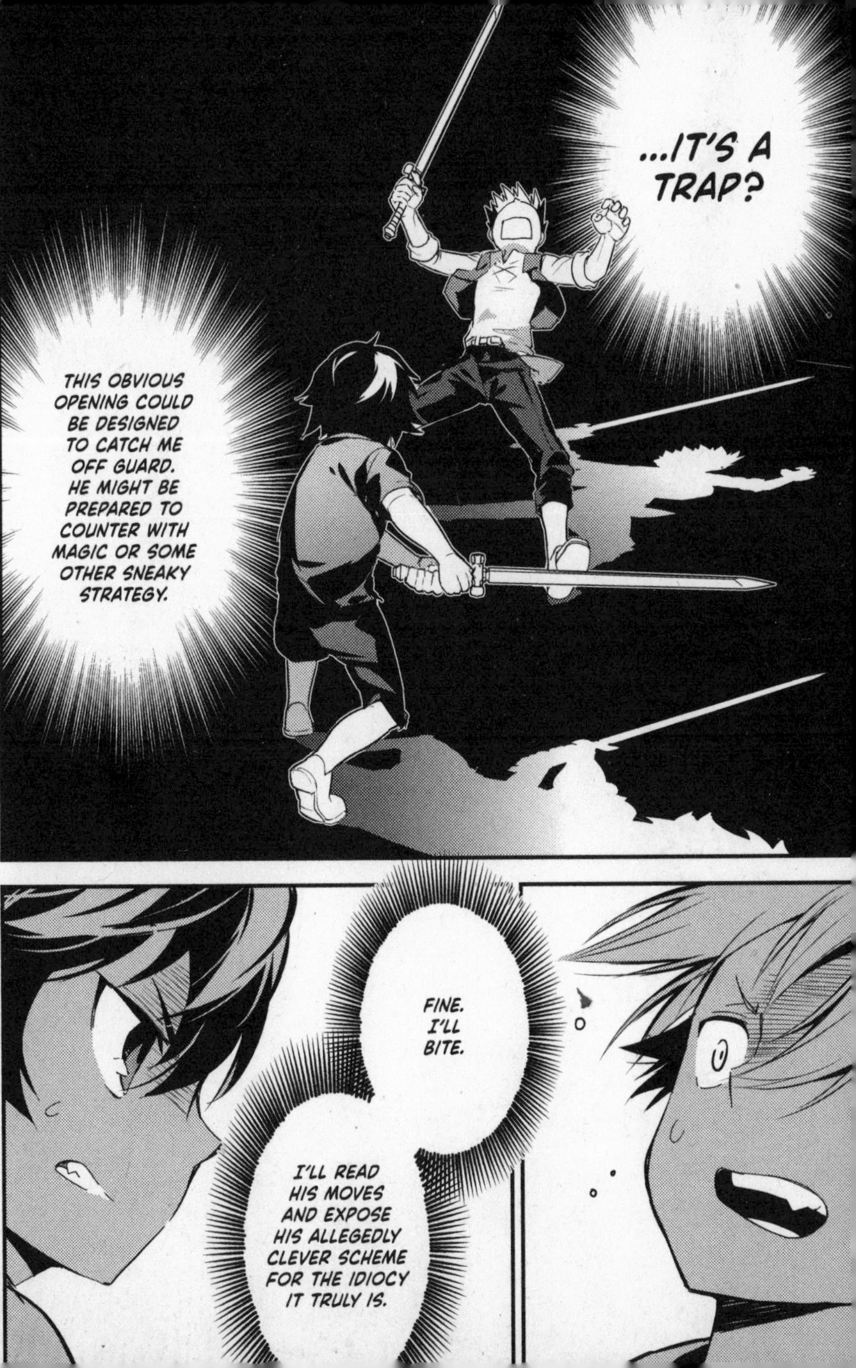
...IT'S A TRAP?
THIS OBVIOUS OPENING COULD BE DESIGNED TO CATCH ME OFF GUARD. HE MIGHT BE PREPARED TO COUNTER WITH MAGIC OR SOME OTHER SNEAKY STRATEGY.
FINE. I'LL BITE.
I'LL READ HIS MOVES AND EXPOSE HIS ALLEGEDLY CLEVER SCHEME FOR THE IDIOCY IT TRULY IS.

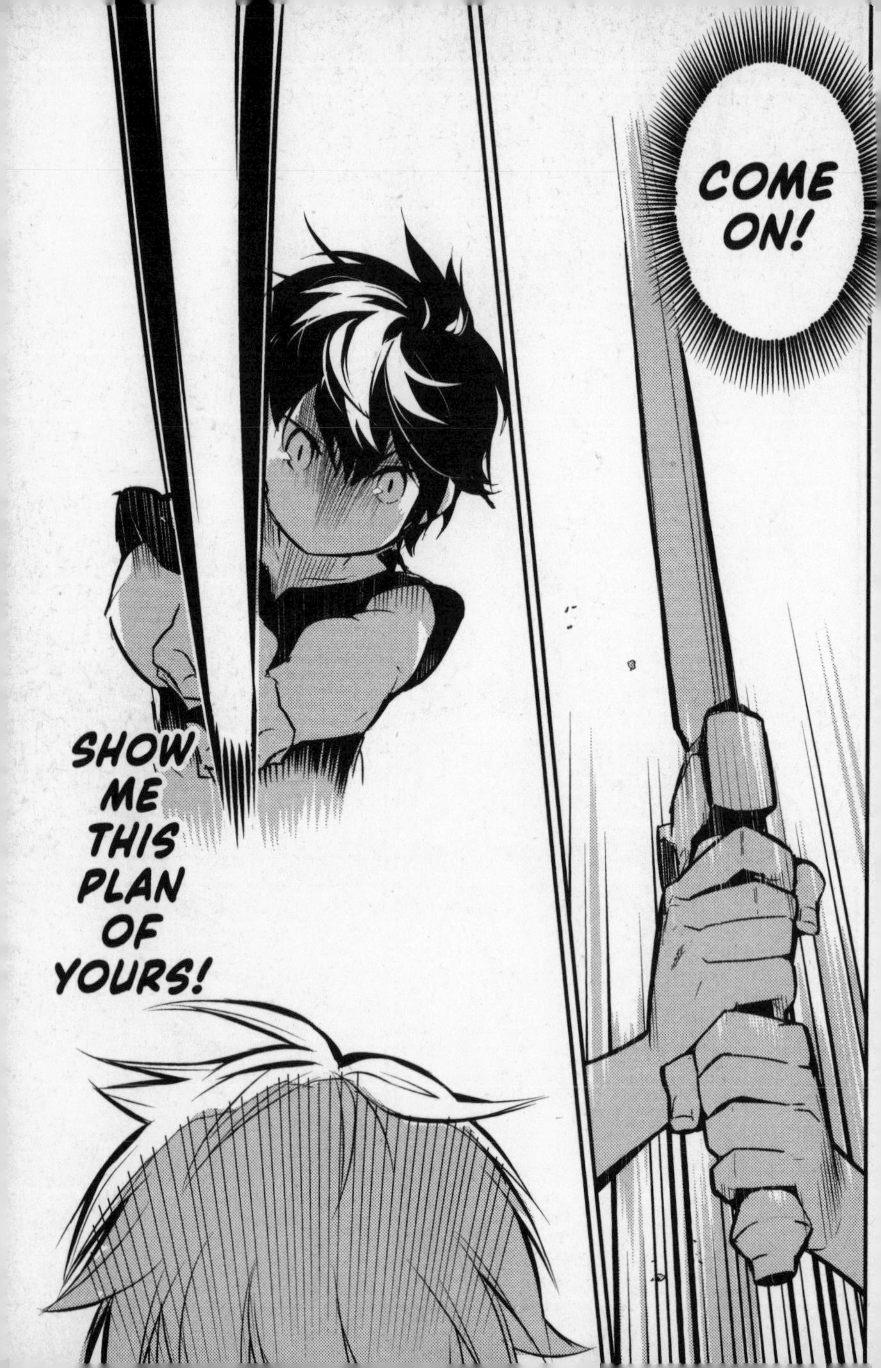
COME ON!
SHOW ME THIS PLAN OF YOURS!

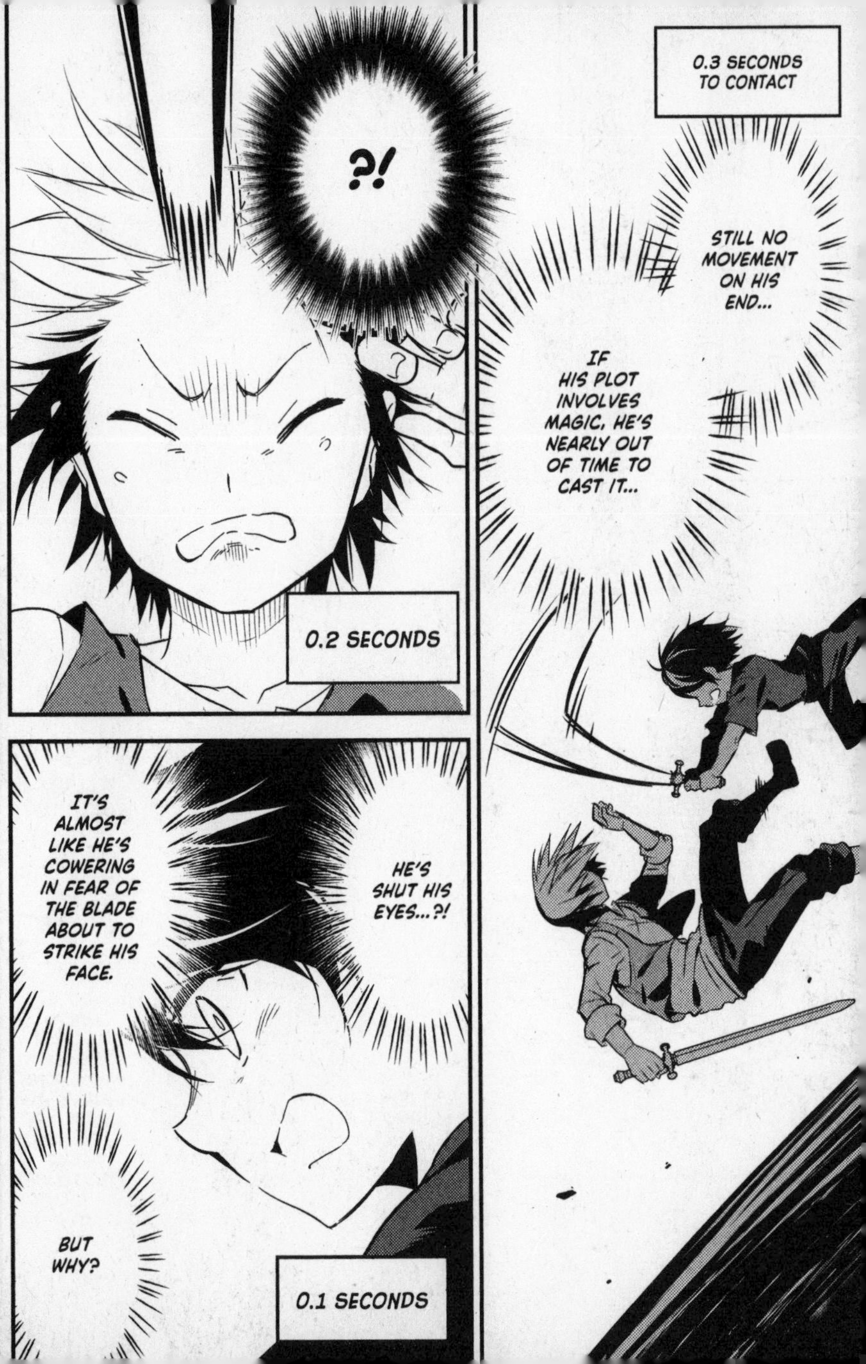
0.3 SECONDS TO CONTACT
STILL NO MOVEMENT ON HIS END...
IF HIS PLOT INVOLVES MAGIC, HE'S NEARLY OUT OF TIME TO CAST IT...
?!
0.2 SECONDS
HE'S SHUT HIS EYES...?!
IT'S ALMOST LIKE HE'S COWERING IN FEAR OF THE BLADE ABOUT TO STRIKE HIS FACE.
BUT WHY?
0.1 SECONDS

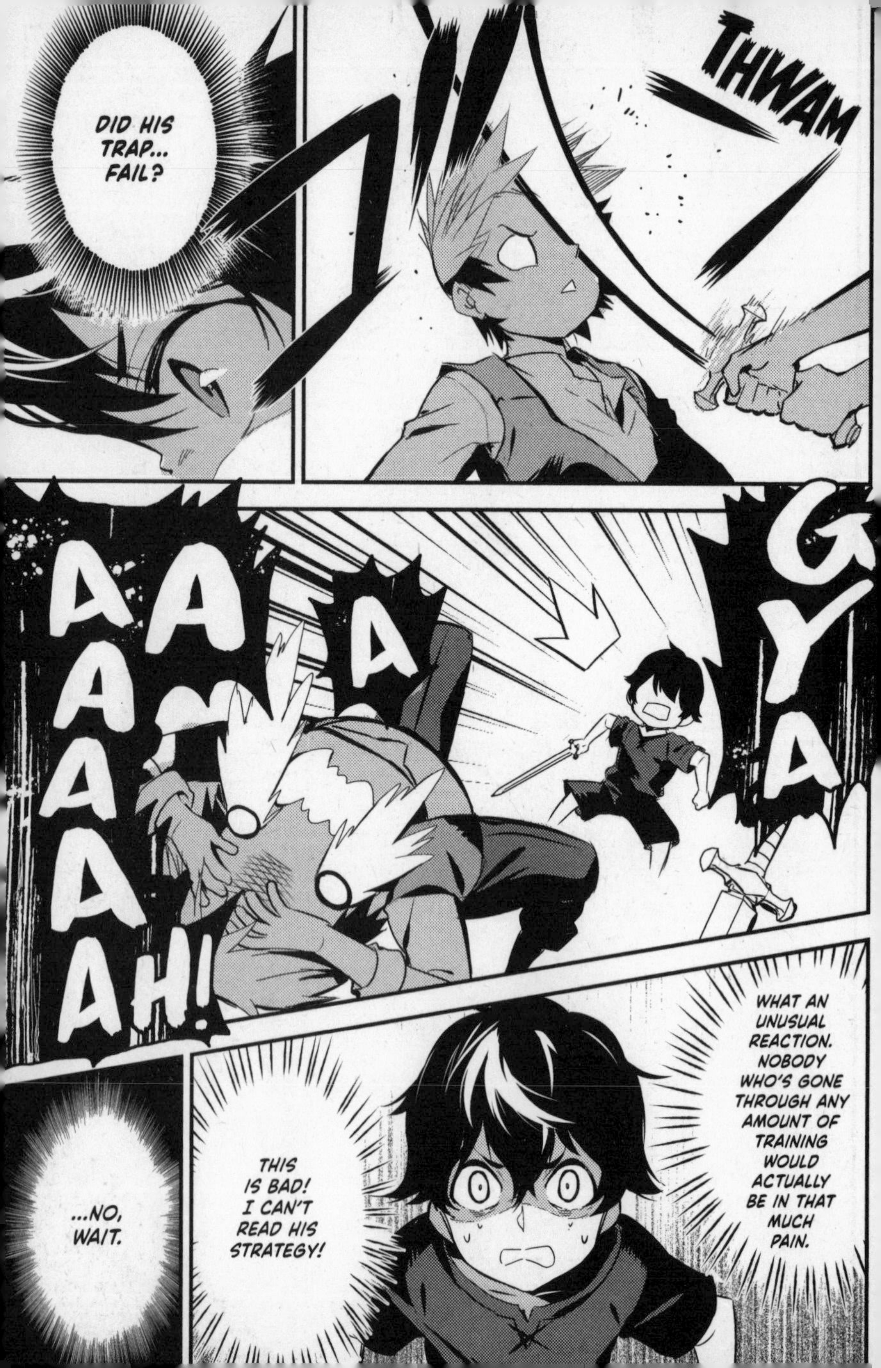
THWAM
DID HIS TRAP... FAIL?
GYA
AAAAAAAAH!
WHAT AN UNUSUAL REACTION. NOBODY WHO'S GONE THROUGH ANY AMOUNT OF TRAINING WOULD ACTUALLY BE IN THAT MUCH PAIN.
THIS IS BAD! I CAN'T READ HIS STRATEGY!
...NO, WAIT.

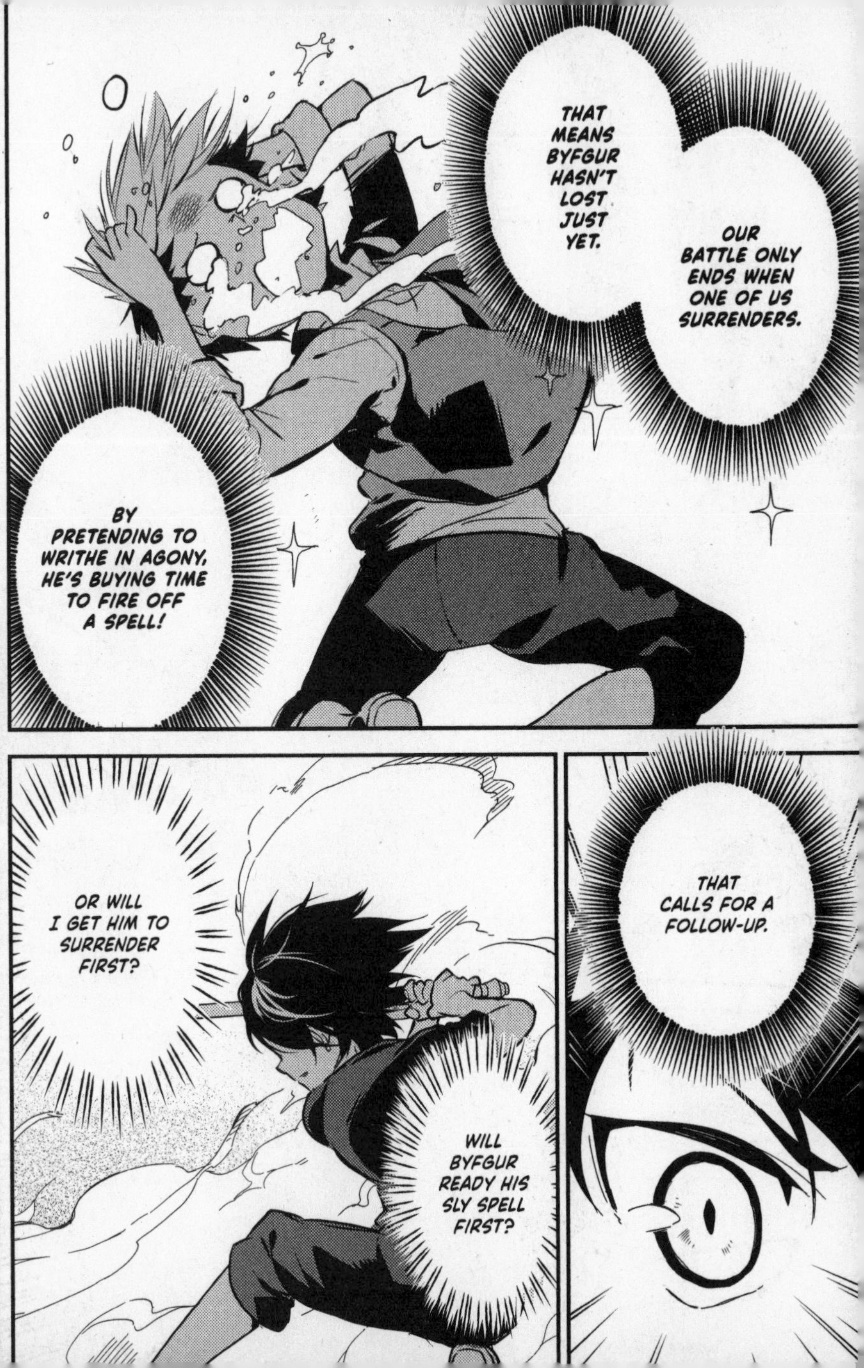
OUR BATTLE ONLY ENDS WHEN ONE OF US SURRENDERS.
THAT MEANS BYFGUR HASN'T LOST JUST YET.
BY PRETENDING TO WRITHE IN AGONY, HE'S BUYING TIME TO FIRE OFF A SPELL!
THAT CALLS FOR A FOLLOW-UP.
WILL BYFGUR READY HIS SLY SPELL FIRST?
OR WILL I GET HIM TO SURRENDER FIRST?

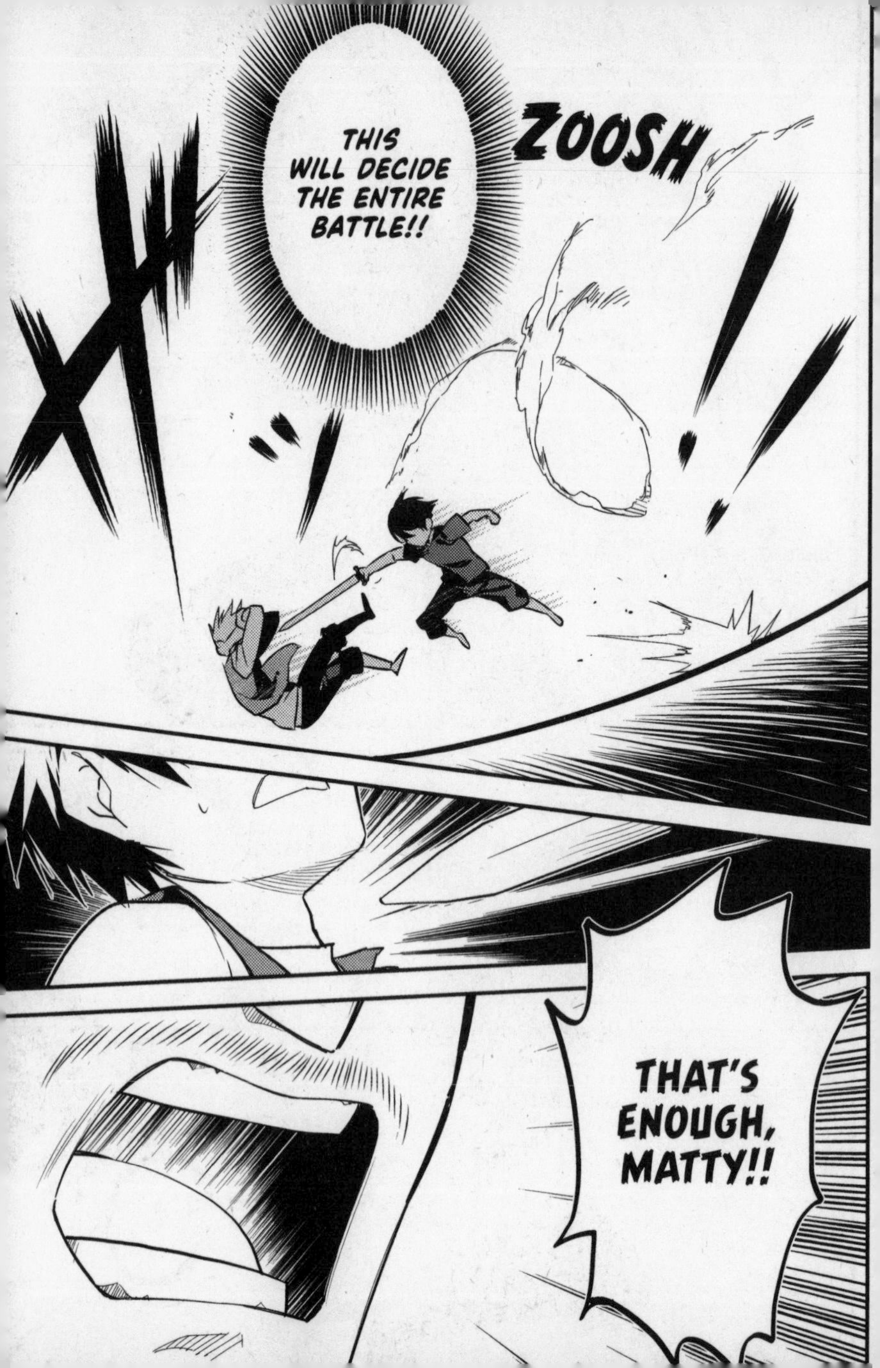
ZOOSH
THIS WILL DECIDE THE ENTIRE BATTLE!!
THAT'S ENOUGH, MATTY!!

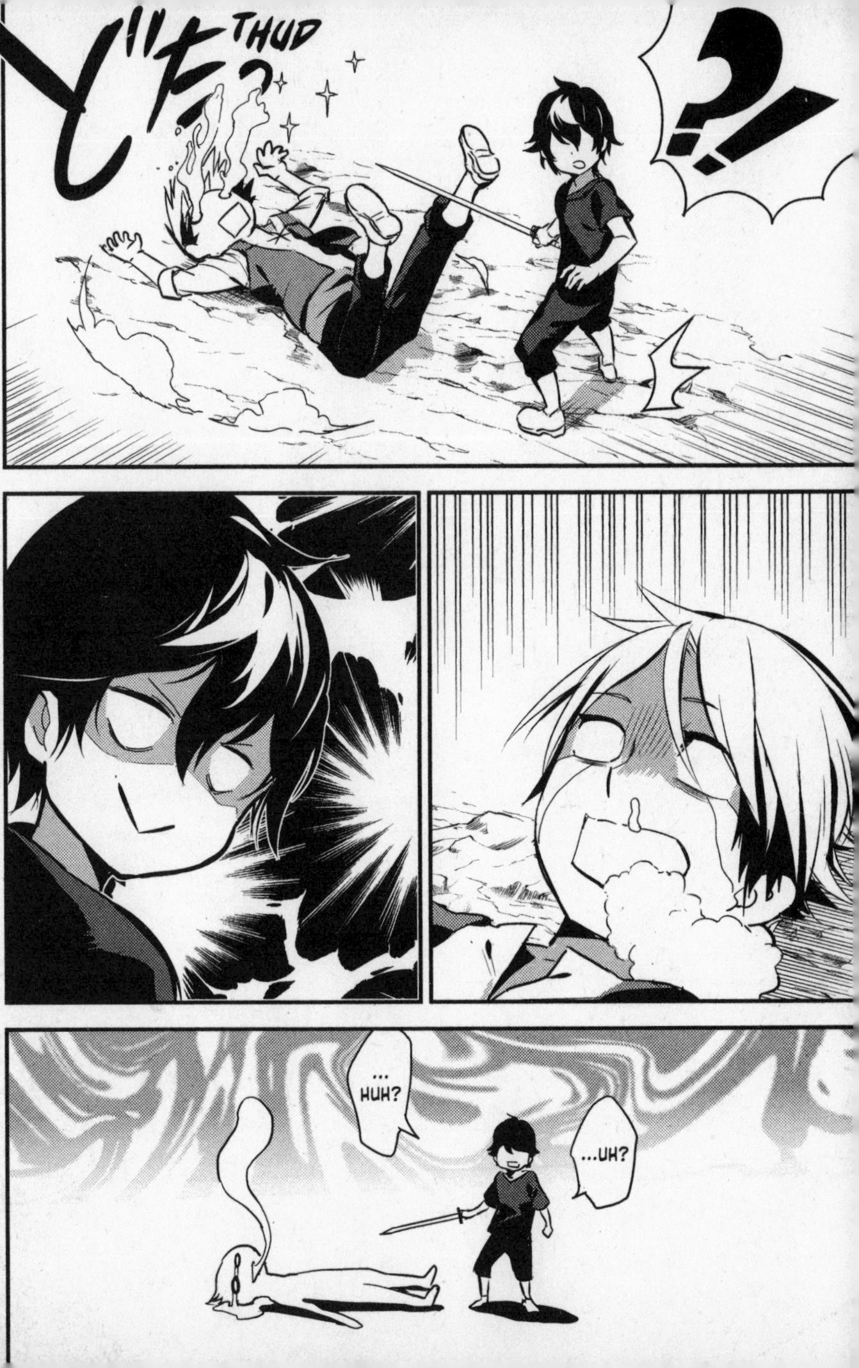
?!
THUD
...UH?
... HUH?

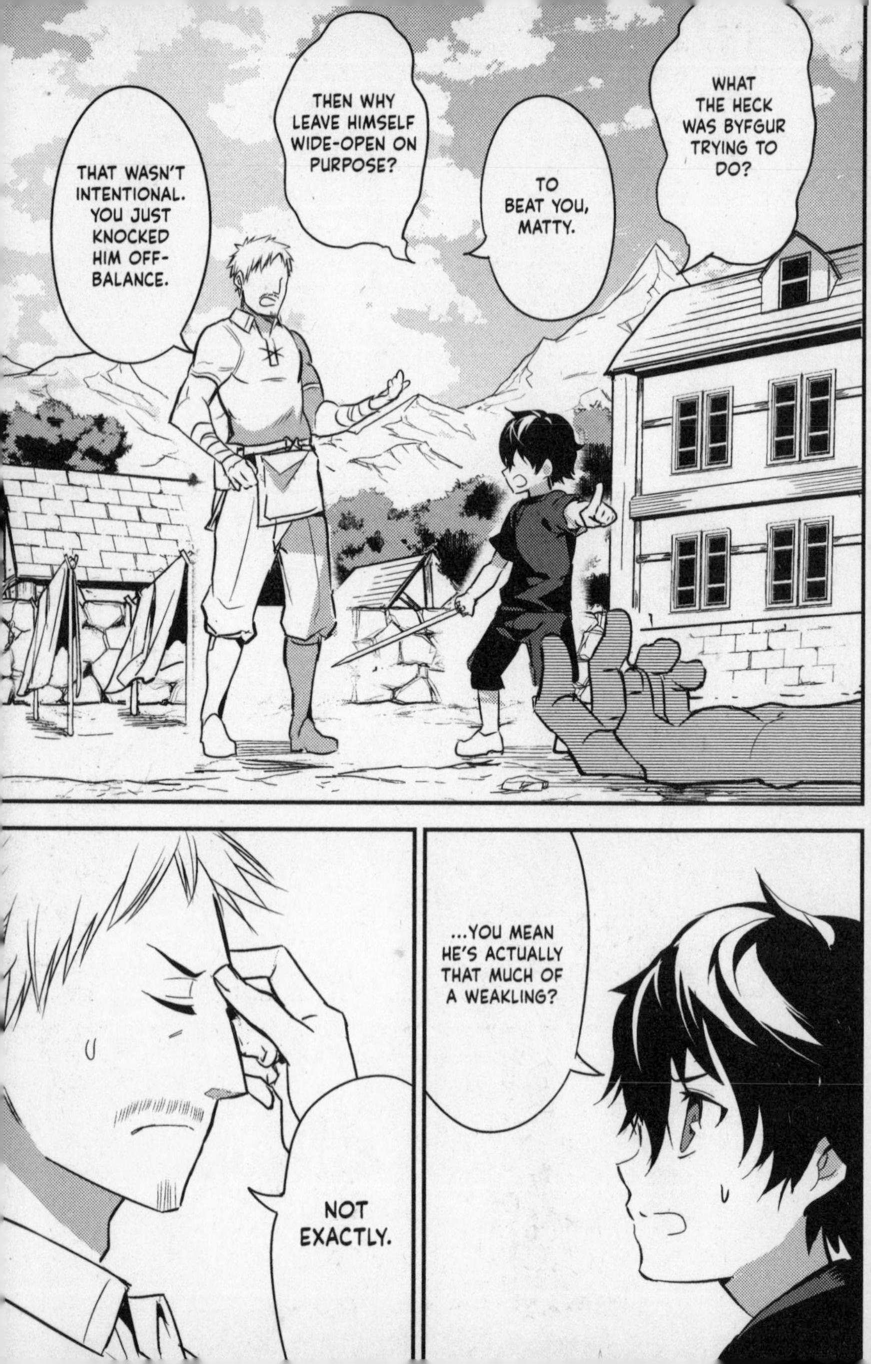
WHAT THE HECK WAS BYFGUR TRYING TO DO?
TO BEAT YOU, MATTY.
THEN WHY LEAVE HIMSELF WIDE-OPEN ON PURPOSE?
THAT WASN'T INTENTIONAL. YOU JUST KNOCKED HIM OFF-BALANCE.
...YOU MEAN HE'S ACTUALLY THAT MUCH OF A WEAKLING?
NOT EXACTLY.

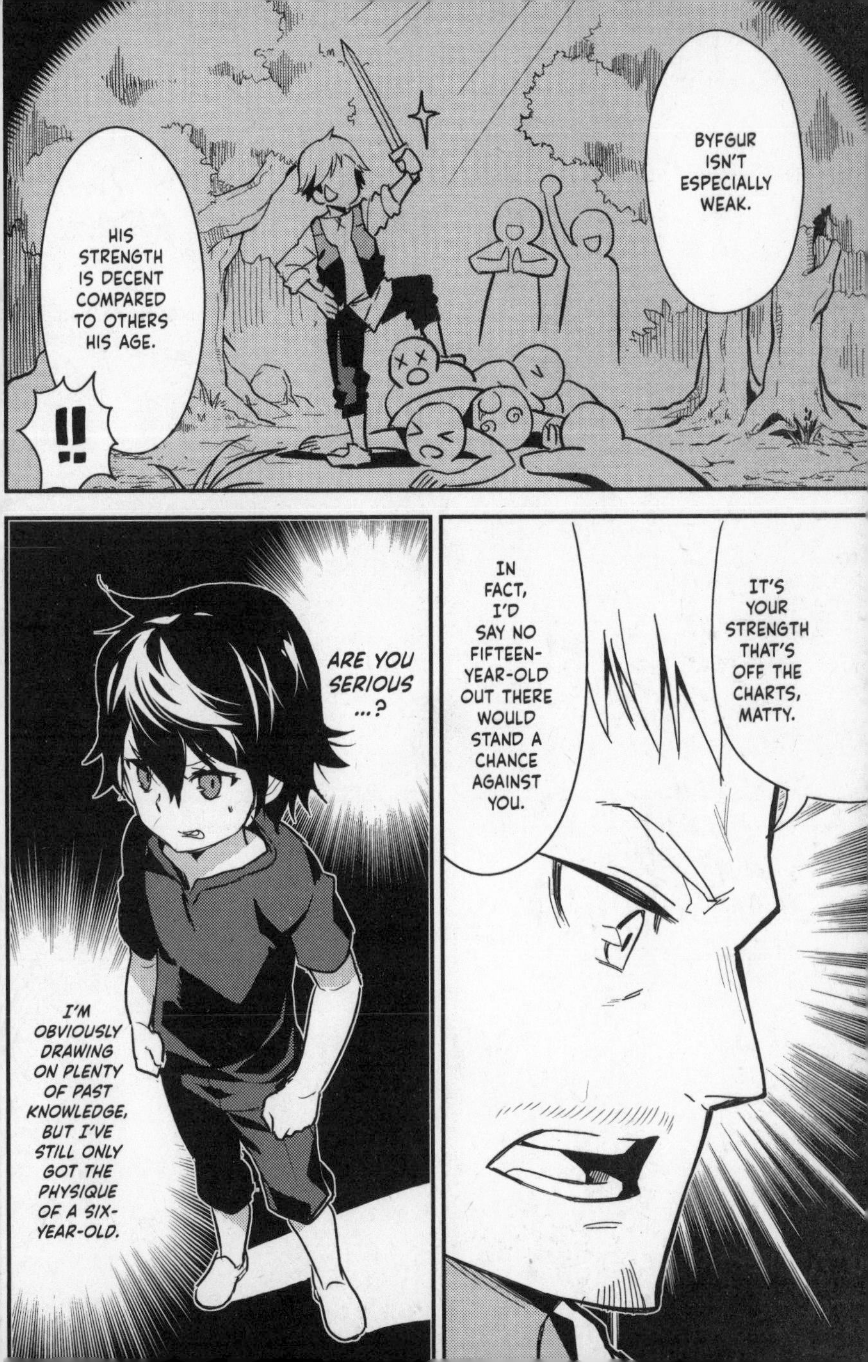
BYFGUR ISN'T ESPECIALLY WEAK.
HIS STRENGTH IS DECENT COMPARED TO OTHERS HIS AGE.
!!
IT'S YOUR STRENGTH THAT'S OFF THE CHARTS, MATTY.
IN FACT, I'D SAY NO FIFTEEN-YEAR-OLD OUT THERE WOULD STAND A CHANCE AGAINST YOU.
ARE YOU SERIOUS ...?
I'M OBVIOUSLY DRAWING ON PLENTY OF PAST KNOWLEDGE, BUT I'VE STILL ONLY GOT THE PHYSIQUE OF A SIX-YEAR-OLD.

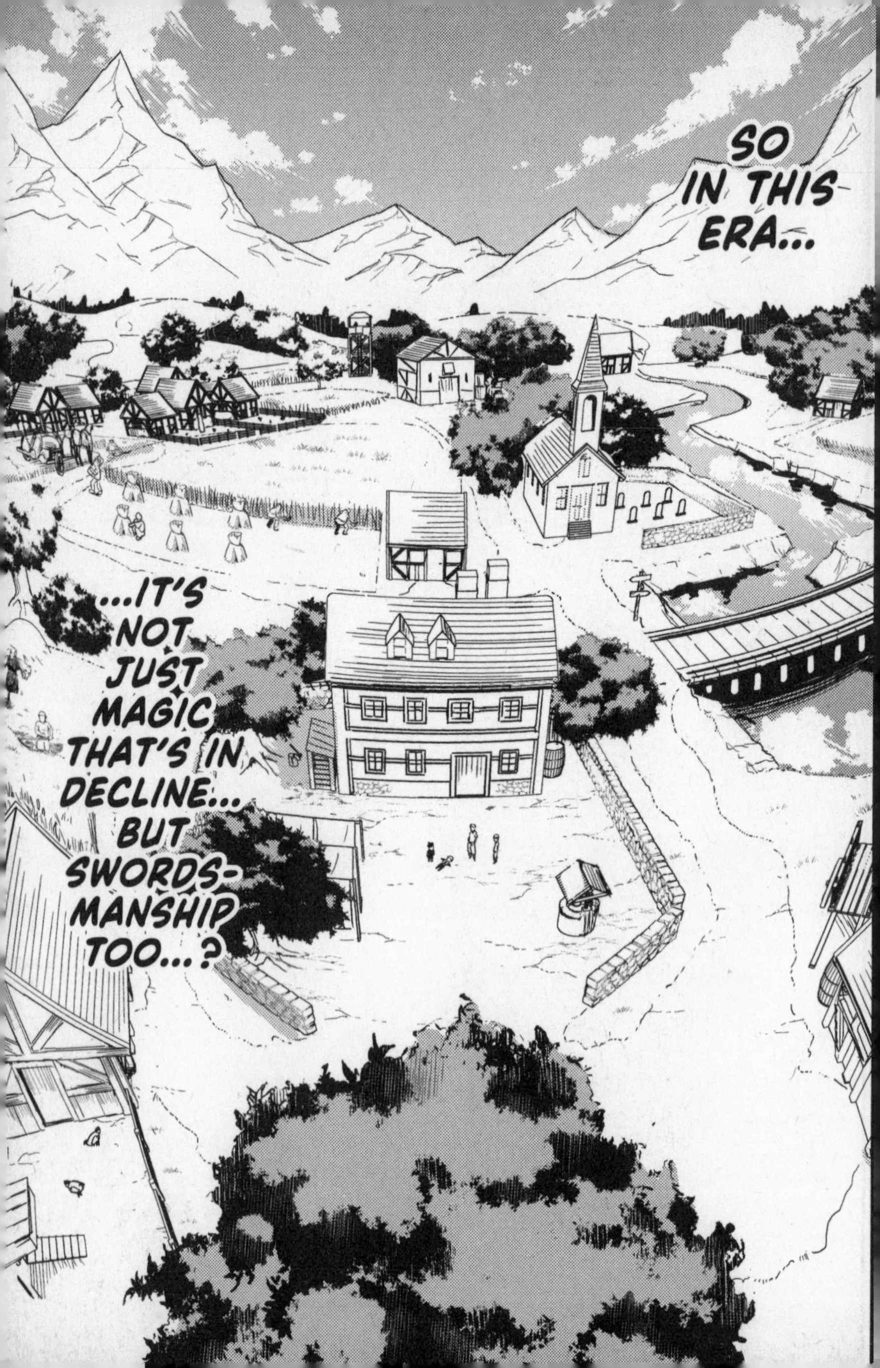
SO IN THIS ERA...
...IT'S NOT JUST MAGIC THAT'S IN DECLINE... BUT SWORDSMANSHIP TOO...?

THE
STRONGEST SAGE
WITH
THE WEAKEST CREST

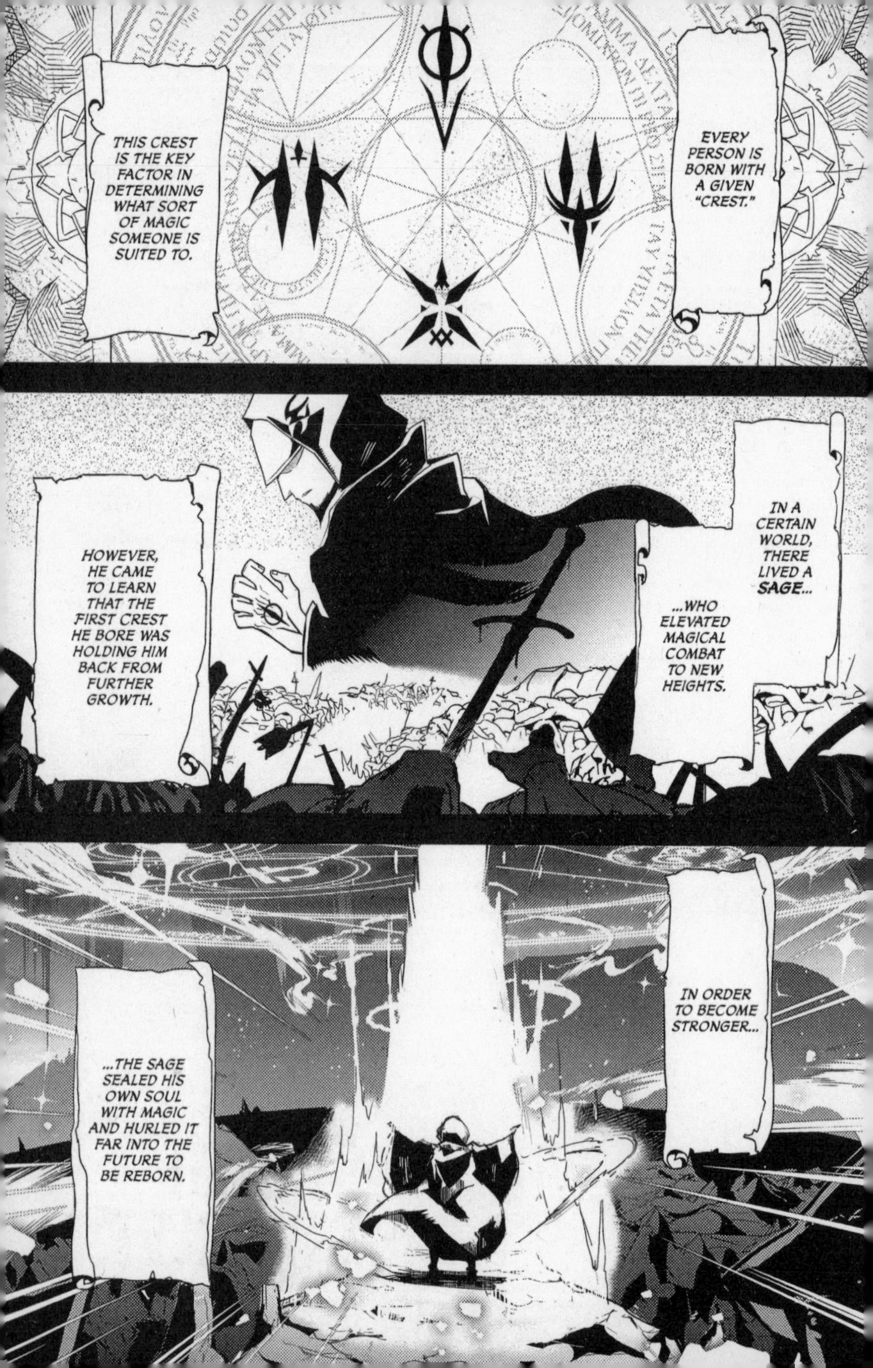
EVERY PERSON IS BORN WITH A GIVEN "CREST."
THIS CREST IS THE KEY FACTOR IN DETERMINING WHAT SORT OF MAGIC SOMEONE IS SUITED TO.
IN A CERTAIN WORLD, THERE LIVED A **SAGE**...
...WHO ELEVATED MAGICAL COMBAT TO NEW HEIGHTS.
HOWEVER, HE CAME TO LEARN THAT THE FIRST CREST HE BORE WAS HOLDING HIM BACK FROM FURTHER GROWTH.
IN ORDER TO BECOME STRONGER...
...THE SAGE SEALED HIS OWN SOUL WITH MAGIC AND HURLED IT FAR INTO THE FUTURE TO BE REBORN.

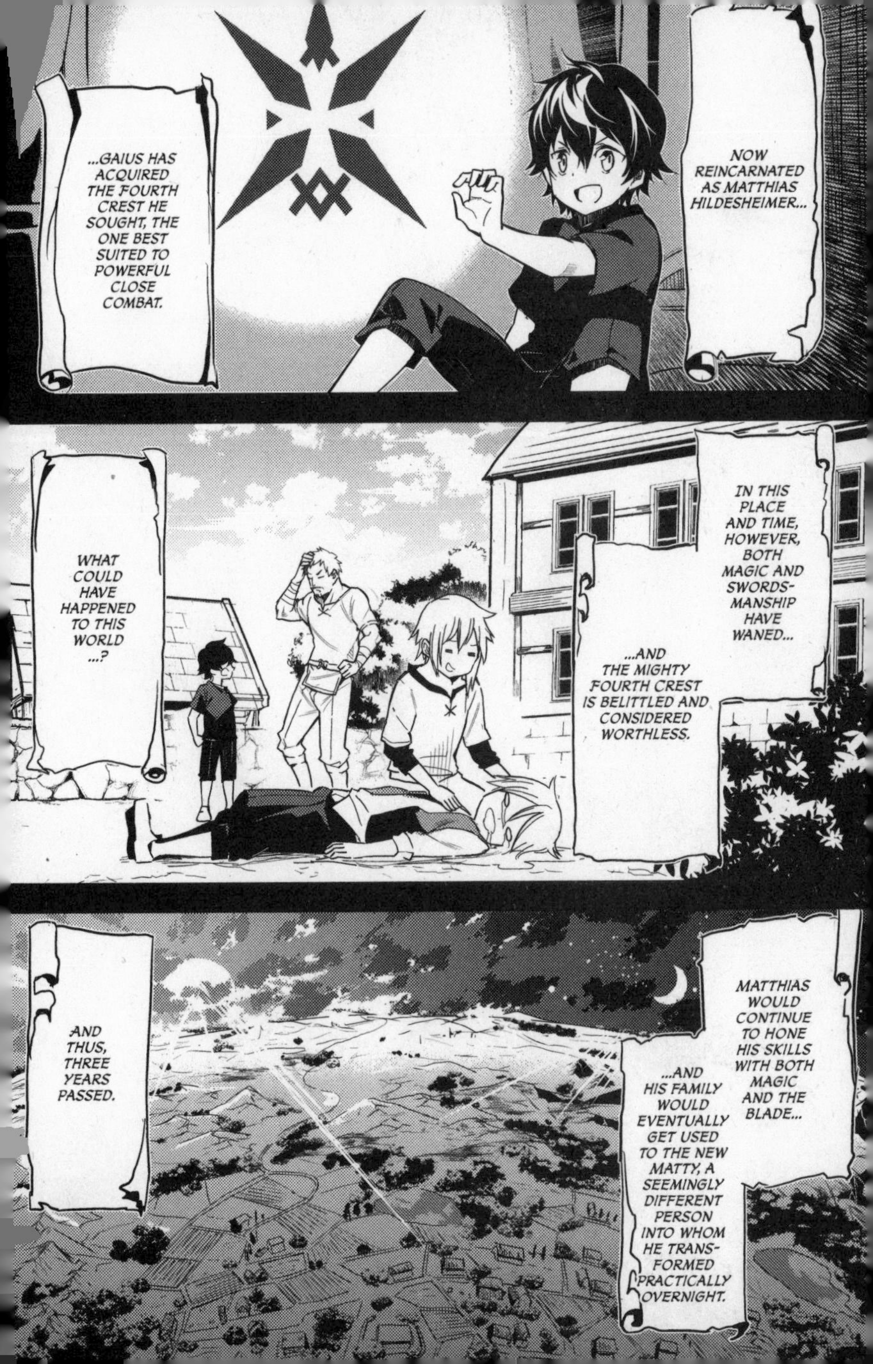
NOW REINCARNATED AS MATTHIAS HILDESHEIMER...
...GAIUS HAS ACQUIRED THE FOURTH CREST HE SOUGHT, THE ONE BEST SUITED TO POWERFUL CLOSE COMBAT.
IN THIS PLACE AND TIME, HOWEVER, BOTH MAGIC AND SWORDS-MANSHIP HAVE WANED...
...AND THE MIGHTY FOURTH CREST IS BELITTLED AND CONSIDERED WORTHLESS.
WHAT COULD HAVE HAPPENED TO THIS WORLD ...?
MATTHIAS WOULD CONTINUE TO HONE HIS SKILLS WITH BOTH MAGIC AND THE BLADE...
...AND HIS FAMILY WOULD EVENTUALLY GET USED TO THE NEW MATTY, A SEEMINGLY DIFFERENT PERSON INTO WHOM HE TRANS-FORMED PRACTICALLY OVERNIGHT.
AND THUS, THREE YEARS PASSED.

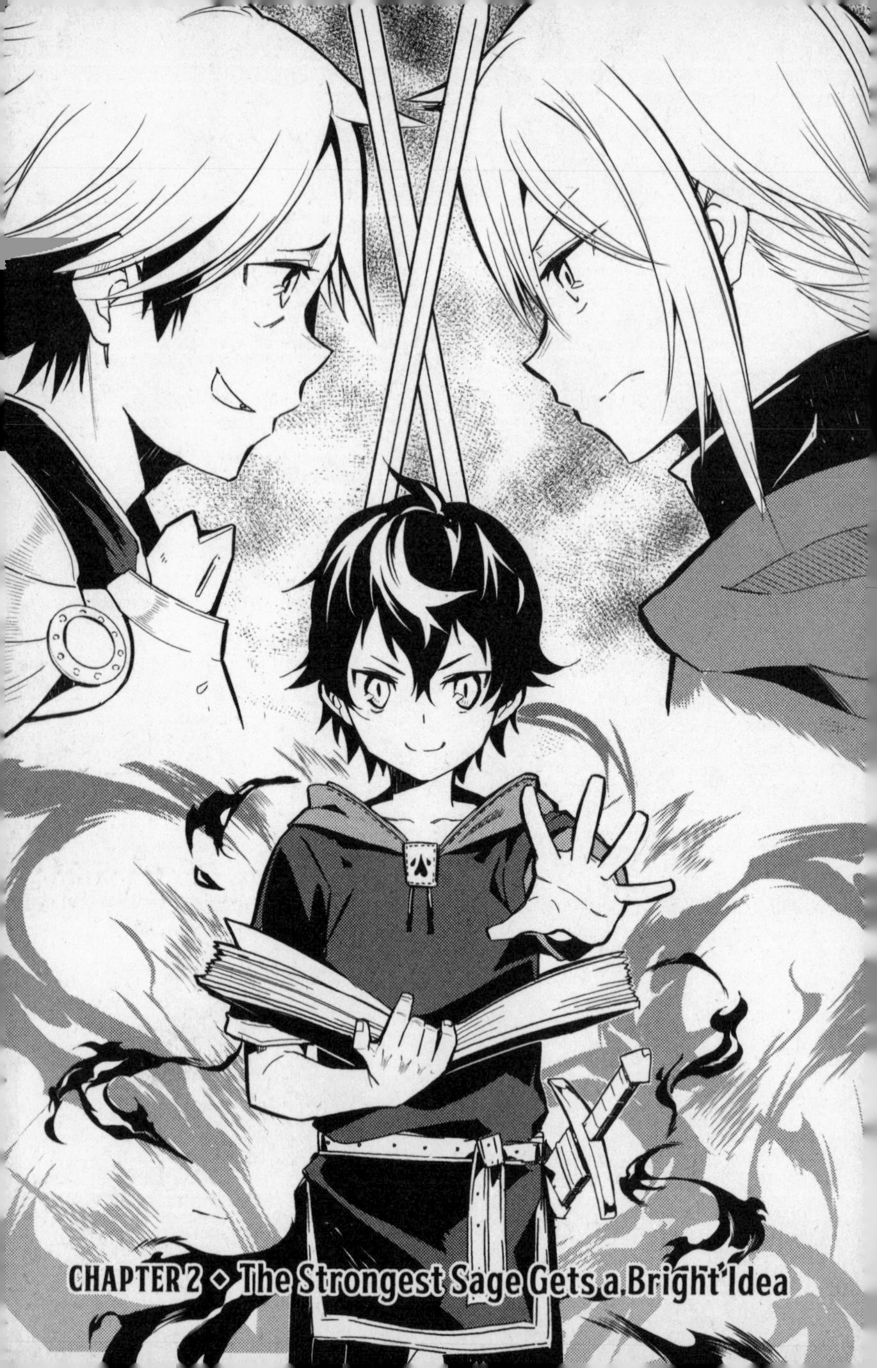
CHAPTER 2 ◆ The Strongest Sage Gets a Bright Idea

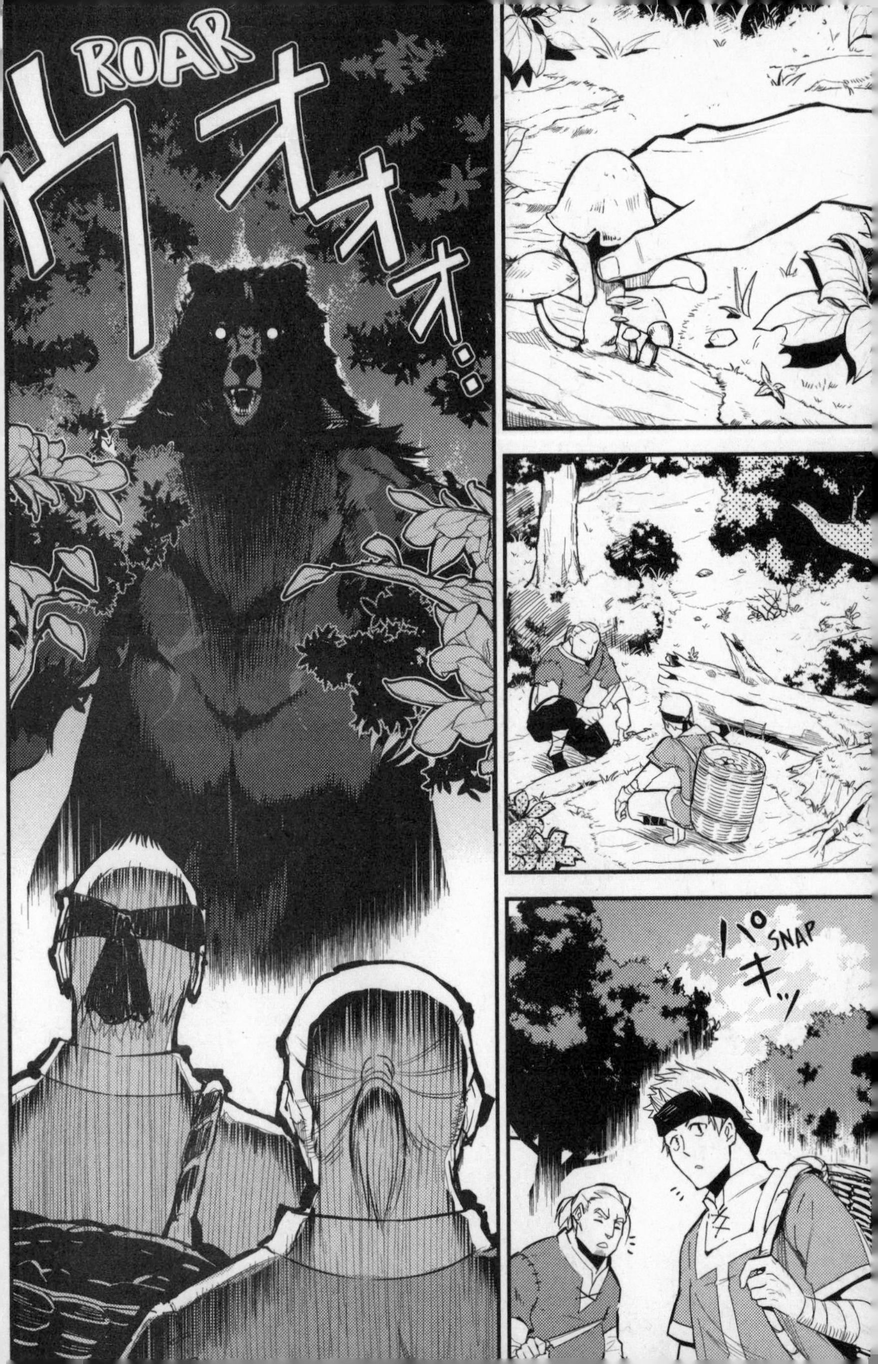
パキッ
SNAP
ウオオオ!!
ROAR

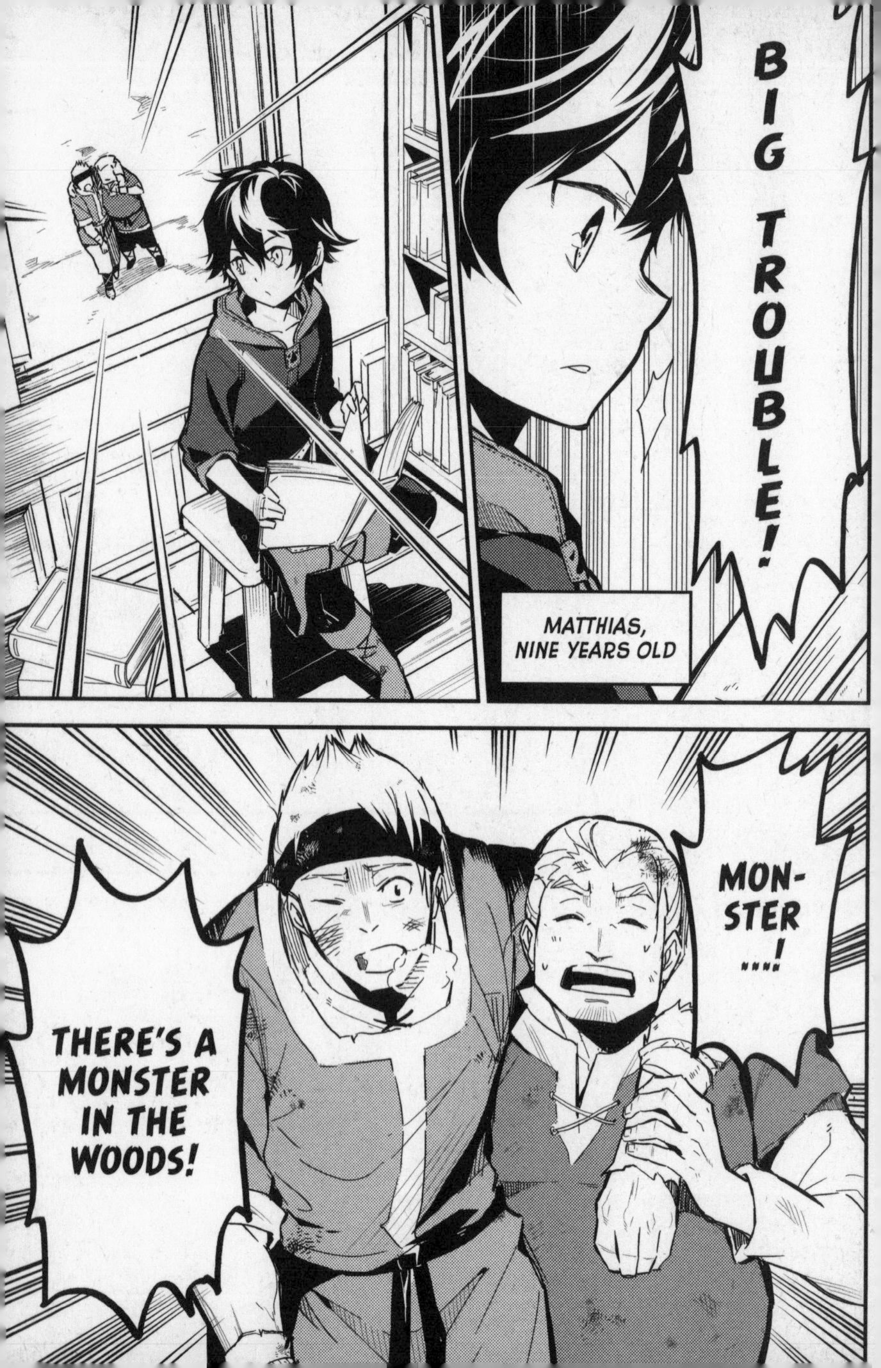
BIG TROUBLE!
MATTHIAS, NINE YEARS OLD
MON-STER...!
THERE'S A MONSTER IN THE WOODS!

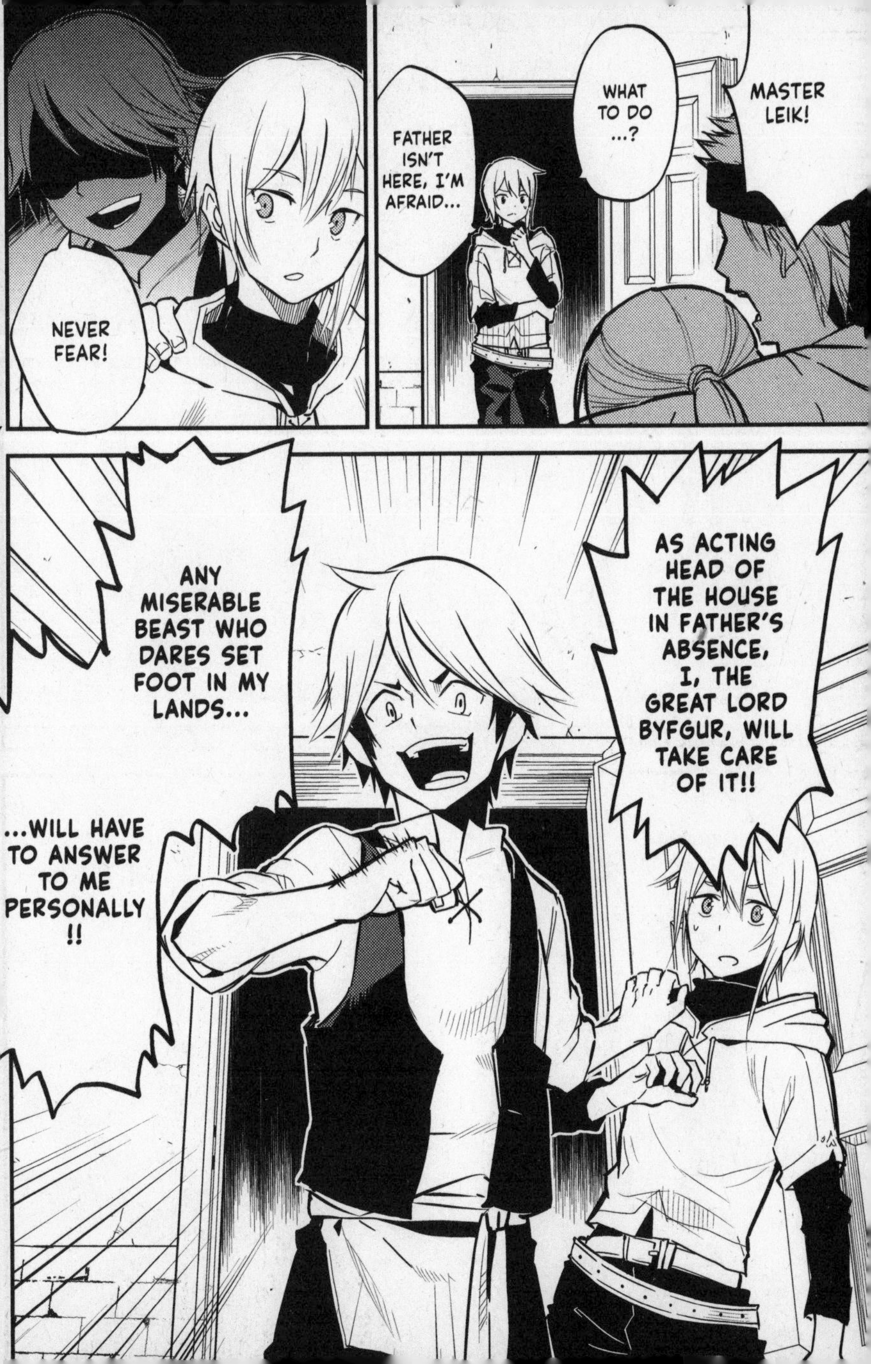
MASTER LEIK!
WHAT TO DO ...?
FATHER ISN'T HERE, I'M AFRAID...
NEVER FEAR!
AS ACTING HEAD OF THE HOUSE IN FATHER'S ABSENCE, I, THE GREAT LORD BYFGUR, WILL TAKE CARE OF IT!!
ANY MISERABLE BEAST WHO DARES SET FOOT IN MY LANDS...
...WILL HAVE TO ANSWER TO ME PERSONALLY!!

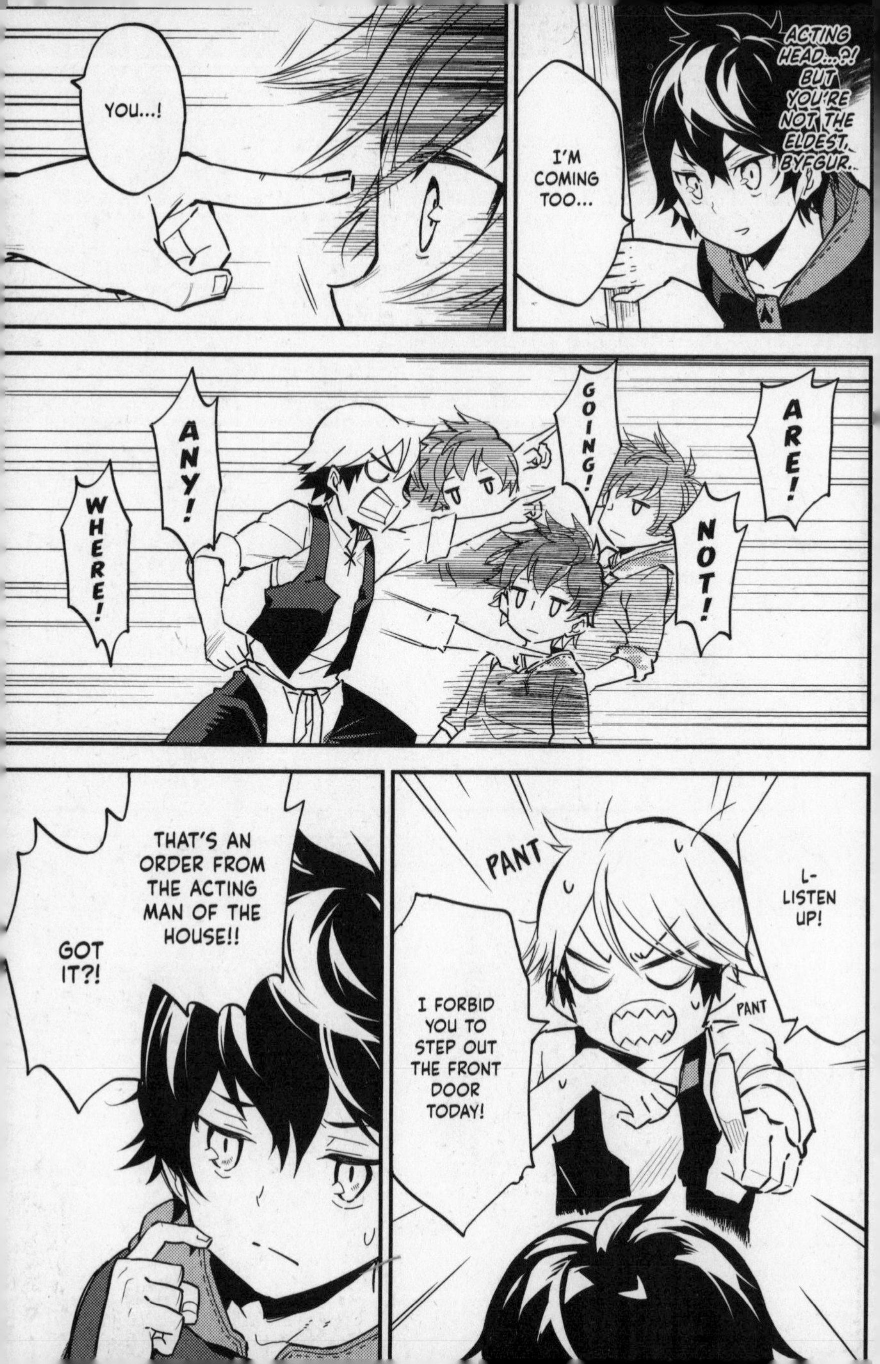
ACTING HEAD...?! BUT YOU'RE NOT THE ELDEST, BYFGUR...
I'M COMING TOO...
YOU...!
ARE!
NOT!
GOING!
ANY!
WHERE!
PANT
L- LISTEN UP!
I FORBID YOU TO STEP OUT THE FRONT DOOR TODAY!
PANT
THAT'S AN ORDER FROM THE ACTING MAN OF THE HOUSE!!
GOT IT?!

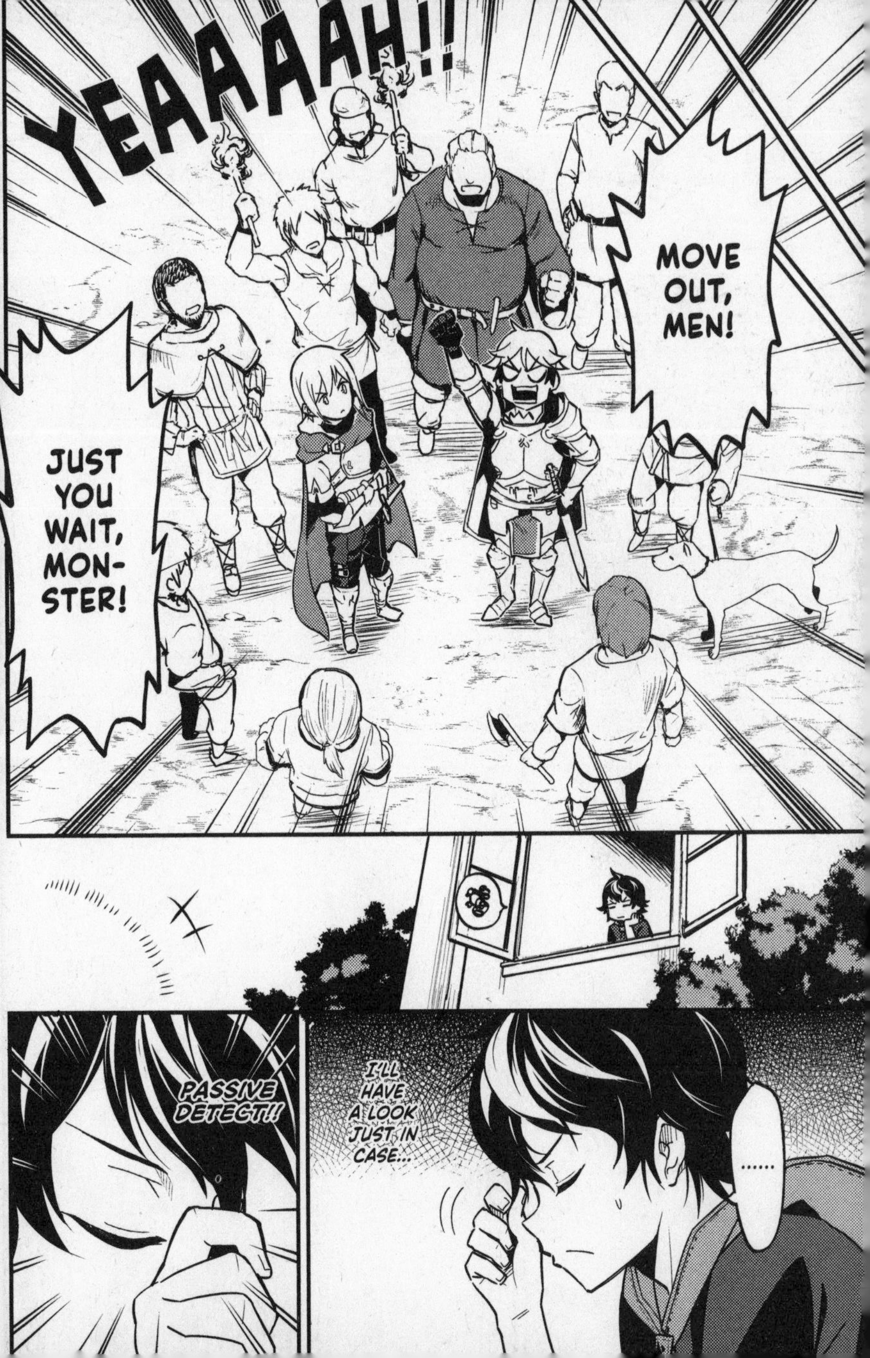
MOVE OUT, MEN!
YEAAAAAH!!
JUST YOU WAIT, MON-STER!
......
I'LL HAVE A LOOK JUST IN CASE...
PASSIVE DETECT!!

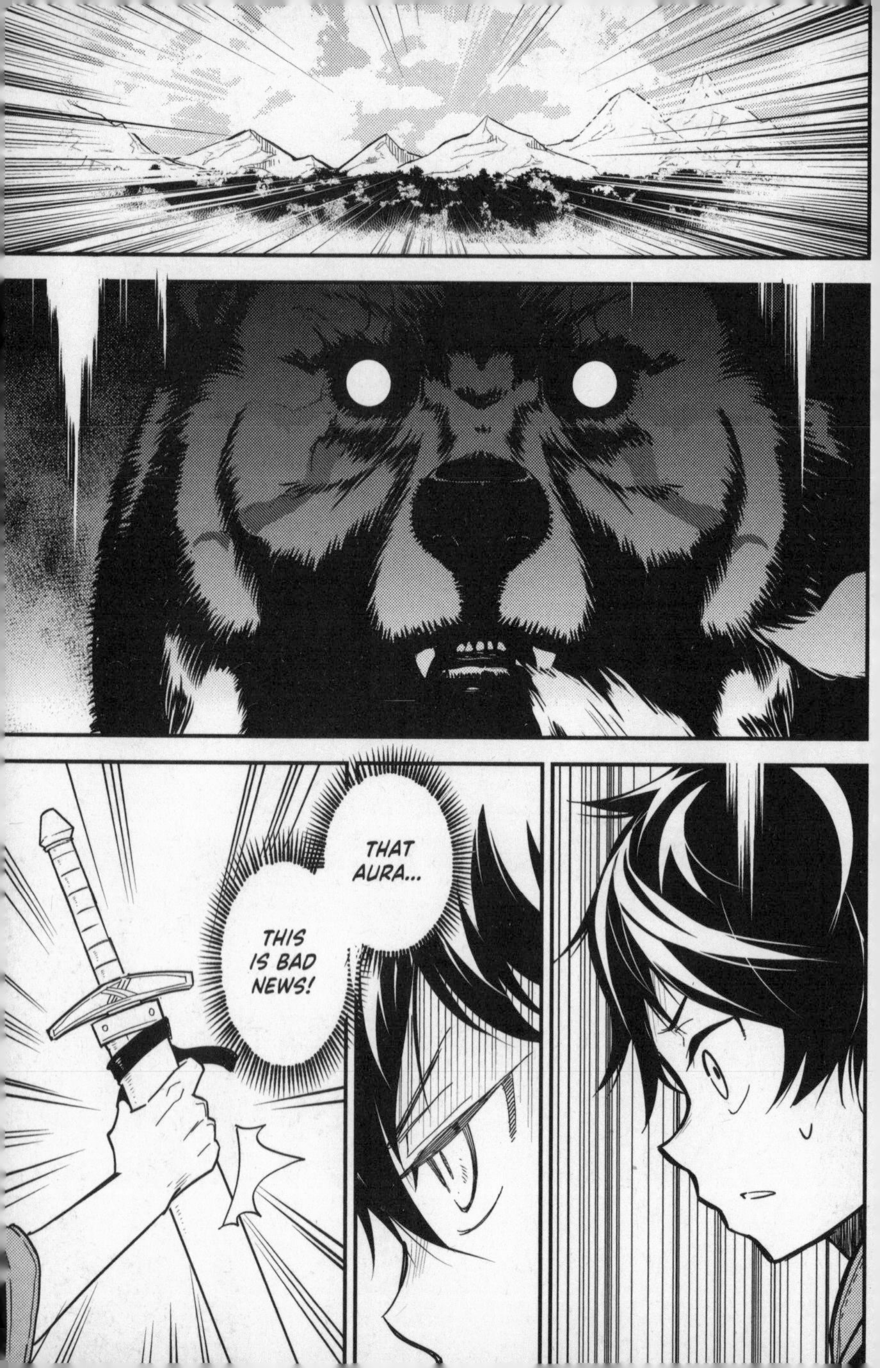
THAT AURA...
THIS IS BAD NEWS!

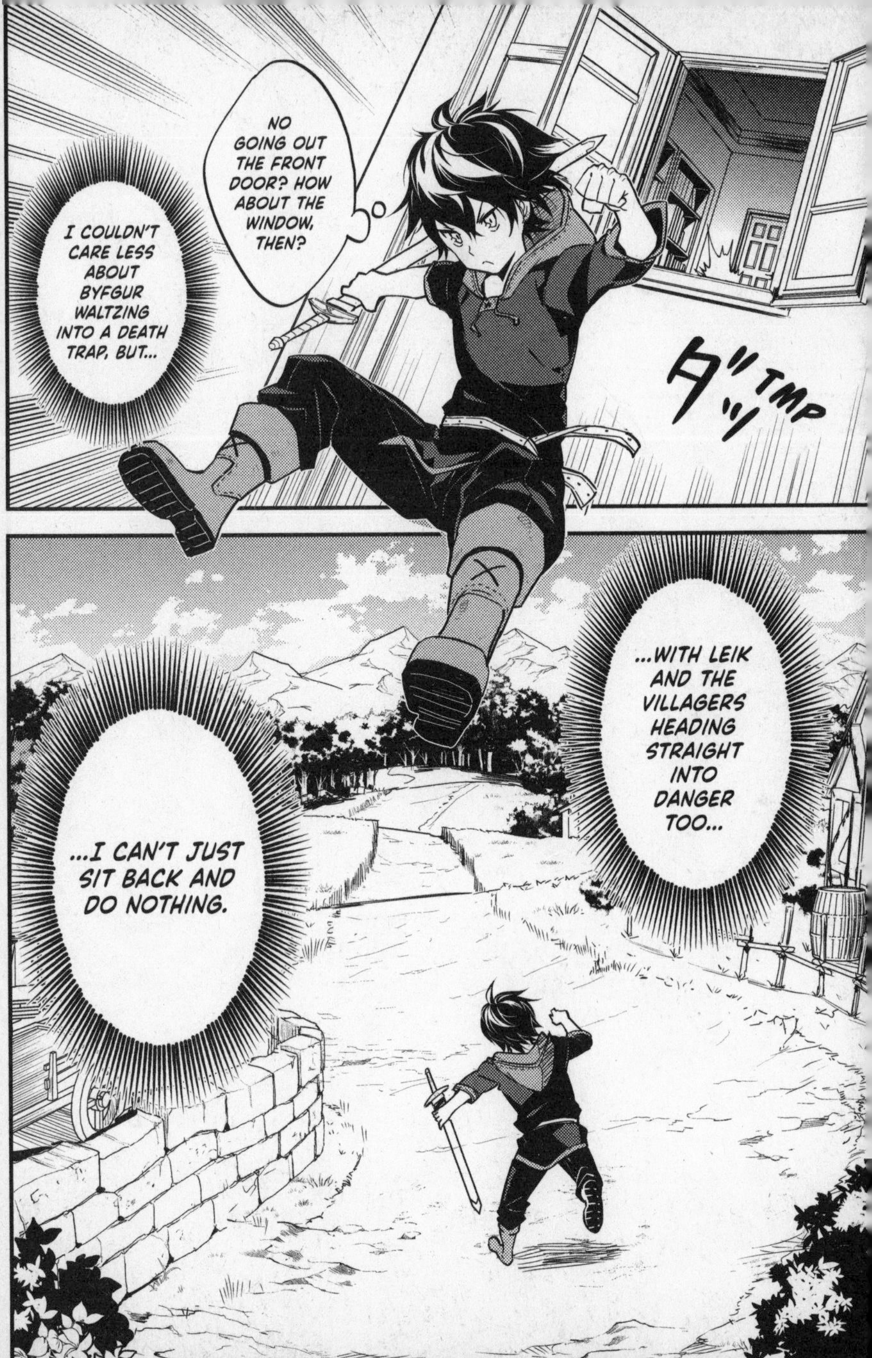
NO GOING OUT THE FRONT DOOR? HOW ABOUT THE WINDOW, THEN?
I COULDN'T CARE LESS ABOUT BYFGUR WALTZING INTO A DEATH TRAP, BUT...
タッ TMP
...WITH LEIK AND THE VILLAGERS HEADING STRAIGHT INTO DANGER TOO...
...I CAN'T JUST SIT BACK AND DO NOTHING.

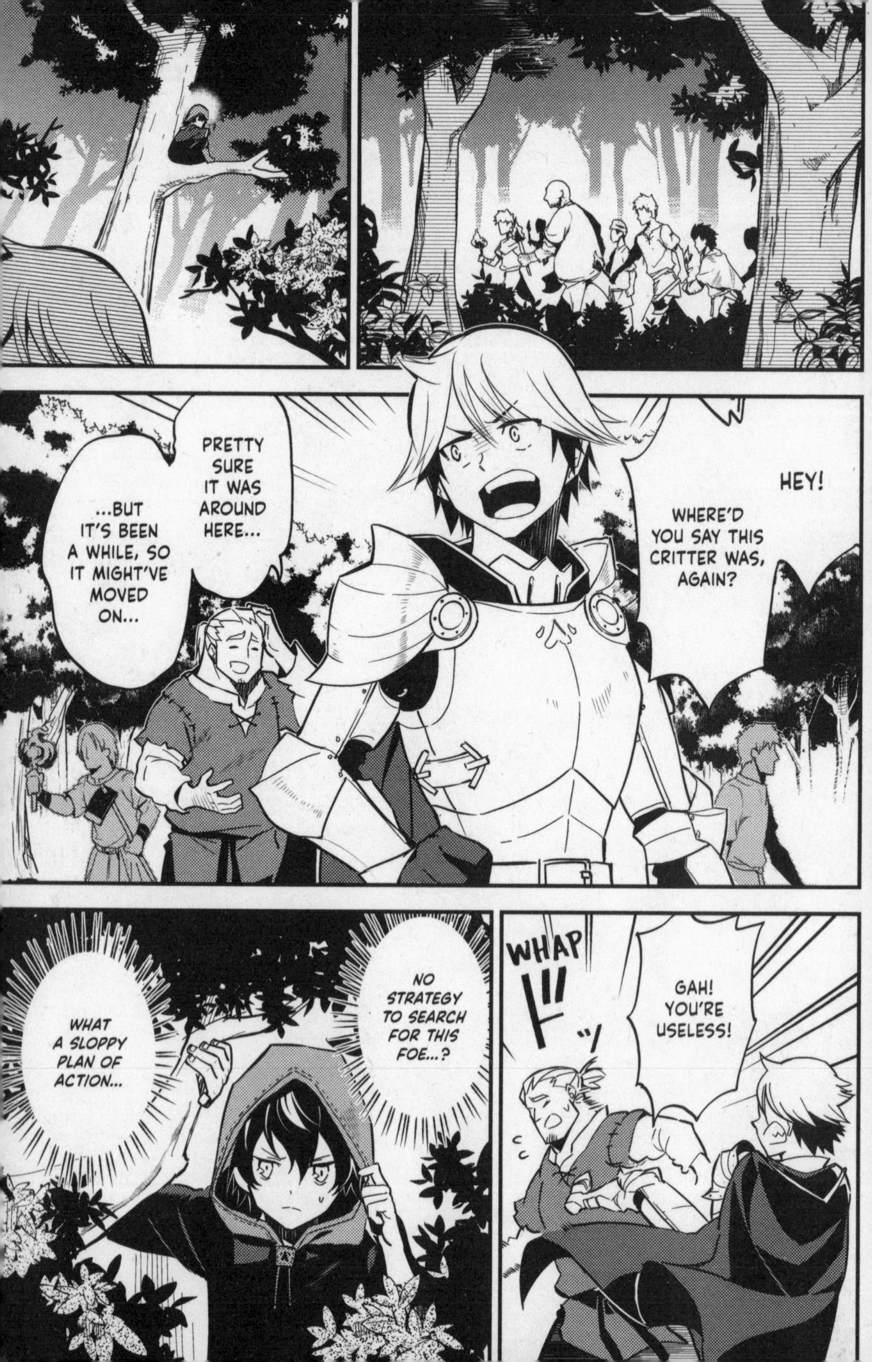
HEY!
WHERE'D YOU SAY THIS CRITTER WAS, AGAIN?
PRETTY SURE IT WAS AROUND HERE...
...BUT IT'S BEEN A WHILE, SO IT MIGHT'VE MOVED ON...
WHAP
ドッ
GAH! YOU'RE USELESS!
NO STRATEGY TO SEARCH FOR THIS FOE...?
WHAT A SLOPPY PLAN OF ACTION...

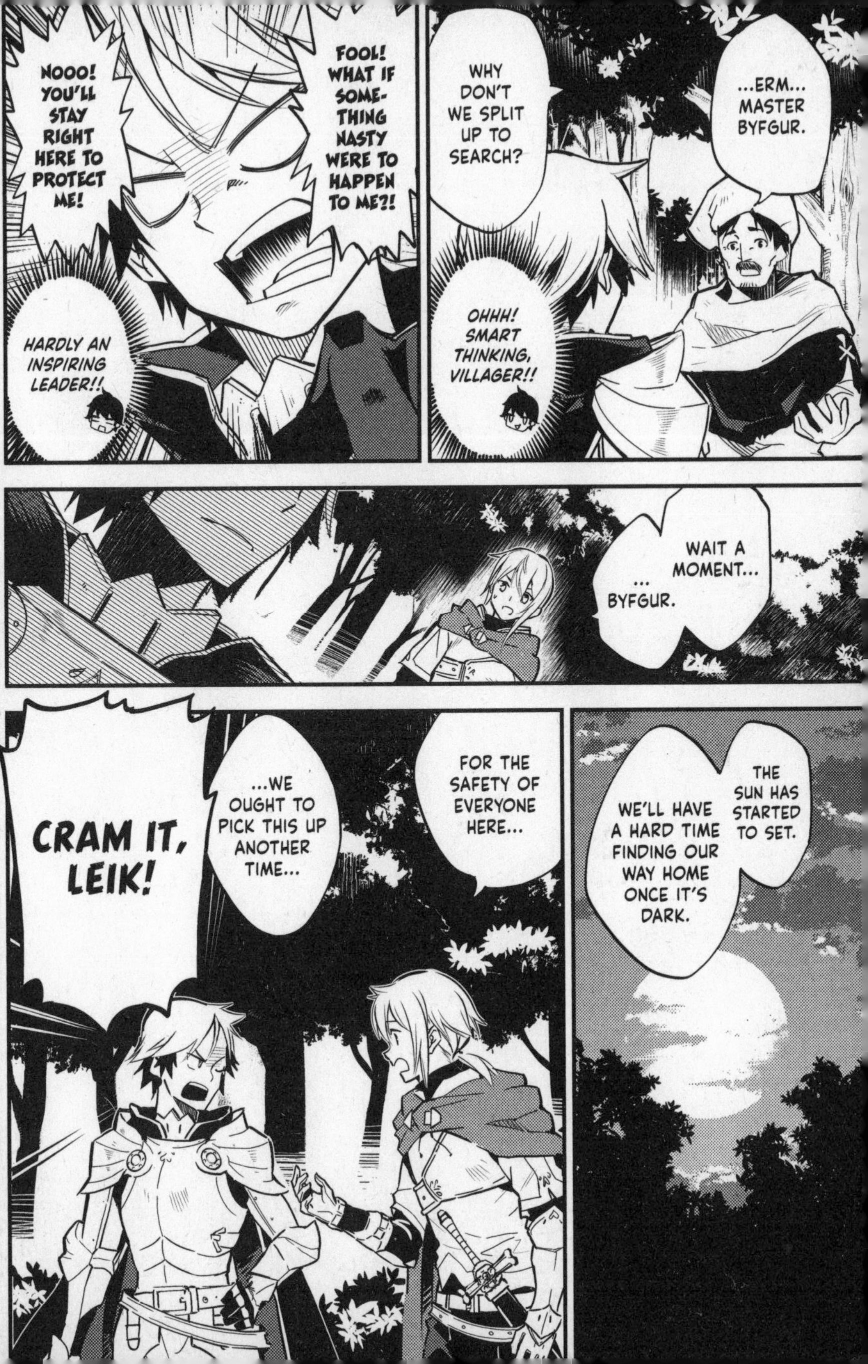
...ERM... MASTER BYFGUR.
WHY DON'T WE SPLIT UP TO SEARCH?
OHHH! SMART THINKING, VILLAGER!!
FOOL! WHAT IF SOME-THING NASTY WERE TO HAPPEN TO ME?!
NOOO! YOU'LL STAY RIGHT HERE TO PROTECT ME!
HARDLY AN INSPIRING LEADER!!
WAIT A MOMENT... ... BYFGUR.
THE SUN HAS STARTED TO SET.
WE'LL HAVE A HARD TIME FINDING OUR WAY HOME ONCE IT'S DARK.
FOR THE SAFETY OF EVERYONE HERE...
...WE OUGHT TO PICK THIS UP ANOTHER TIME...
CRAM IT, LEIK!

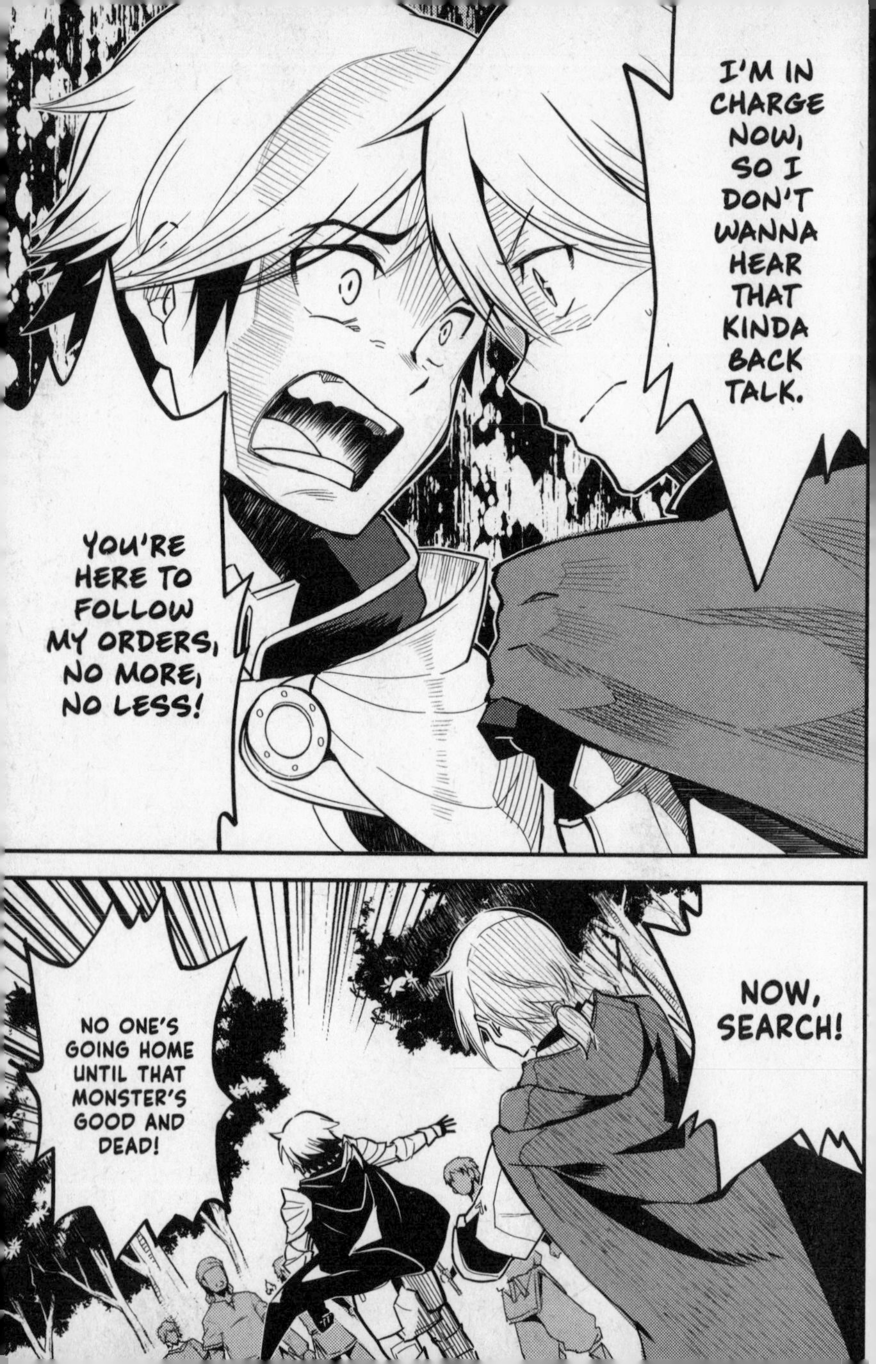
I'M IN CHARGE NOW, SO I DON'T WANNA HEAR THAT KINDA BACK TALK.
YOU'RE HERE TO FOLLOW MY ORDERS, NO MORE, NO LESS!
NOW, SEARCH!
NO ONE'S GOING HOME UNTIL THAT MONSTER'S GOOD AND DEAD!

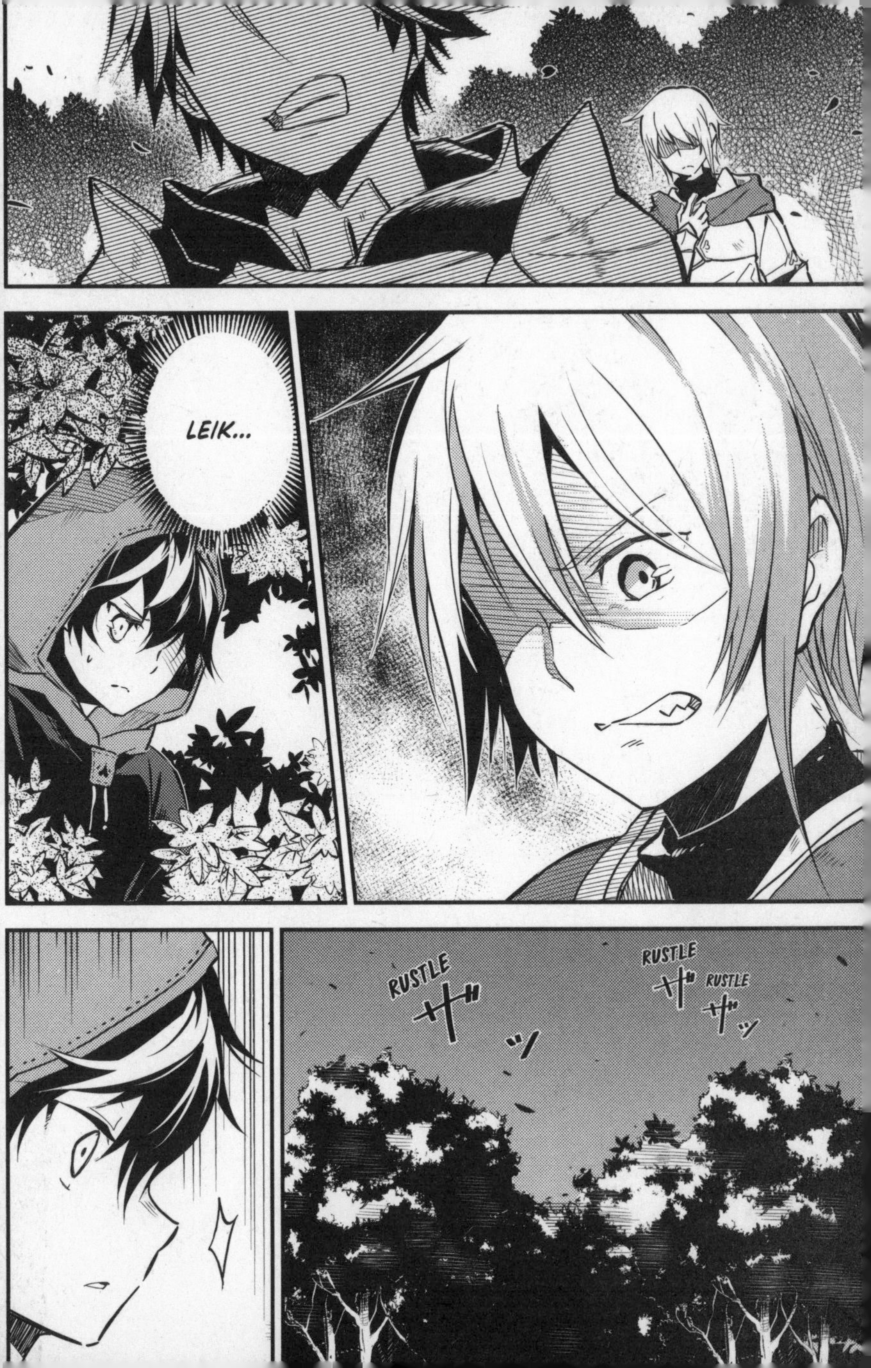
LEIK...
RUSTLE
ザッ
RUSTLE
ザッ
RUSTLE
ザッ

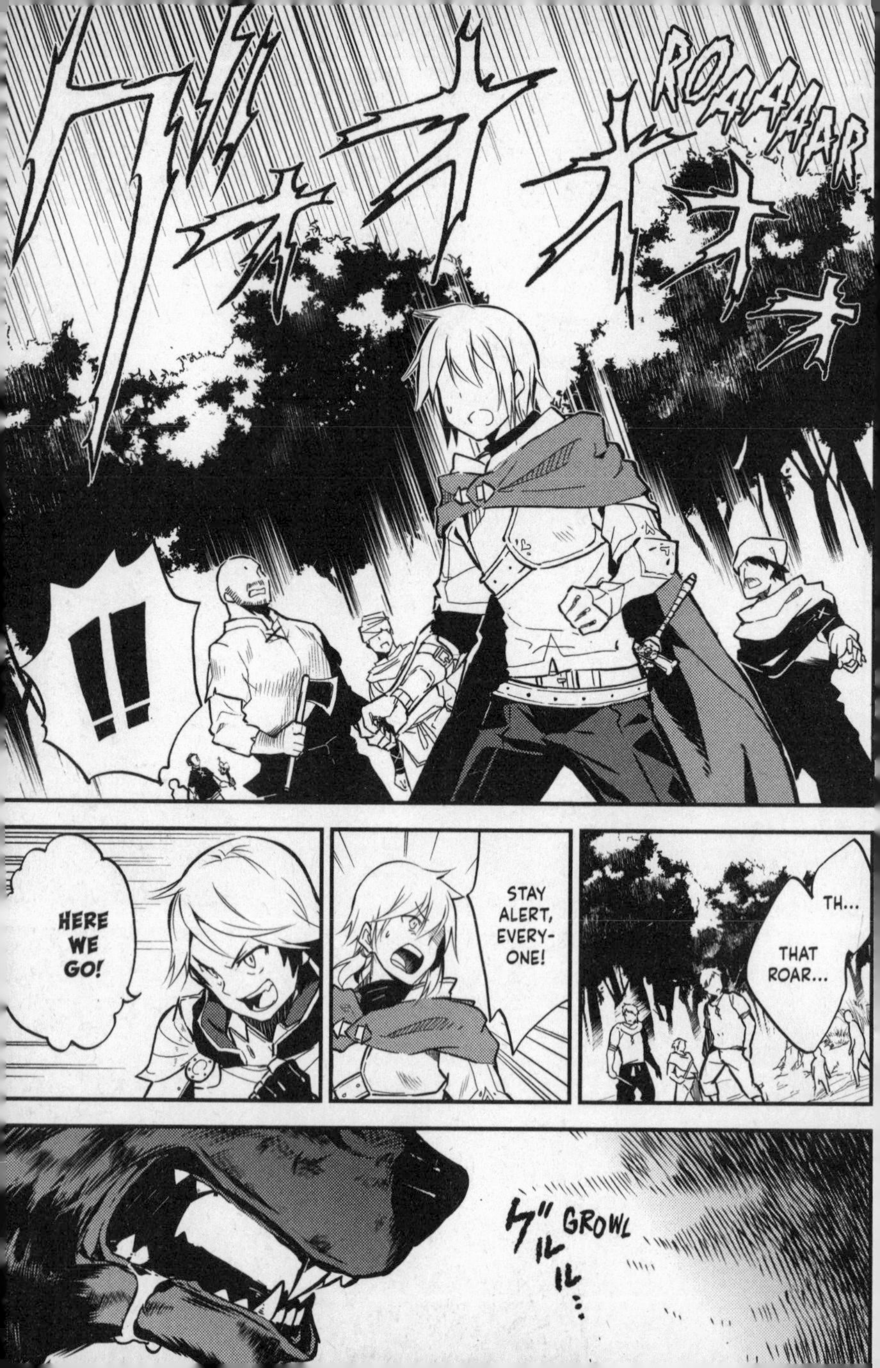
ROAAAAR
!!
TH...
THAT ROAR...
STAY ALERT, EVERY-ONE!
HERE WE GO!
GROWL

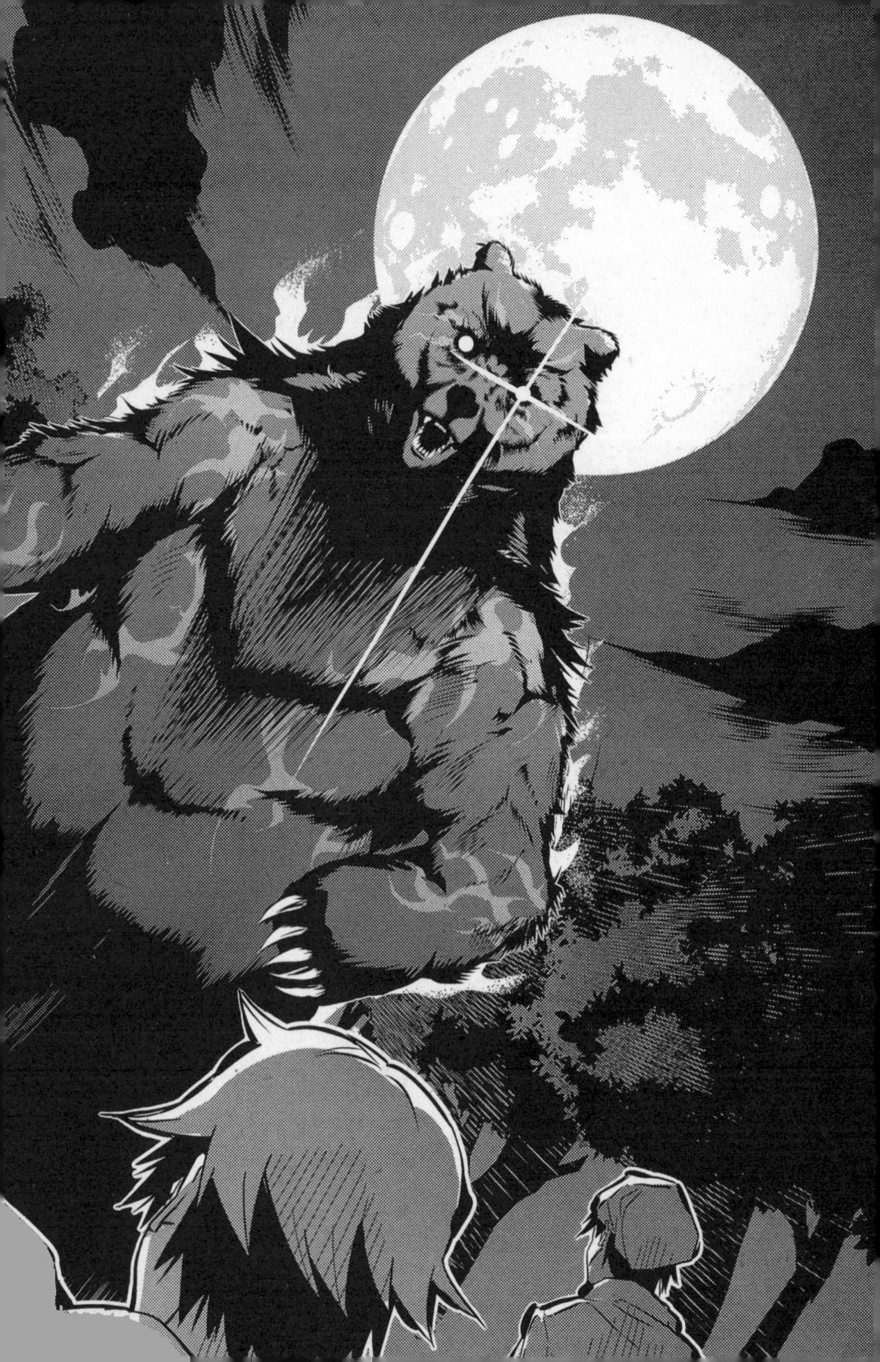

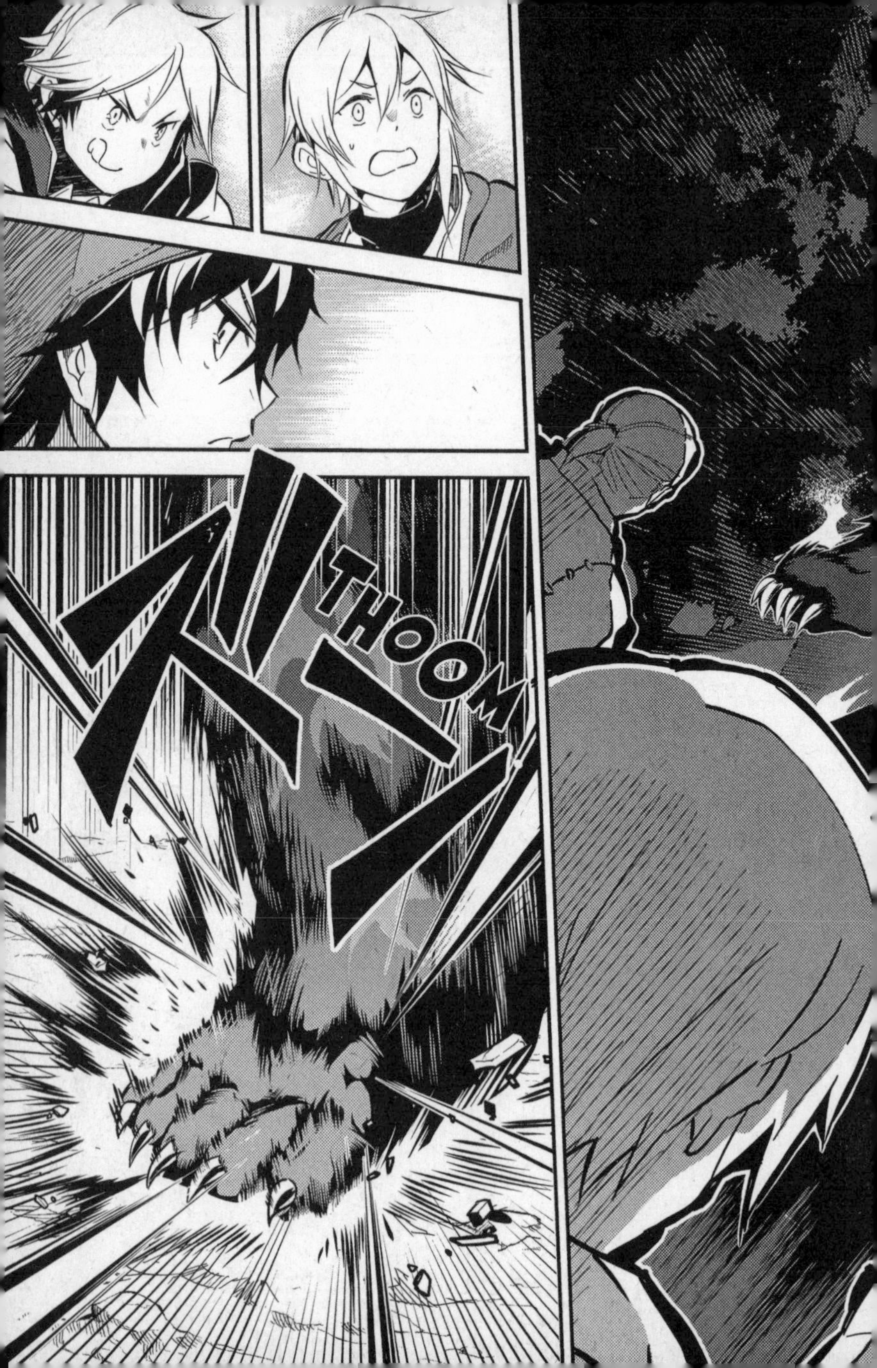
THOOM

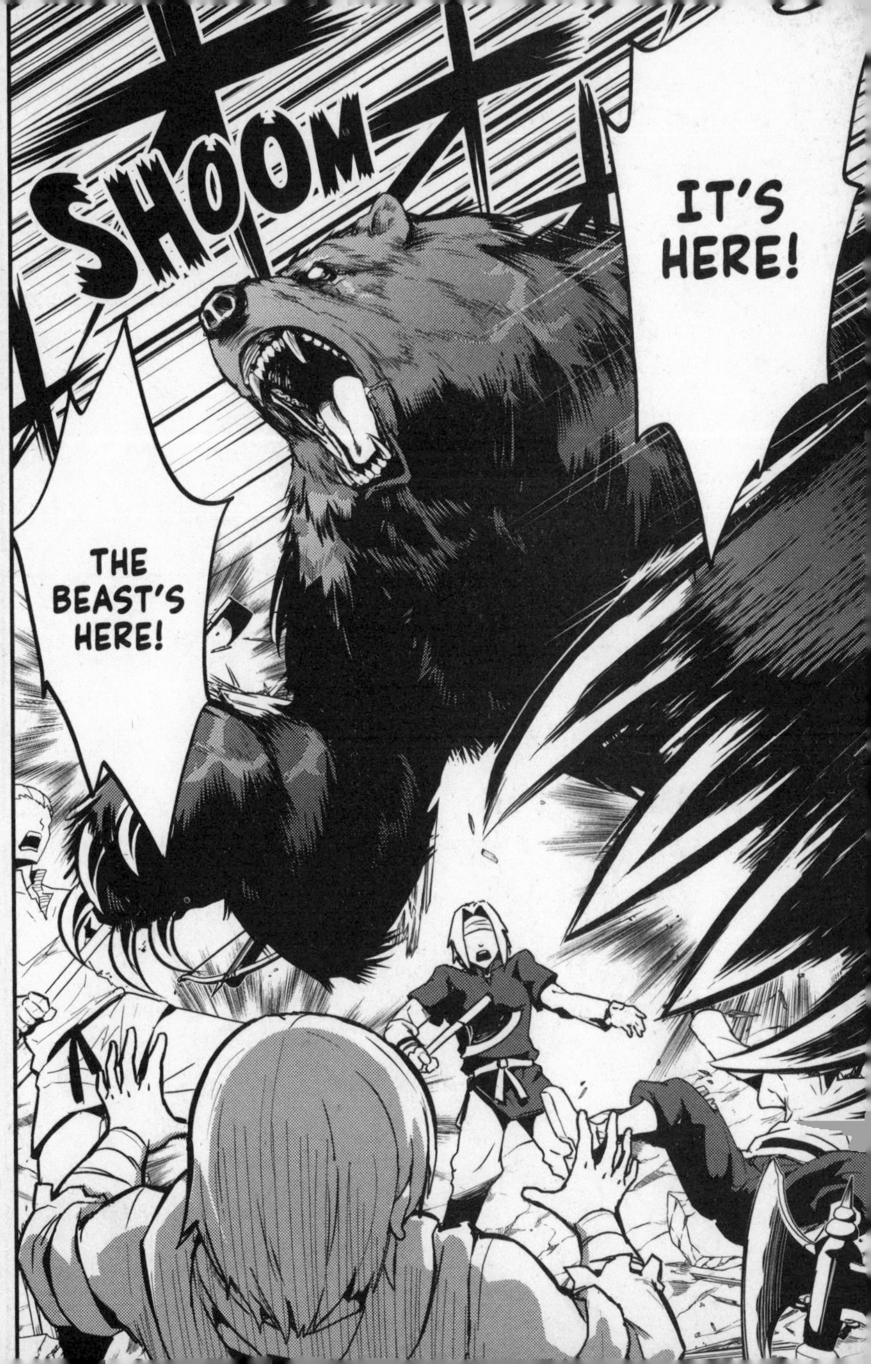
IT'S HERE!
SHOOM
THE BEAST'S HERE!

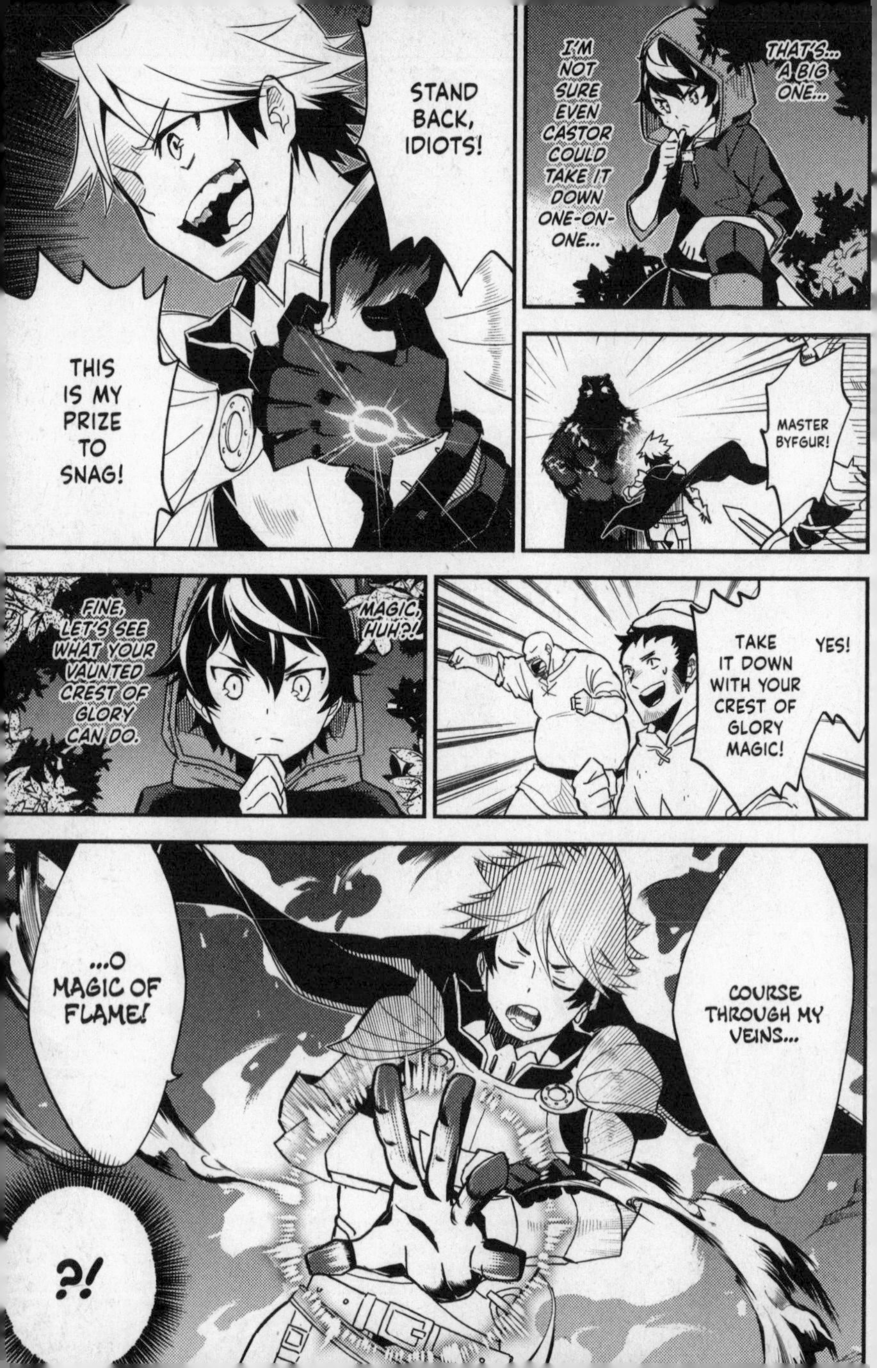
THAT'S... A BIG ONE...
I'M NOT SURE EVEN CASTOR COULD TAKE IT DOWN ONE-ON-ONE...
MASTER BYFGUR!
STAND BACK, IDIOTS!
THIS IS MY PRIZE TO SNAG!
YES!
TAKE IT DOWN WITH YOUR CREST OF GLORY MAGIC!
MAGIC, HUH?!
FINE, LET'S SEE WHAT YOUR VAUNTED CREST OF GLORY CAN DO.
COURSE THROUGH MY VEINS...
...O MAGIC OF FLAME!
?!

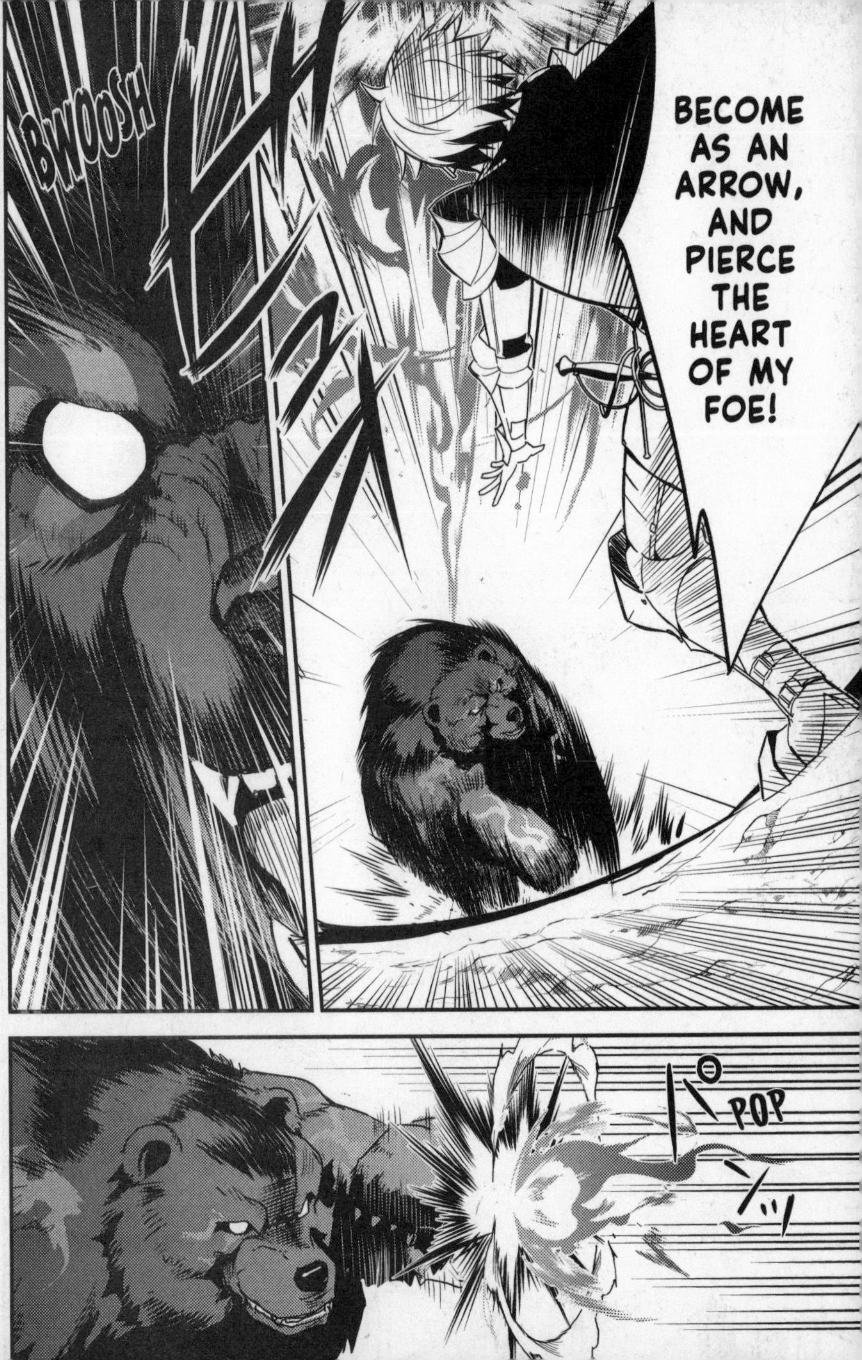
BECOME AS AN ARROW, AND PIERCE THE HEART OF MY FOE!
BWOOSH
POP

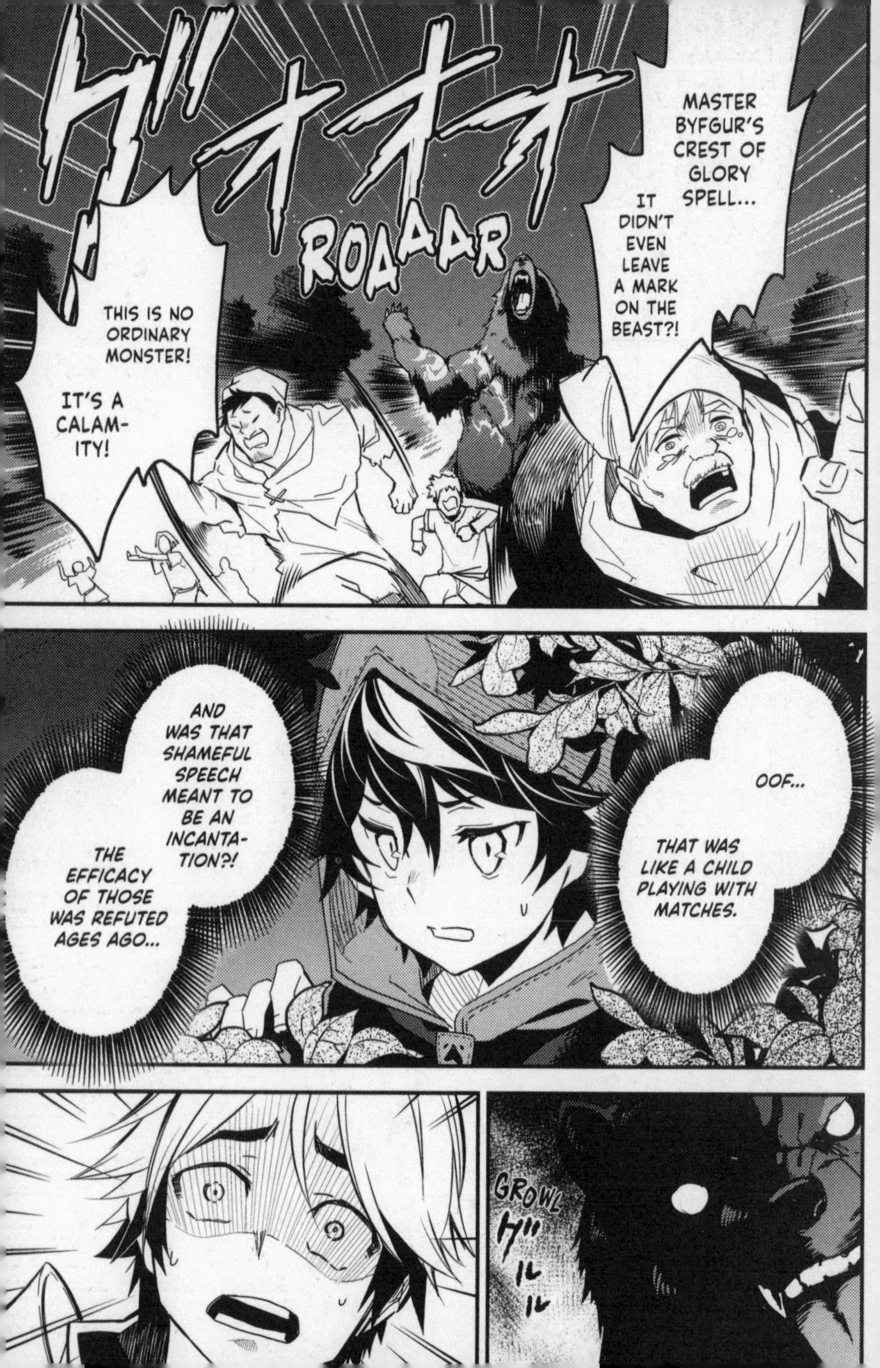
MASTER BYFGUR'S CREST OF GLORY SPELL...
IT DIDN'T EVEN LEAVE A MARK ON THE BEAST?!
ガオオオ
ROAAAR
THIS IS NO ORDINARY MONSTER!
IT'S A CALAMITY!
OOF...
THAT WAS LIKE A CHILD PLAYING WITH MATCHES.
AND WAS THAT SHAMEFUL SPEECH MEANT TO BE AN INCANTATION?!
THE EFFICACY OF THOSE WAS REFUTED AGES AGO...
GROWL

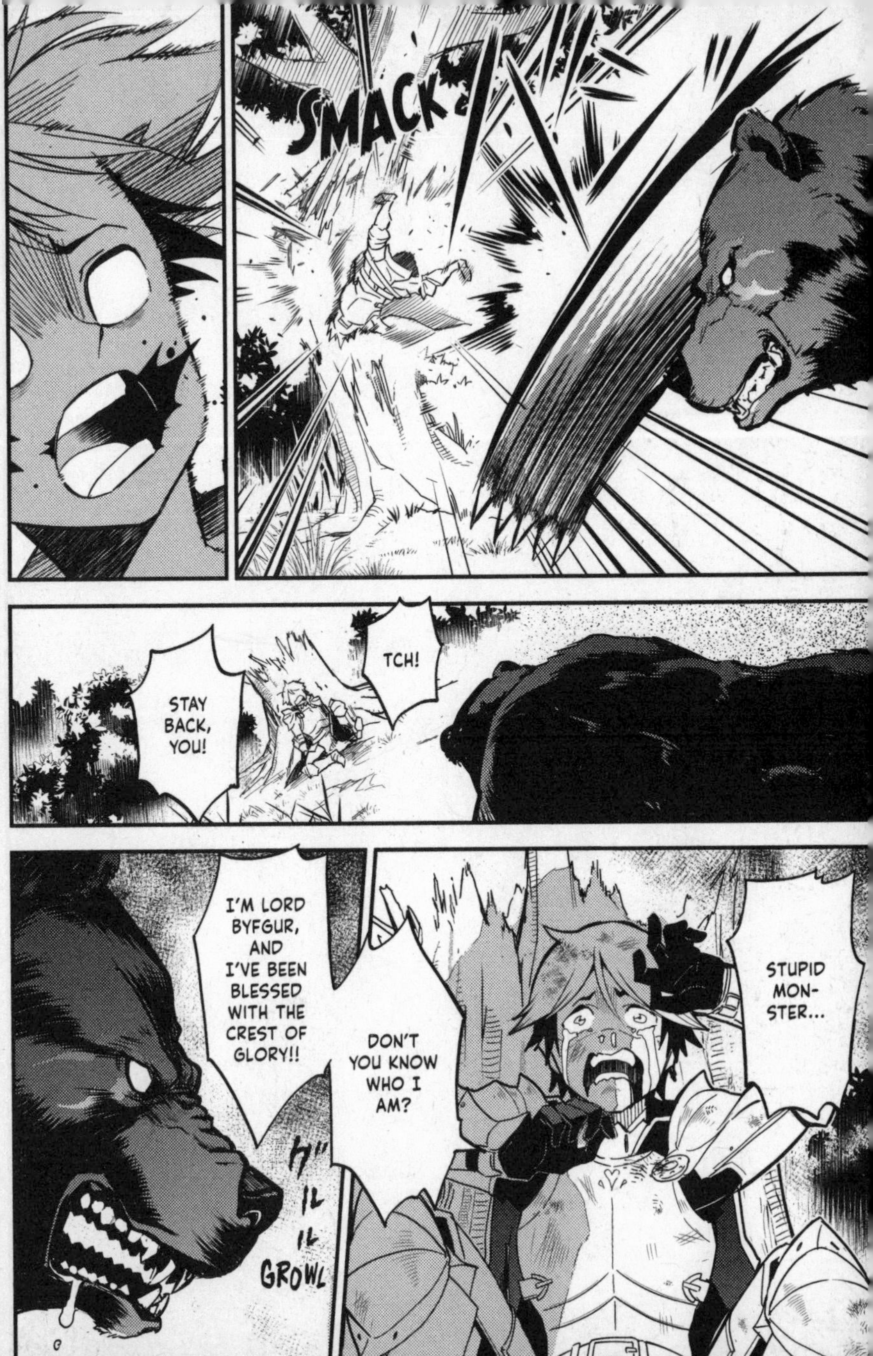
SMACK
TCH!
STAY BACK, YOU!
STUPID MON-STER...
DON'T YOU KNOW WHO I AM?
I'M LORD BYFGUR, AND I'VE BEEN BLESSED WITH THE CREST OF GLORY!!
GROWL

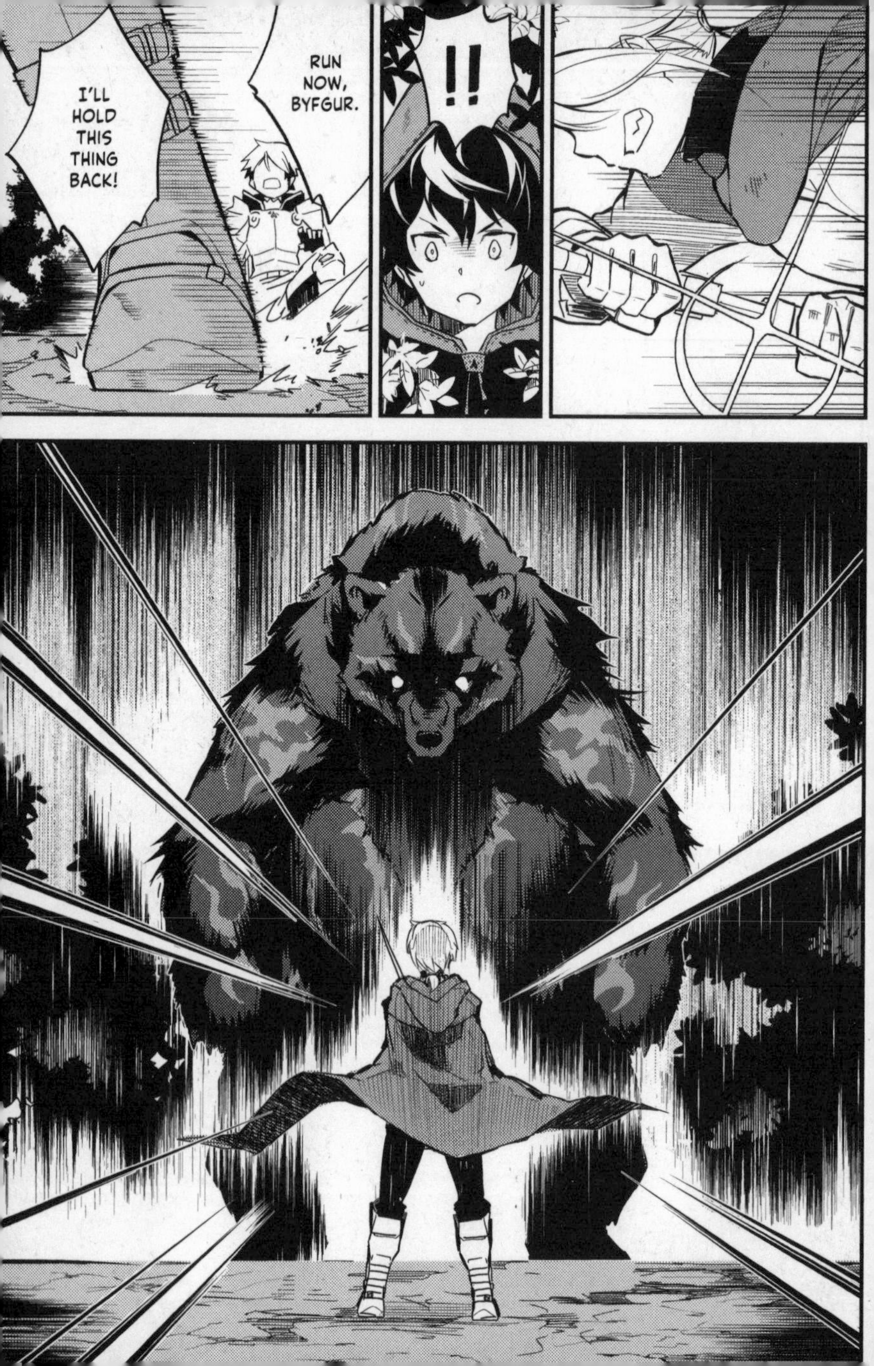
!!
RUN NOW, BYFGUR.
I'LL HOLD THIS THING BACK!

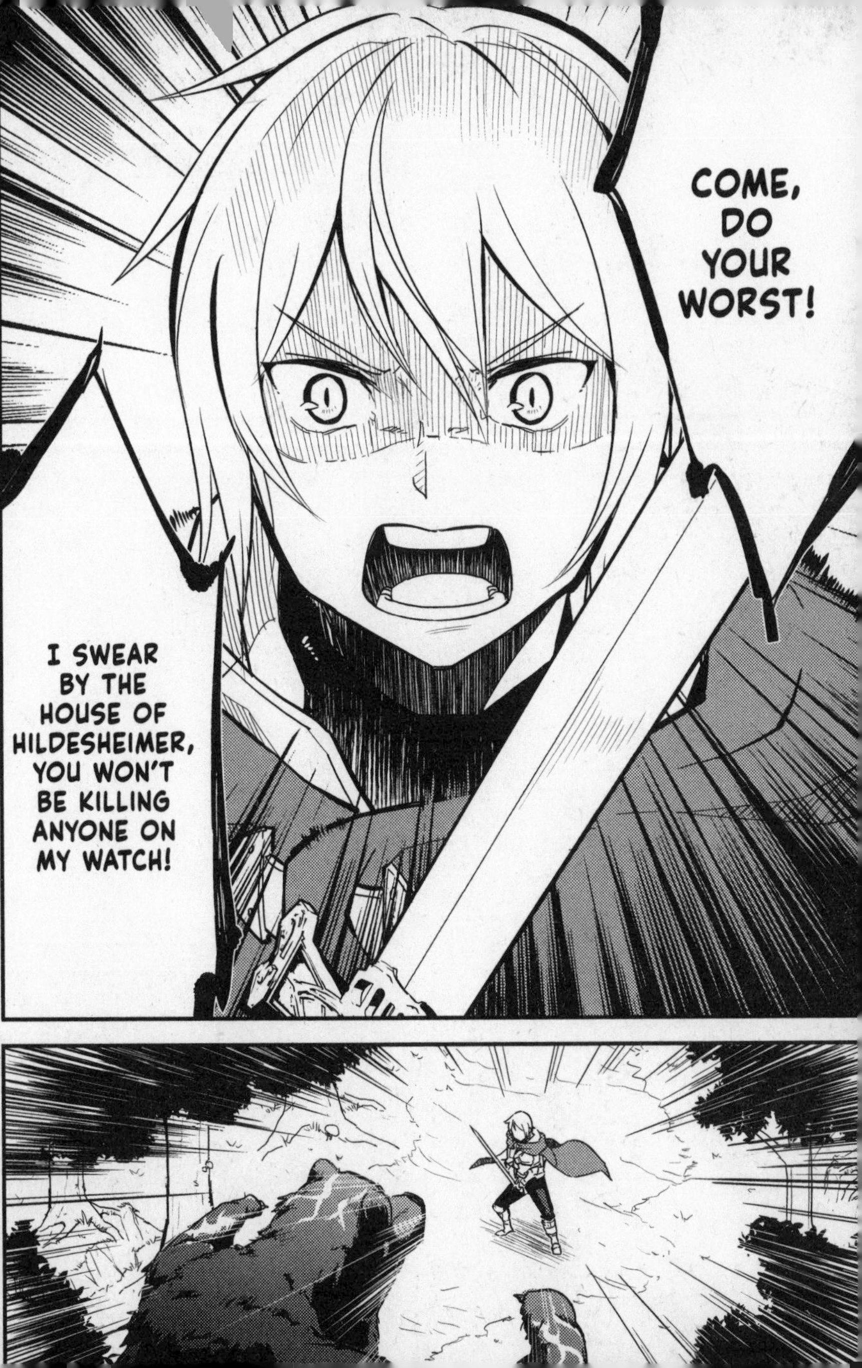
COME, DO YOUR WORST!
I SWEAR BY THE HOUSE OF HILDESHEIMER, YOU WON'T BE KILLING ANYONE ON MY WATCH!

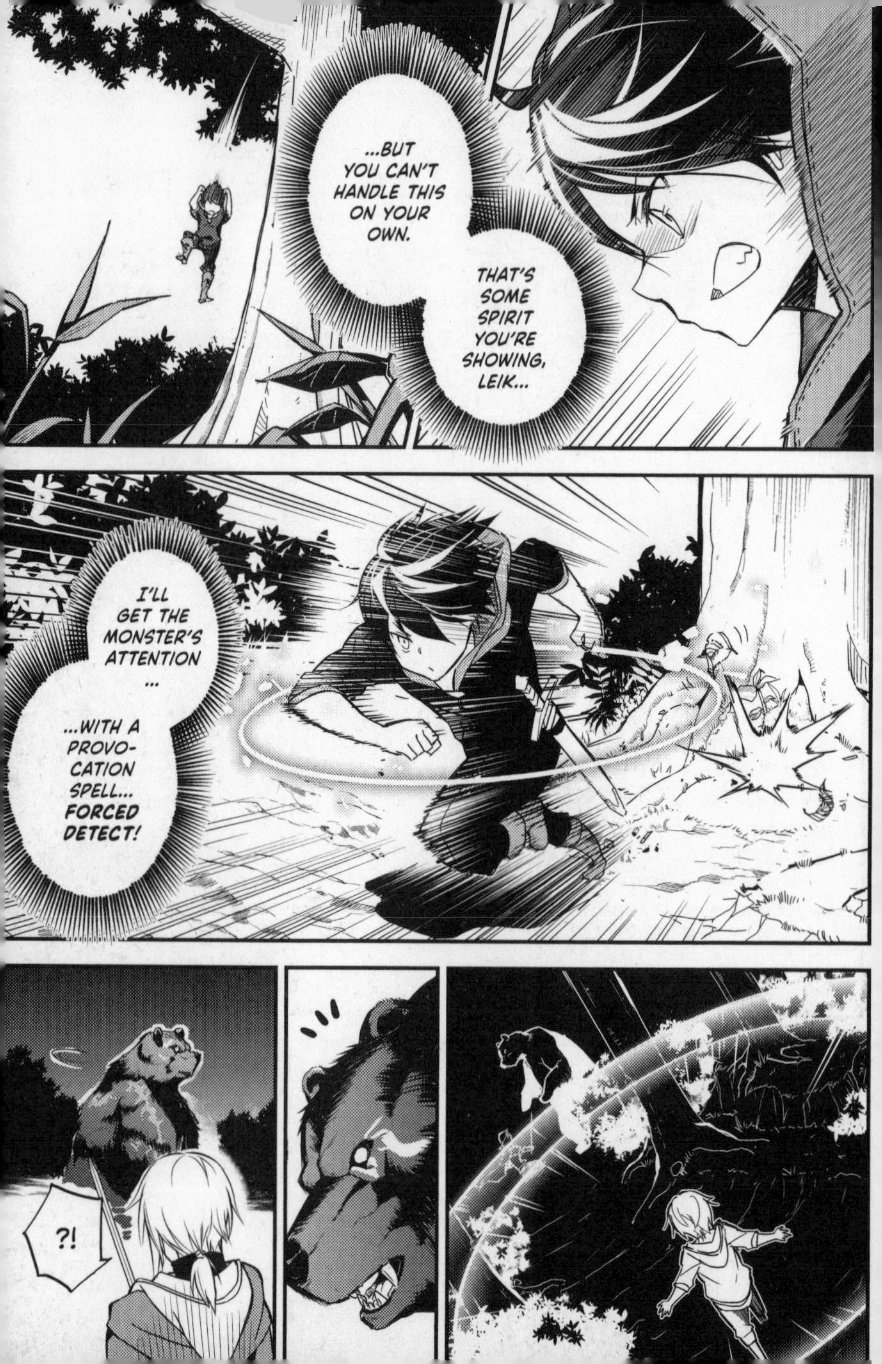
...BUT YOU CAN'T HANDLE THIS ON YOUR OWN.
THAT'S SOME SPIRIT YOU'RE SHOWING, LEIK...
I'LL GET THE MONSTER'S ATTENTION ...
...WITH A PROVO-CATION SPELL... FORCED DETECT!
?!

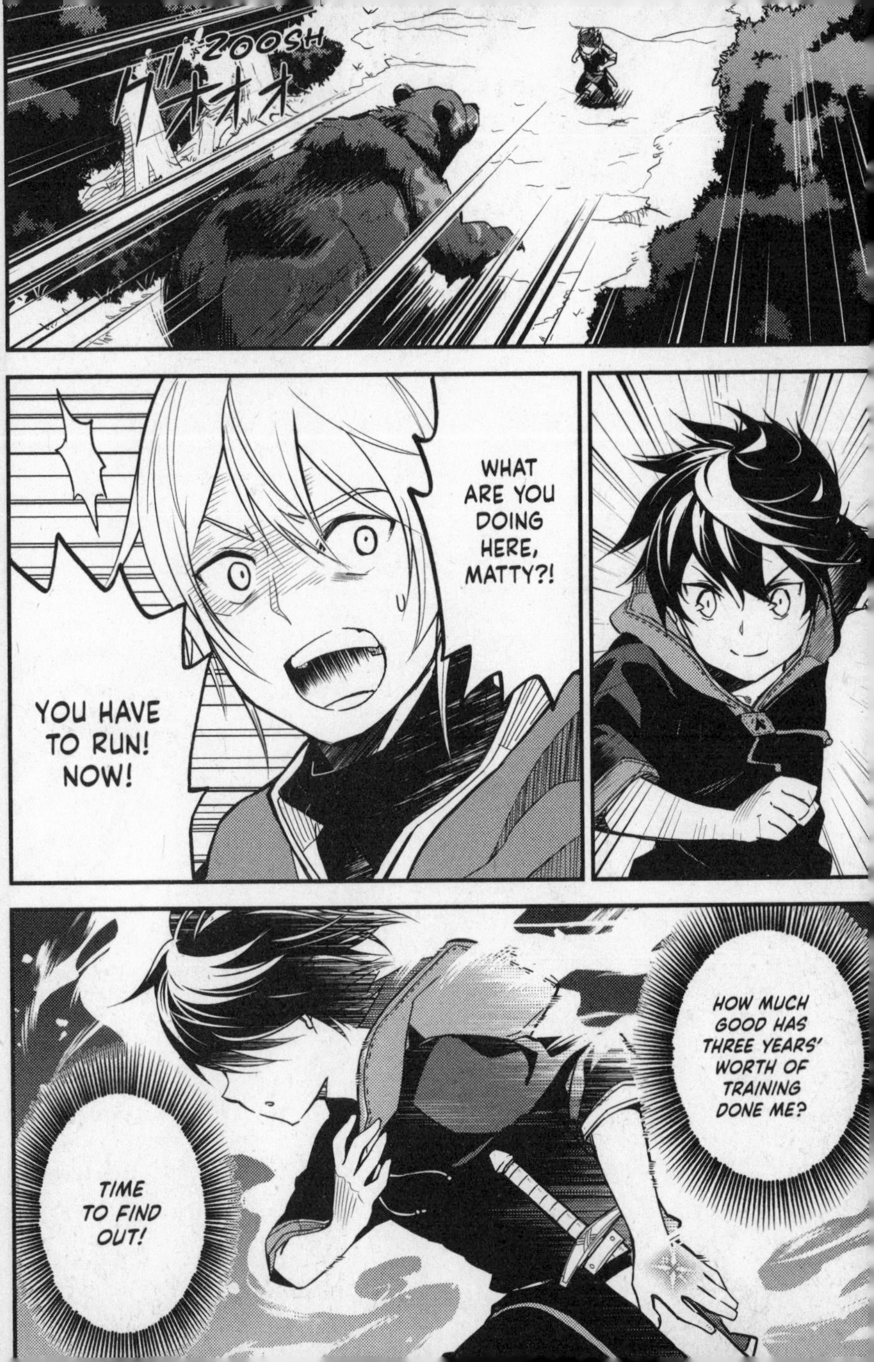
ZOOSH
グオオオ
WHAT ARE YOU DOING HERE, MATTY?!
YOU HAVE TO RUN! NOW!
HOW MUCH GOOD HAS THREE YEARS' WORTH OF TRAINING DONE ME?
TIME TO FIND OUT!

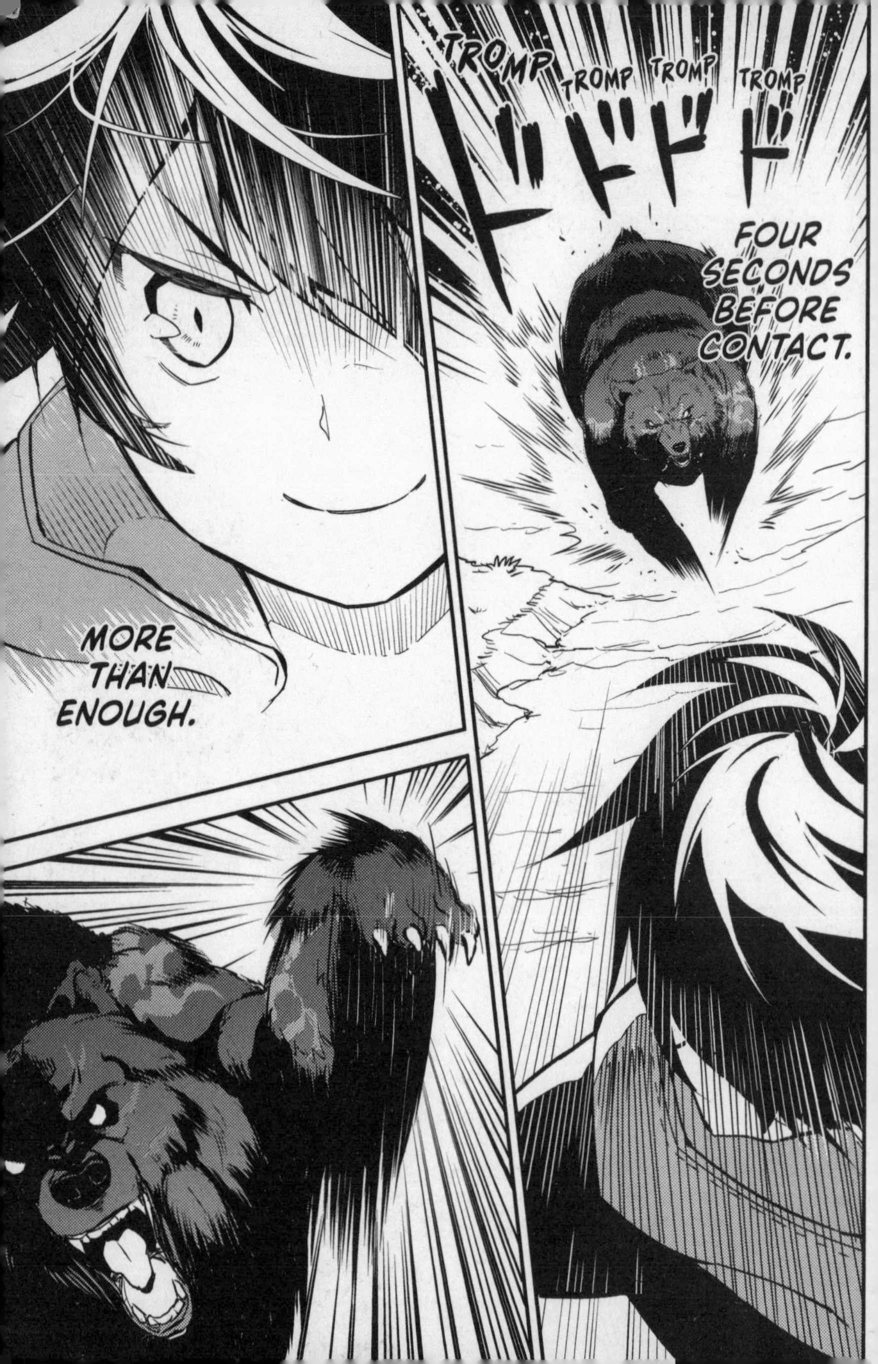
TROMP TROMP TROMP TROMP
ドドドド
FOUR SECONDS BEFORE CONTACT.
MORE THAN ENOUGH.

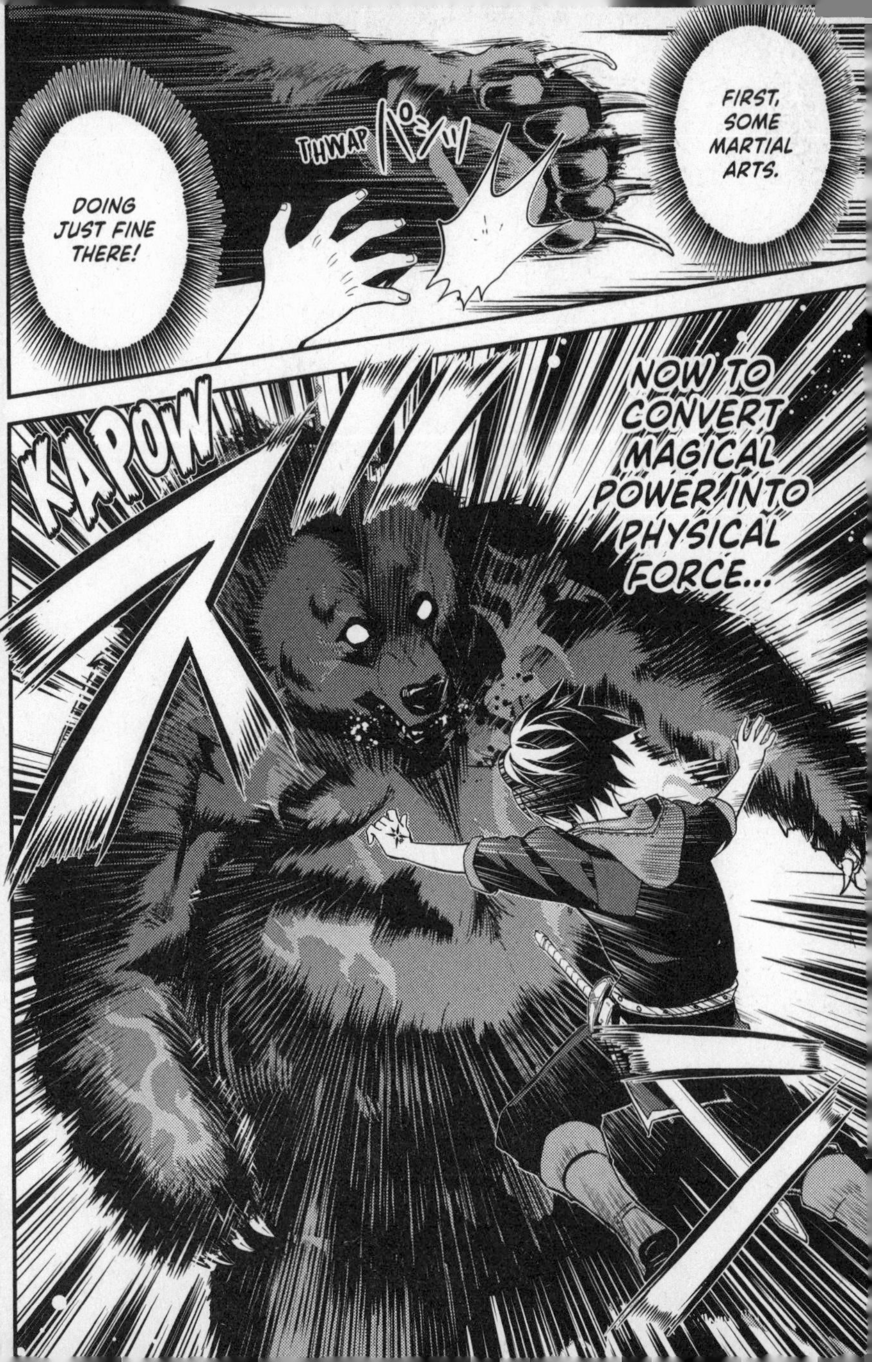
FIRST, SOME MARTIAL ARTS.
THWAP
DOING JUST FINE THERE!
NOW TO CONVERT MAGICAL POWER INTO PHYSICAL FORCE...
KAPOW

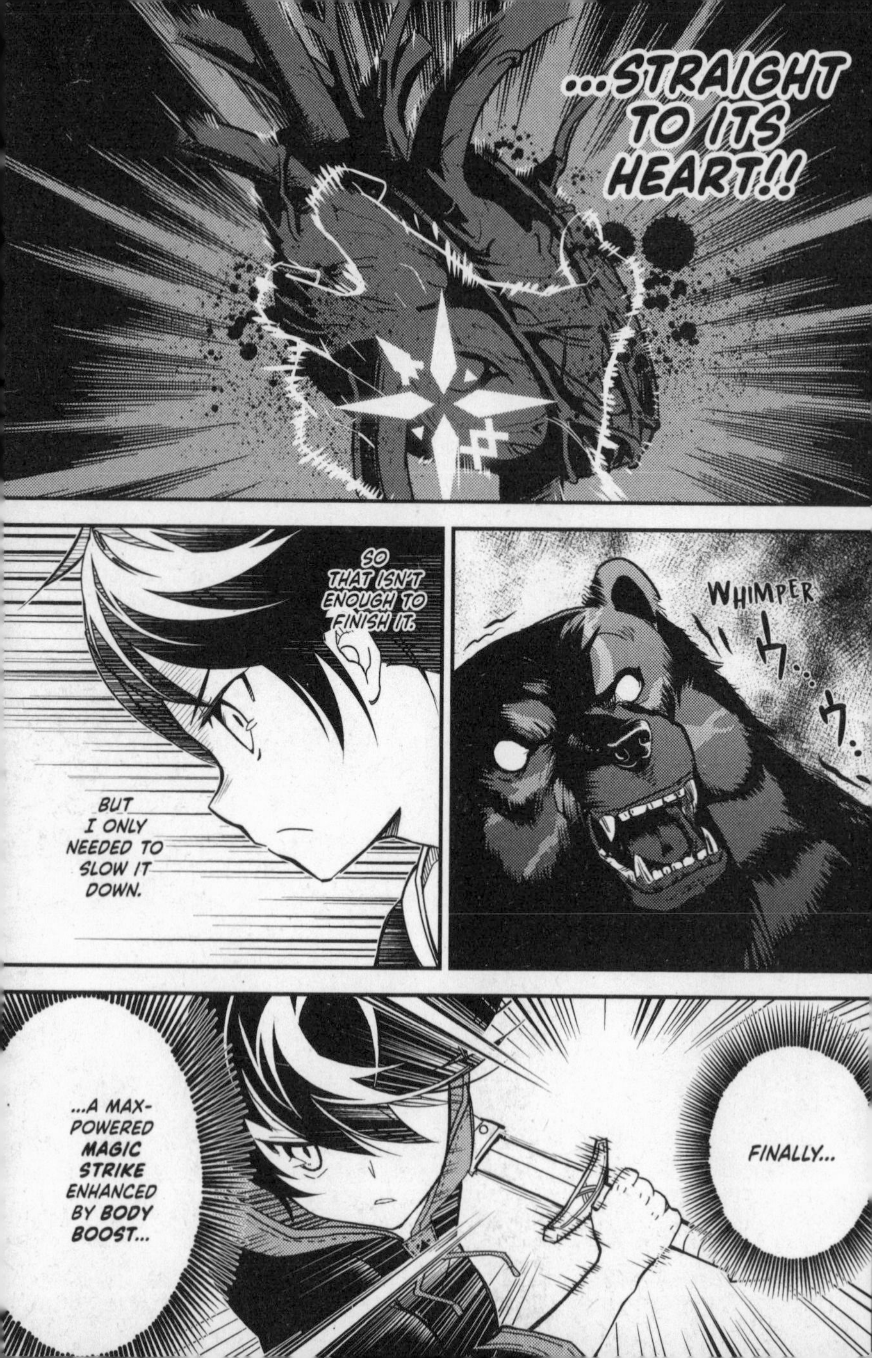
...STRAIGHT TO ITS HEART!!
WHIMPER
ウ...ウ...
SO THAT ISN'T ENOUGH TO FINISH IT.
BUT I ONLY NEEDED TO SLOW IT DOWN.
FINALLY...
...A MAX-POWERED MAGIC STRIKE ENHANCED BY BODY BOOST...

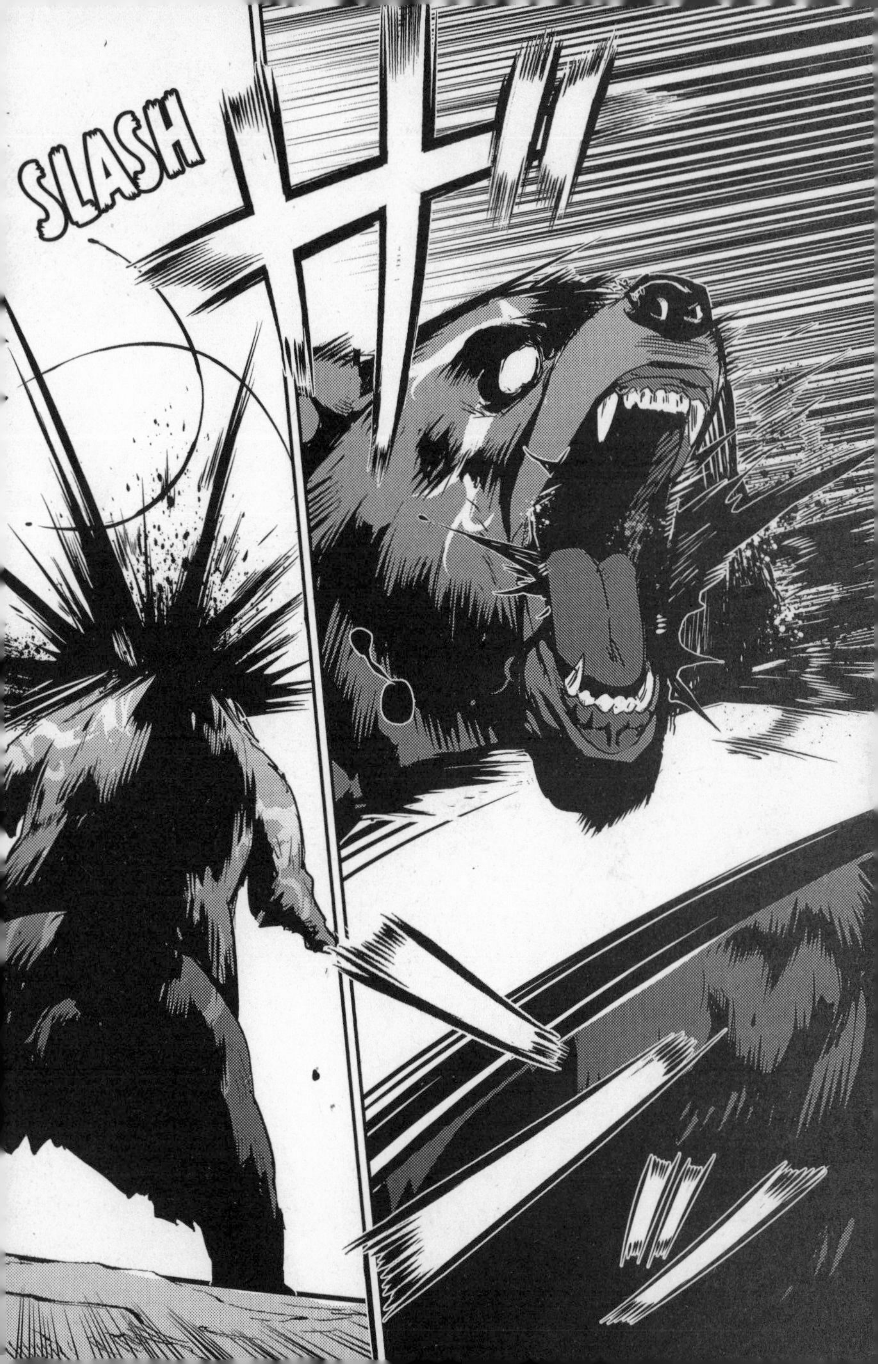
SLASH

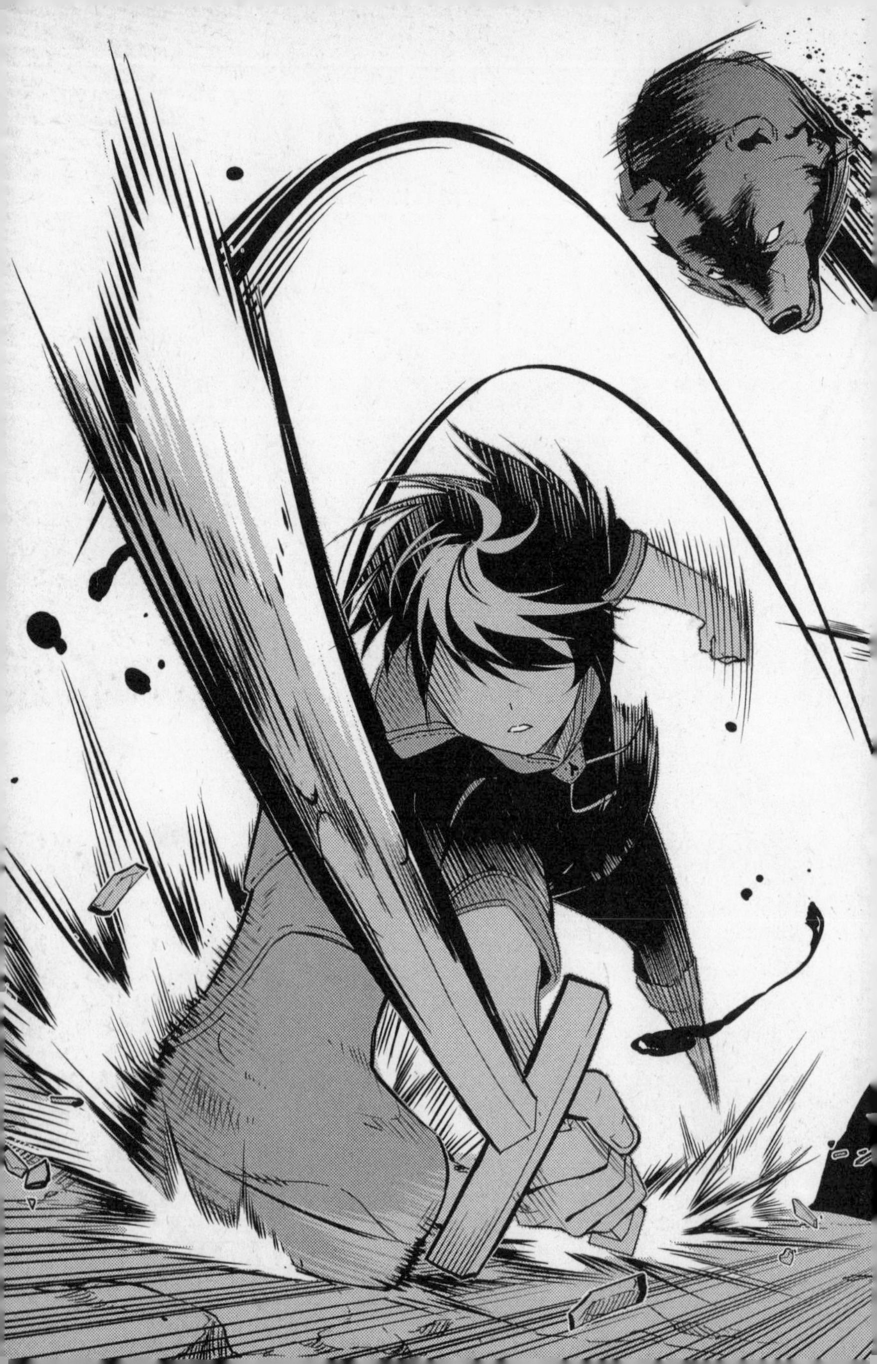

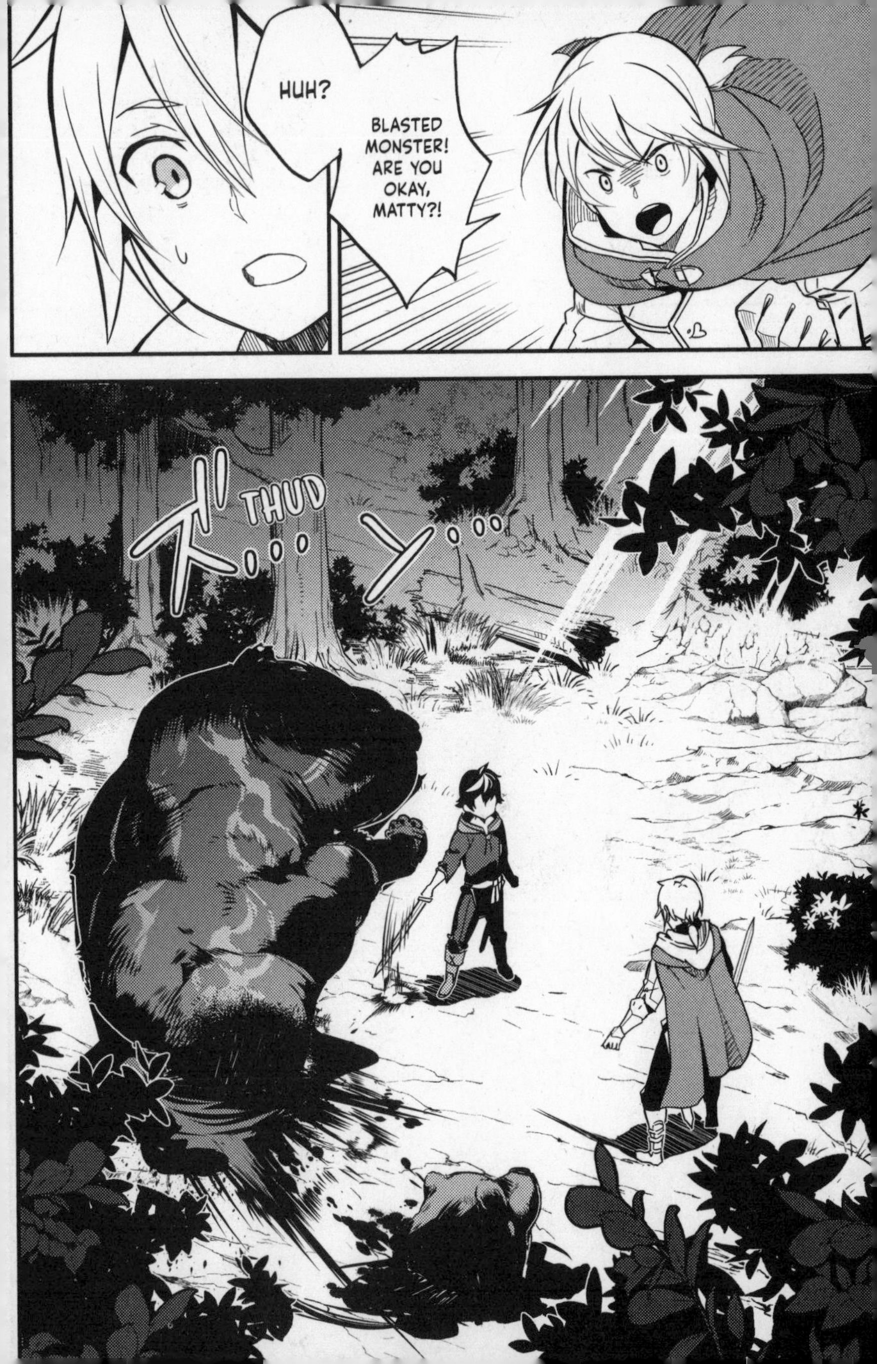
BLASTED MONSTER! ARE YOU OKAY, MATTY?!
HUH?
THUD

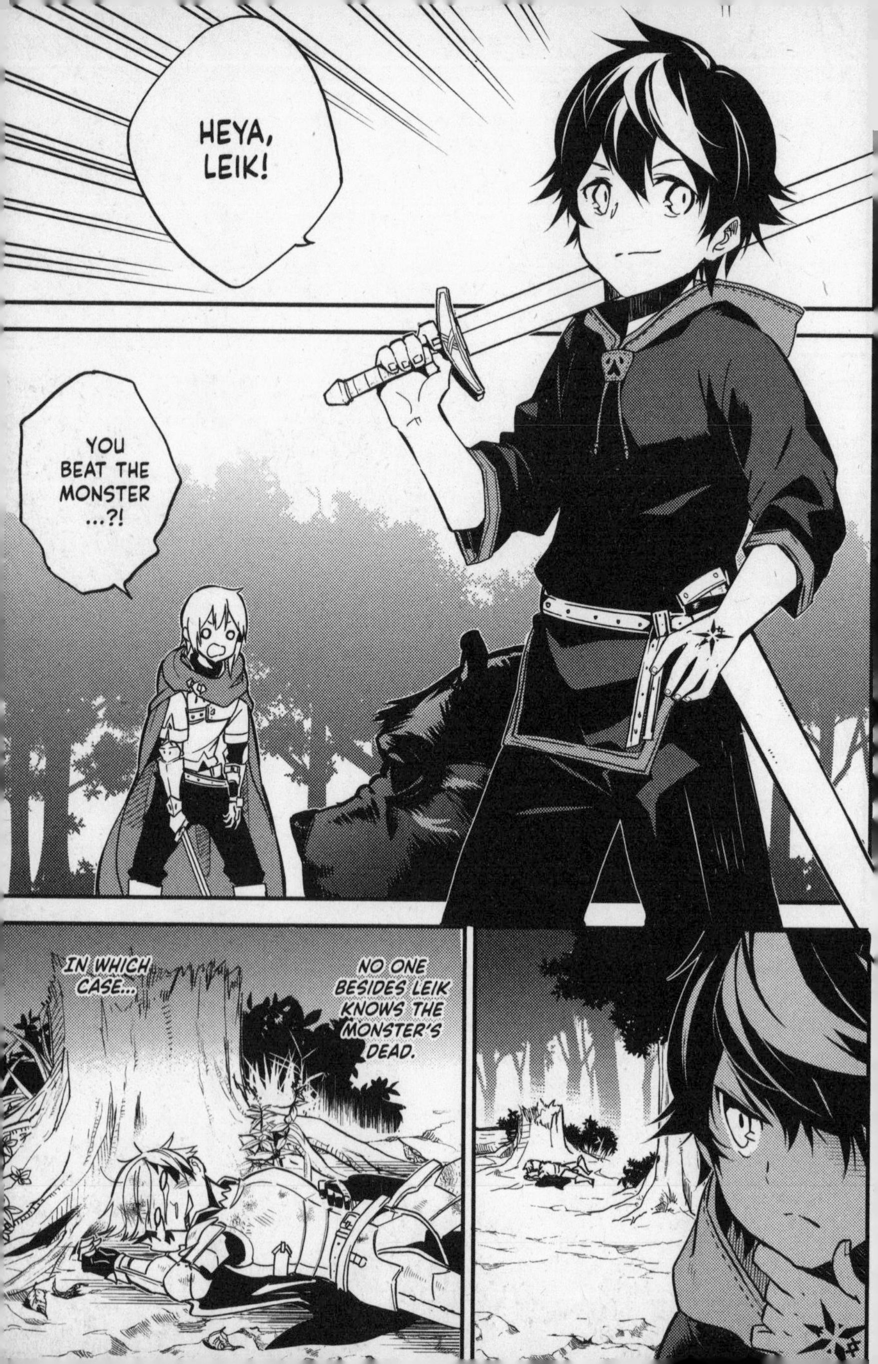
HEYA, LEIK!
YOU BEAT THE MONSTER ...?!
NO ONE BESIDES LEIK KNOWS THE MONSTER'S DEAD.
IN WHICH CASE...

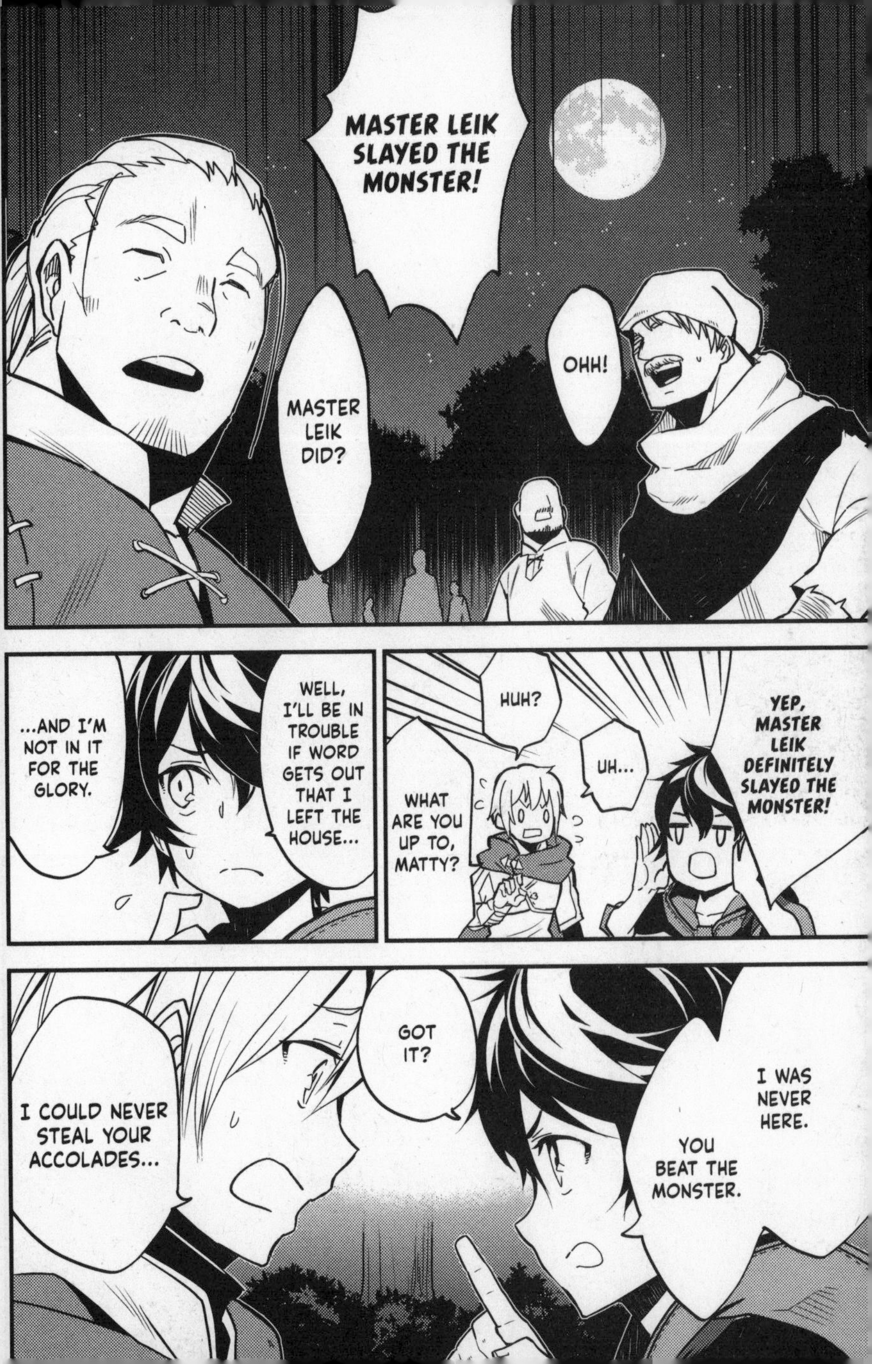
MASTER LEIK SLAYED THE MONSTER!
OHH!
MASTER LEIK DID?
YEP, MASTER LEIK DEFINITELY SLAYED THE MONSTER!
HUH?
UH...
WHAT ARE YOU UP TO, MATTY?
WELL, I'LL BE IN TROUBLE IF WORD GETS OUT THAT I LEFT THE HOUSE...
...AND I'M NOT IN IT FOR THE GLORY.
I WAS NEVER HERE.
YOU BEAT THE MONSTER.
GOT IT?
I COULD NEVER STEAL YOUR ACCOLADES...

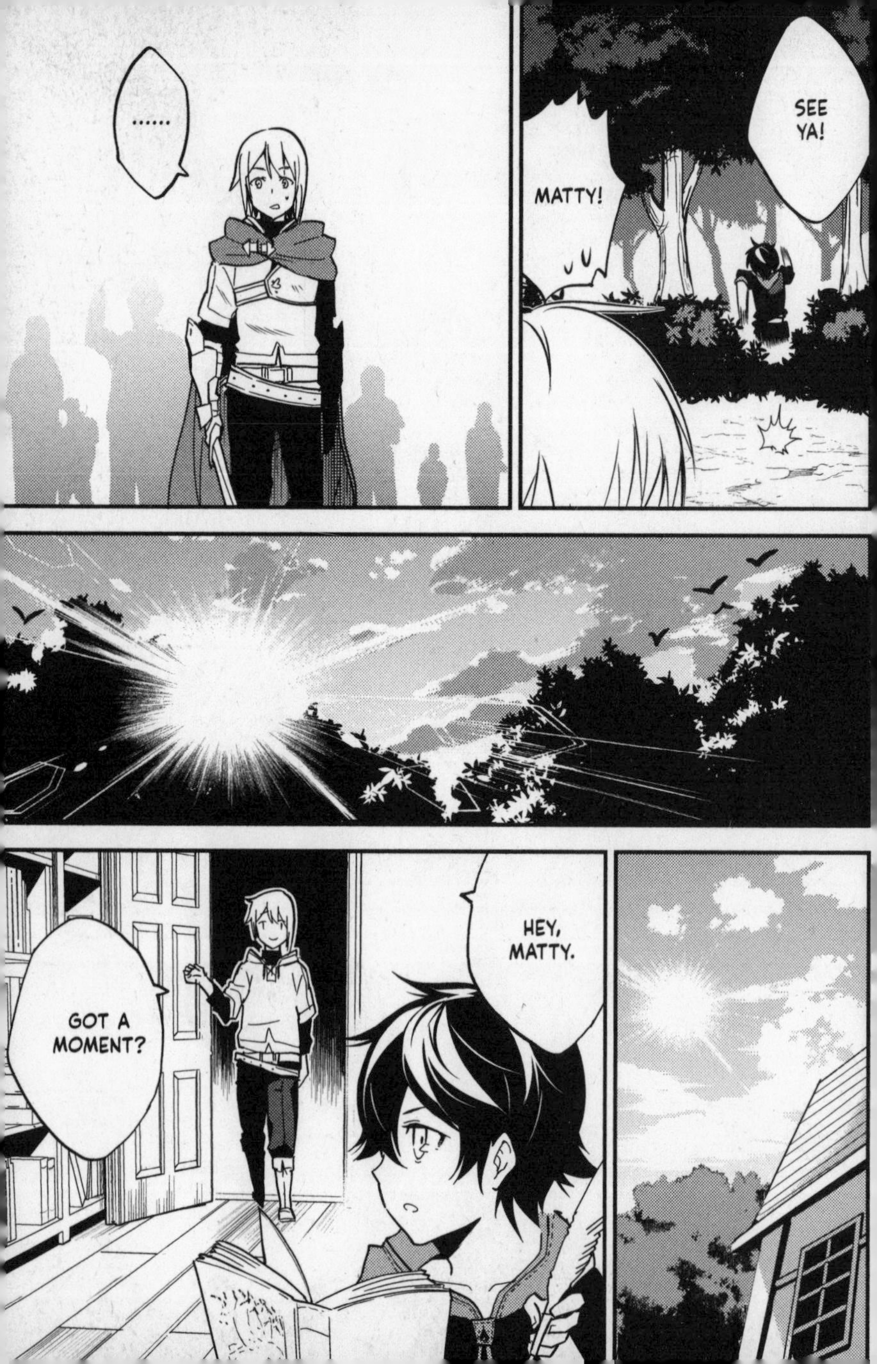
SEE YA!
MATTY!
......
HEY, MATTY.
GOT A MOMENT?

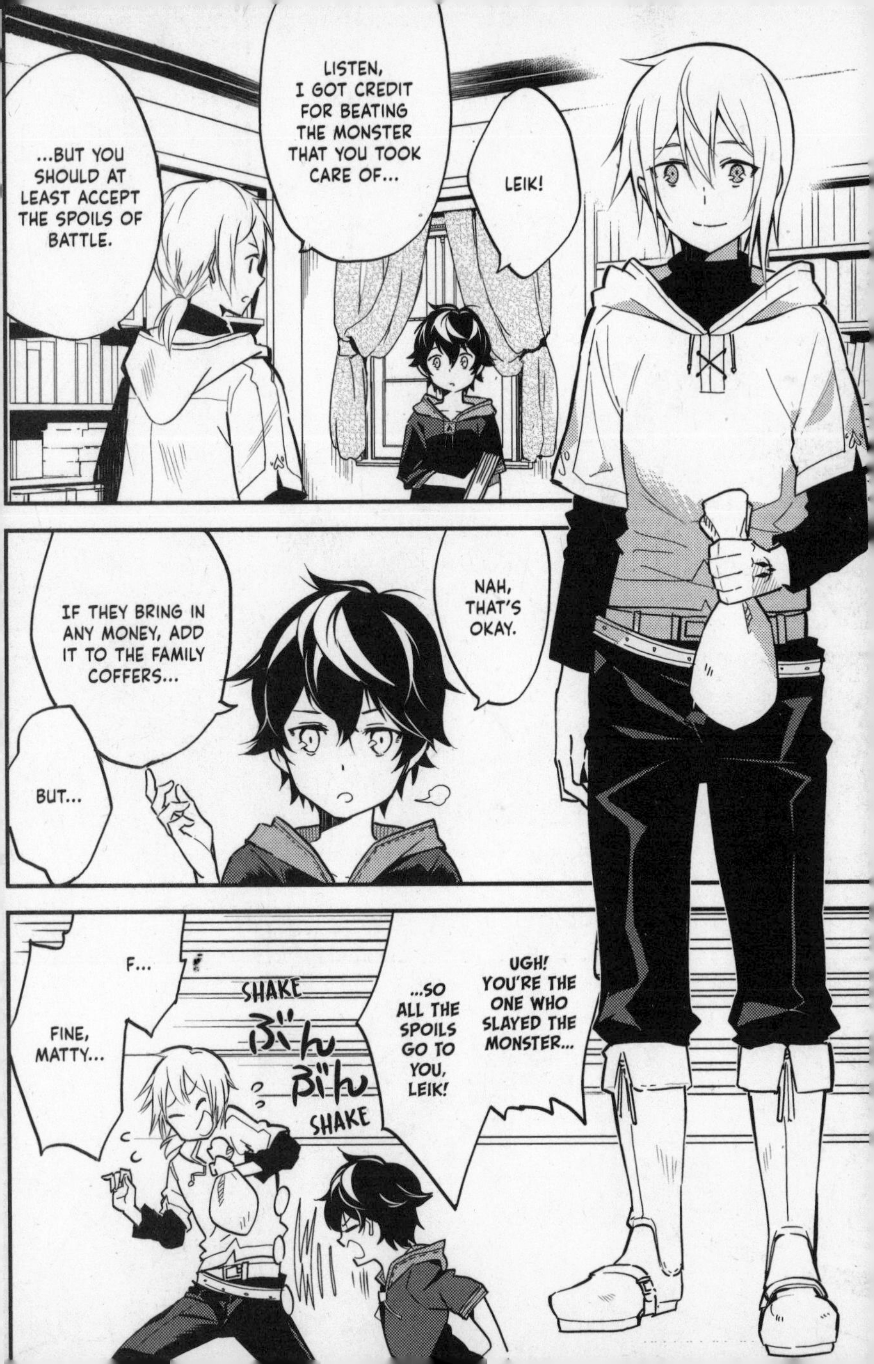
LEIK!
LISTEN, I GOT CREDIT FOR BEATING THE MONSTER THAT YOU TOOK CARE OF...
...BUT YOU SHOULD AT LEAST ACCEPT THE SPOILS OF BATTLE.
NAH, THAT'S OKAY.
IF THEY BRING IN ANY MONEY, ADD IT TO THE FAMILY COFFERS...
BUT...
UGH! YOU'RE THE ONE WHO SLAYED THE MONSTER...
...SO ALL THE SPOILS GO TO YOU, LEIK!
SHAKE
ぶん
ぶん
SHAKE
F...
FINE, MATTY...

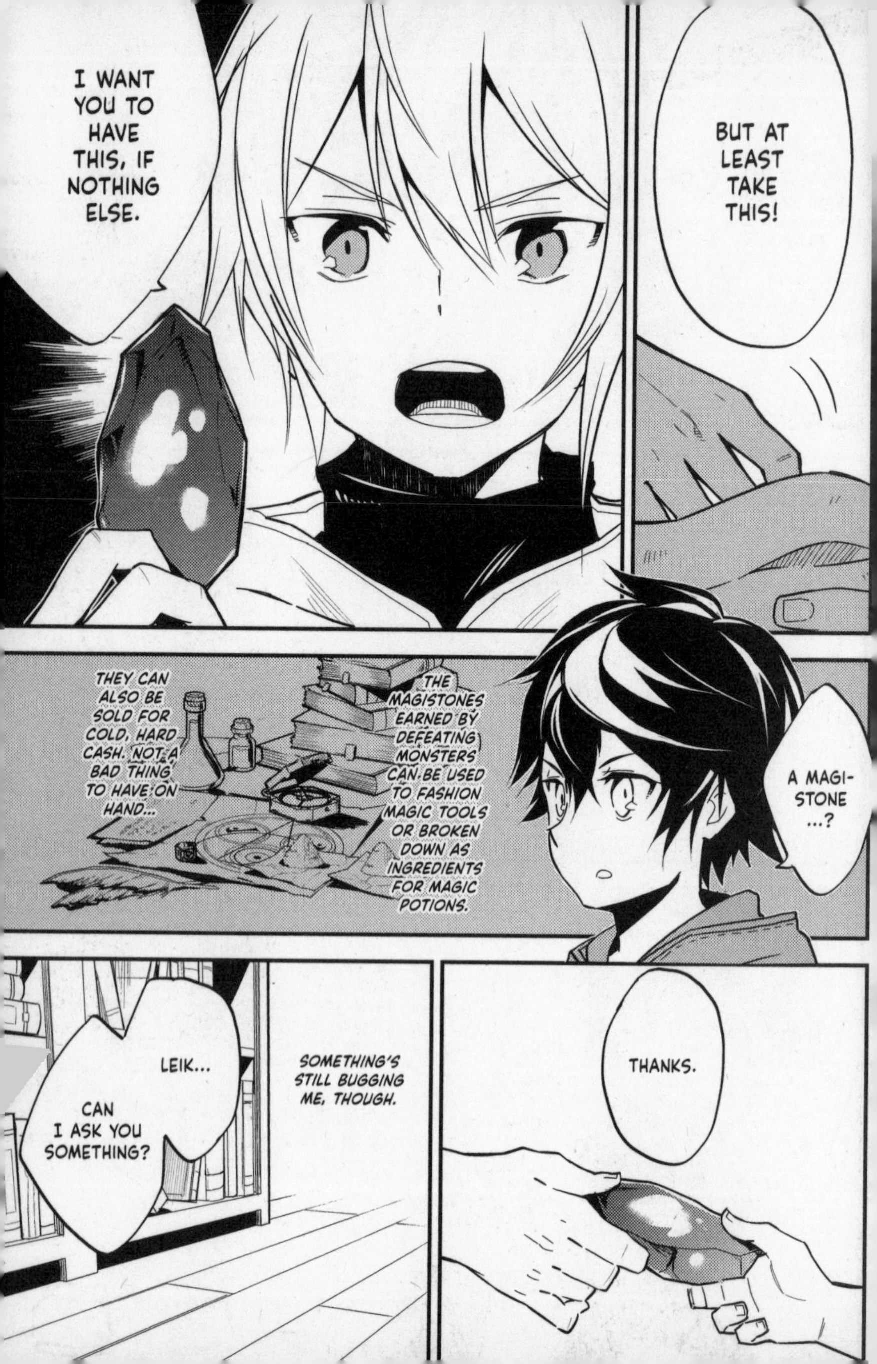
BUT AT LEAST TAKE THIS!
I WANT YOU TO HAVE THIS, IF NOTHING ELSE.
A MAGI-STONE ...?
THE MAGISTONES EARNED BY DEFEATING MONSTERS CAN BE USED TO FASHION MAGIC TOOLS OR BROKEN DOWN AS INGREDIENTS FOR MAGIC POTIONS.
THEY CAN ALSO BE SOLD FOR COLD, HARD CASH. NOT A BAD THING TO HAVE ON HAND...
THANKS.
SOMETHING'S STILL BUGGING ME, THOUGH.
LEIK...
CAN I ASK YOU SOMETHING?

WHY IS BYFGUR ACTING HEAD OF THE HOUSE...

...WHEN YOU'RE THE OLDEST SON?

THERE ARE A FEW FACTORS THAT DETERMINE WHICH CHILD WILL TAKE OVER THE FAMILY.

RIGHT... THAT.

...A POINT SYSTEM...?

CRITERIA FOR SUCCESSION IN NOBLE HOUSES OF THE EIS KINGDOM

WHEN DECIDING WHICH HEIR SHALL BECOME THE NEXT HEAD, REFER TO THE FOLLOWING CRITERIA AND GRANT PRIORITY TO THE HEIR WITH THE MOST POINTS. LET IT BE KNOWN THAT EXCEPTIONAL CIRCUMSTANCES MAY SUPERSEDE EVEN THESE CRITERIA.

[ELDEST SON]	+5 POINTS
[OTHER HEIRS]	−1 POINT FOR EACH YEAR YOUNGER THAN THE ELDEST SON THE HEIR IN QUESTION IS
[CREST OF GLORY]	+5 POINTS
[MAGIC PROFICIENCY]	+3 POINTS TO THE MOST ADEPT HEIR
[WOMAN]	−2 POINTS
[CREST OF FAILURE]	−200 POINTS

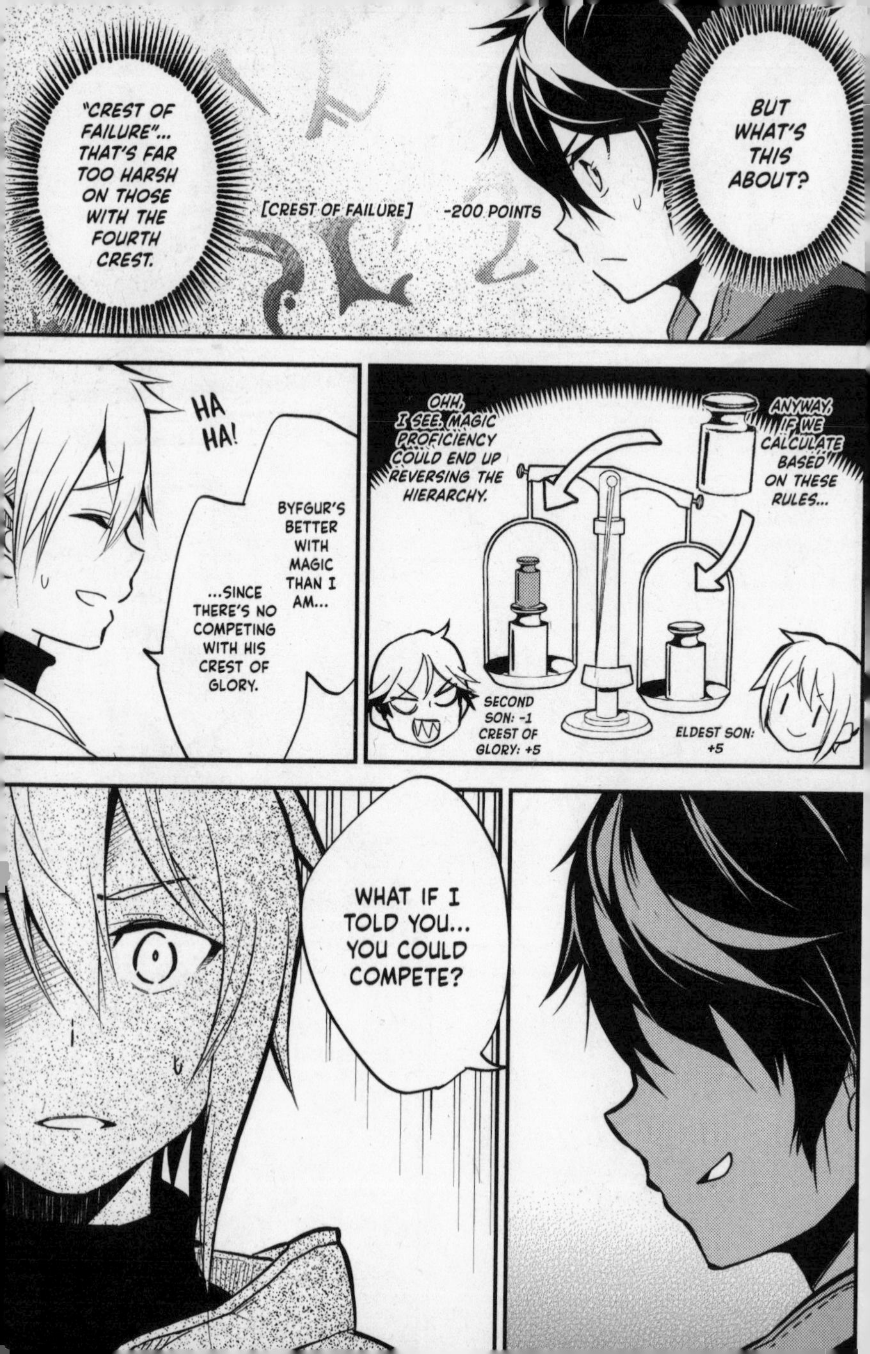
BUT WHAT'S THIS ABOUT?
[CREST OF FAILURE] -200 POINTS
"CREST OF FAILURE"... THAT'S FAR TOO HARSH ON THOSE WITH THE FOURTH CREST.
ANYWAY, IF WE CALCULATE BASED ON THESE RULES...
OHH, I SEE. MAGIC PROFICIENCY COULD END UP REVERSING THE HIERARCHY.
ELDEST SON: +5
SECOND SON: -1 CREST OF GLORY: +5
BYFGUR'S BETTER WITH MAGIC THAN I AM...
...SINCE THERE'S NO COMPETING WITH HIS CREST OF GLORY.
HA HA!
WHAT IF I TOLD YOU... YOU COULD COMPETE?

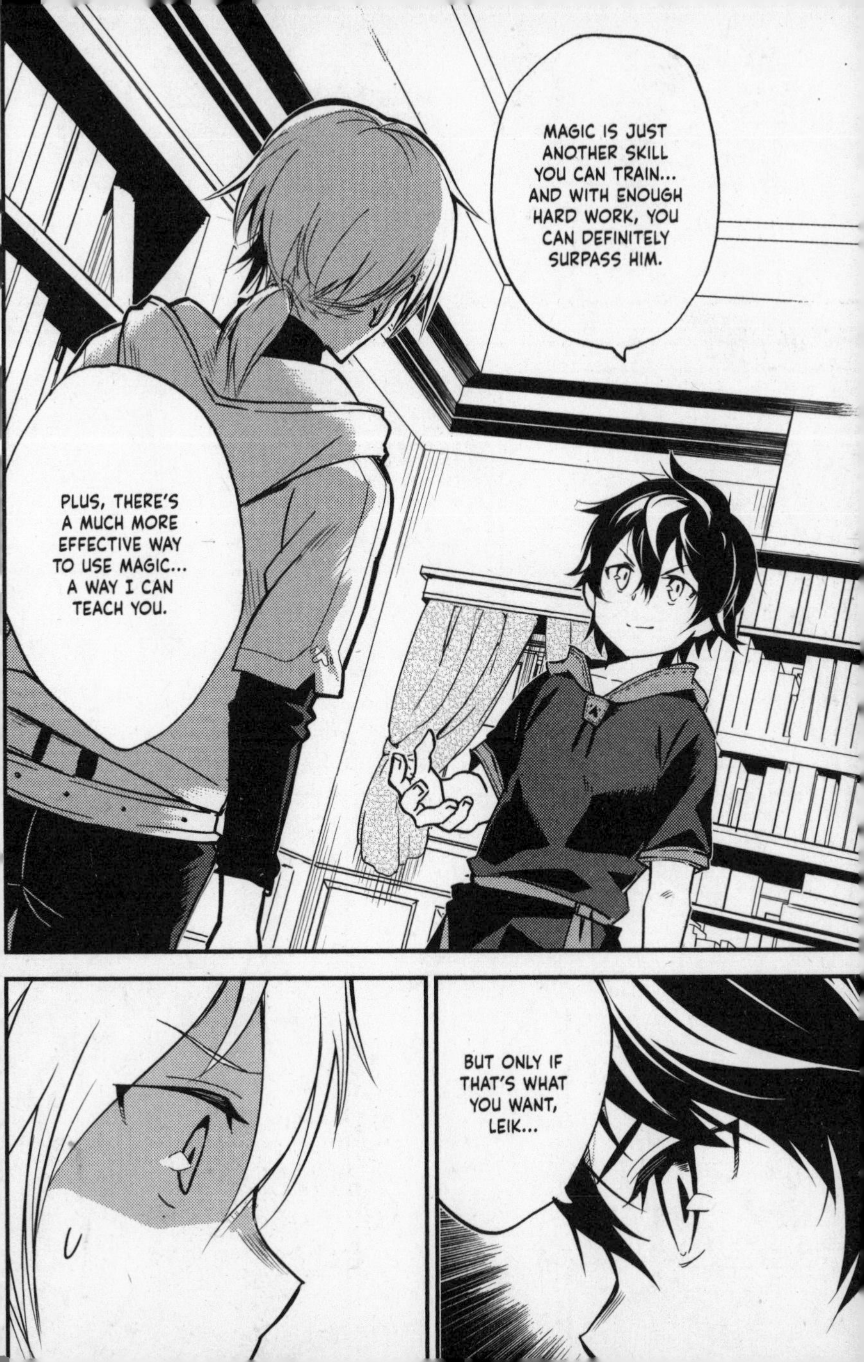
MAGIC IS JUST ANOTHER SKILL YOU CAN TRAIN... AND WITH ENOUGH HARD WORK, YOU CAN DEFINITELY SURPASS HIM.
PLUS, THERE'S A MUCH MORE EFFECTIVE WAY TO USE MAGIC... A WAY I CAN TEACH YOU.
BUT ONLY IF THAT'S WHAT YOU WANT, LEIK...

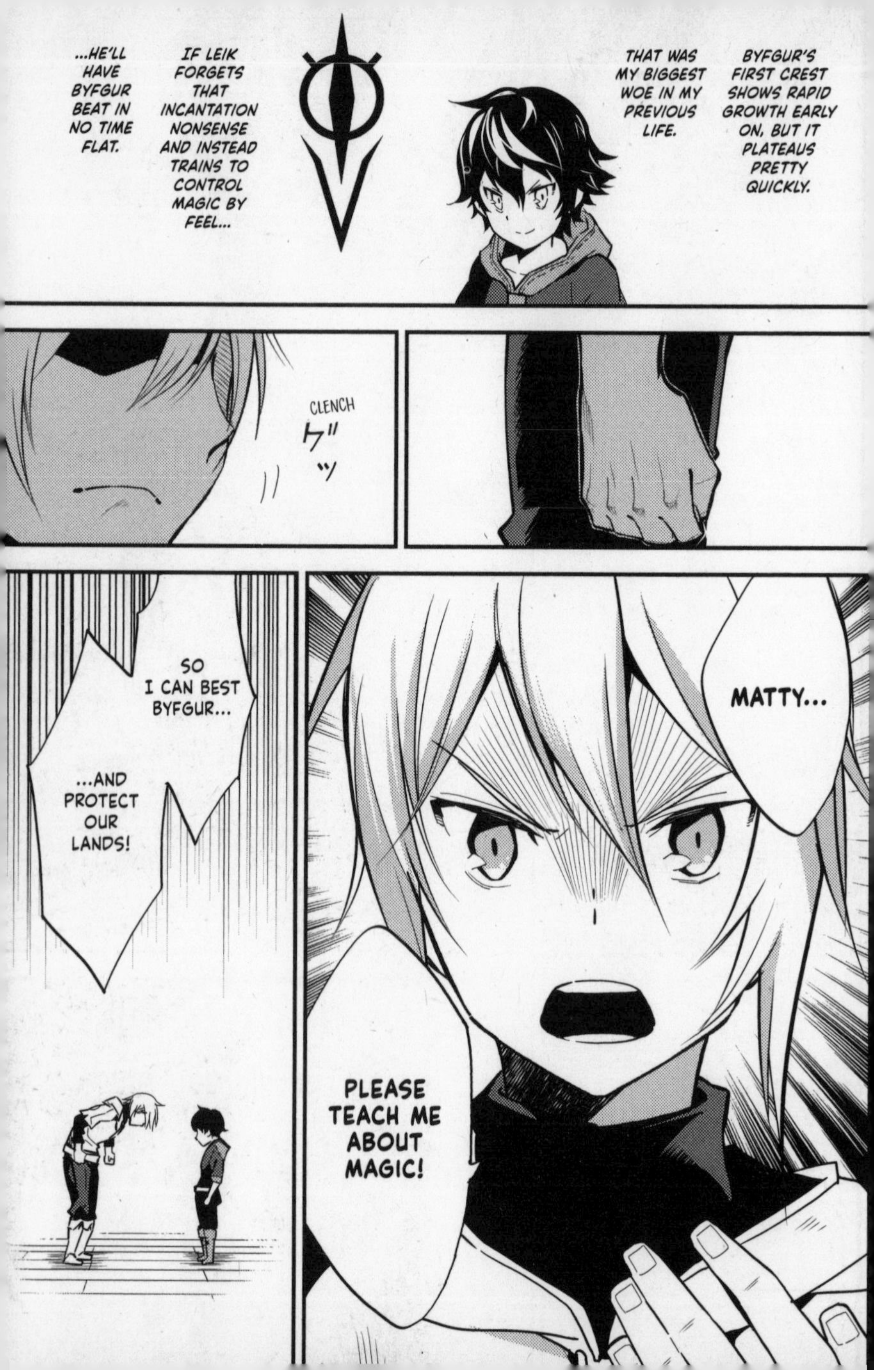
BYFGUR'S FIRST CREST SHOWS RAPID GROWTH EARLY ON, BUT IT PLATEAUS PRETTY QUICKLY.
THAT WAS MY BIGGEST WOE IN MY PREVIOUS LIFE.
IF LEIK FORGETS THAT INCANTATION NONSENSE AND INSTEAD TRAINS TO CONTROL MAGIC BY FEEL...
...HE'LL HAVE BYFGUR BEAT IN NO TIME FLAT.
CLENCH
グッ
MATTY...
PLEASE TEACH ME ABOUT MAGIC!
SO I CAN BEST BYFGUR...
...AND PROTECT OUR LANDS!

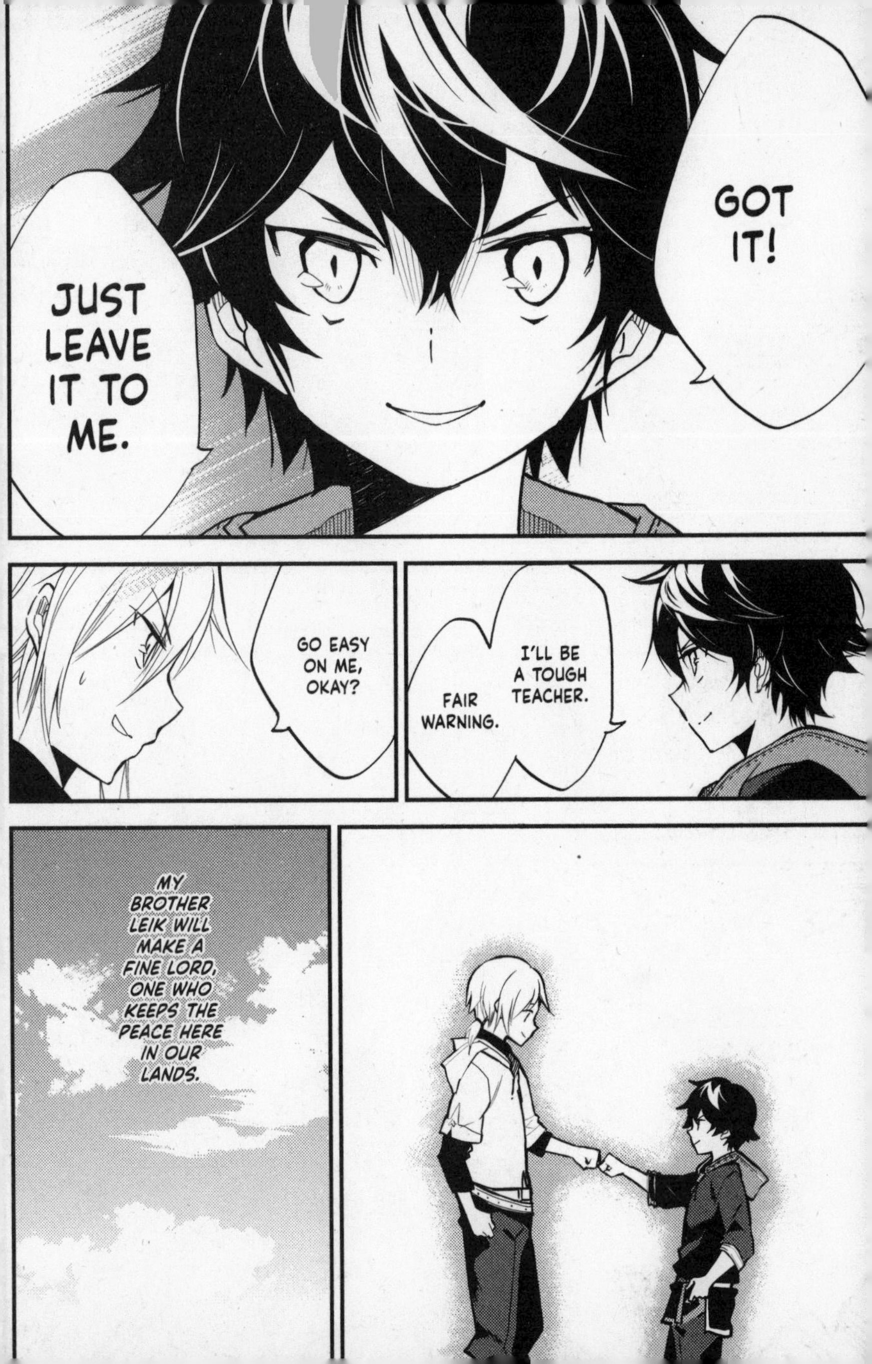
GOT IT!
JUST LEAVE IT TO ME.
I'LL BE A TOUGH TEACHER.
FAIR WARNING.
GO EASY ON ME, OKAY?
MY BROTHER LEIK WILL MAKE A FINE LORD, ONE WHO KEEPS THE PEACE HERE IN OUR LANDS.

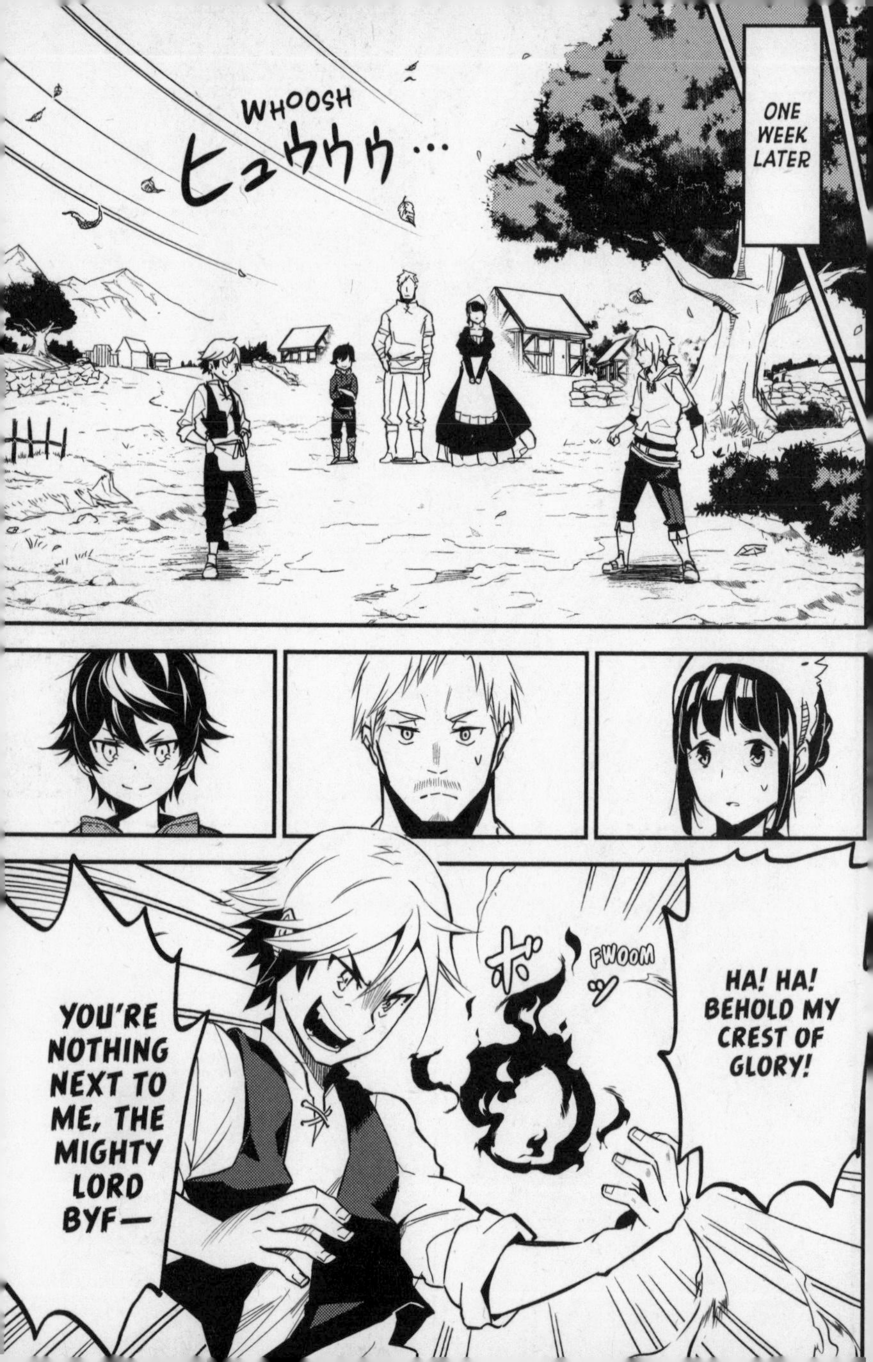
ONE WEEK LATER
WHOOSH
ヒュウウウ…
HA! HA! BEHOLD MY CREST OF GLORY!
ボッ
FWOOM
YOU'RE NOTHING NEXT TO ME, THE MIGHTY LORD BYF—

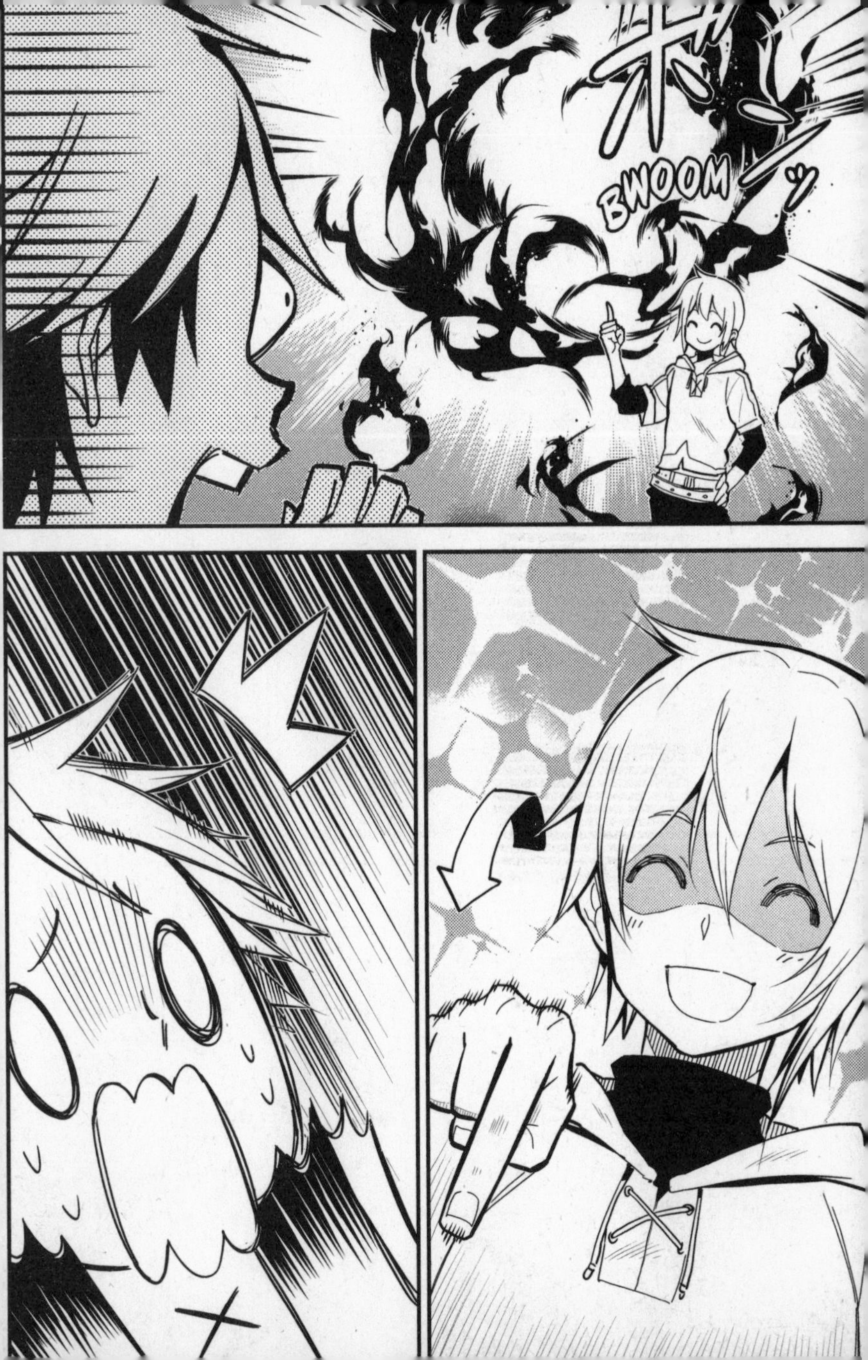
BWOOM

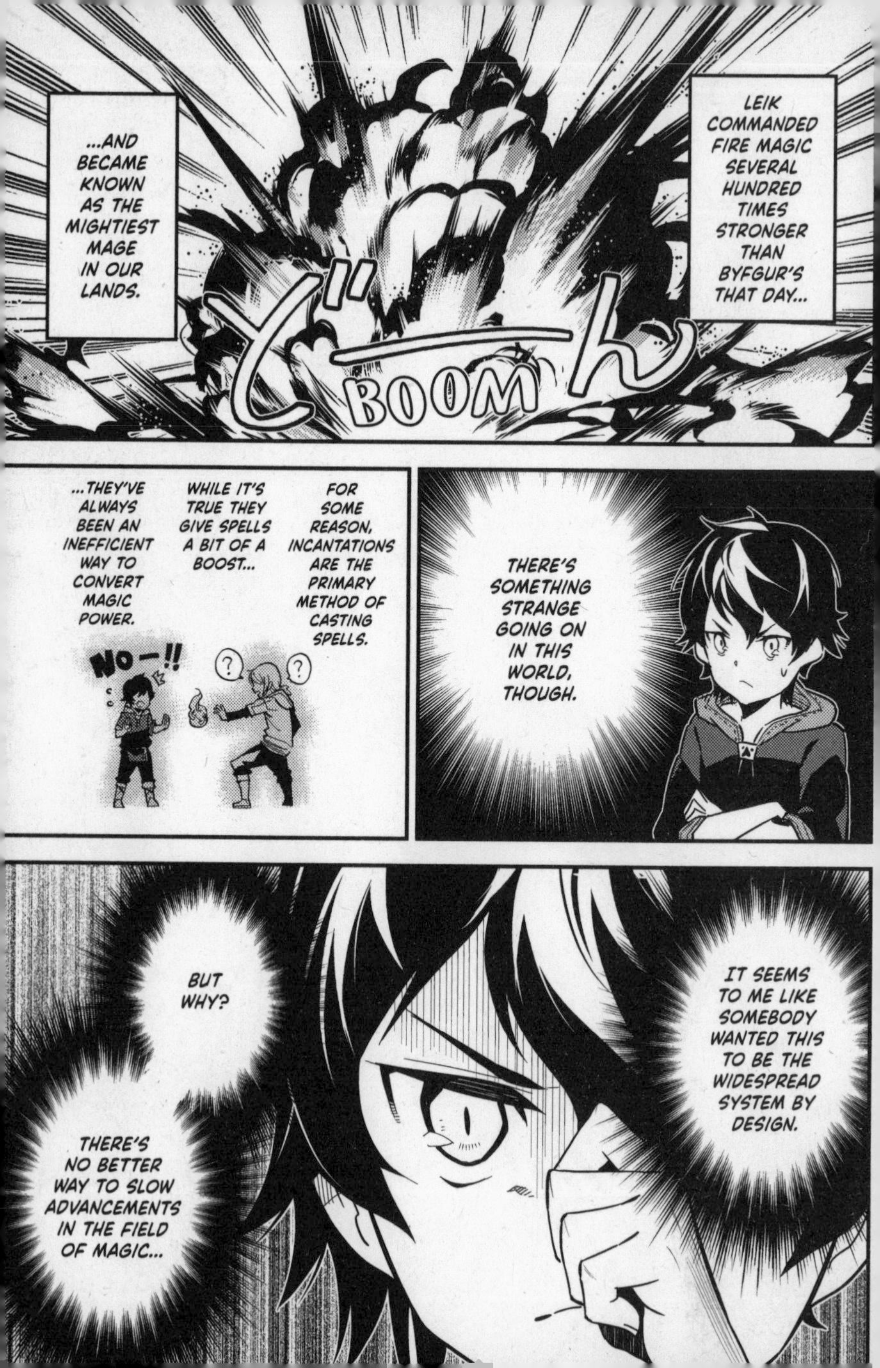
LEIK COMMANDED FIRE MAGIC SEVERAL HUNDRED TIMES STRONGER THAN BYFGUR'S THAT DAY...
...AND BECAME KNOWN AS THE MIGHTIEST MAGE IN OUR LANDS.
ドーン
BOOM
THERE'S SOMETHING STRANGE GOING ON IN THIS WORLD, THOUGH.
FOR SOME REASON, INCANTATIONS ARE THE PRIMARY METHOD OF CASTING SPELLS.
WHILE IT'S TRUE THEY GIVE SPELLS A BIT OF A BOOST...
...THEY'VE ALWAYS BEEN AN INEFFICIENT WAY TO CONVERT MAGIC POWER.
NO—!!
?
?
IT SEEMS TO ME LIKE SOMEBODY WANTED THIS TO BE THE WIDESPREAD SYSTEM BY DESIGN.
BUT WHY?
THERE'S NO BETTER WAY TO SLOW ADVANCEMENTS IN THE FIELD OF MAGIC...

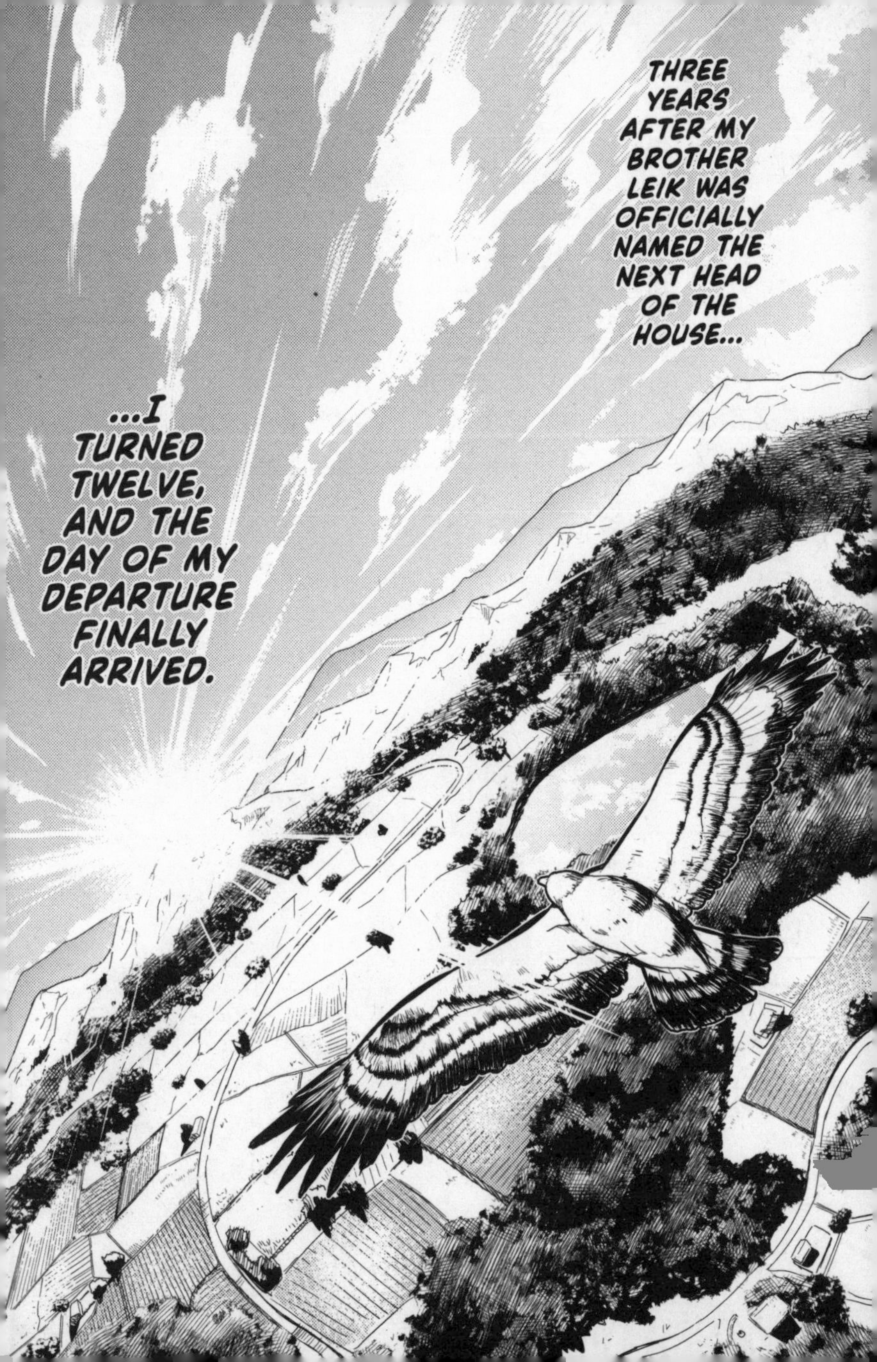
THREE YEARS AFTER MY BROTHER LEIK WAS OFFICIALLY NAMED THE NEXT HEAD OF THE HOUSE...
...I TURNED TWELVE, AND THE DAY OF MY DEPARTURE FINALLY ARRIVED.

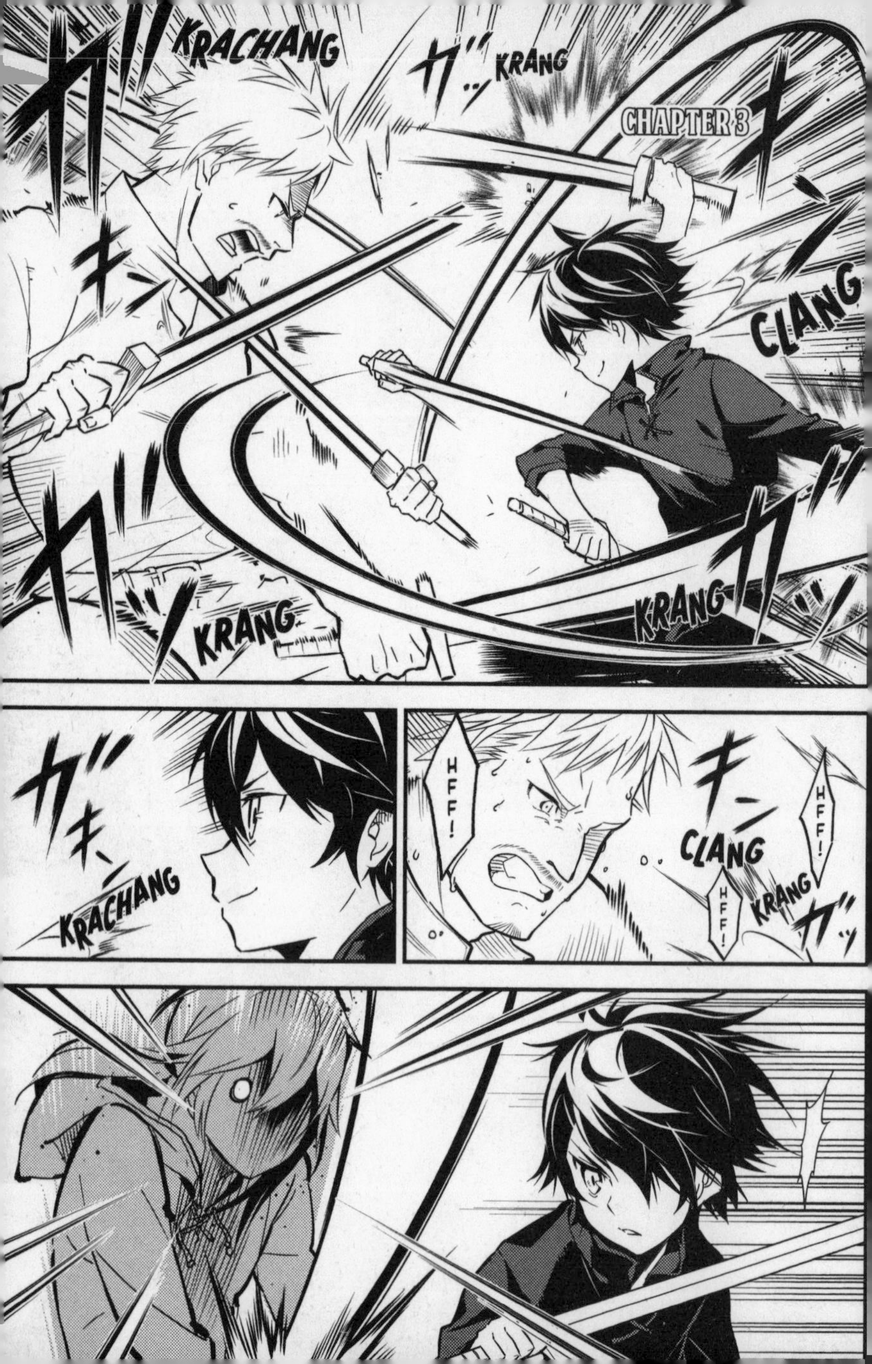
CHAPTER 3
KRANG
KRACHANG
CLANG
KRANG
KRANG
HFF!
CLANG
KRANG
HFF!
HFF!
KRACHANG

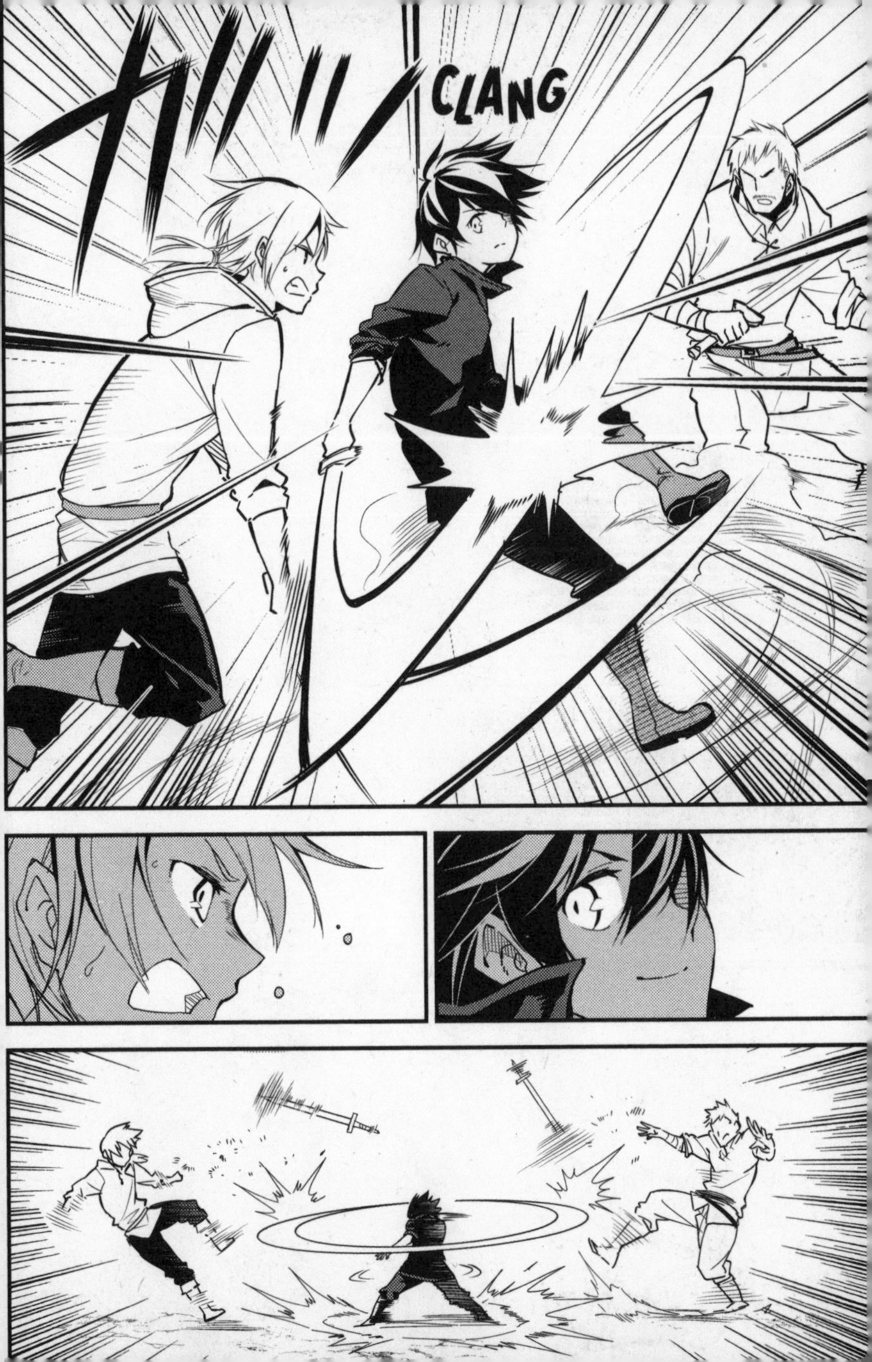
CLANG

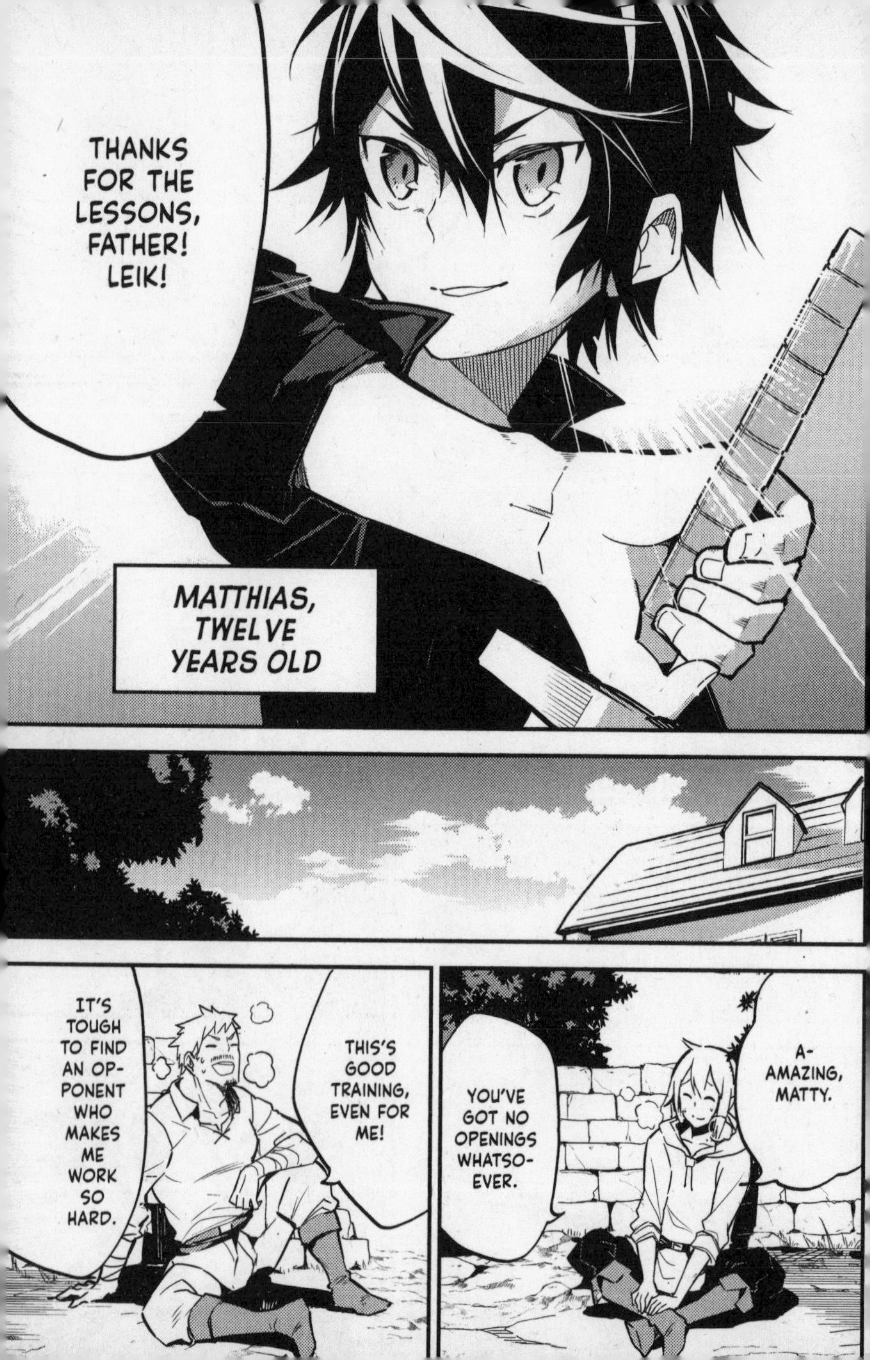
THANKS FOR THE LESSONS, FATHER! LEIK!
MATTHIAS, TWELVE YEARS OLD
A-AMAZING, MATTY.
YOU'VE GOT NO OPENINGS WHATSO-EVER.
THIS'S GOOD TRAINING, EVEN FOR ME!
IT'S TOUGH TO FIND AN OP-PONENT WHO MAKES ME WORK SO HARD.

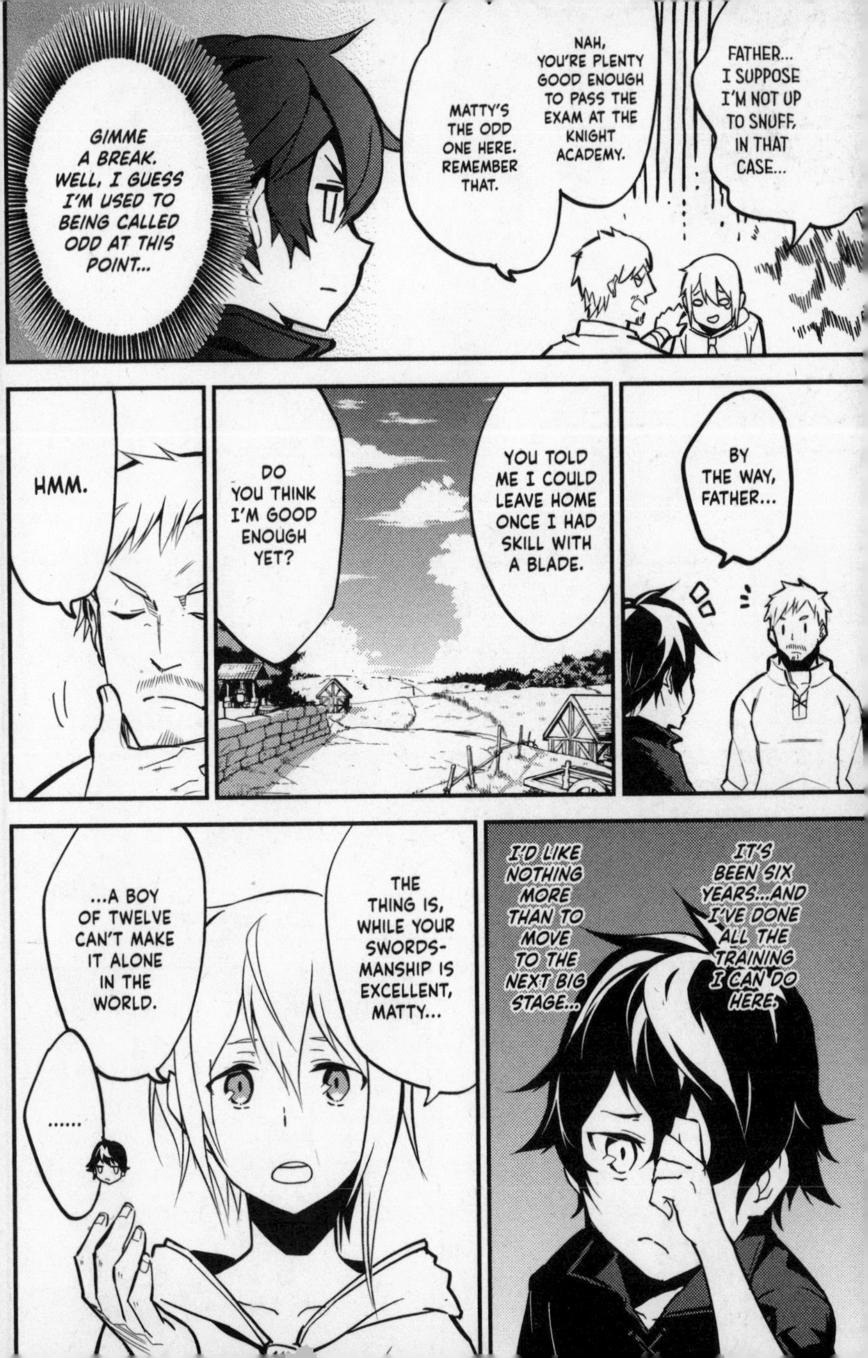
FATHER... I SUPPOSE I'M NOT UP TO SNUFF, IN THAT CASE...
NAH, YOU'RE PLENTY GOOD ENOUGH TO PASS THE EXAM AT THE KNIGHT ACADEMY.
MATTY'S THE ODD ONE HERE. REMEMBER THAT.
GIMME A BREAK. WELL, I GUESS I'M USED TO BEING CALLED ODD AT THIS POINT...
BY THE WAY, FATHER...
YOU TOLD ME I COULD LEAVE HOME ONCE I HAD SKILL WITH A BLADE.
DO YOU THINK I'M GOOD ENOUGH YET?
HMM.
IT'S BEEN SIX YEARS...AND I'VE DONE ALL THE TRAINING I CAN DO HERE.
I'D LIKE NOTHING MORE THAN TO MOVE TO THE NEXT BIG STAGE...
THE THING IS, WHILE YOUR SWORDS-MANSHIP IS EXCELLENT, MATTY...
...A BOY OF TWELVE CAN'T MAKE IT ALONE IN THE WORLD.
......

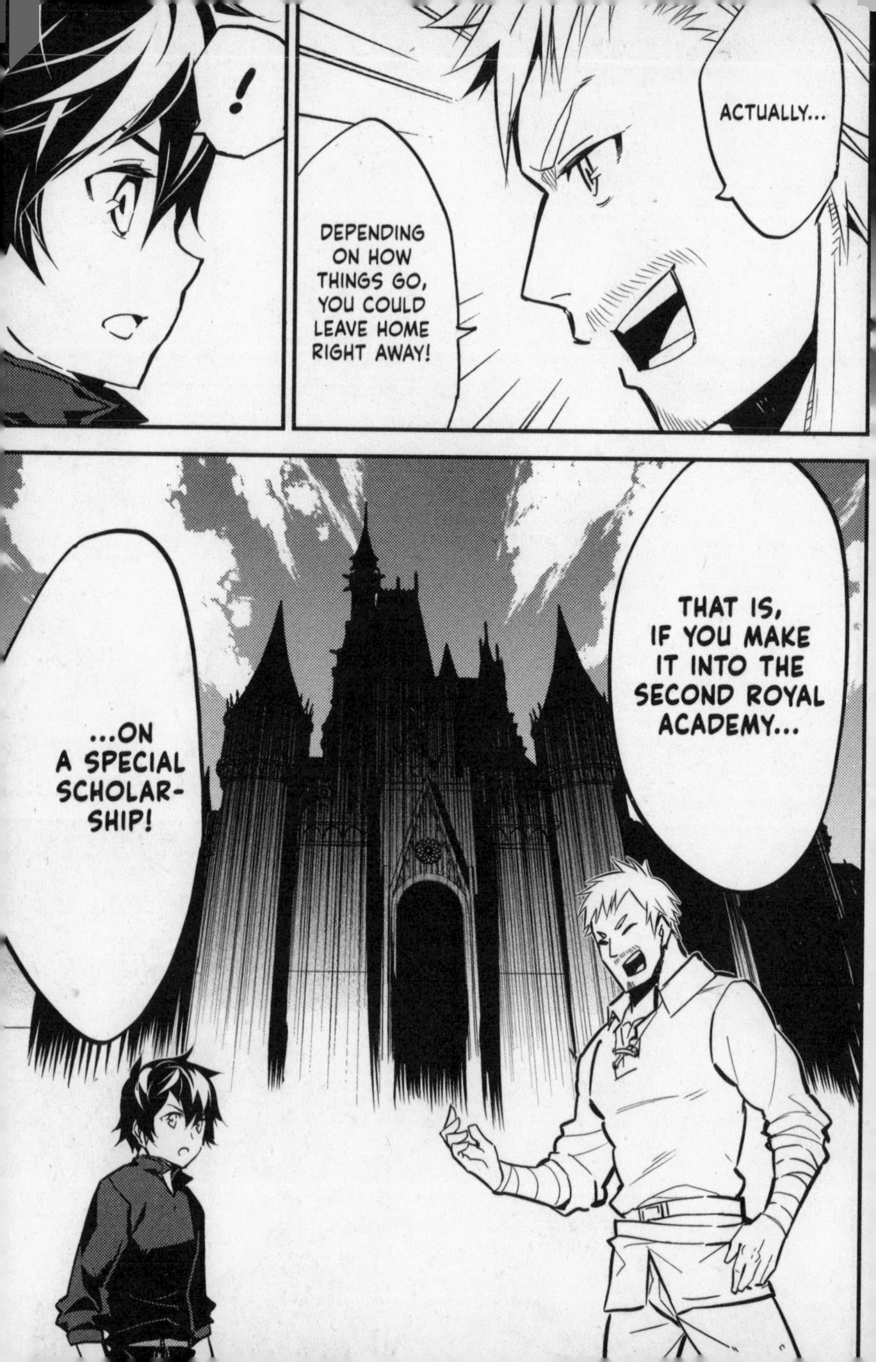
ACTUALLY...
DEPENDING ON HOW THINGS GO, YOU COULD LEAVE HOME RIGHT AWAY!
!
THAT IS, IF YOU MAKE IT INTO THE SECOND ROYAL ACADEMY...
...ON A SPECIAL SCHOLAR-SHIP!

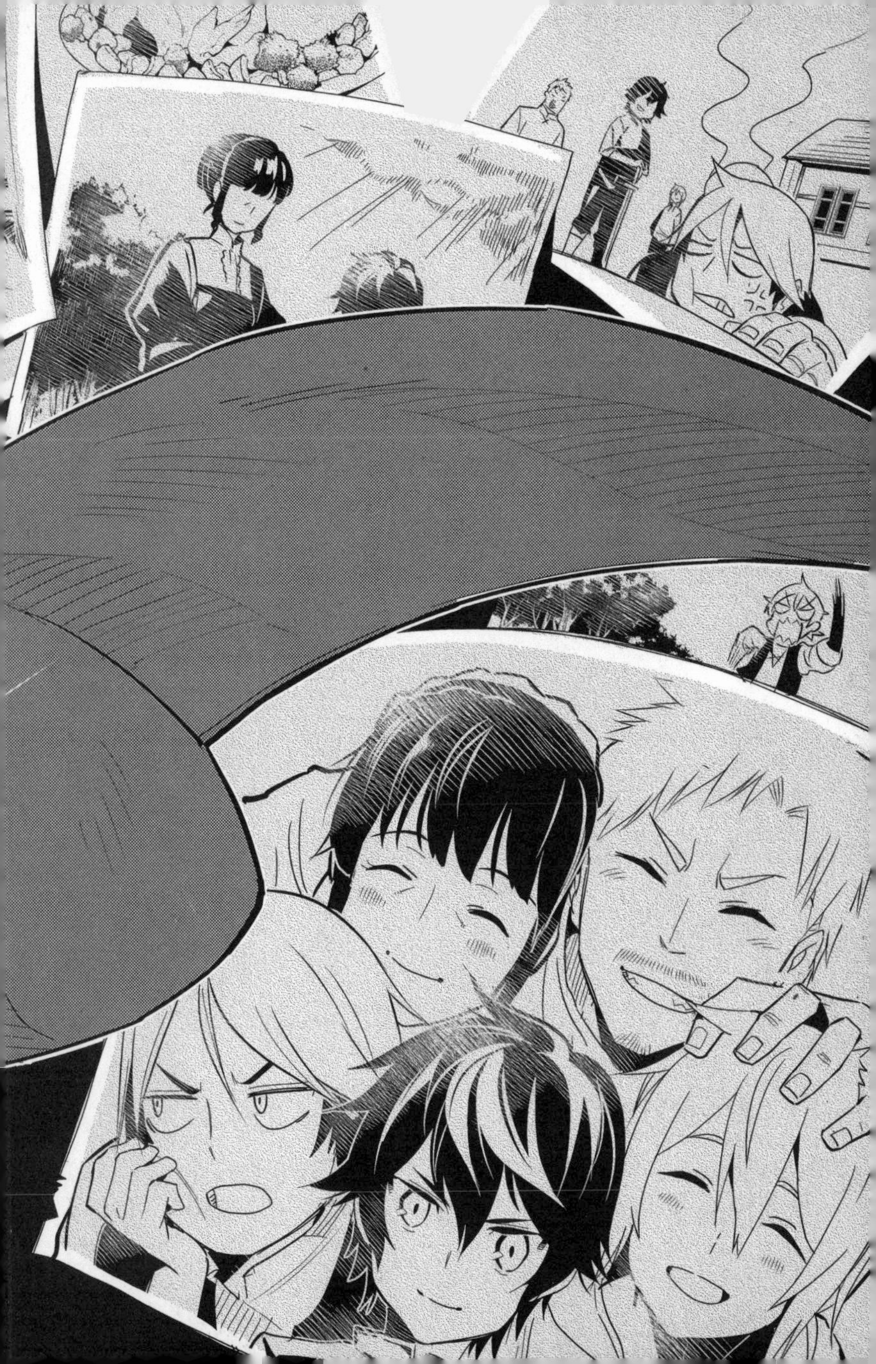

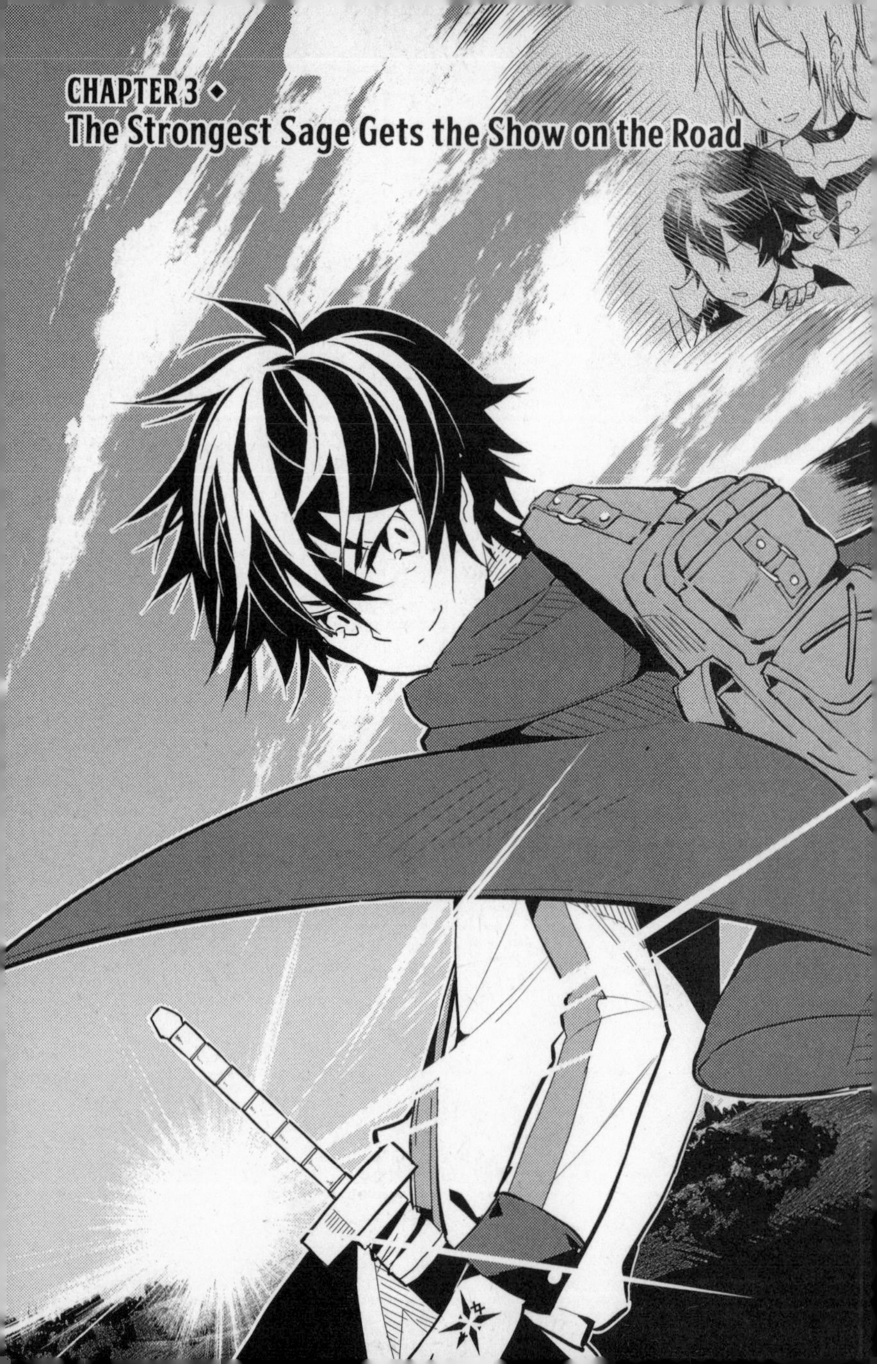
CHAPTER 3 ◆
The Strongest Sage Gets the Show on the Road

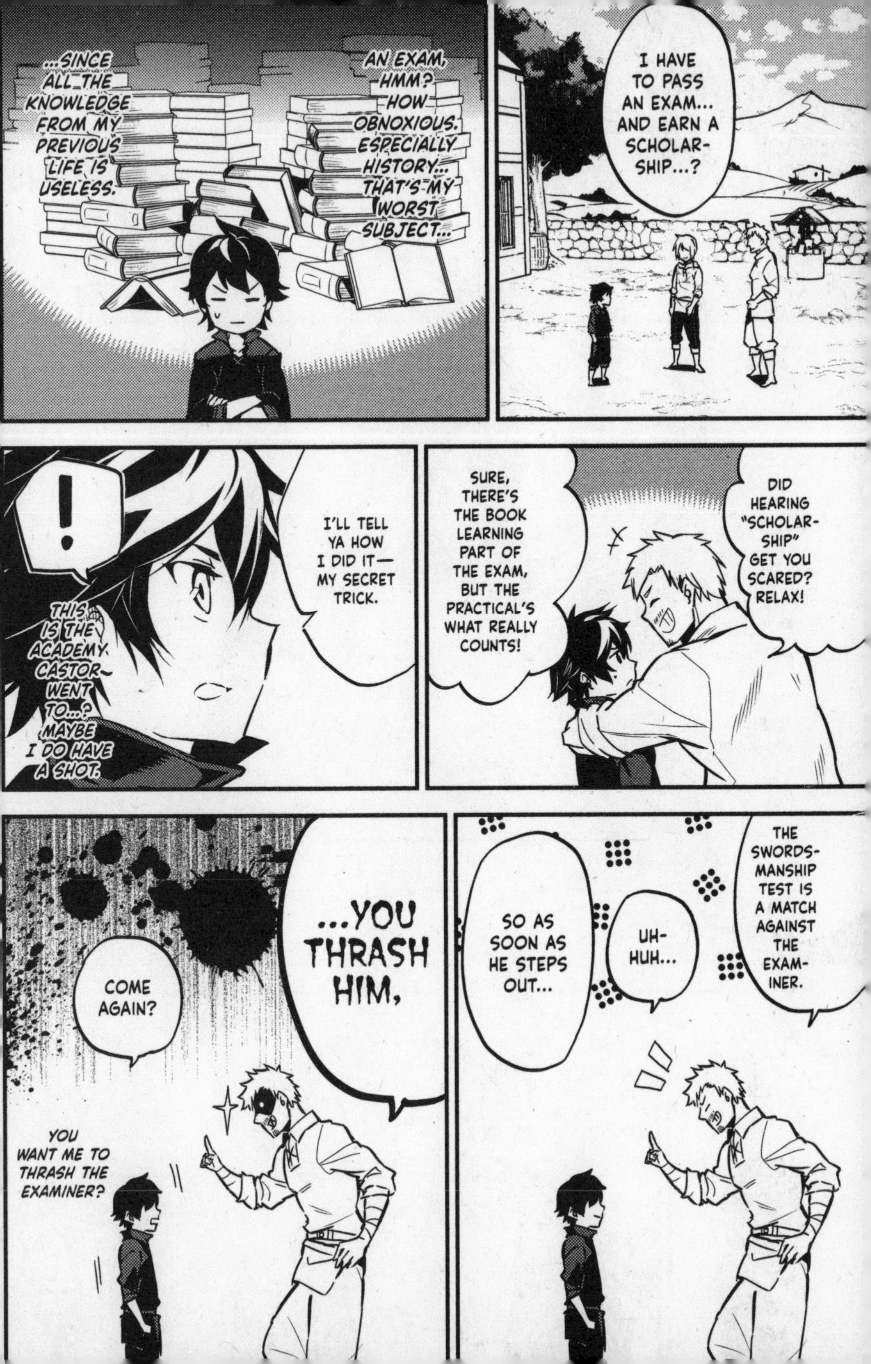
I HAVE TO PASS AN EXAM... AND EARN A SCHOLARSHIP...?
AN EXAM, HMM? HOW OBNOXIOUS. ESPECIALLY HISTORY... THAT'S MY WORST SUBJECT...
...SINCE ALL THE KNOWLEDGE FROM MY PREVIOUS LIFE IS USELESS.
DID HEARING "SCHOLARSHIP" GET YOU SCARED? RELAX!
SURE, THERE'S THE BOOK LEARNING PART OF THE EXAM, BUT THE PRACTICAL'S WHAT REALLY COUNTS!
I'LL TELL YA HOW I DID IT—MY SECRET TRICK.
!
THIS IS THE ACADEMY CASTOR WENT TO...? MAYBE I DO HAVE A SHOT.
THE SWORDSMANSHIP TEST IS A MATCH AGAINST THE EXAMINER.
UH-HUH...
SO AS SOON AS HE STEPS OUT...
...YOU THRASH HIM,
COME AGAIN?
YOU WANT ME TO THRASH THE EXAMINER?

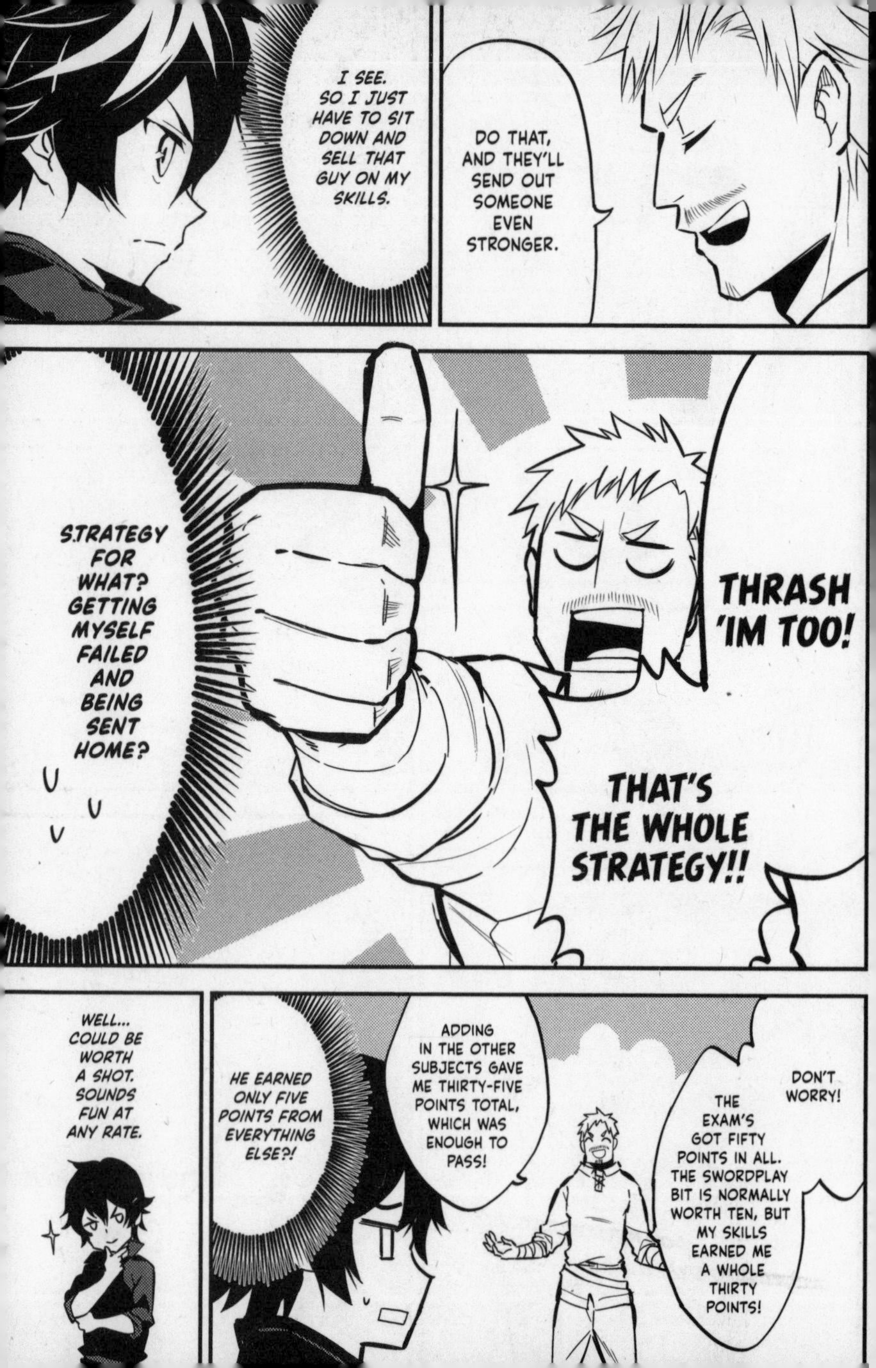
DO THAT, AND THEY'LL SEND OUT SOMEONE EVEN STRONGER.
I SEE. SO I JUST HAVE TO SIT DOWN AND SELL THAT GUY ON MY SKILLS.
THRASH 'IM TOO!
THAT'S THE WHOLE STRATEGY!!
S.TRATEGY FOR WHAT? GETTING MYSELF FAILED AND BEING SENT HOME?
DON'T WORRY!
THE EXAM'S GOT FIFTY POINTS IN ALL. THE SWORDPLAY BIT IS NORMALLY WORTH TEN, BUT MY SKILLS EARNED ME A WHOLE THIRTY POINTS!
ADDING IN THE OTHER SUBJECTS GAVE ME THIRTY-FIVE POINTS TOTAL, WHICH WAS ENOUGH TO PASS!
HE EARNED ONLY FIVE POINTS FROM EVERYTHING ELSE?!
WELL... COULD BE WORTH A SHOT. SOUNDS FUN AT ANY RATE.

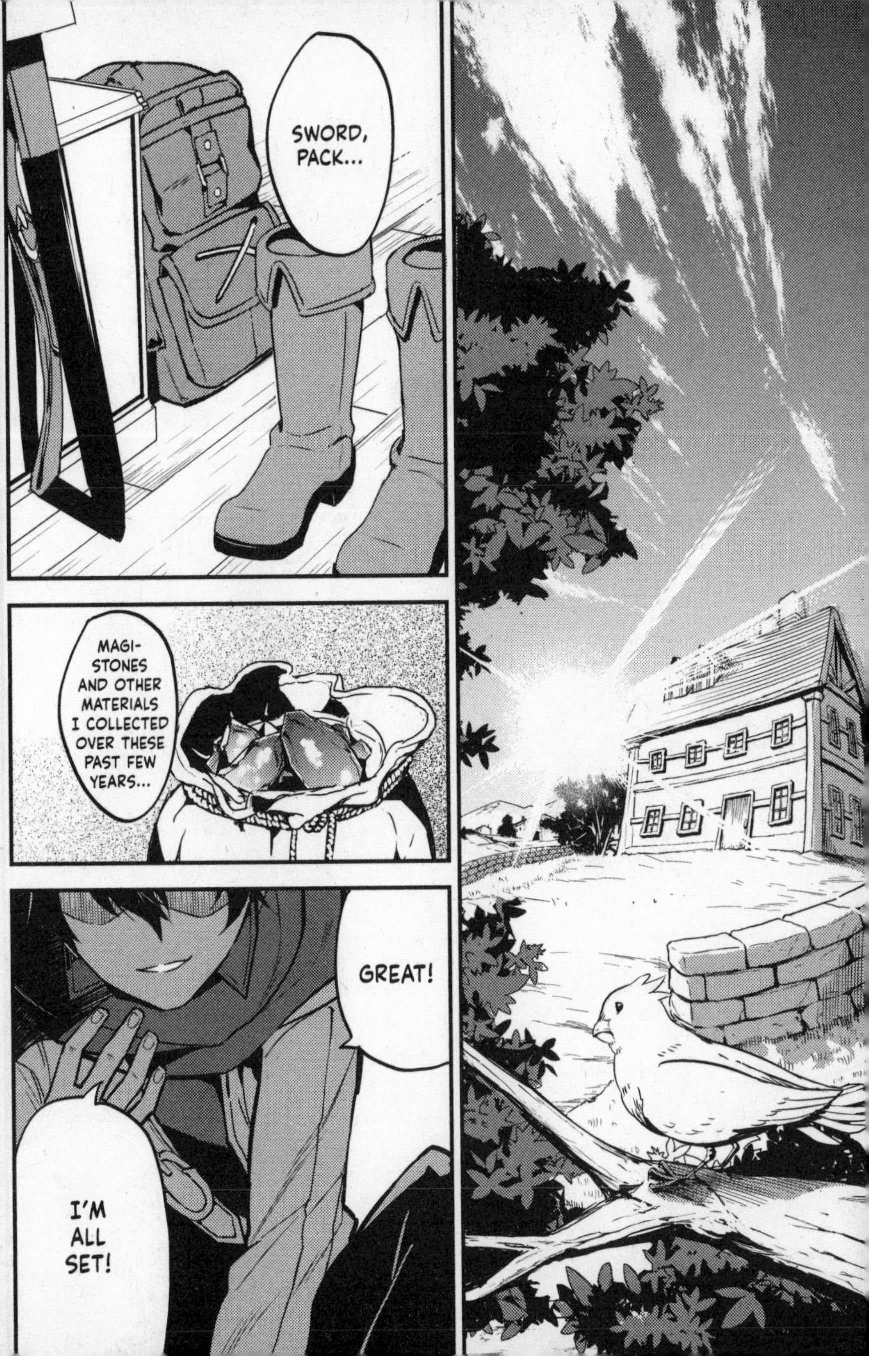
SWORD, PACK...
MAGI-STONES AND OTHER MATERIALS I COLLECTED OVER THESE PAST FEW YEARS...
GREAT!
I'M ALL SET!

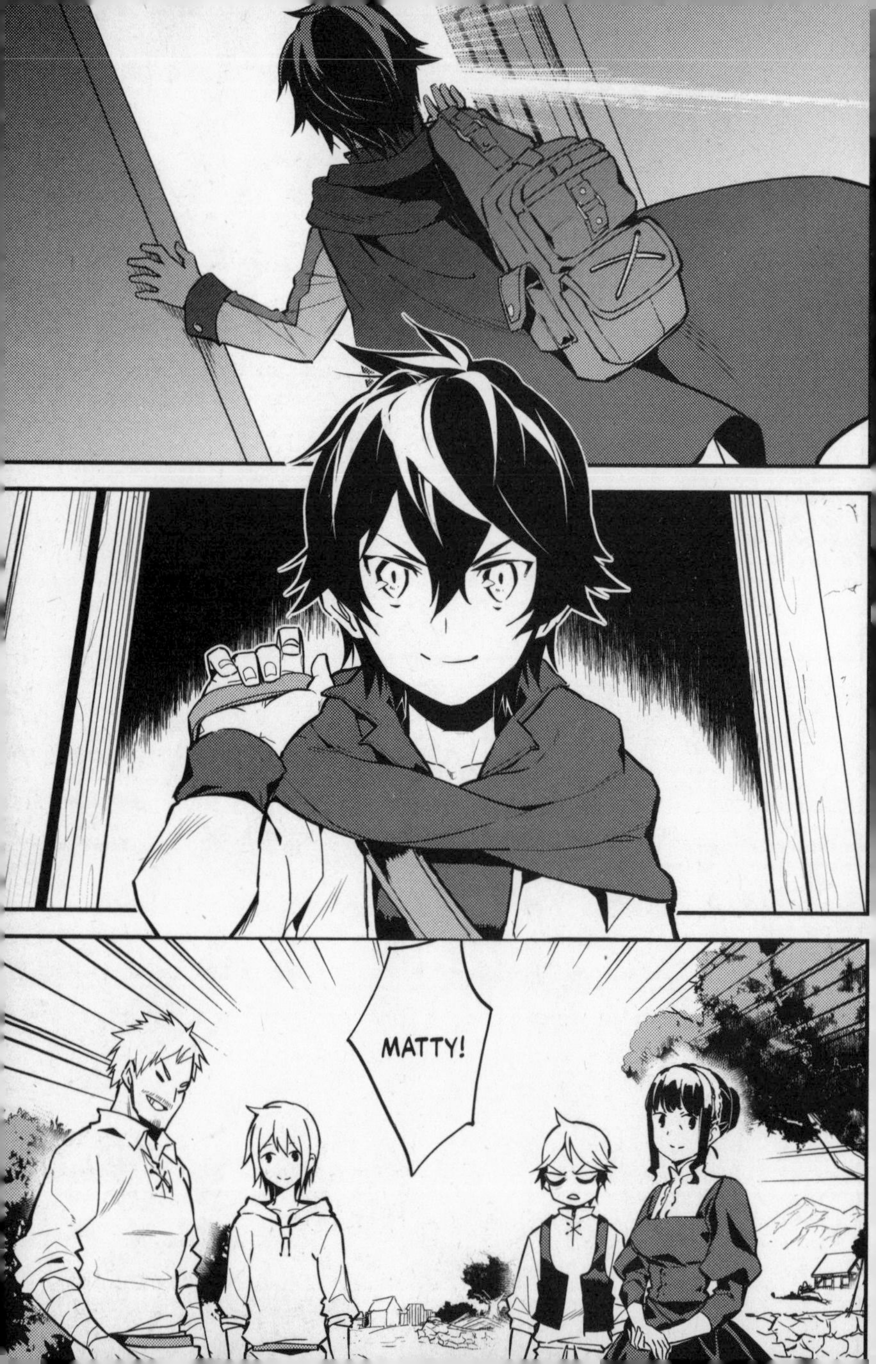
MATTY!

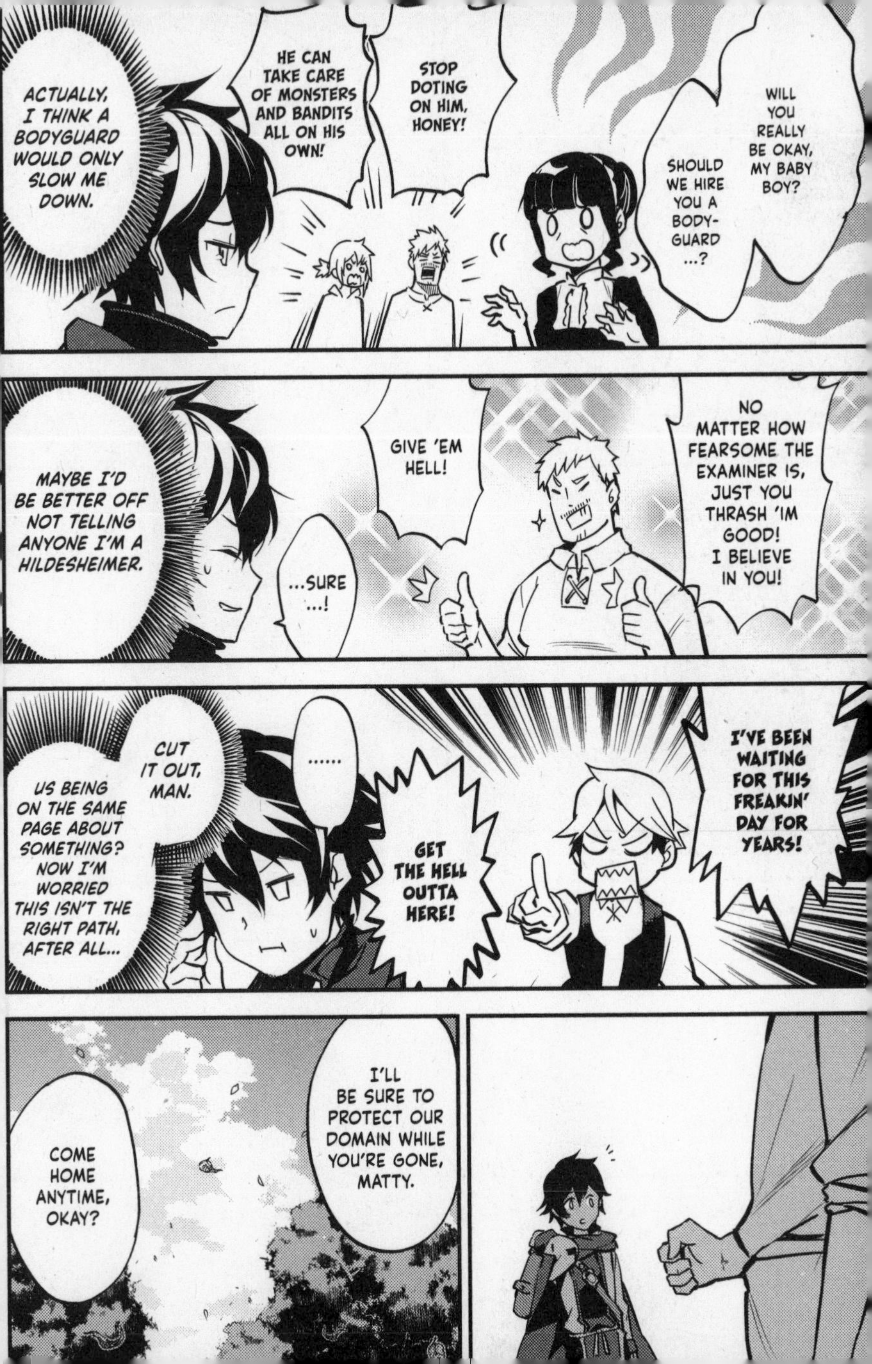
WILL YOU REALLY BE OKAY, MY BABY BOY?
SHOULD WE HIRE YOU A BODY-GUARD ...?
STOP DOTING ON HIM, HONEY!
HE CAN TAKE CARE OF MONSTERS AND BANDITS ALL ON HIS OWN!
ACTUALLY, I THINK A BODYGUARD WOULD ONLY SLOW ME DOWN.
NO MATTER HOW FEARSOME THE EXAMINER IS, JUST YOU THRASH 'IM GOOD! I BELIEVE IN YOU!
GIVE 'EM HELL!
...SURE ...!
MAYBE I'D BE BETTER OFF NOT TELLING ANYONE I'M A HILDESHEIMER.
I'VE BEEN WAITING FOR THIS FREAKIN' DAY FOR YEARS!
GET THE HELL OUTTA HERE!
......
CUT IT OUT, MAN.
US BEING ON THE SAME PAGE ABOUT SOMETHING? NOW I'M WORRIED THIS ISN'T THE RIGHT PATH, AFTER ALL...
I'LL BE SURE TO PROTECT OUR DOMAIN WHILE YOU'RE GONE, MATTY.
COME HOME ANYTIME, OKAY?

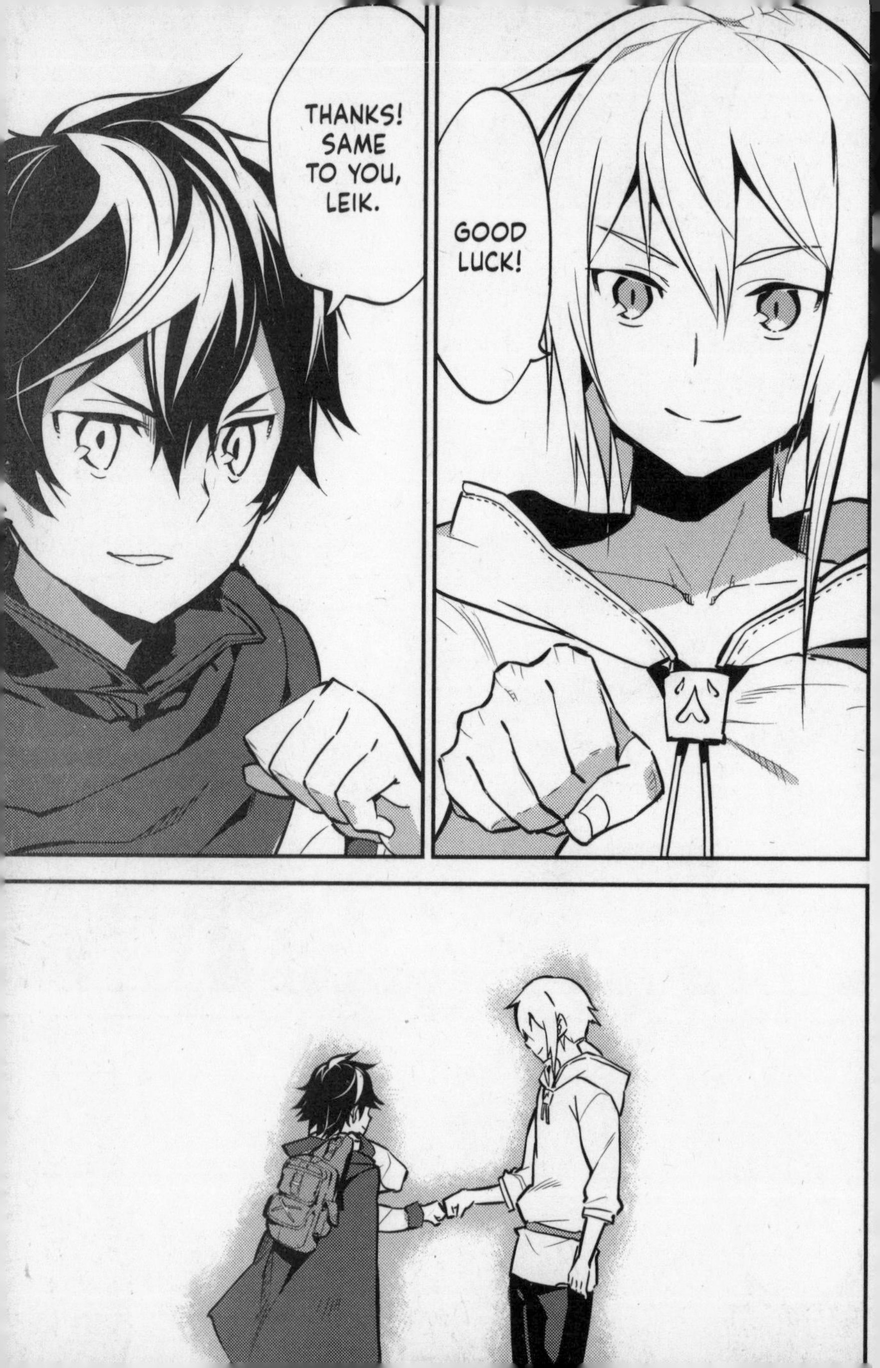
GOOD LUCK!
THANKS! SAME TO YOU, LEIK.

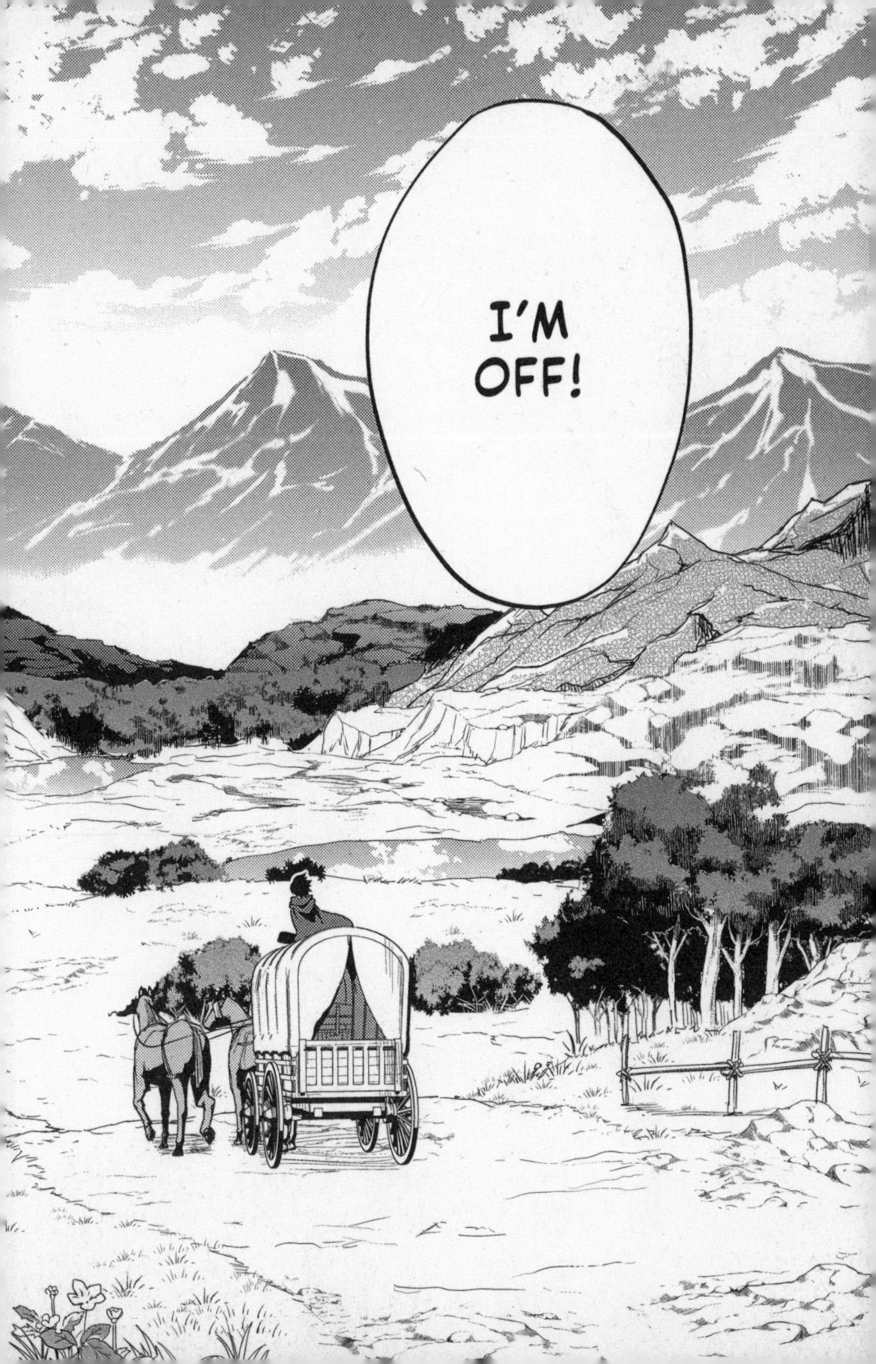
I'M OFF!

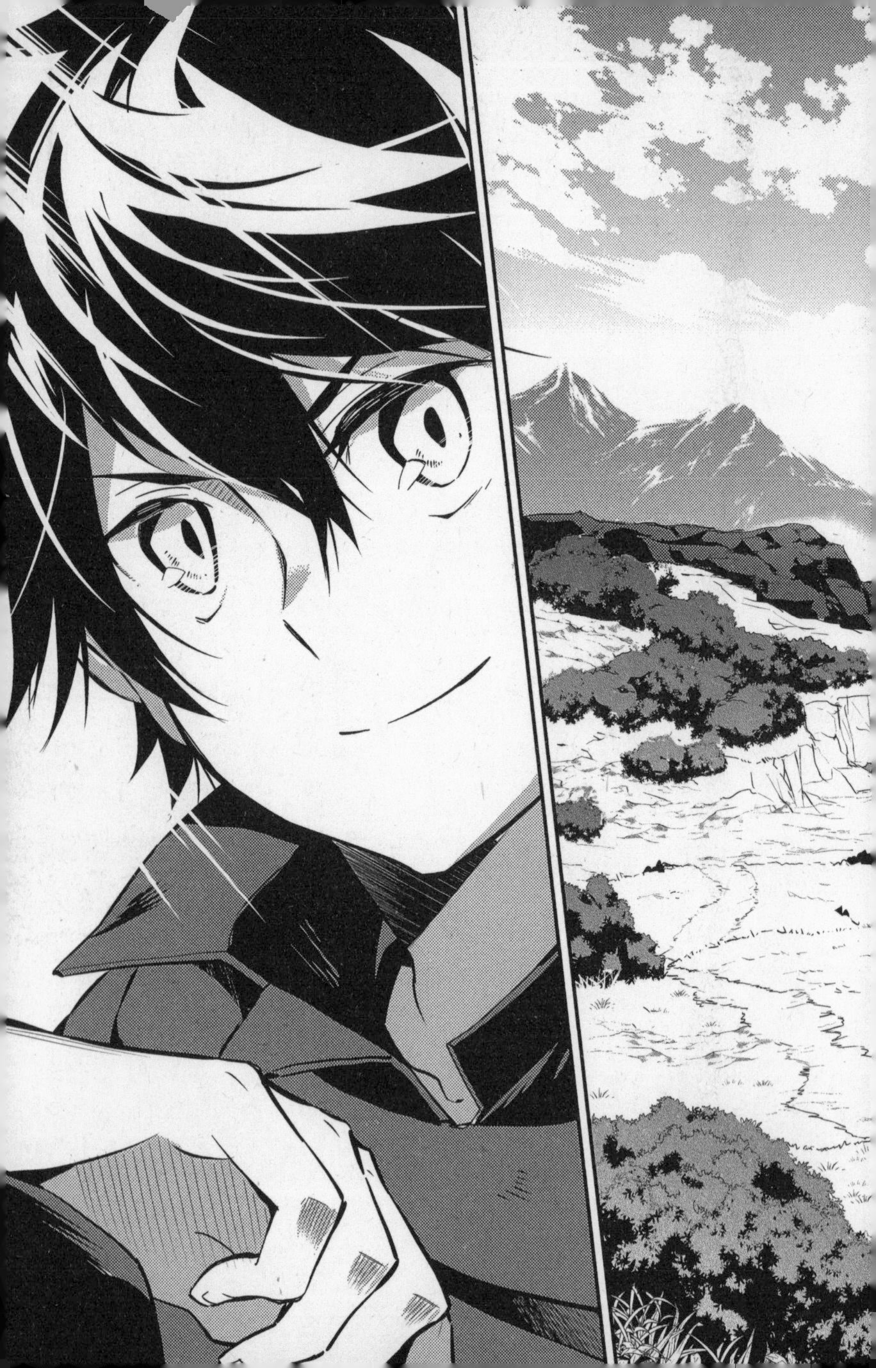

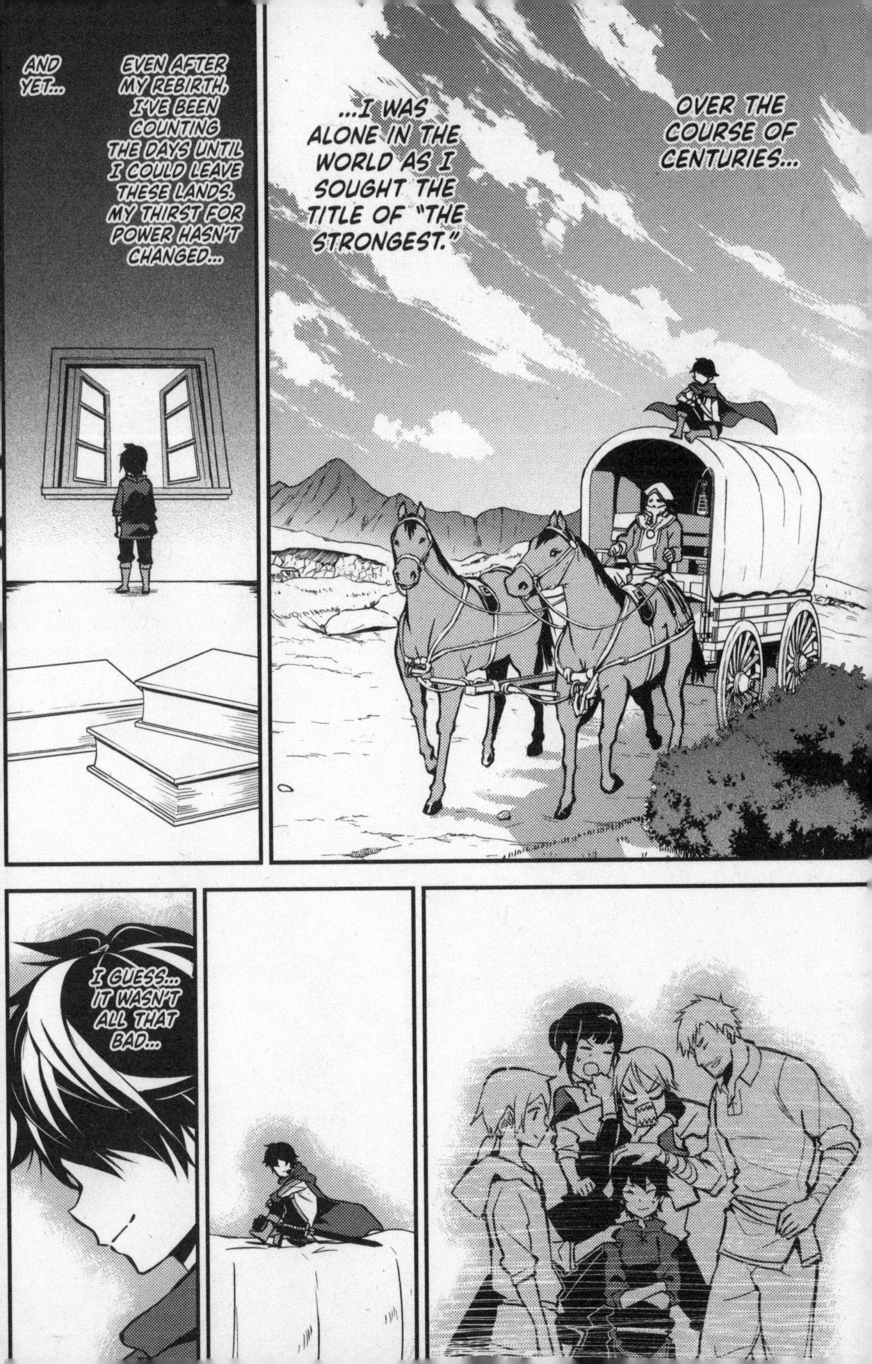
OVER THE COURSE OF CENTURIES...
...I WAS ALONE IN THE WORLD AS I SOUGHT THE TITLE OF "THE STRONGEST."
EVEN AFTER MY REBIRTH, I'VE BEEN COUNTING THE DAYS UNTIL I COULD LEAVE THESE LANDS. MY THIRST FOR POWER HASN'T CHANGED...
AND YET...
I GUESS... IT WASN'T ALL THAT BAD...

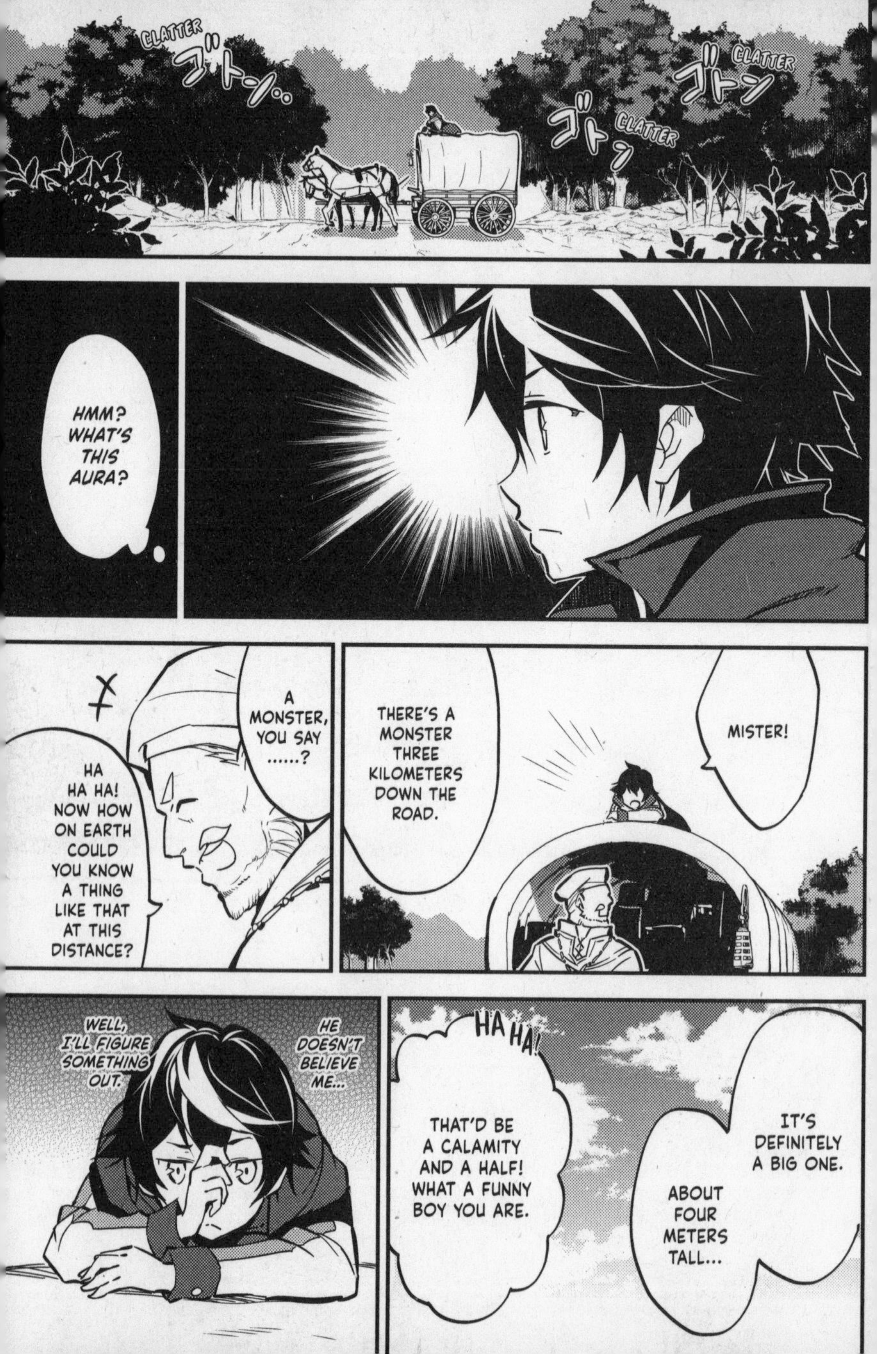
ゴトン
CLATTER
ゴトン
CLATTER
ゴトン..
CLATTER
HMM? WHAT'S THIS AURA?
MISTER!
THERE'S A MONSTER THREE KILOMETERS DOWN THE ROAD.
A MONSTER, YOU SAY ......?
HA HA HA! NOW HOW ON EARTH COULD YOU KNOW A THING LIKE THAT AT THIS DISTANCE?
IT'S DEFINITELY A BIG ONE.
ABOUT FOUR METERS TALL...
HA HA!
THAT'D BE A CALAMITY AND A HALF! WHAT A FUNNY BOY YOU ARE.
HE DOESN'T BELIEVE ME...
WELL, I'LL FIGURE SOMETHING OUT.

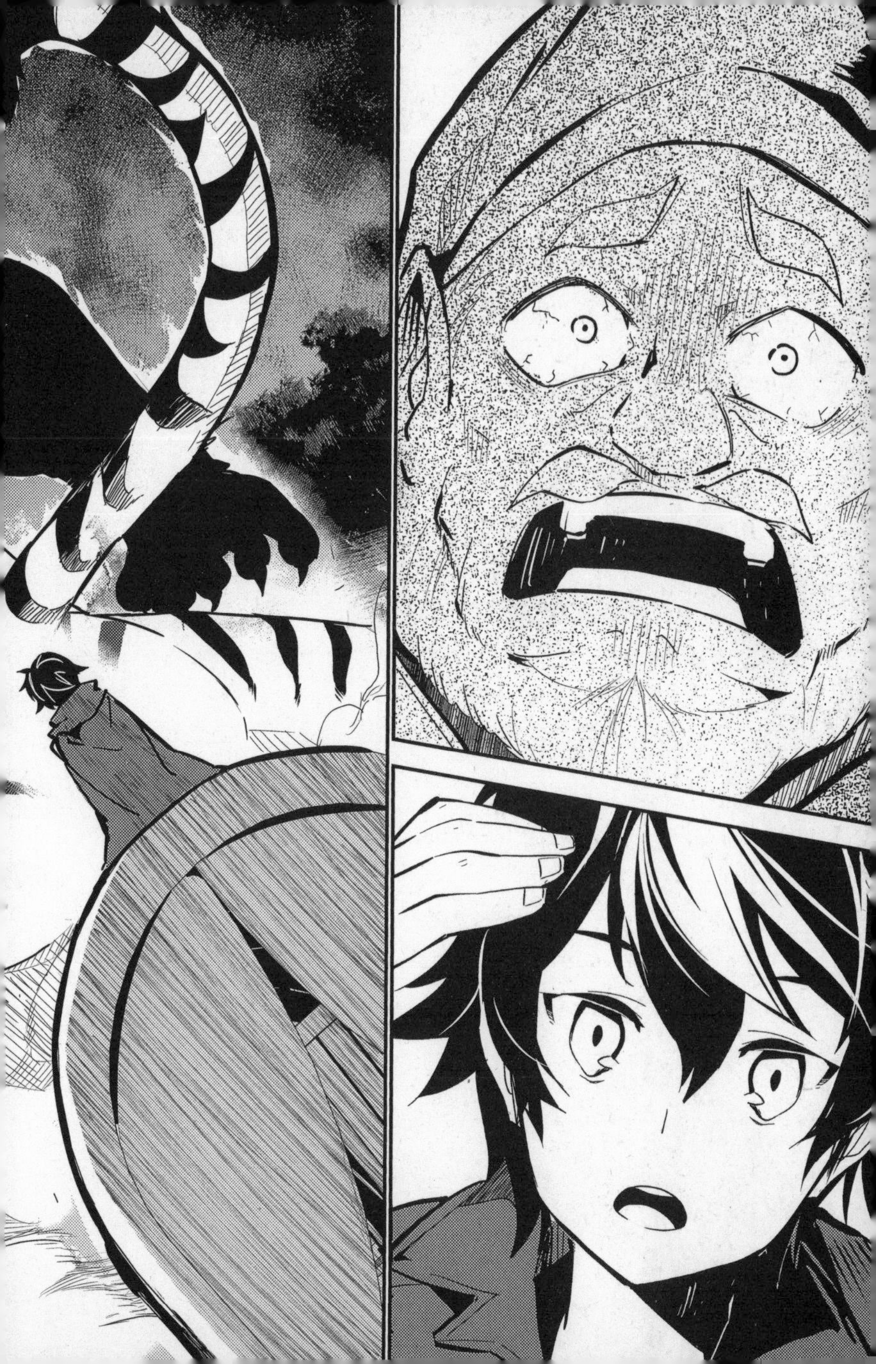

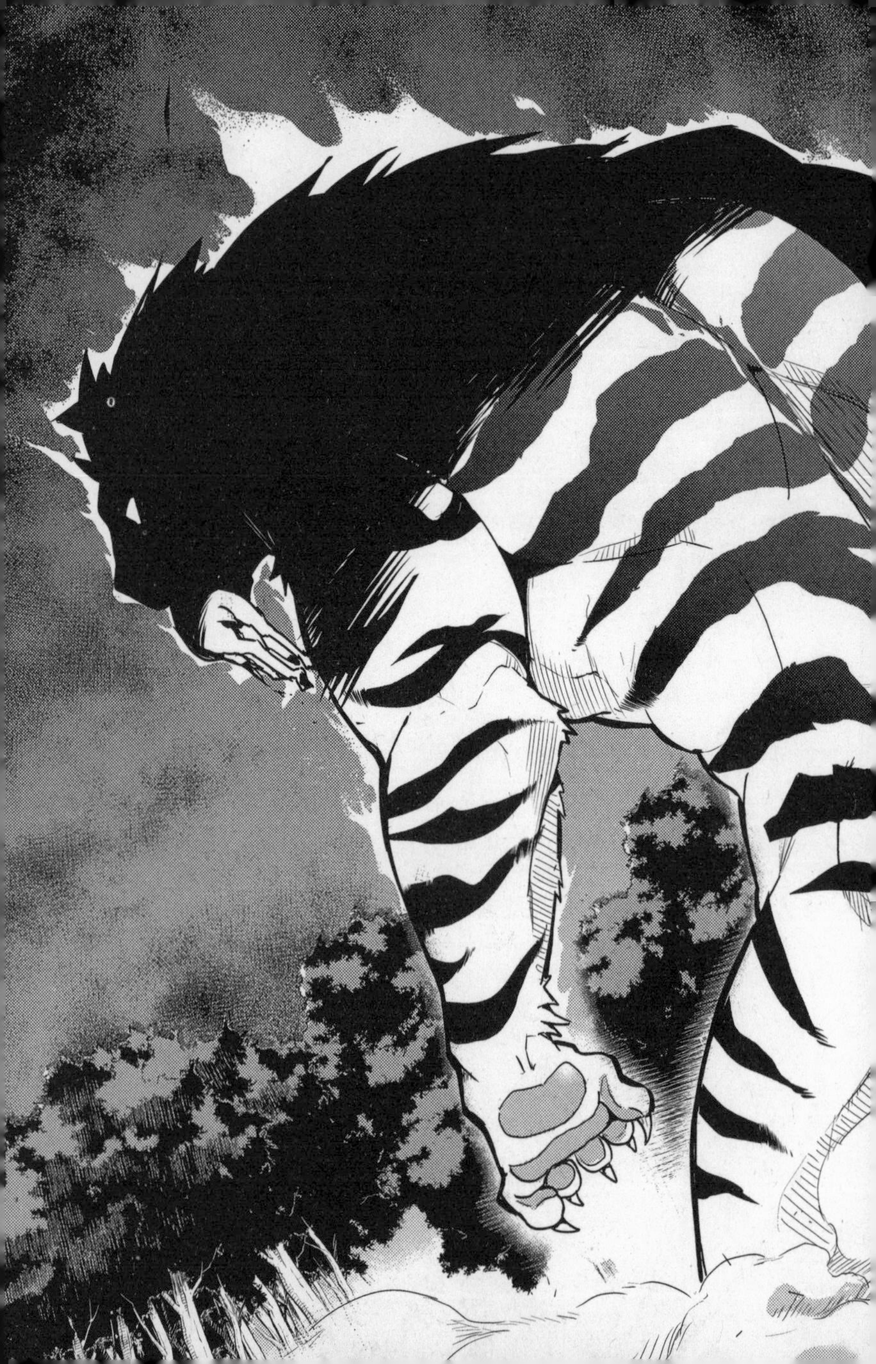

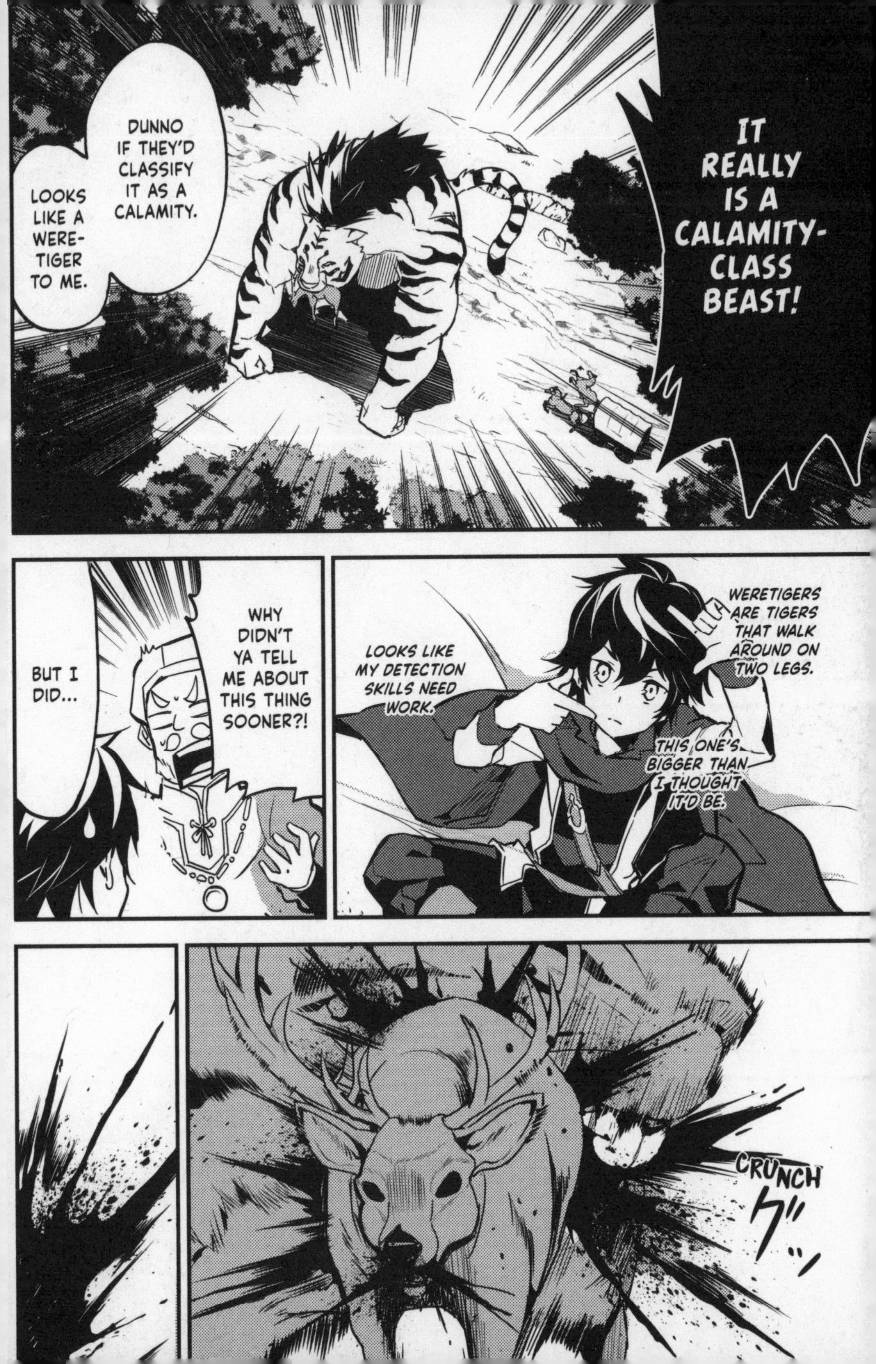
IT REALLY IS A CALAMITY-CLASS BEAST!
DUNNO IF THEY'D CLASSIFY IT AS A CALAMITY.
LOOKS LIKE A WERE-TIGER TO ME.
WERETIGERS ARE TIGERS THAT WALK AROUND ON TWO LEGS.
LOOKS LIKE MY DETECTION SKILLS NEED WORK.
THIS ONE'S BIGGER THAN I THOUGHT IT'D BE.
WHY DIDN'T YA TELL ME ABOUT THIS THING SOONER?!
BUT I DID...
CRUNCH

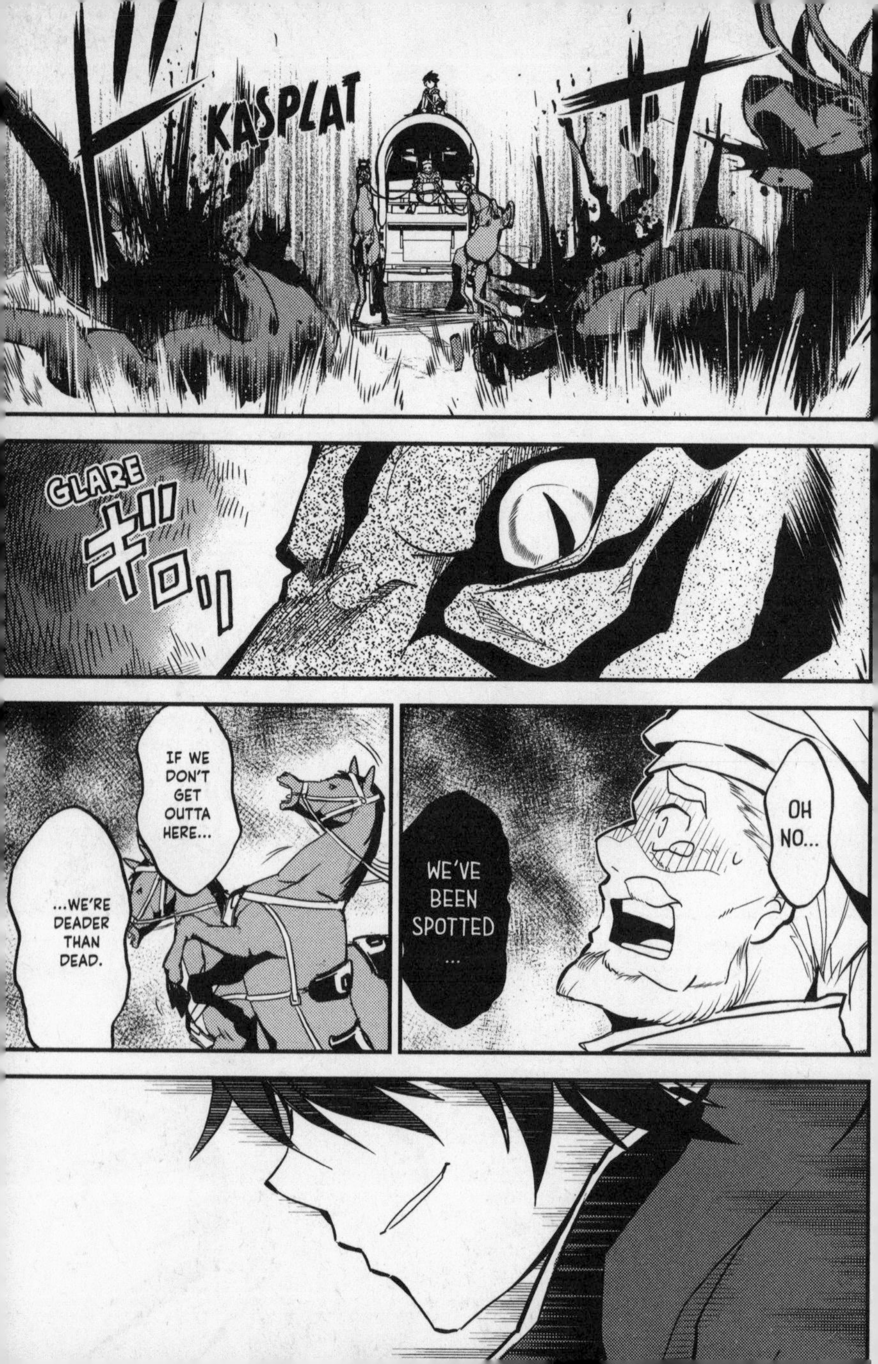
KASPLAT
GLARE
ギロッ
OH NO...
WE'VE BEEN SPOTTED ...
IF WE DON'T GET OUTTA HERE...
...WE'RE DEADER THAN DEAD.

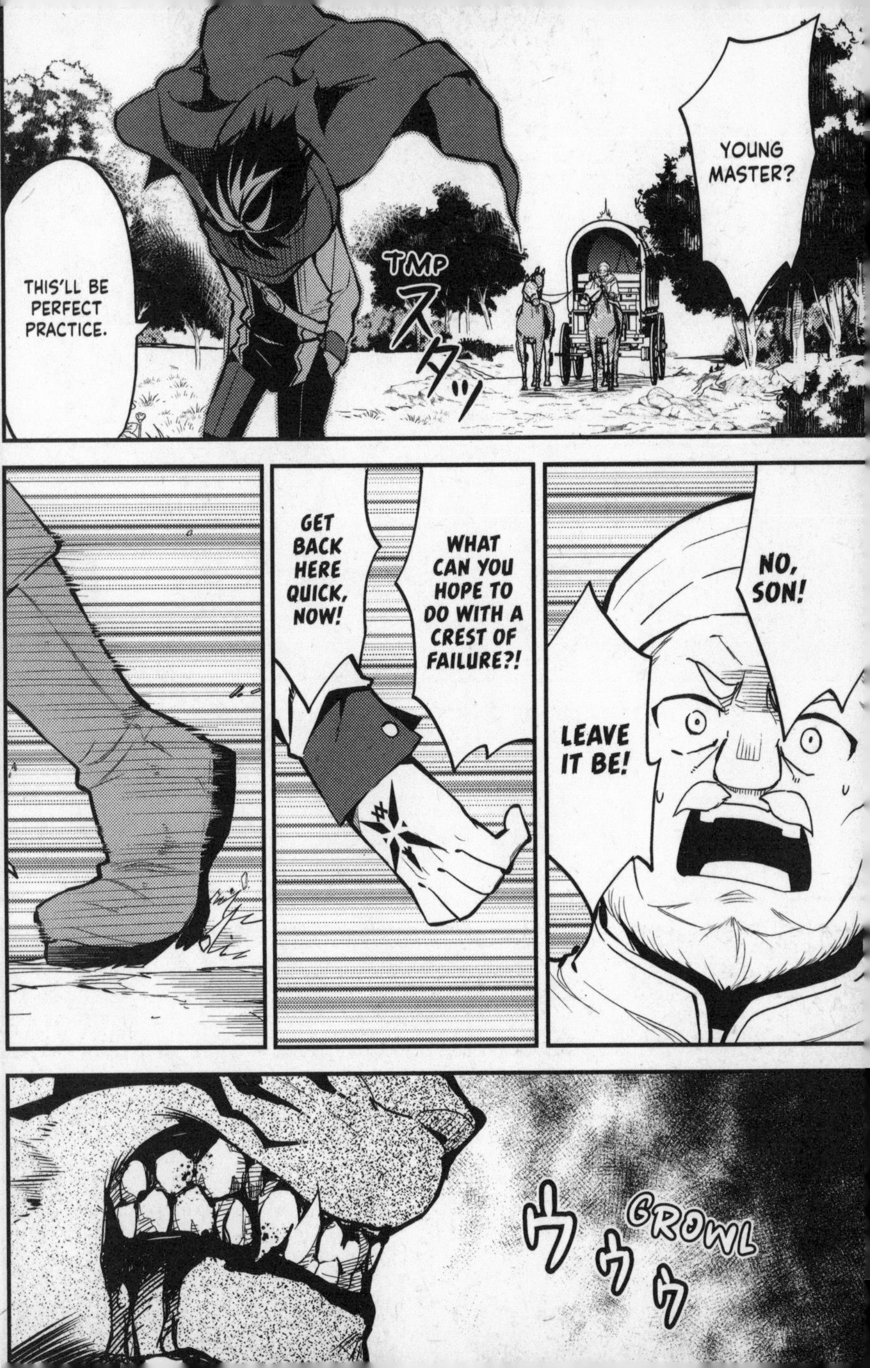
YOUNG MASTER?
TMP
スタッ
THIS'LL BE PERFECT PRACTICE.
NO, SON!
LEAVE IT BE!
WHAT CAN YOU HOPE TO DO WITH A CREST OF FAILURE?!
GET BACK HERE QUICK, NOW!
GROWL
ウウウ

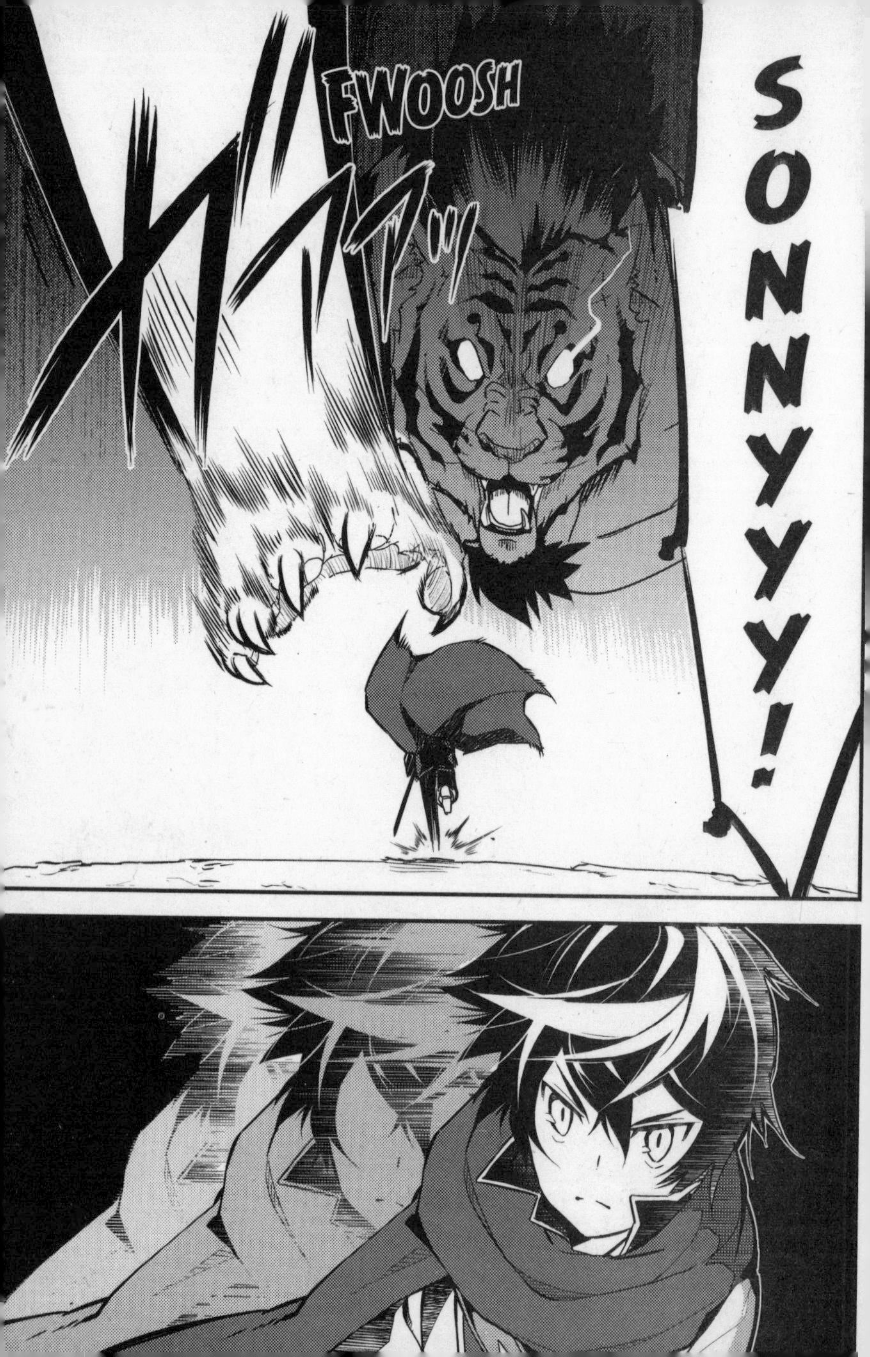
SONNYYY!!
FWOOSH

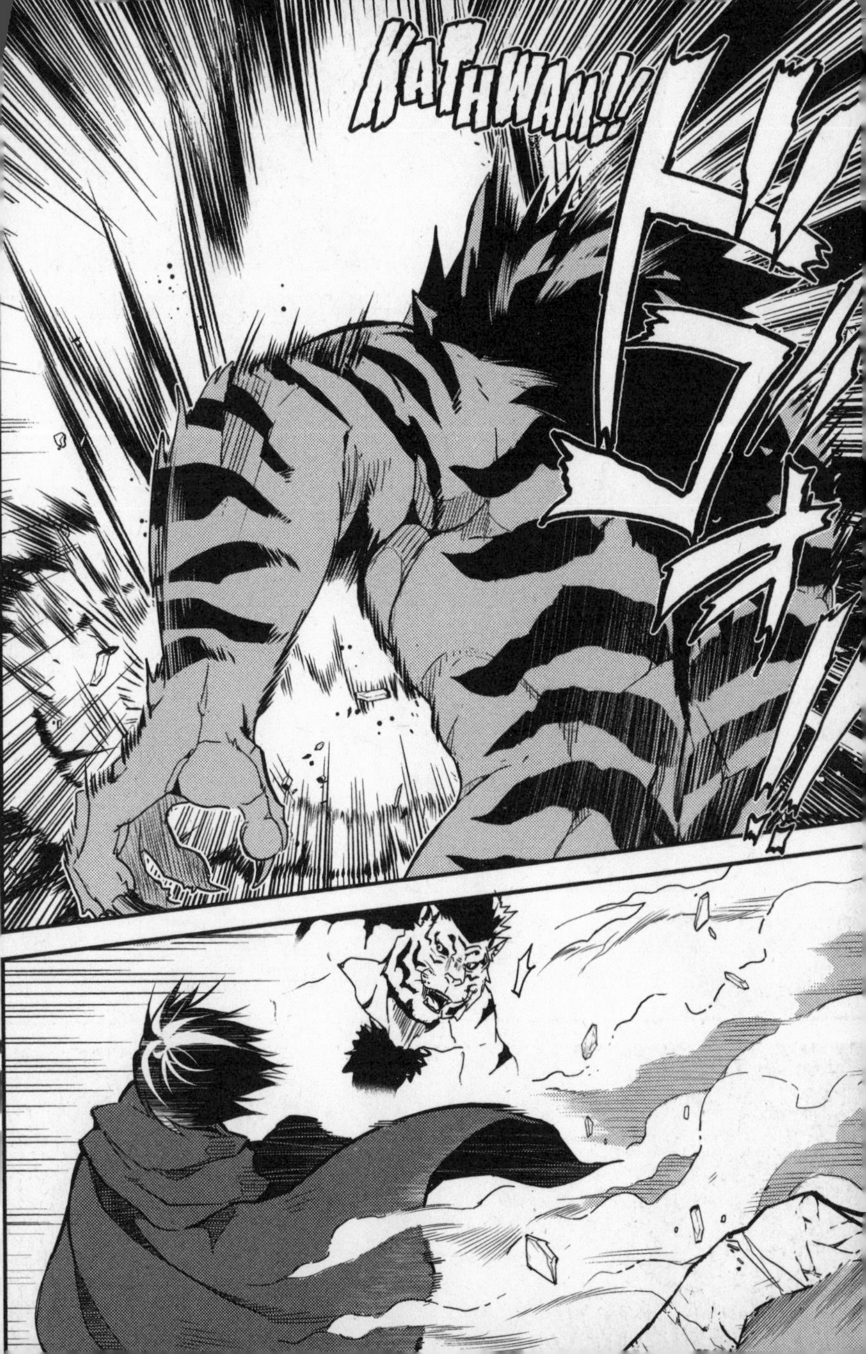
KATHWAM!!

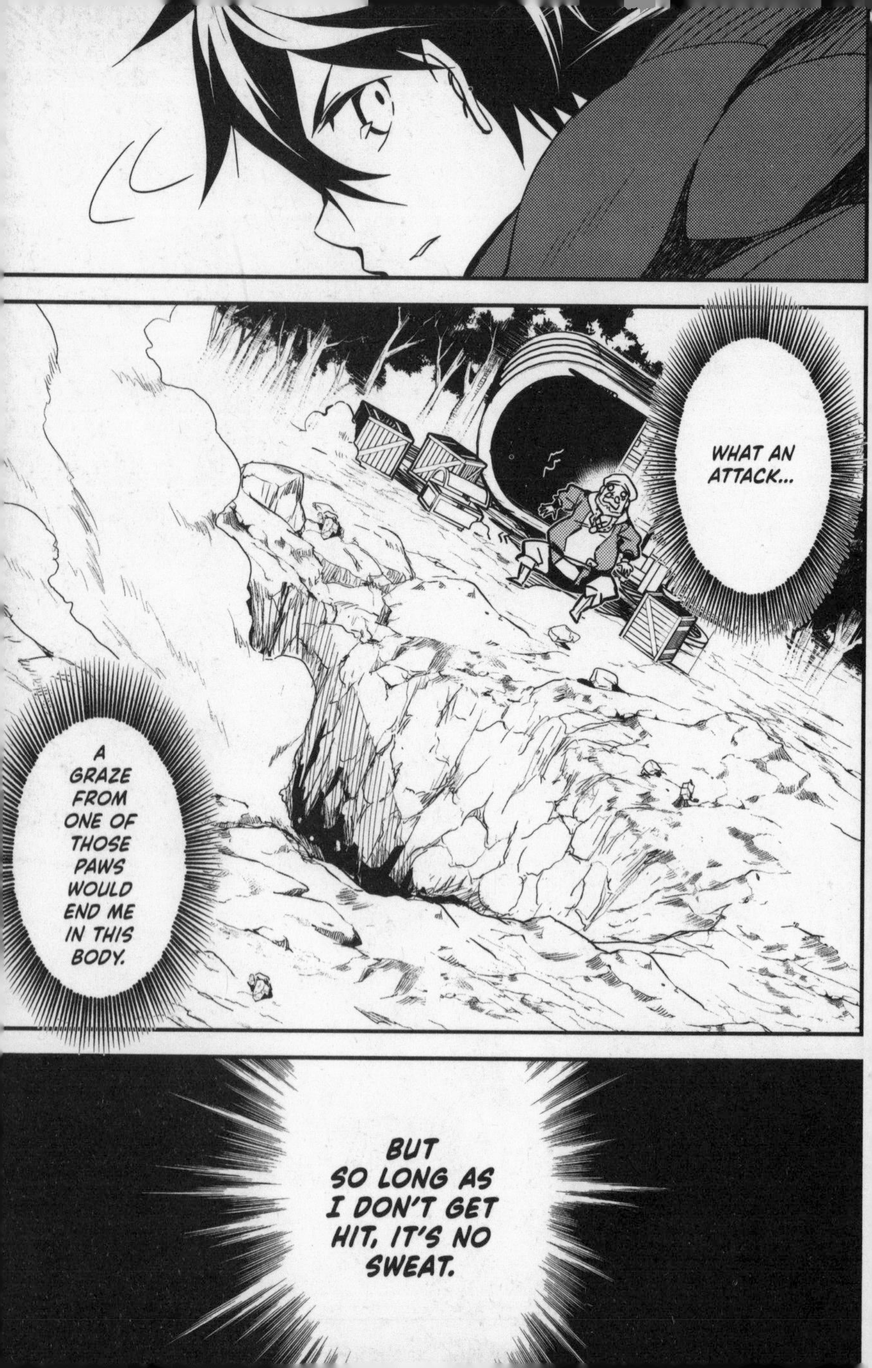
WHAT AN ATTACK...
A GRAZE FROM ONE OF THOSE PAWS WOULD END ME IN THIS BODY.
BUT SO LONG AS I DON'T GET HIT, IT'S NO SWEAT.

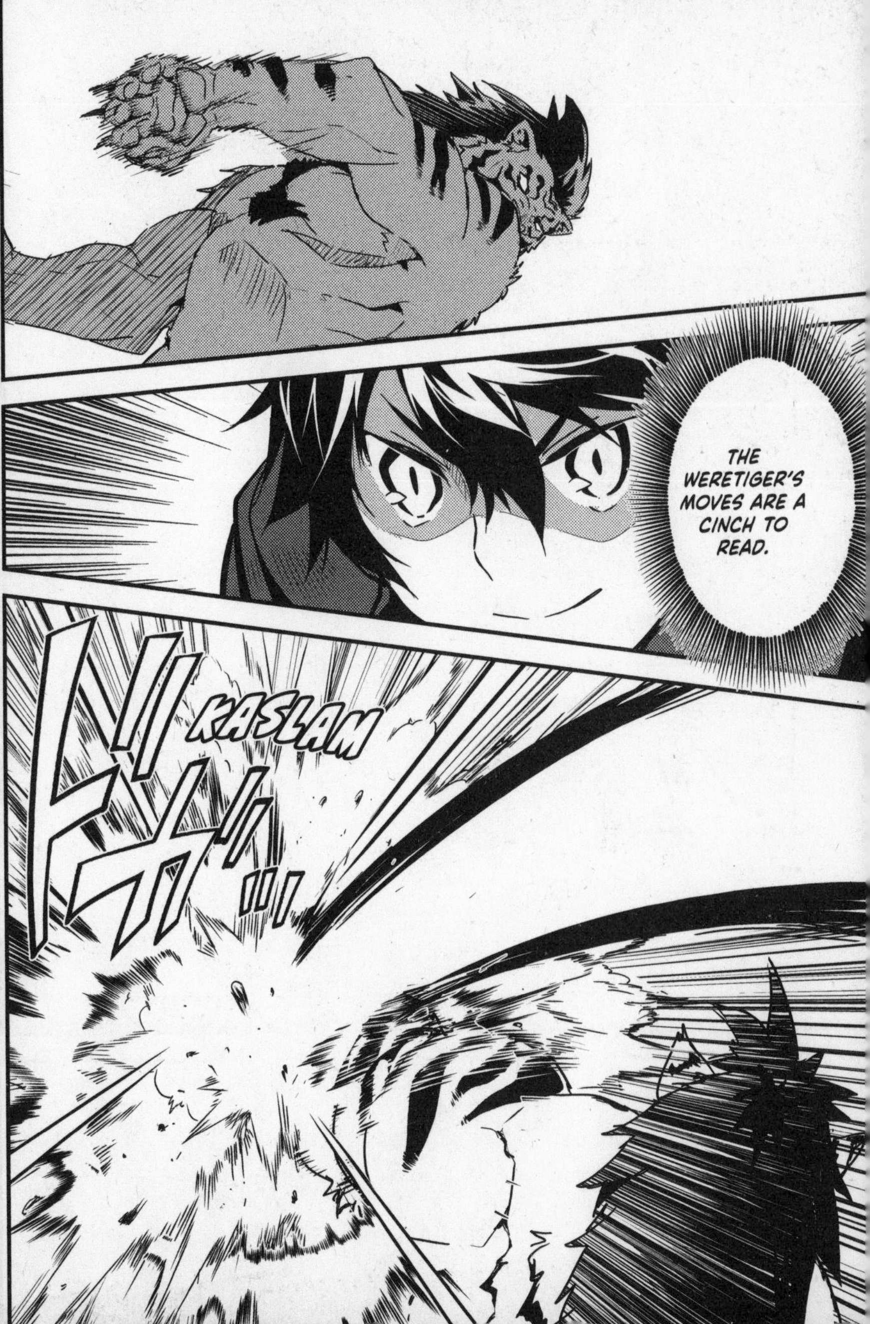
THE WERETIGER'S MOVES ARE A CINCH TO READ.
KASLAM

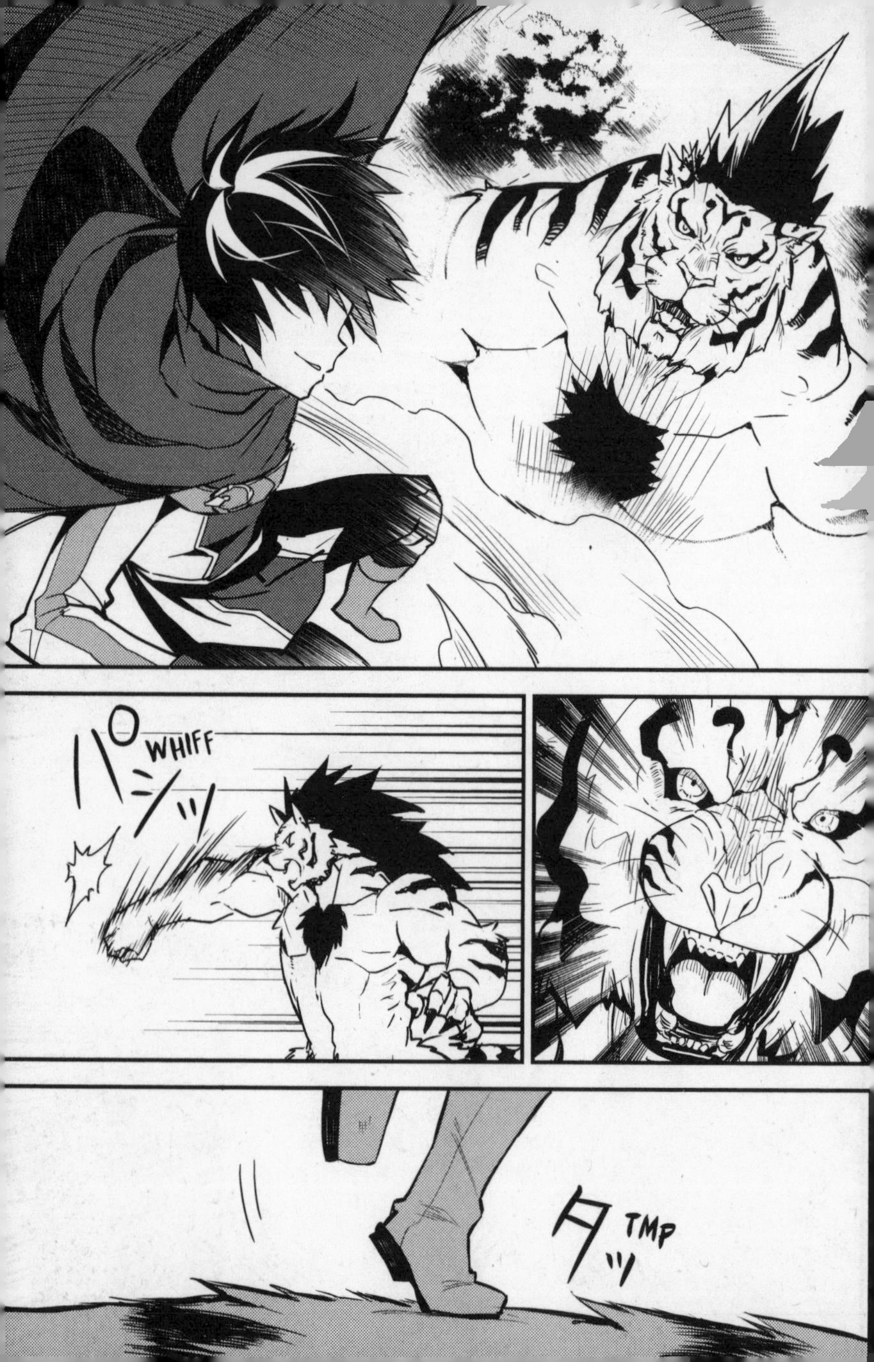
パシッ
WHIFF
タッ
TMP

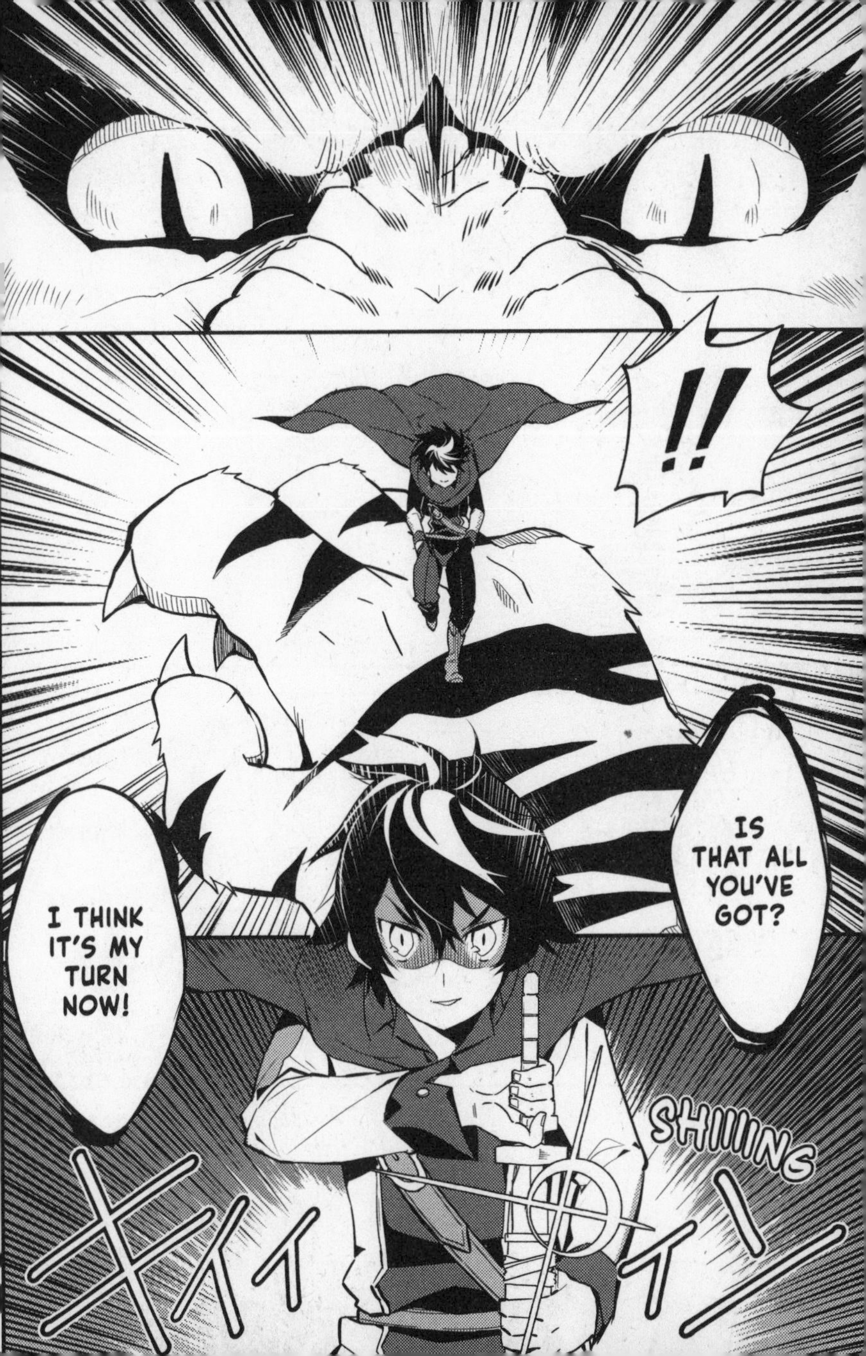
!!
IS THAT ALL YOU'VE GOT?
I THINK IT'S MY TURN NOW!
SHIIIING

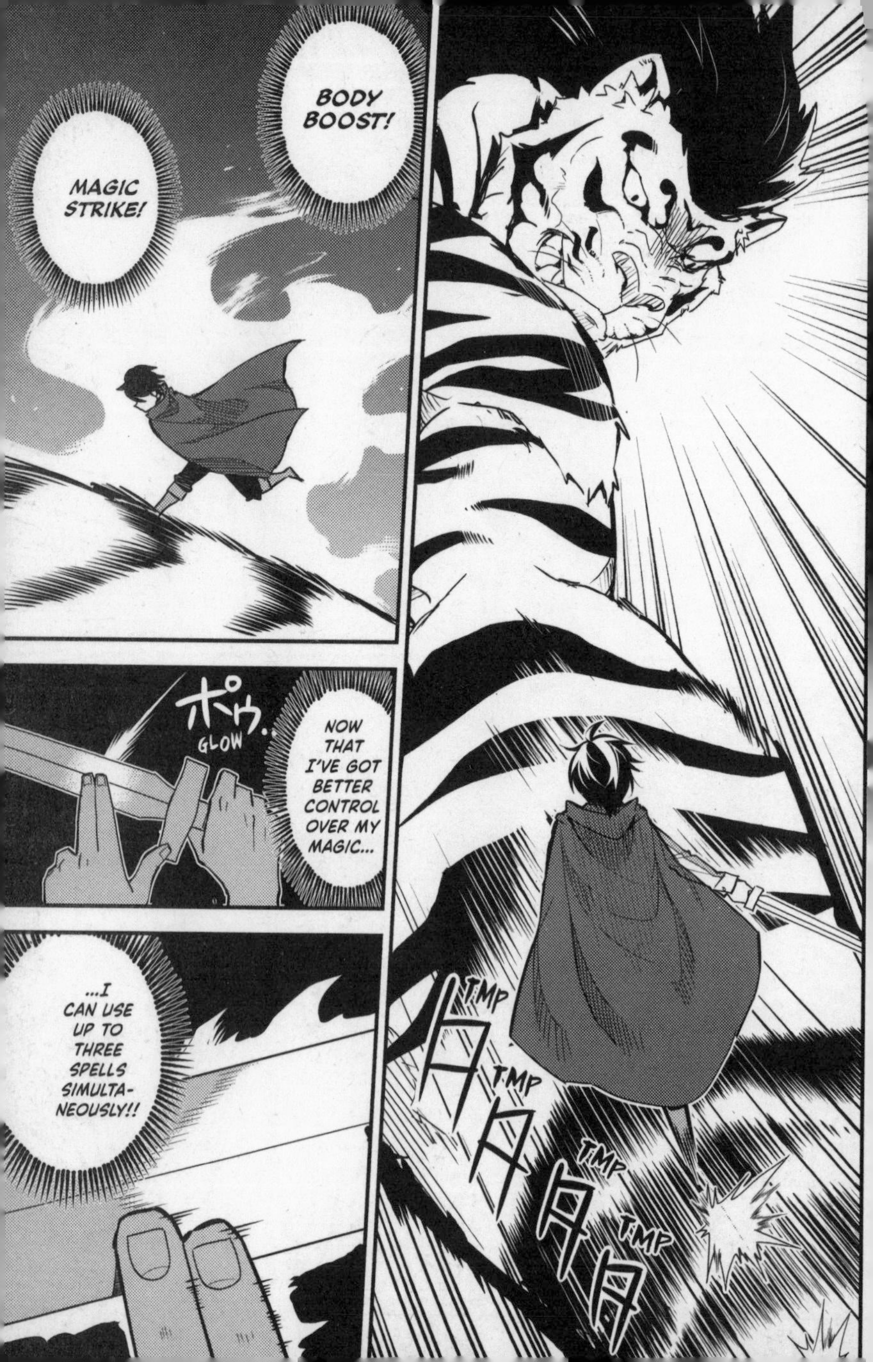
TMP
TMP
TMP
TMP
BODY BOOST!
MAGIC STRIKE!
NOW THAT I'VE GOT BETTER CONTROL OVER MY MAGIC...
ポウ.. GLOW
...I CAN USE UP TO THREE SPELLS SIMULTA-NEOUSLY!!

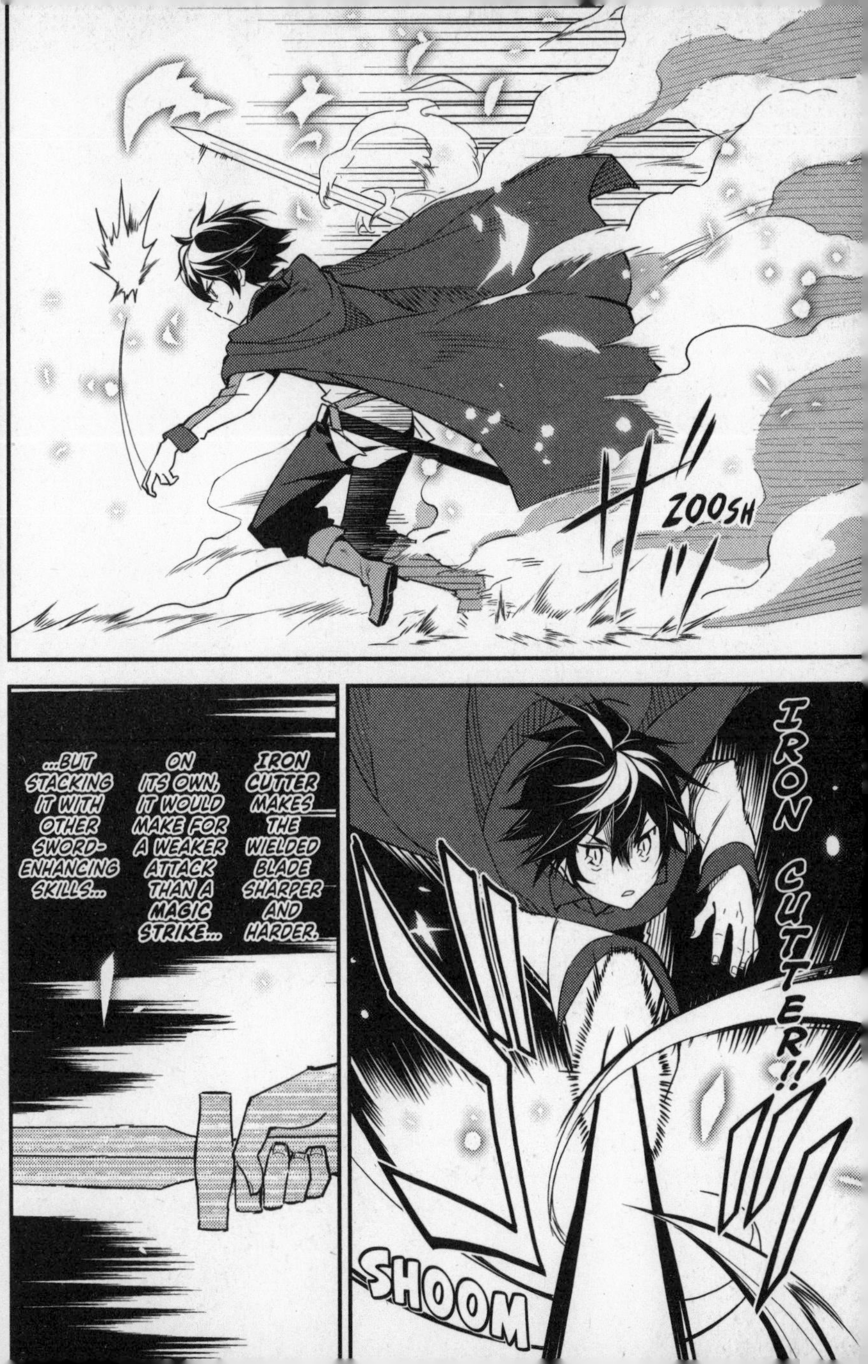
ZOOSH
IRON CUTTER!!
SHOOM
IRON CUTTER MAKES THE WIELDED BLADE SHARPER AND HARDER.
ON ITS OWN, IT WOULD MAKE FOR A WEAKER ATTACK THAN A MAGIC STRIKE...
...BUT STACKING IT WITH OTHER SWORD-ENHANCING SKILLS...

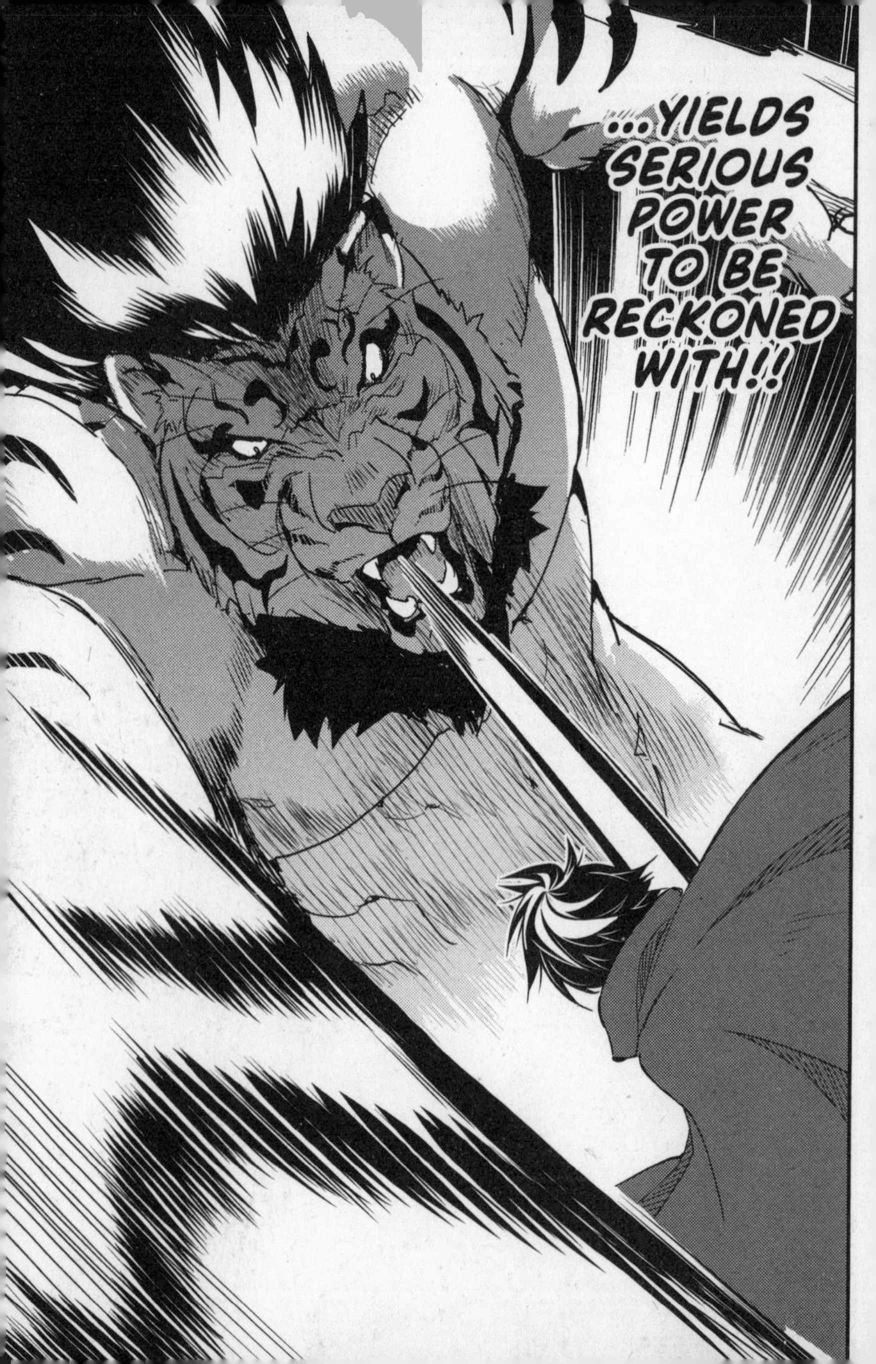
...YIELDS SERIOUS POWER TO BE RECKONED WITH!!

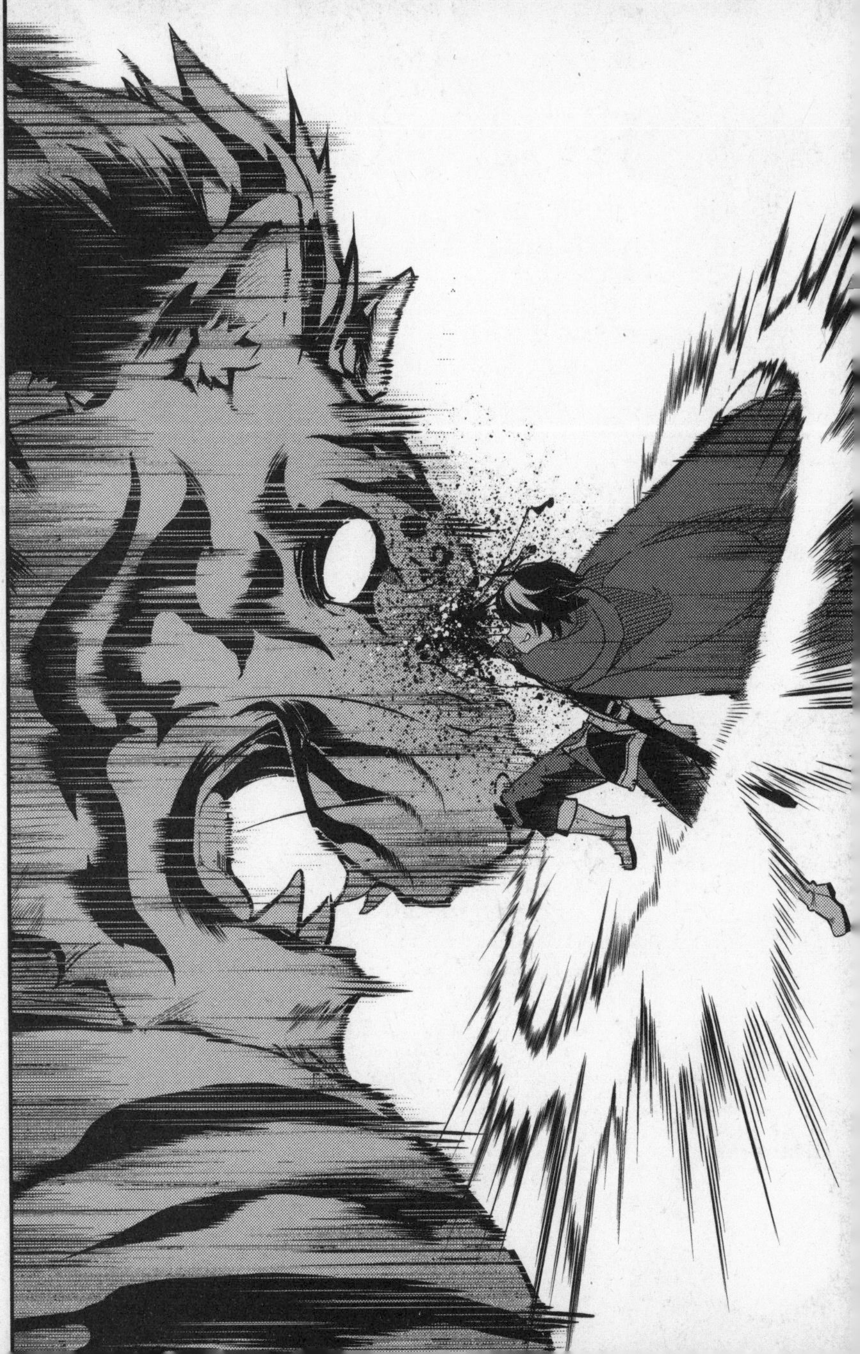

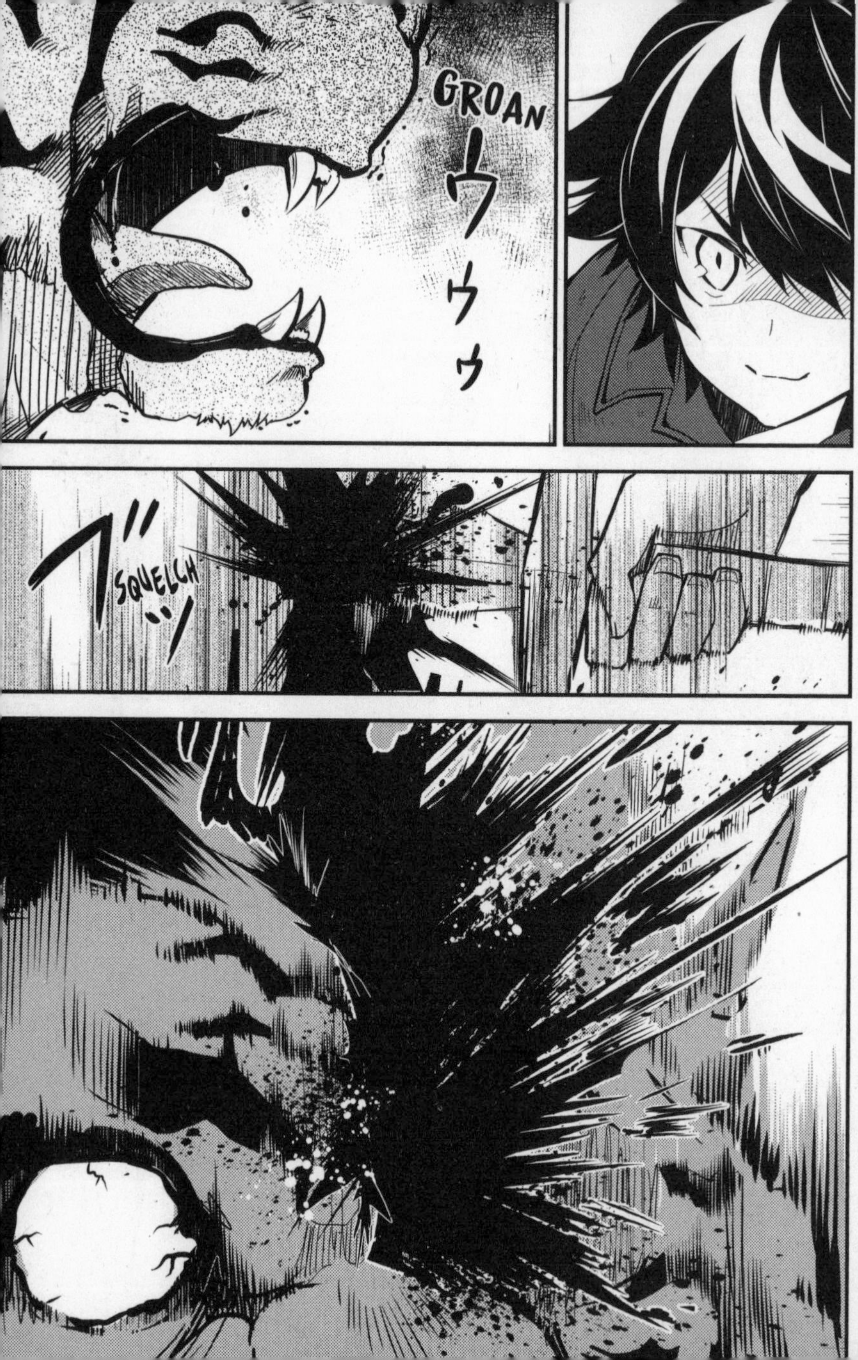
GROAN
ウゥゥゥ
SQUELCH
ブジッ

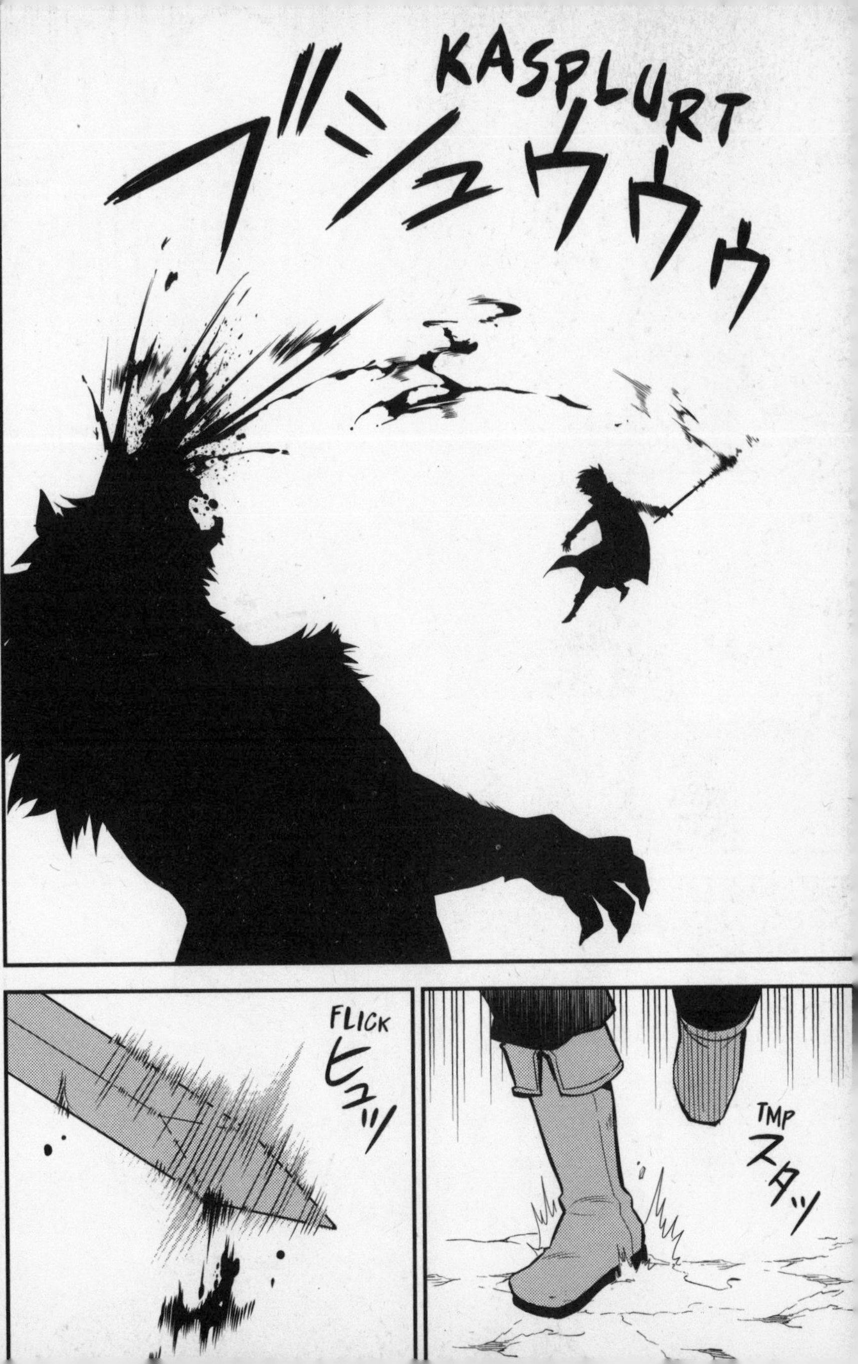
KASPLURT
ブシュウウウ
TMP
スタッ
FLICK
ヒュッ

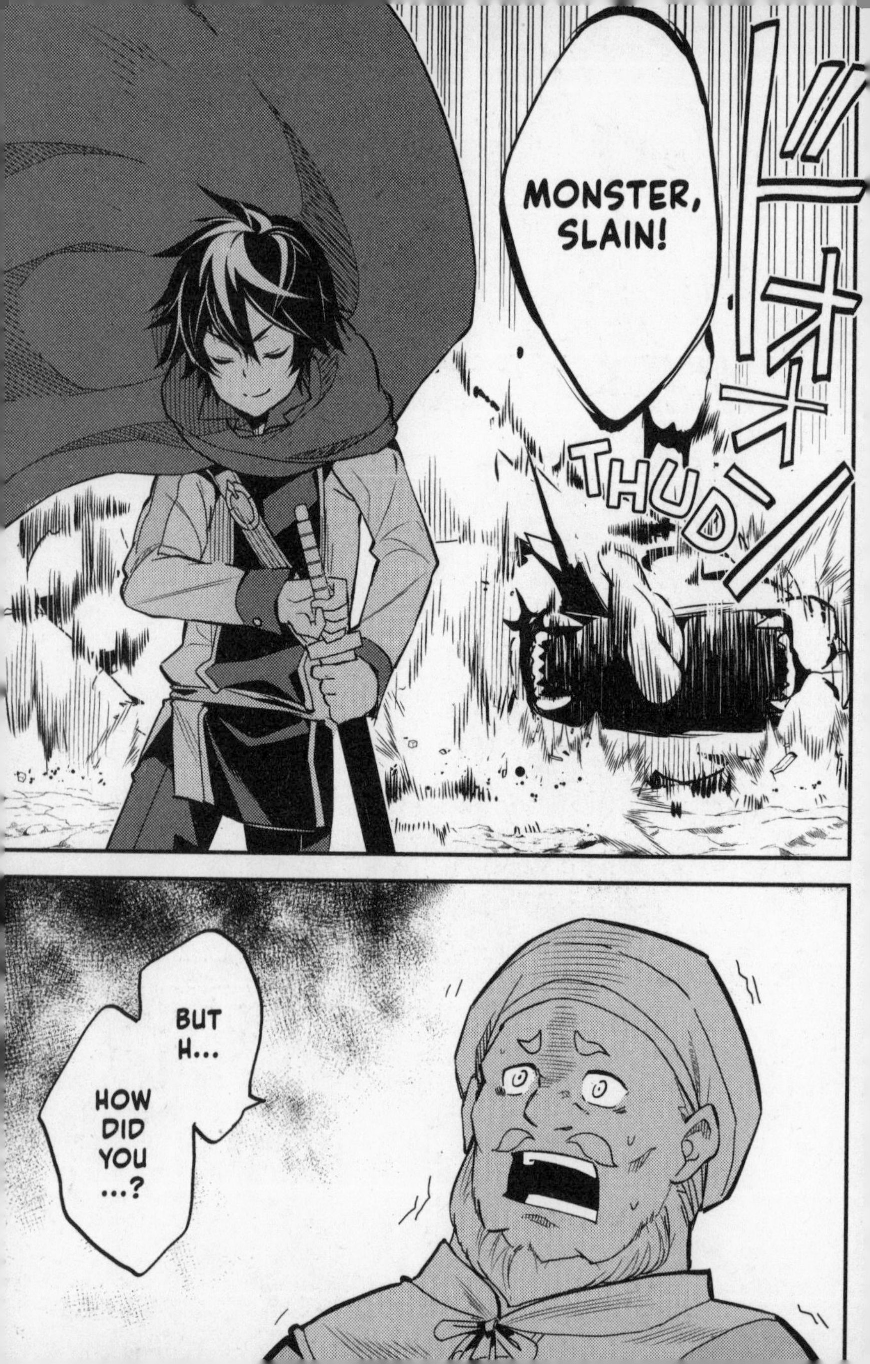
MONSTER, SLAIN!
THUD—
BUT H... HOW DID YOU ...?

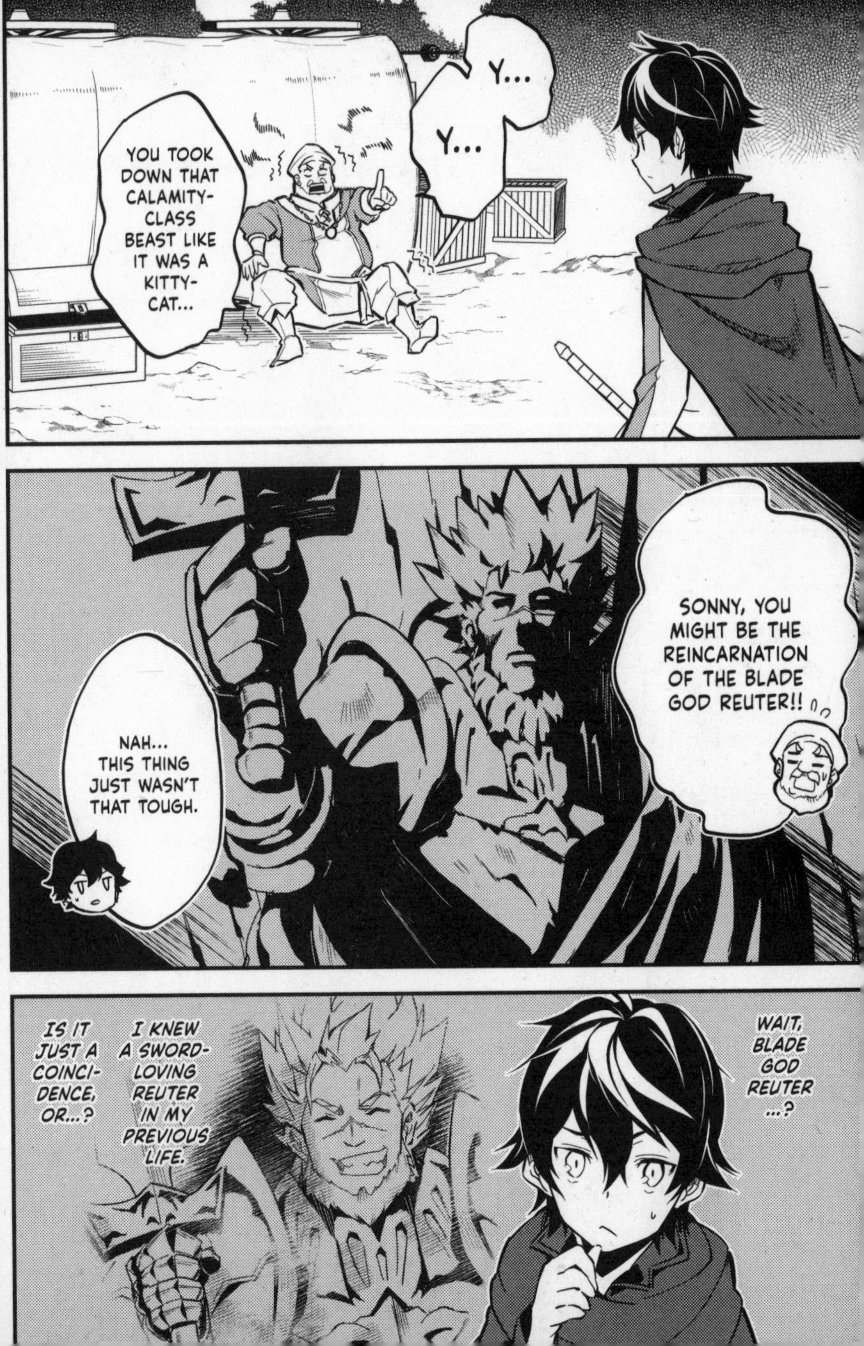
Y... Y...
YOU TOOK DOWN THAT CALAMITY-CLASS BEAST LIKE IT WAS A KITTY-CAT...
SONNY, YOU MIGHT BE THE REINCARNATION OF THE BLADE GOD REUTER!!
NAH... THIS THING JUST WASN'T THAT TOUGH.
WAIT, BLADE GOD REUTER...?
I KNEW A SWORD-LOVING REUTER IN MY PREVIOUS LIFE.
IS IT JUST A COINCIDENCE, OR...?

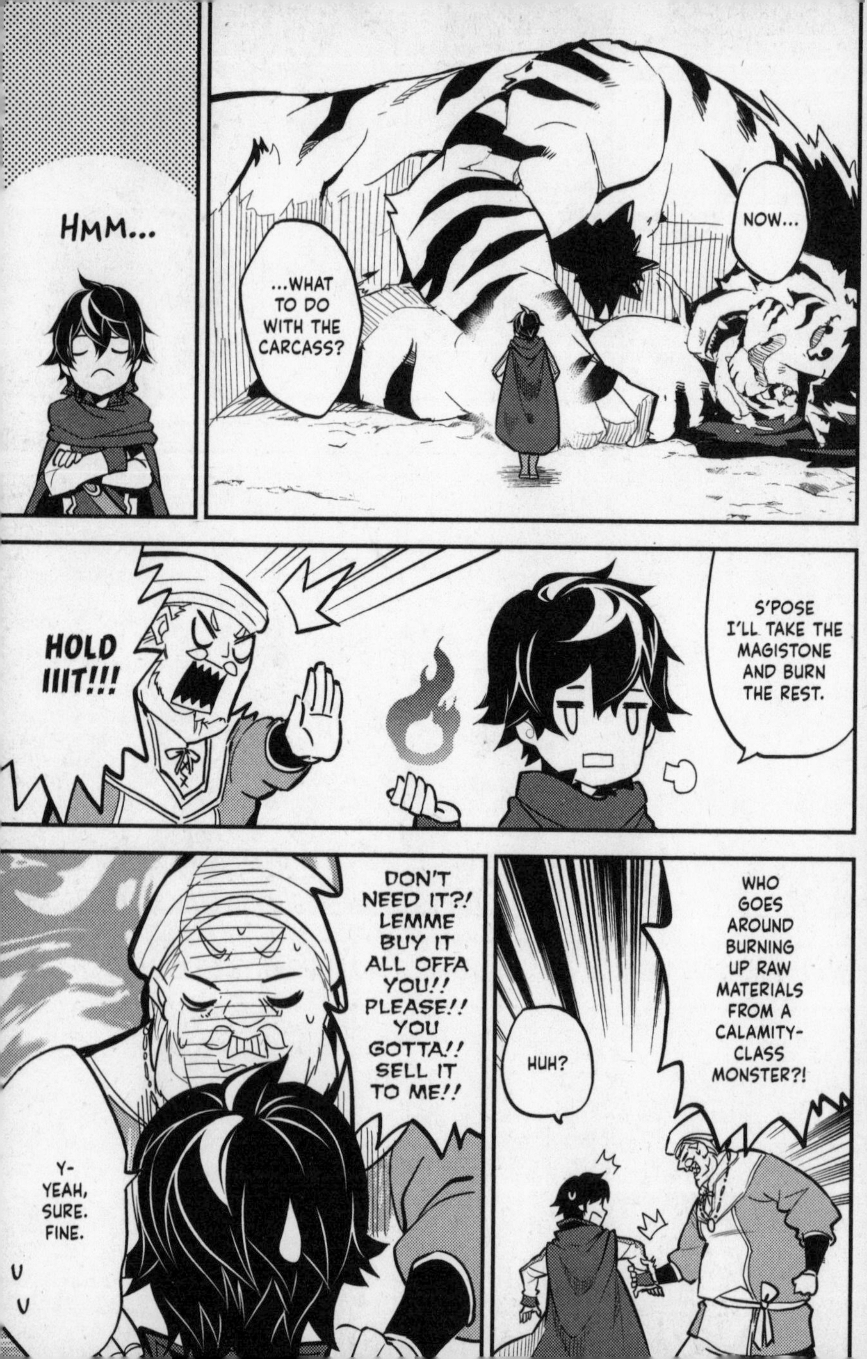
NOW...
...WHAT TO DO WITH THE CARCASS?
HMM...
S'POSE I'LL TAKE THE MAGISTONE AND BURN THE REST.
HOLD IIIT!!!
WHO GOES AROUND BURNING UP RAW MATERIALS FROM A CALAMITY-CLASS MONSTER?!
HUH?
DON'T NEED IT?! LEMME BUY IT ALL OFFA YOU!! PLEASE!! YOU GOTTA!! SELL IT TO ME!!
Y-YEAH, SURE. FINE.

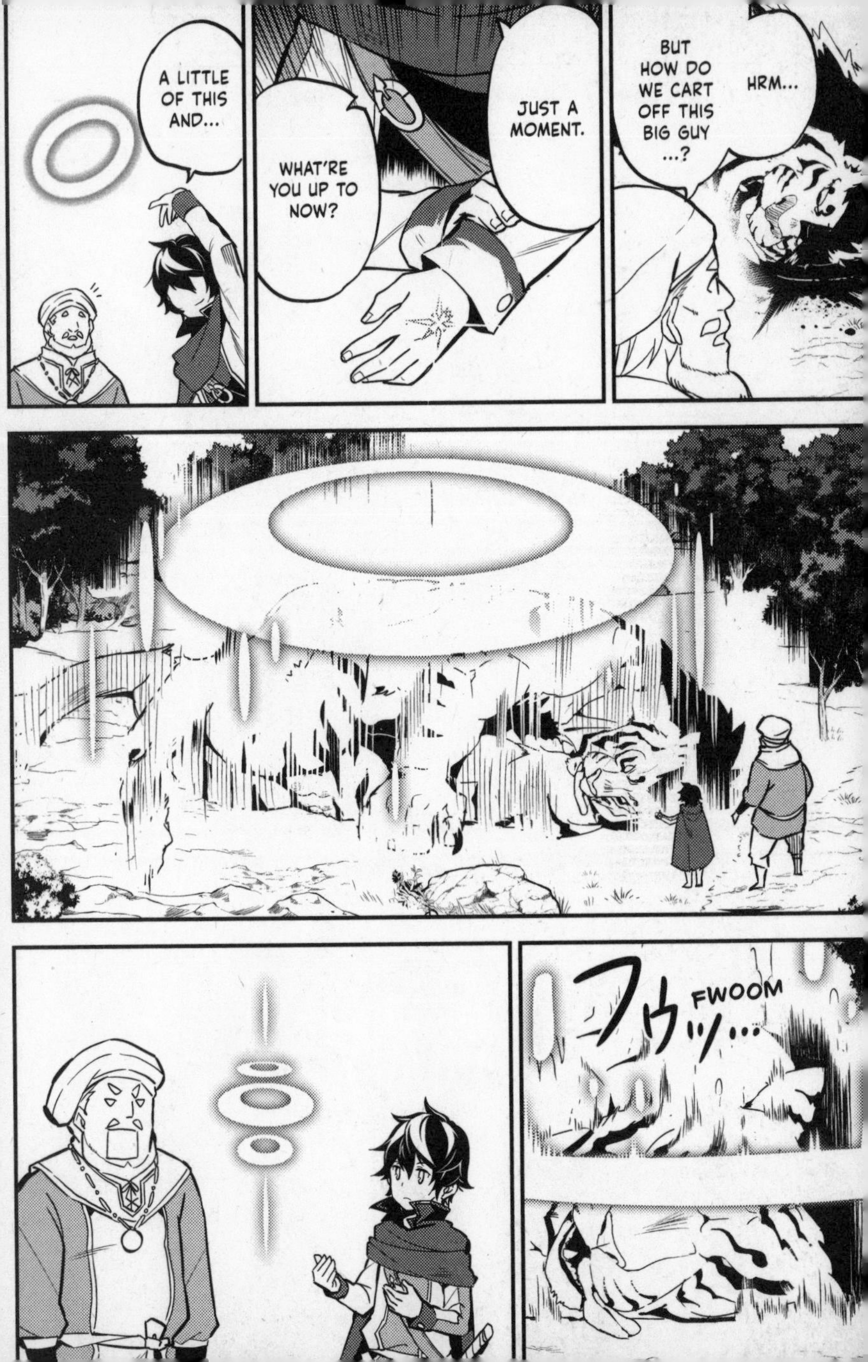
HRM...
BUT HOW DO WE CART OFF THIS BIG GUY ...?
JUST A MOMENT.
WHAT'RE YOU UP TO NOW?
A LITTLE OF THIS AND...
フウッ...
FWOOM

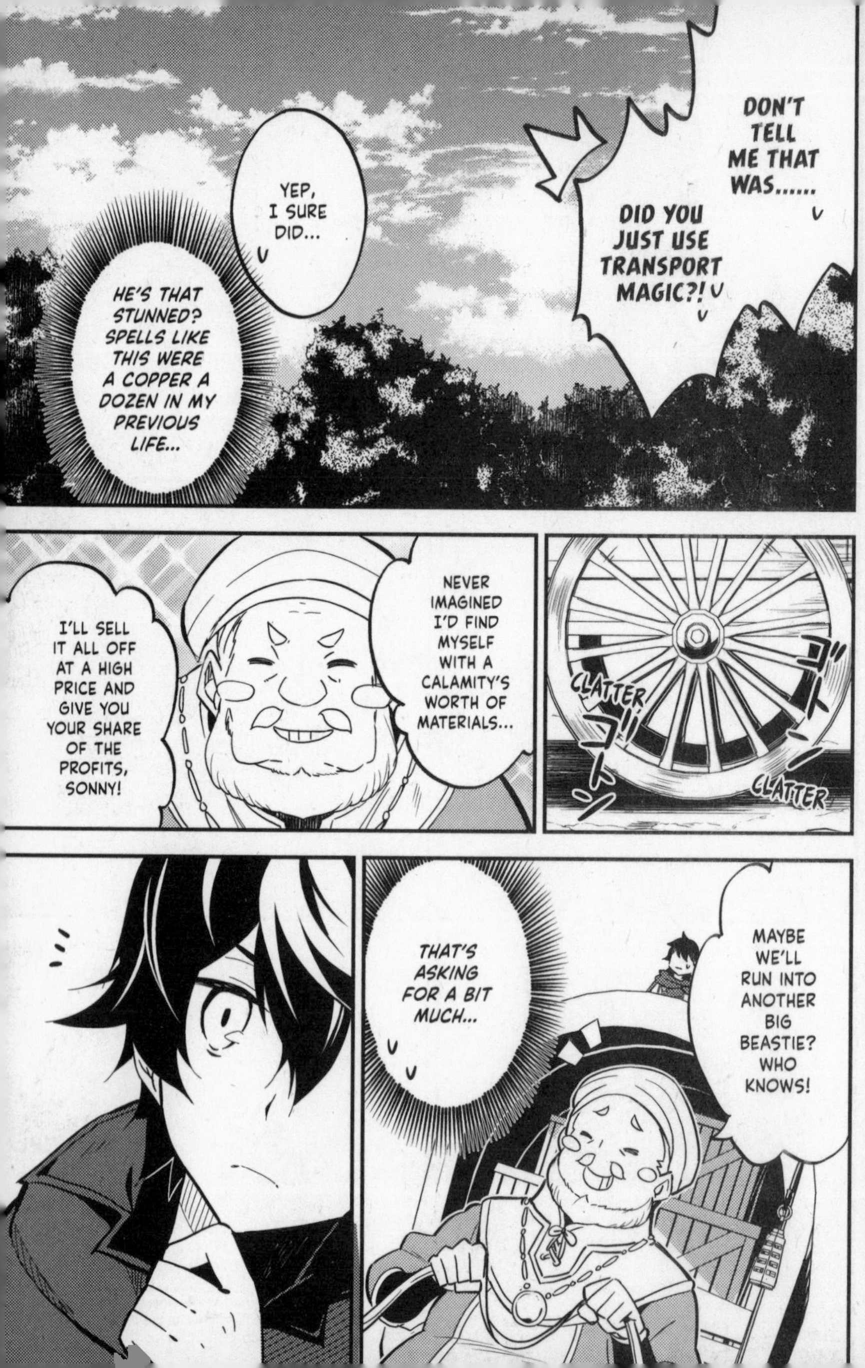
DON'T TELL ME THAT WAS......
DID YOU JUST USE TRANSPORT MAGIC?!
YEP, I SURE DID...
HE'S THAT STUNNED? SPELLS LIKE THIS WERE A COPPER A DOZEN IN MY PREVIOUS LIFE...
CLATTER
CLATTER
NEVER IMAGINED I'D FIND MYSELF WITH A CALAMITY'S WORTH OF MATERIALS...
I'LL SELL IT ALL OFF AT A HIGH PRICE AND GIVE YOU YOUR SHARE OF THE PROFITS, SONNY!
MAYBE WE'LL RUN INTO ANOTHER BIG BEASTIE? WHO KNOWS!
THAT'S ASKING FOR A BIT MUCH...

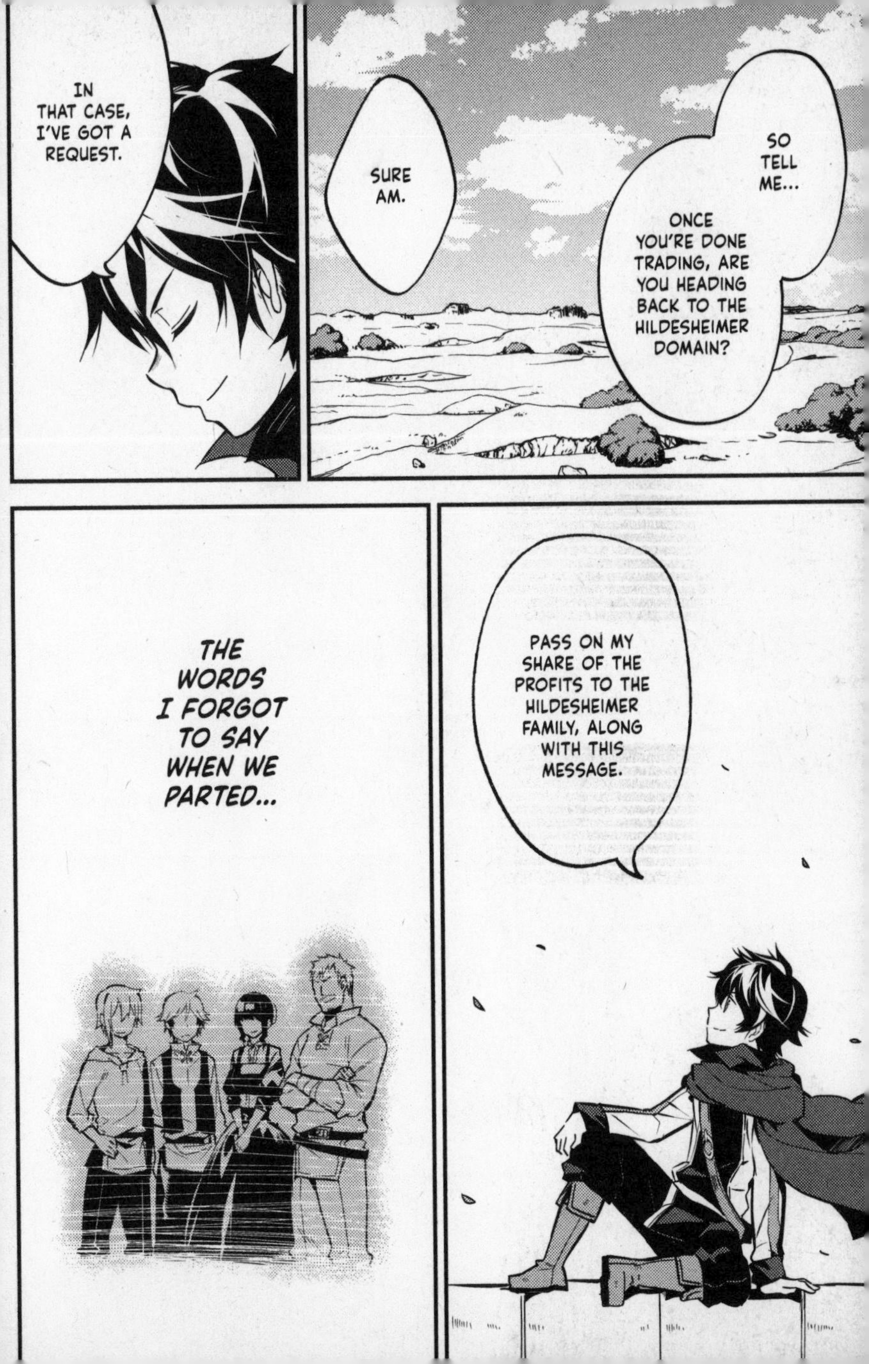
SO TELL ME...
ONCE YOU'RE DONE TRADING, ARE YOU HEADING BACK TO THE HILDESHEIMER DOMAIN?
SURE AM.
IN THAT CASE, I'VE GOT A REQUEST.
PASS ON MY SHARE OF THE PROFITS TO THE HILDESHEIMER FAMILY, ALONG WITH THIS MESSAGE.
THE WORDS I FORGOT TO SAY WHEN WE PARTED...

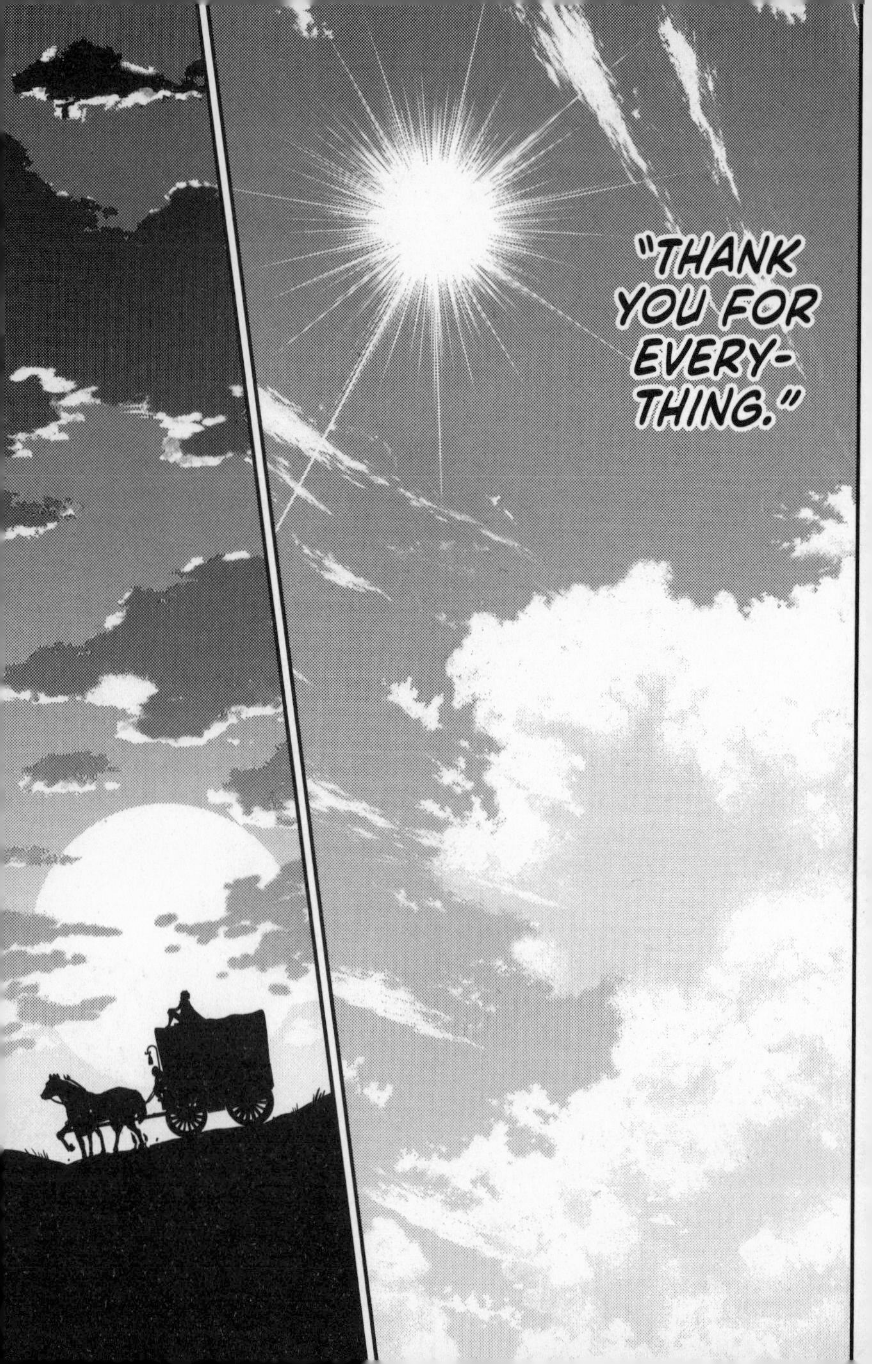
"THANK YOU FOR EVERY-THING."

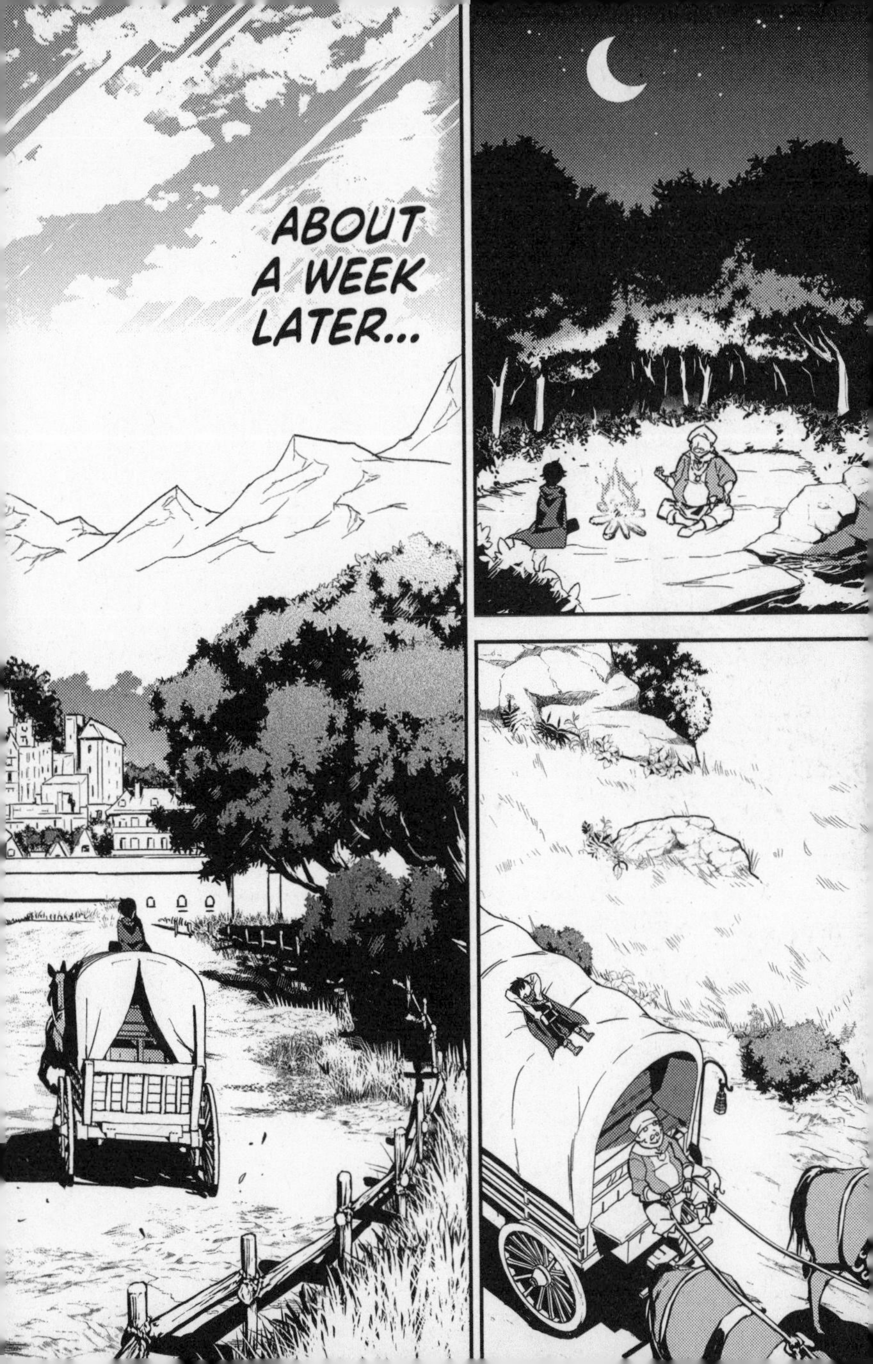
ABOUT A WEEK LATER...

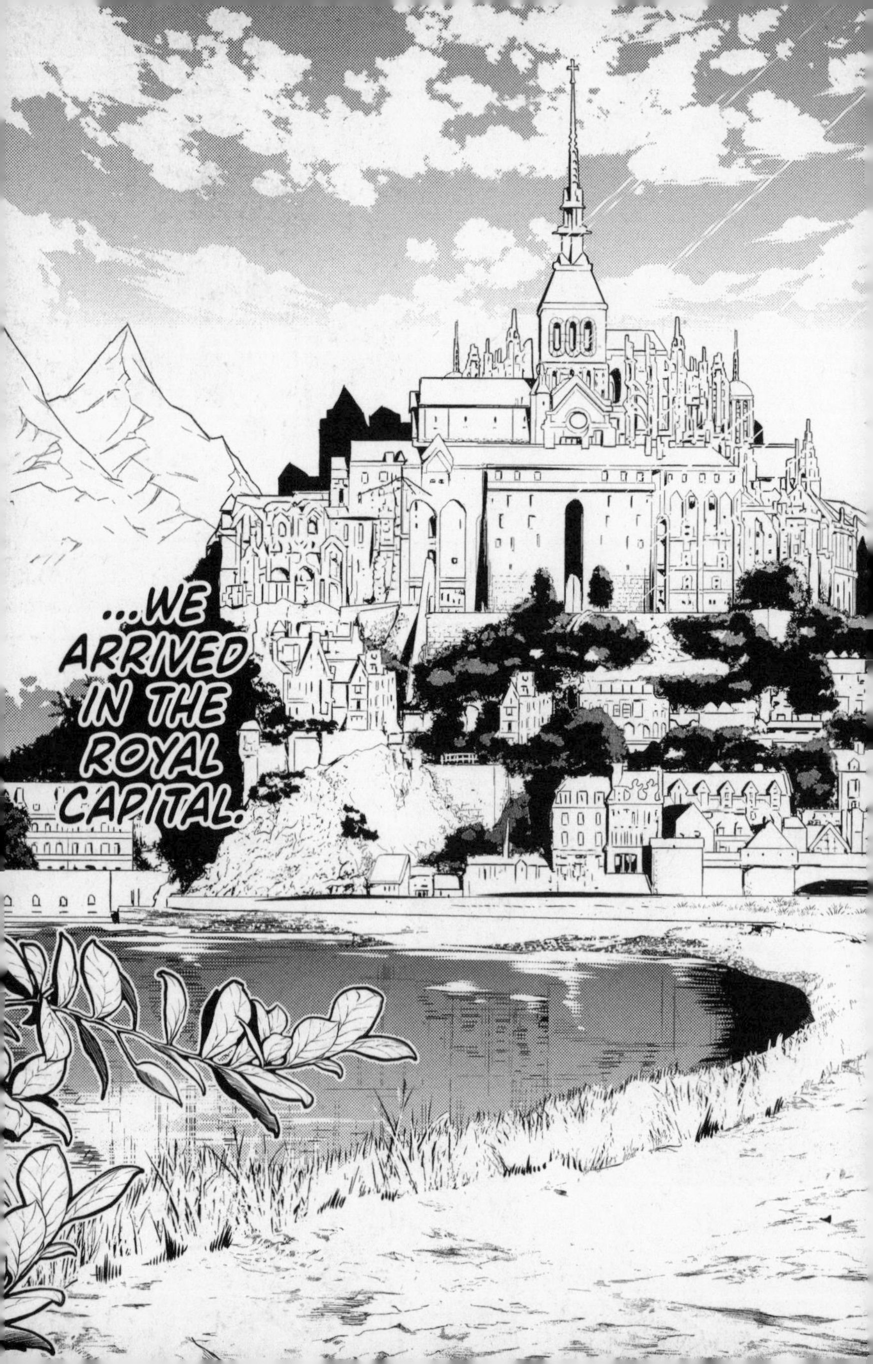
...WE ARRIVED IN THE ROYAL CAPITAL.

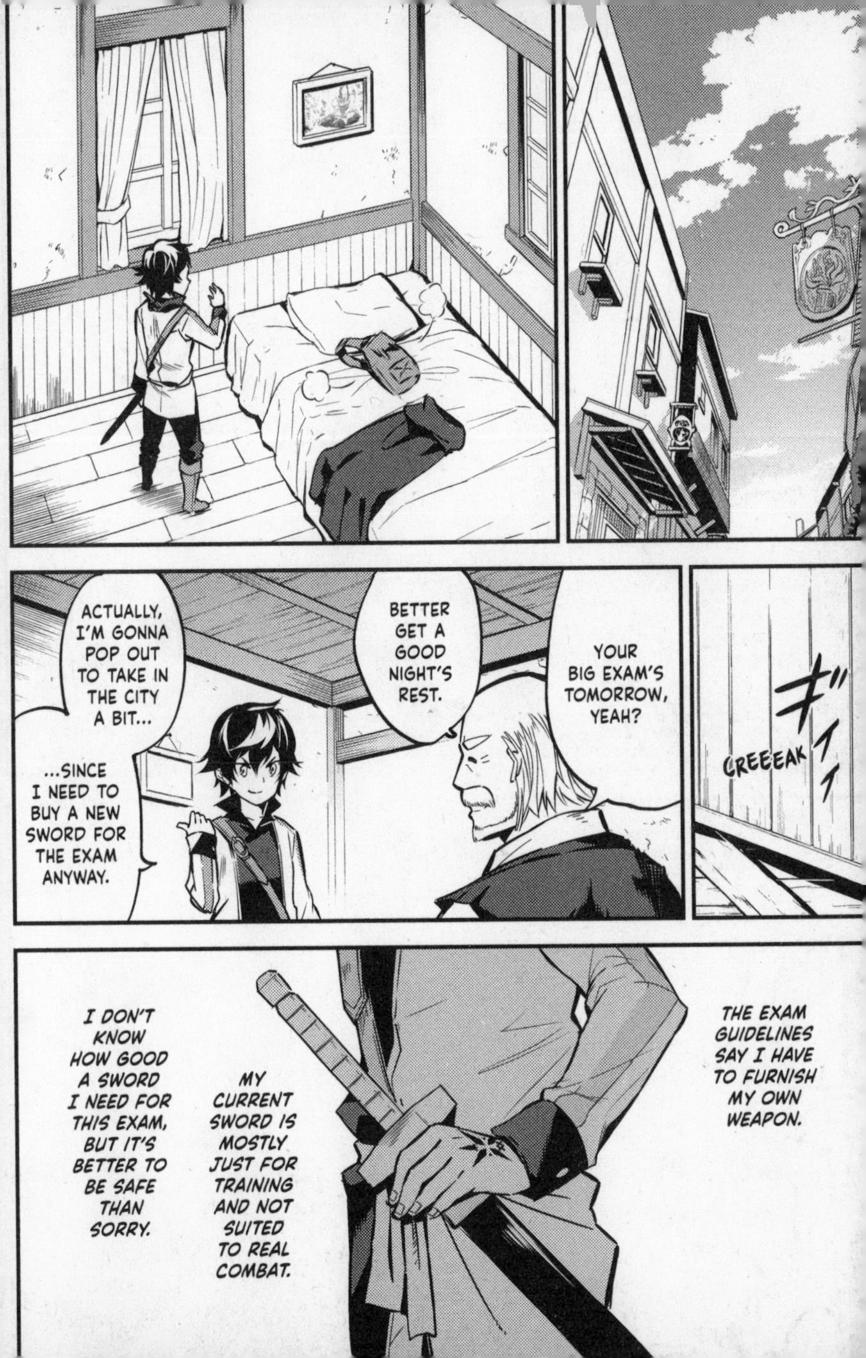
CREEEAK
YOUR BIG EXAM'S TOMORROW, YEAH?
BETTER GET A GOOD NIGHT'S REST.
ACTUALLY, I'M GONNA POP OUT TO TAKE IN THE CITY A BIT...
...SINCE I NEED TO BUY A NEW SWORD FOR THE EXAM ANYWAY.
THE EXAM GUIDELINES SAY I HAVE TO FURNISH MY OWN WEAPON.
MY CURRENT SWORD IS MOSTLY JUST FOR TRAINING AND NOT SUITED TO REAL COMBAT.
I DON'T KNOW HOW GOOD A SWORD I NEED FOR THIS EXAM, BUT IT'S BETTER TO BE SAFE THAN SORRY.

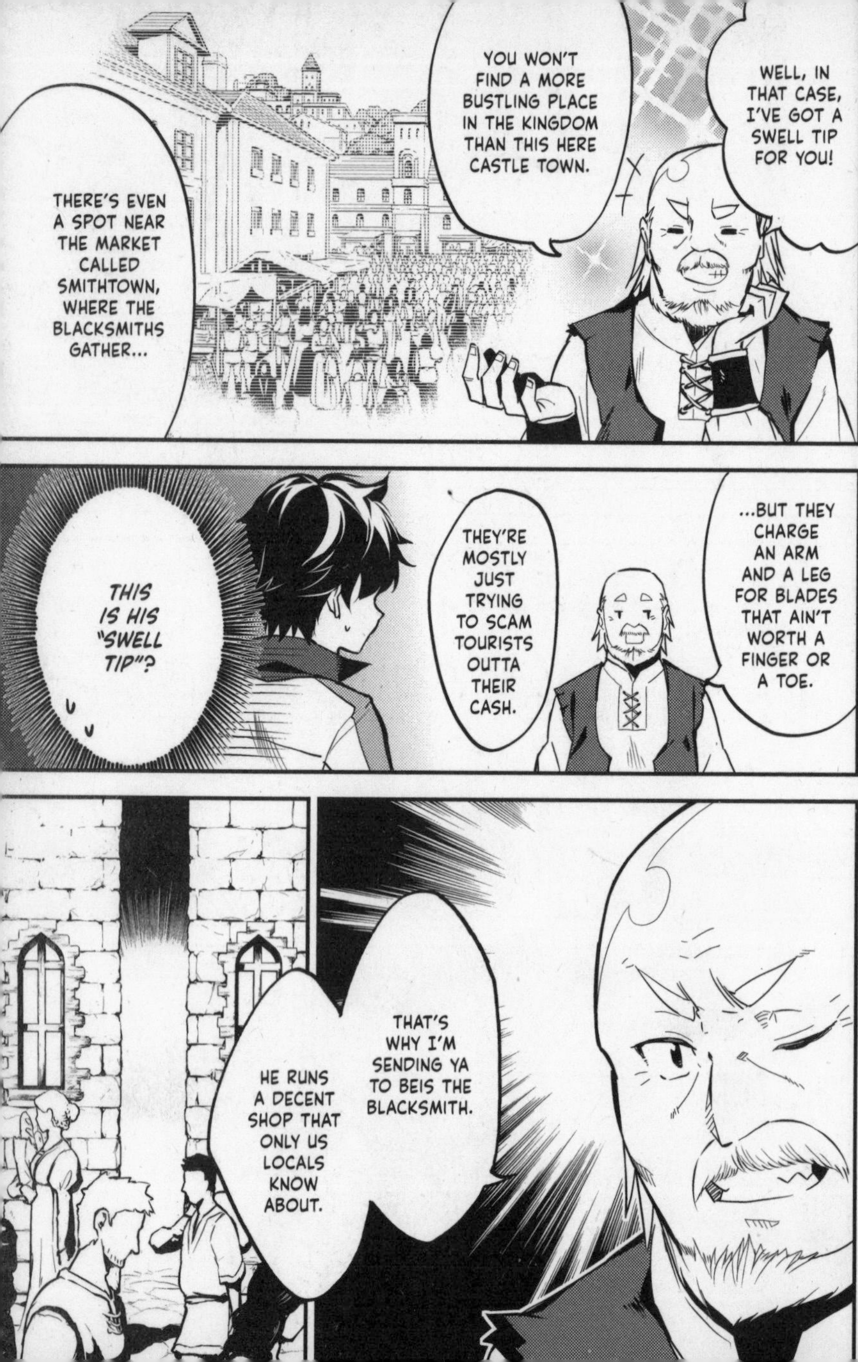
WELL, IN THAT CASE, I'VE GOT A SWELL TIP FOR YOU!
YOU WON'T FIND A MORE BUSTLING PLACE IN THE KINGDOM THAN THIS HERE CASTLE TOWN.
THERE'S EVEN A SPOT NEAR THE MARKET CALLED SMITHTOWN, WHERE THE BLACKSMITHS GATHER...
...BUT THEY CHARGE AN ARM AND A LEG FOR BLADES THAT AIN'T WORTH A FINGER OR A TOE.
THEY'RE MOSTLY JUST TRYING TO SCAM TOURISTS OUTTA THEIR CASH.
THIS IS HIS "SWELL TIP"?
THAT'S WHY I'M SENDING YA TO BEIS THE BLACKSMITH.
HE RUNS A DECENT SHOP THAT ONLY US LOCALS KNOW ABOUT.

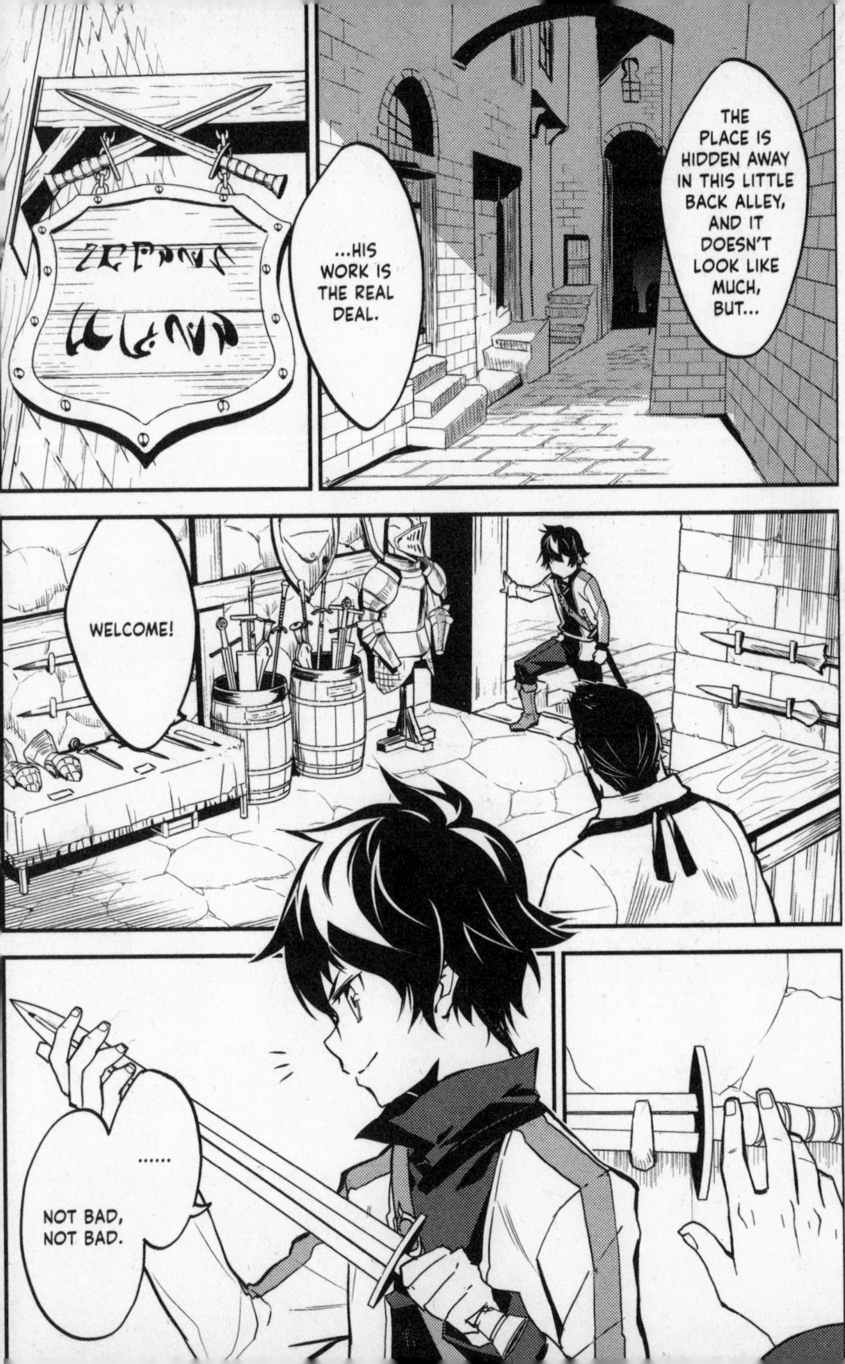
THE PLACE IS HIDDEN AWAY IN THIS LITTLE BACK ALLEY, AND IT DOESN'T LOOK LIKE MUCH, BUT...
...HIS WORK IS THE REAL DEAL.
WELCOME!
......
NOT BAD, NOT BAD.

I COULDN'T PRODUCE WORK THIS FINE AS I AM NOW AND WITHOUT ACCESS TO THE PROPER TOOLS.

NO LEMONS IN THE BUNCH.

IN FACT, ALL THE WEAPONS HERE LOOK PRETTY STURDY.

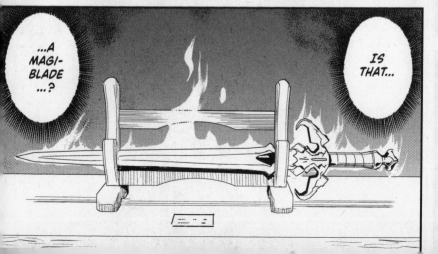

...A MAGI-BLADE...?

IS THAT...

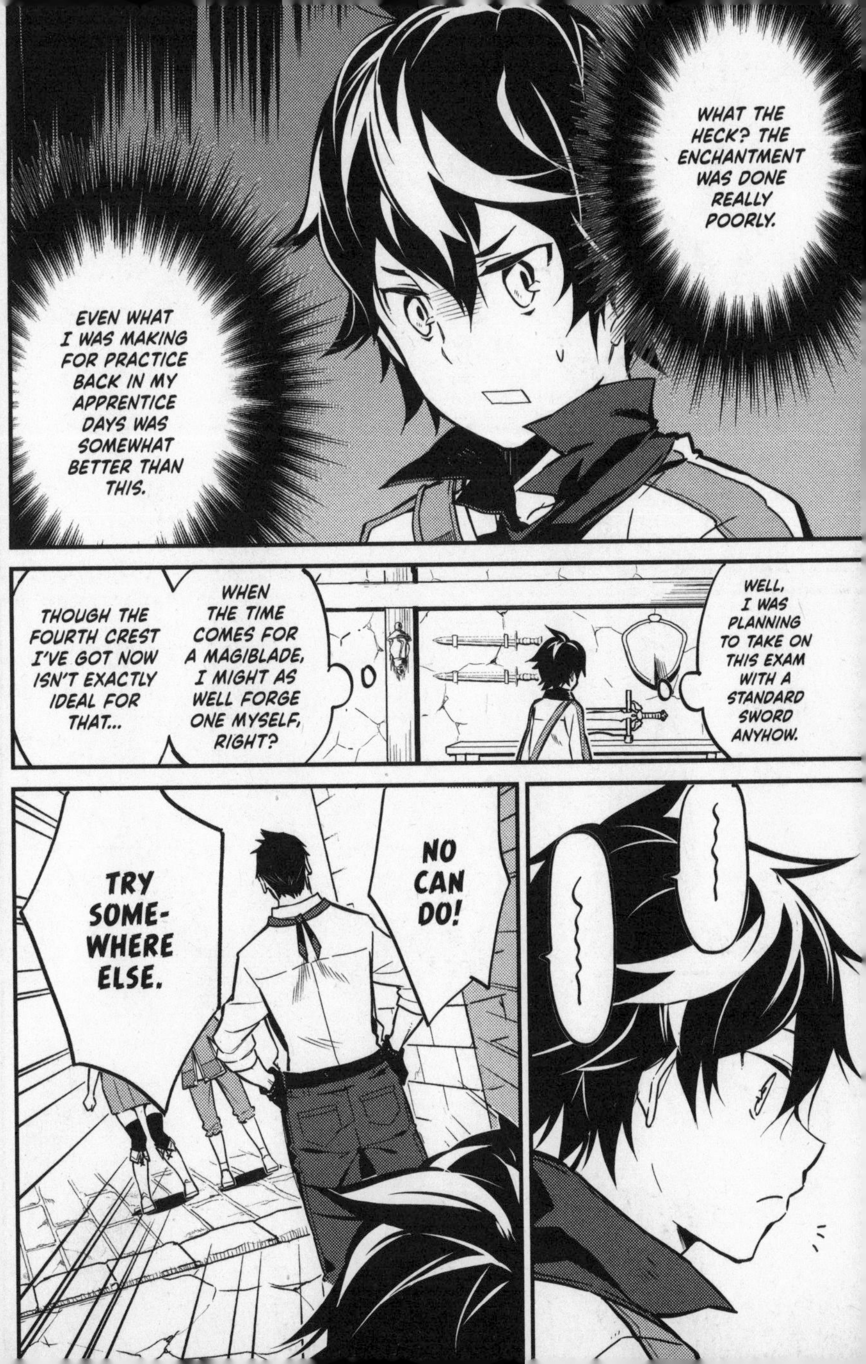
WHAT THE HECK? THE ENCHANTMENT WAS DONE REALLY POORLY.
EVEN WHAT I WAS MAKING FOR PRACTICE BACK IN MY APPRENTICE DAYS WAS SOMEWHAT BETTER THAN THIS.
WELL, I WAS PLANNING TO TAKE ON THIS EXAM WITH A STANDARD SWORD ANYHOW.
WHEN THE TIME COMES FOR A MAGIBLADE, I MIGHT AS WELL FORGE ONE MYSELF, RIGHT?
THOUGH THE FOURTH CREST I'VE GOT NOW ISN'T EXACTLY IDEAL FOR THAT...
NO CAN DO!
TRY SOME-WHERE ELSE.

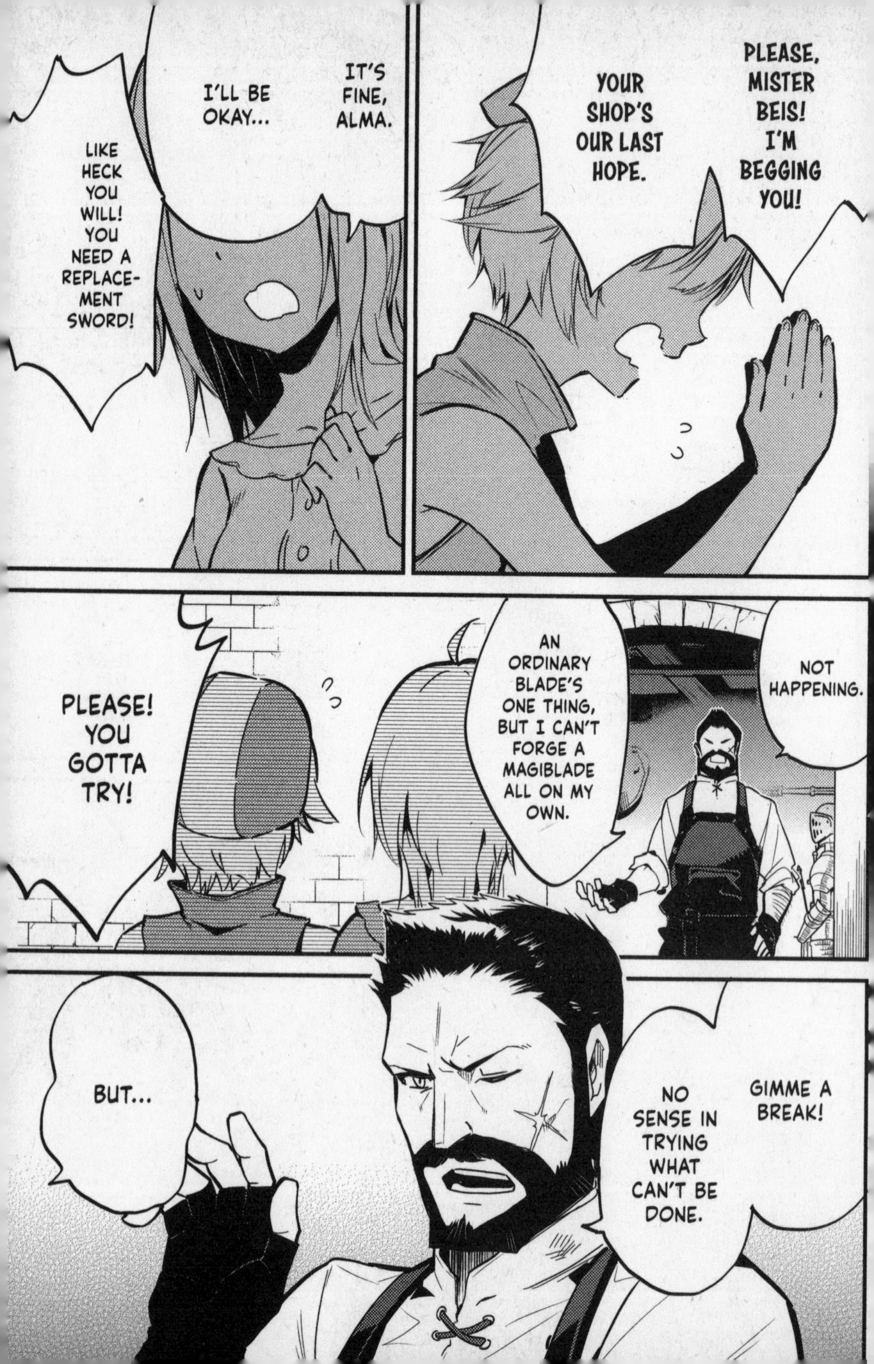
PLEASE, MISTER BEIS! I'M BEGGING YOU!
YOUR SHOP'S OUR LAST HOPE.
IT'S FINE, ALMA.
I'LL BE OKAY...
LIKE HECK YOU WILL! YOU NEED A REPLACEMENT SWORD!
NOT HAPPENING.
AN ORDINARY BLADE'S ONE THING, BUT I CAN'T FORGE A MAGIBLADE ALL ON MY OWN.
PLEASE! YOU GOTTA TRY!
GIMME A BREAK!
NO SENSE IN TRYING WHAT CAN'T BE DONE.
BUT...

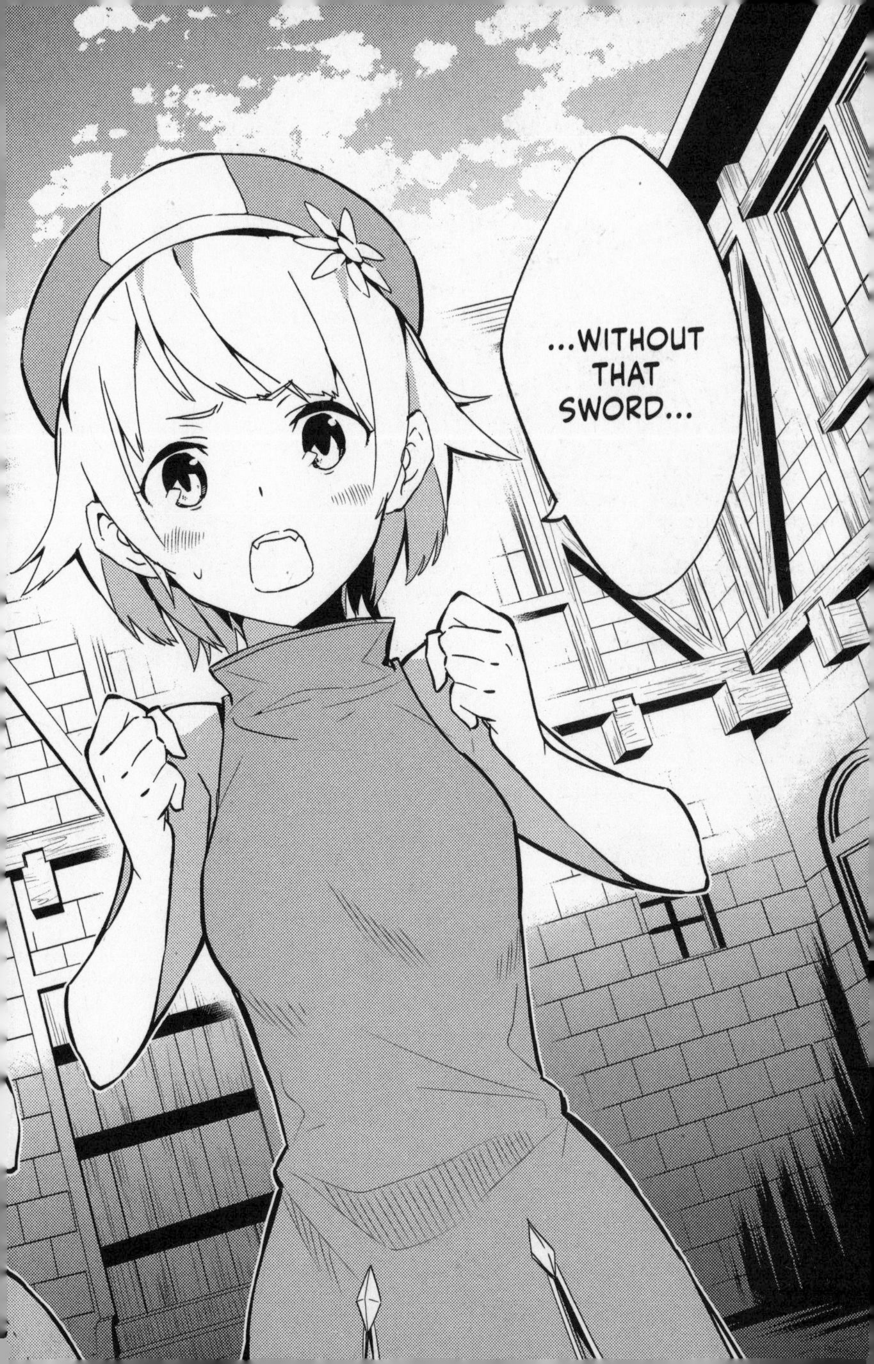
...WITHOUT THAT SWORD...

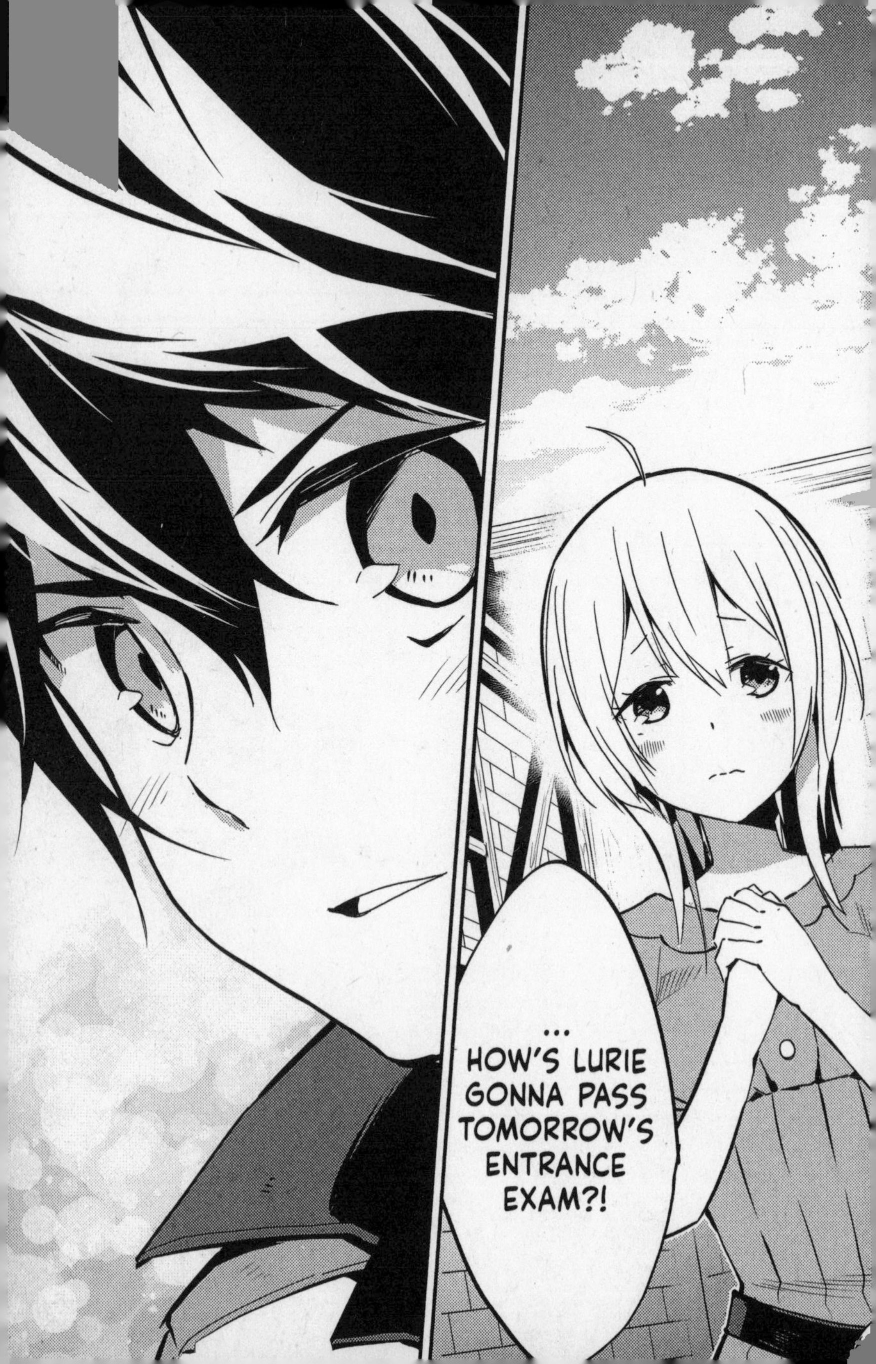
...
HOW'S LURIE GONNA PASS TOMORROW'S ENTRANCE EXAM?!

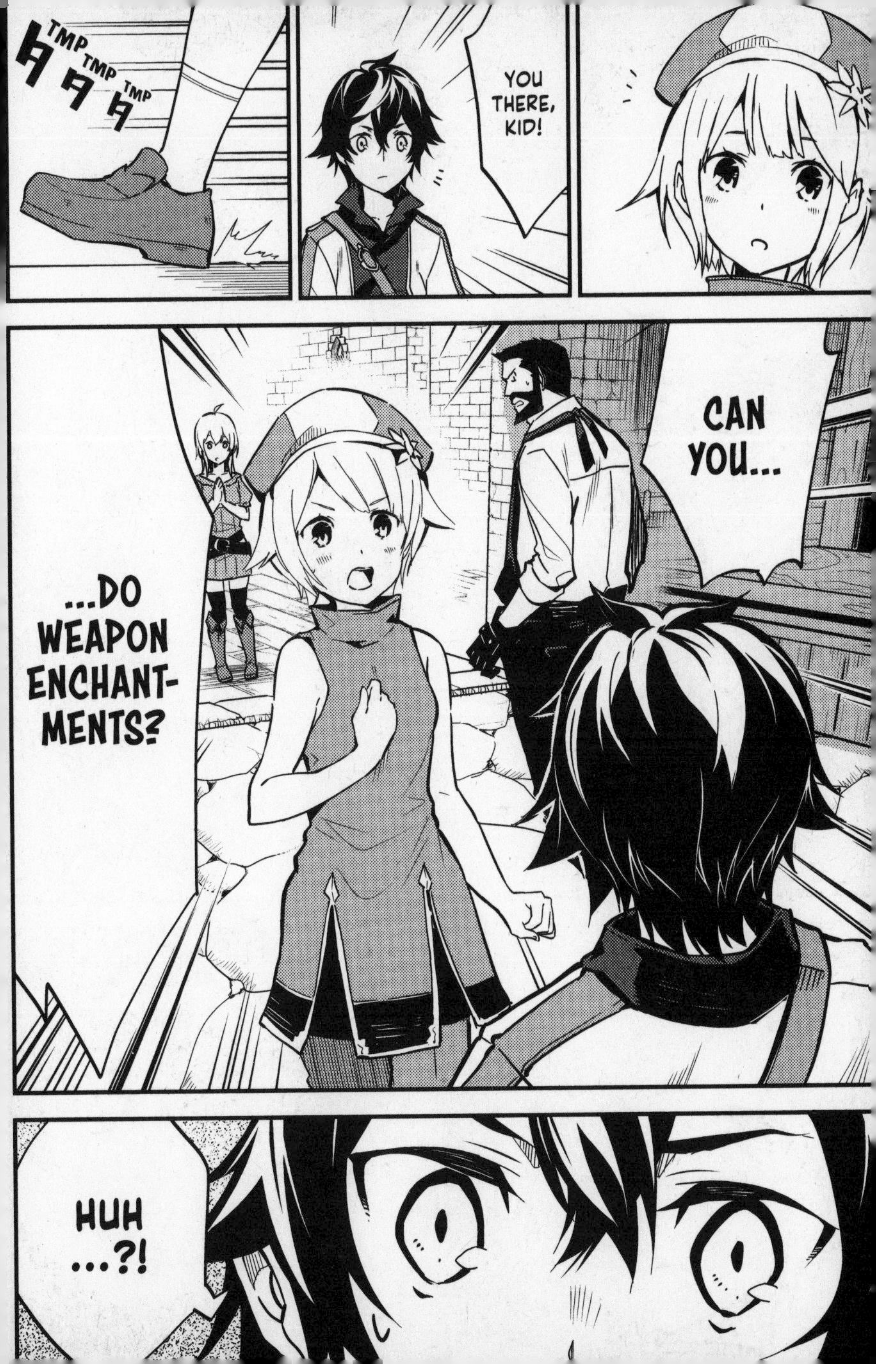
YOU THERE, KID!
TMP TMP TMP
タタタ
CAN YOU...
...DO WEAPON ENCHANT-MENTS?
HUH ...?!

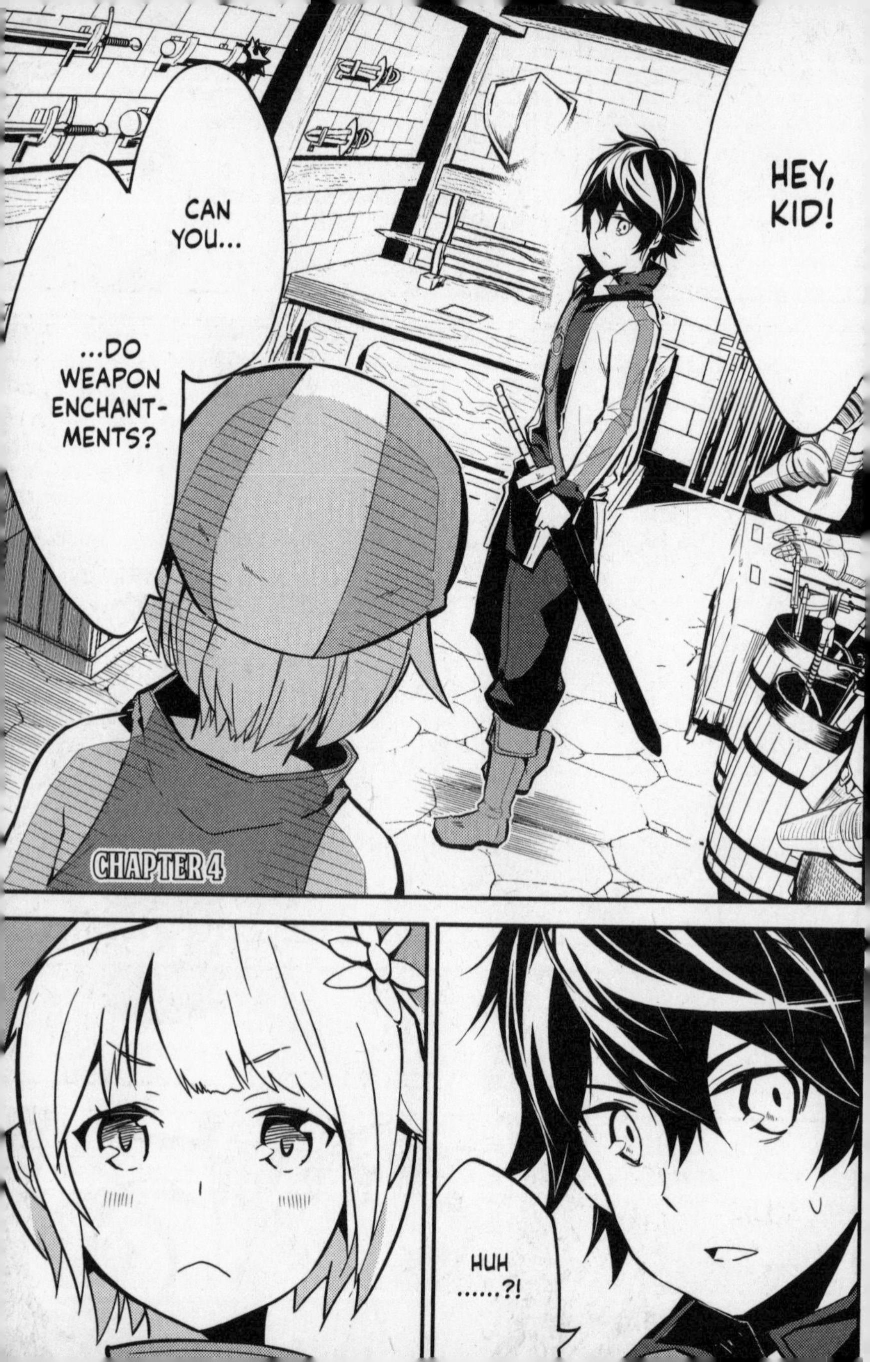
HEY, KID!
CAN YOU...
...DO WEAPON ENCHANT-MENTS?
CHAPTER 4
HUH ......?!

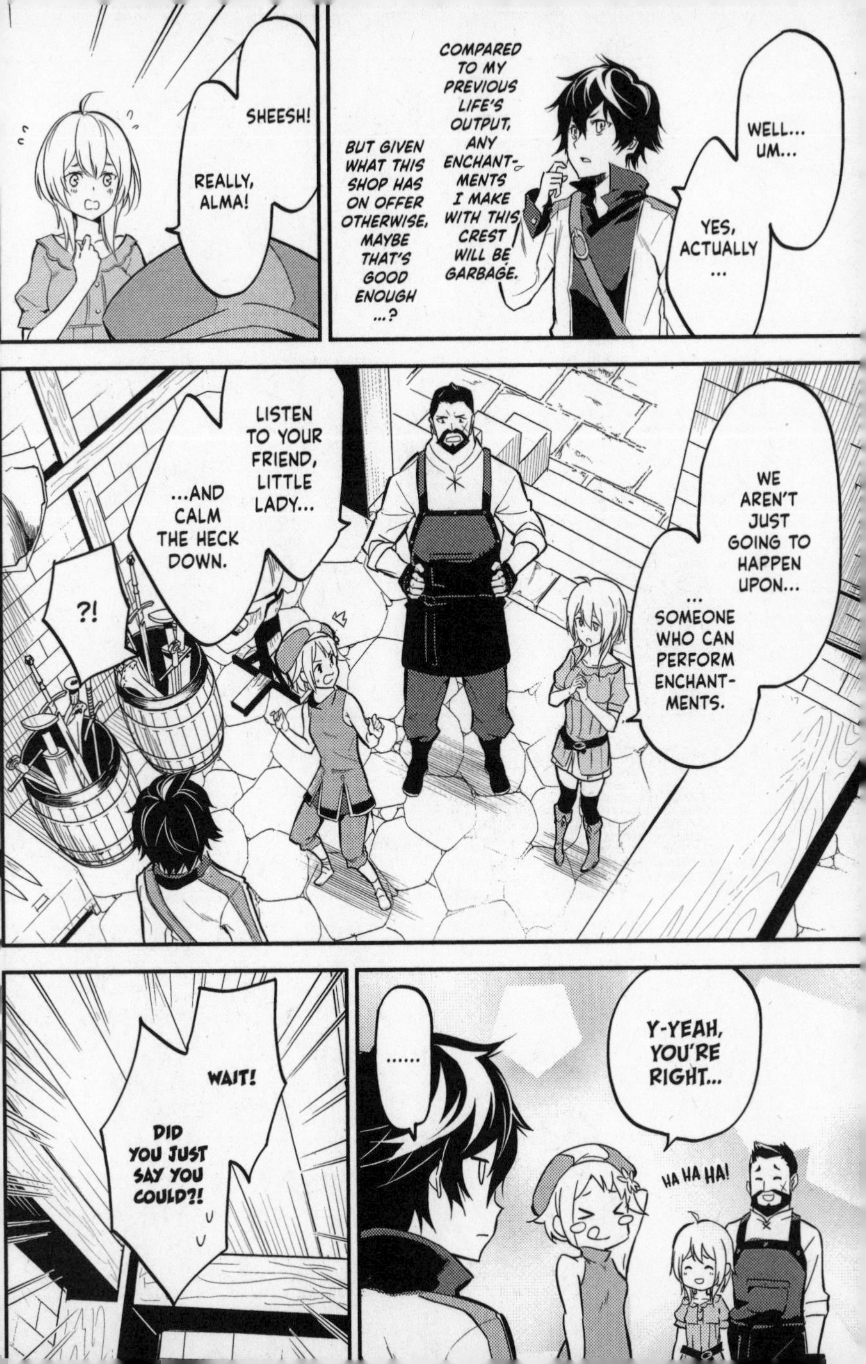
WELL... UM...
YES, ACTUALLY ...
COMPARED TO MY PREVIOUS LIFE'S OUTPUT, ANY ENCHANTMENTS I MAKE WITH THIS CREST WILL BE GARBAGE.
BUT GIVEN WHAT THIS SHOP HAS ON OFFER OTHERWISE, MAYBE THAT'S GOOD ENOUGH ...?
SHEESH!
REALLY, ALMA!
WE AREN'T JUST GOING TO HAPPEN UPON...
...SOMEONE WHO CAN PERFORM ENCHANTMENTS.
LISTEN TO YOUR FRIEND, LITTLE LADY...
...AND CALM THE HECK DOWN.
?!
Y-YEAH, YOU'RE RIGHT...
HA HA HA!
......
WAIT!
DID YOU JUST SAY YOU COULD?!

CHAPTER 4 ◆ The Strongest Sage Gets Tested

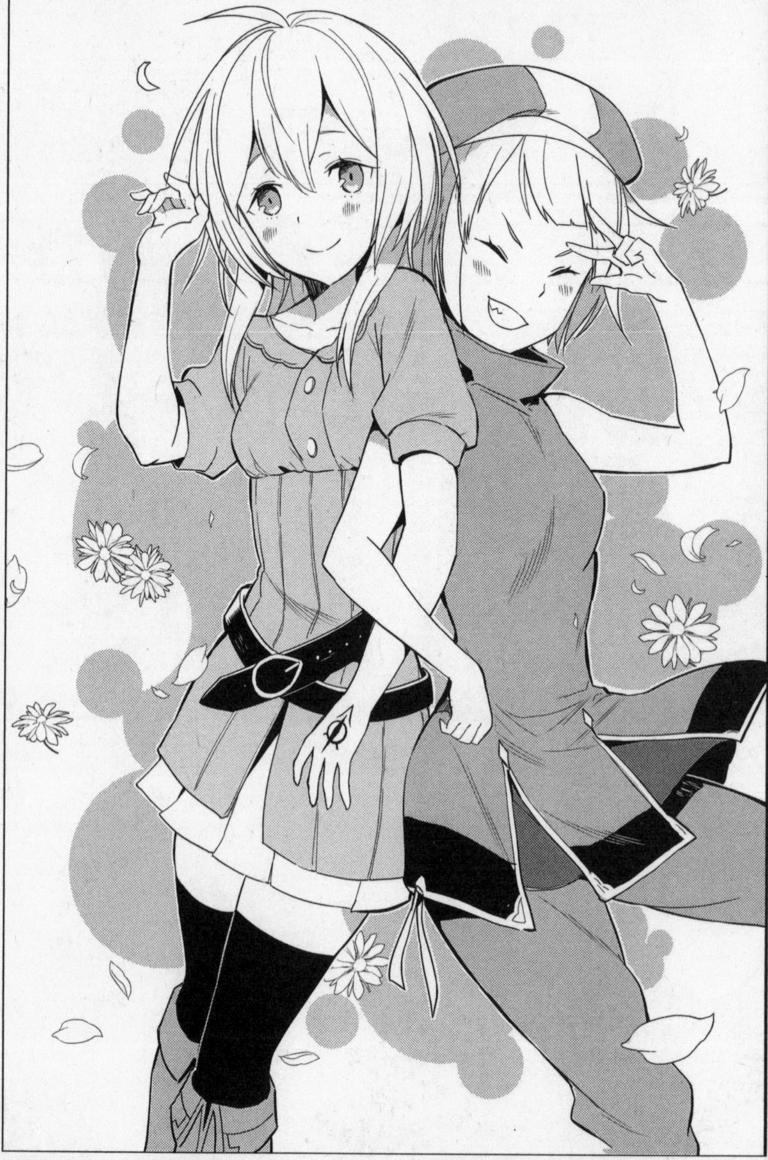

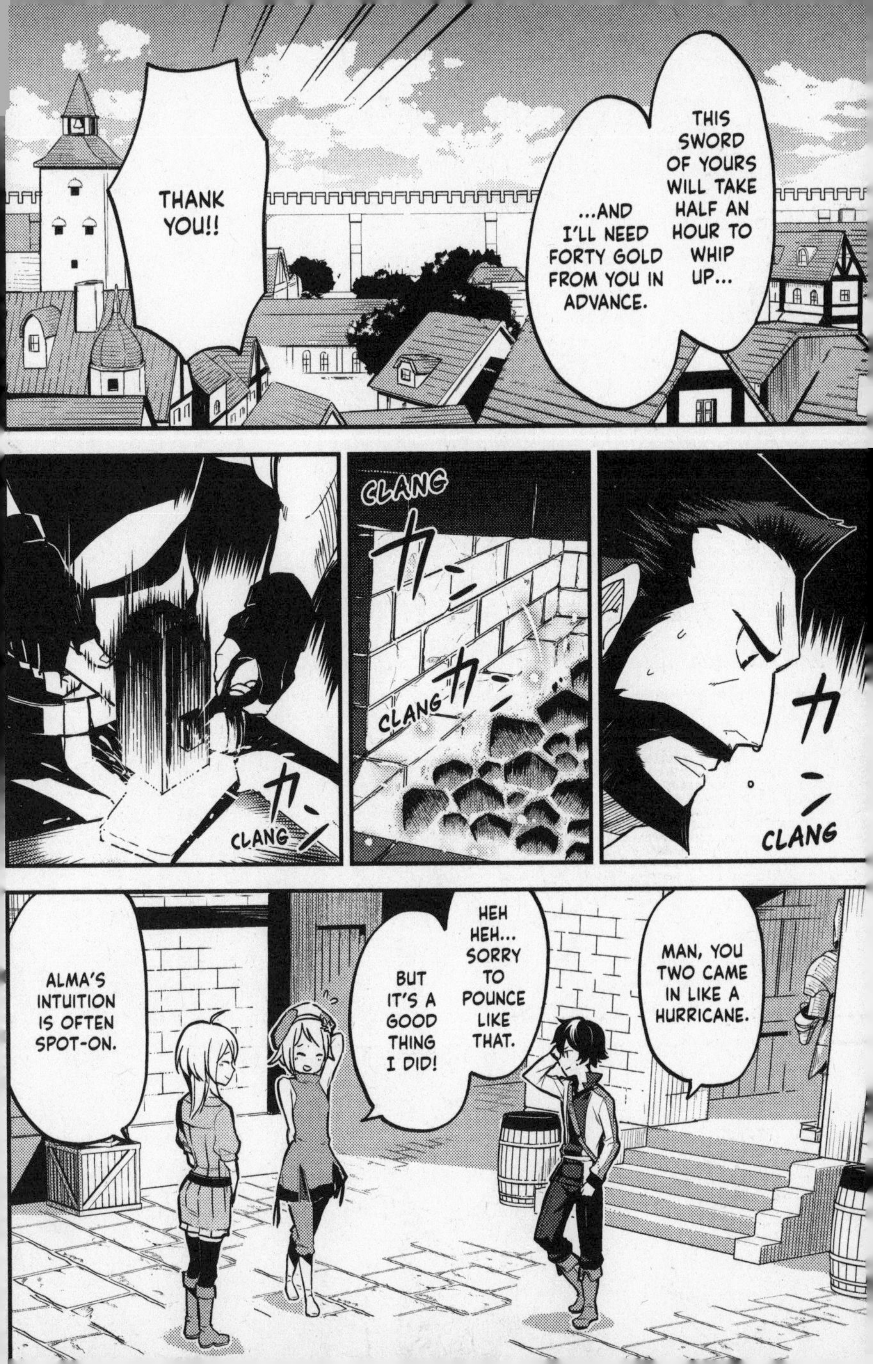
THIS SWORD OF YOURS WILL TAKE HALF AN HOUR TO WHIP UP...
...AND I'LL NEED FORTY GOLD FROM YOU IN ADVANCE.
THANK YOU!!
CLANG
CLANG
CLANG
CLANG
MAN, YOU TWO CAME IN LIKE A HURRICANE.
HEH HEH... SORRY TO POUNCE LIKE THAT.
BUT IT'S A GOOD THING I DID!
ALMA'S INTUITION IS OFTEN SPOT-ON.

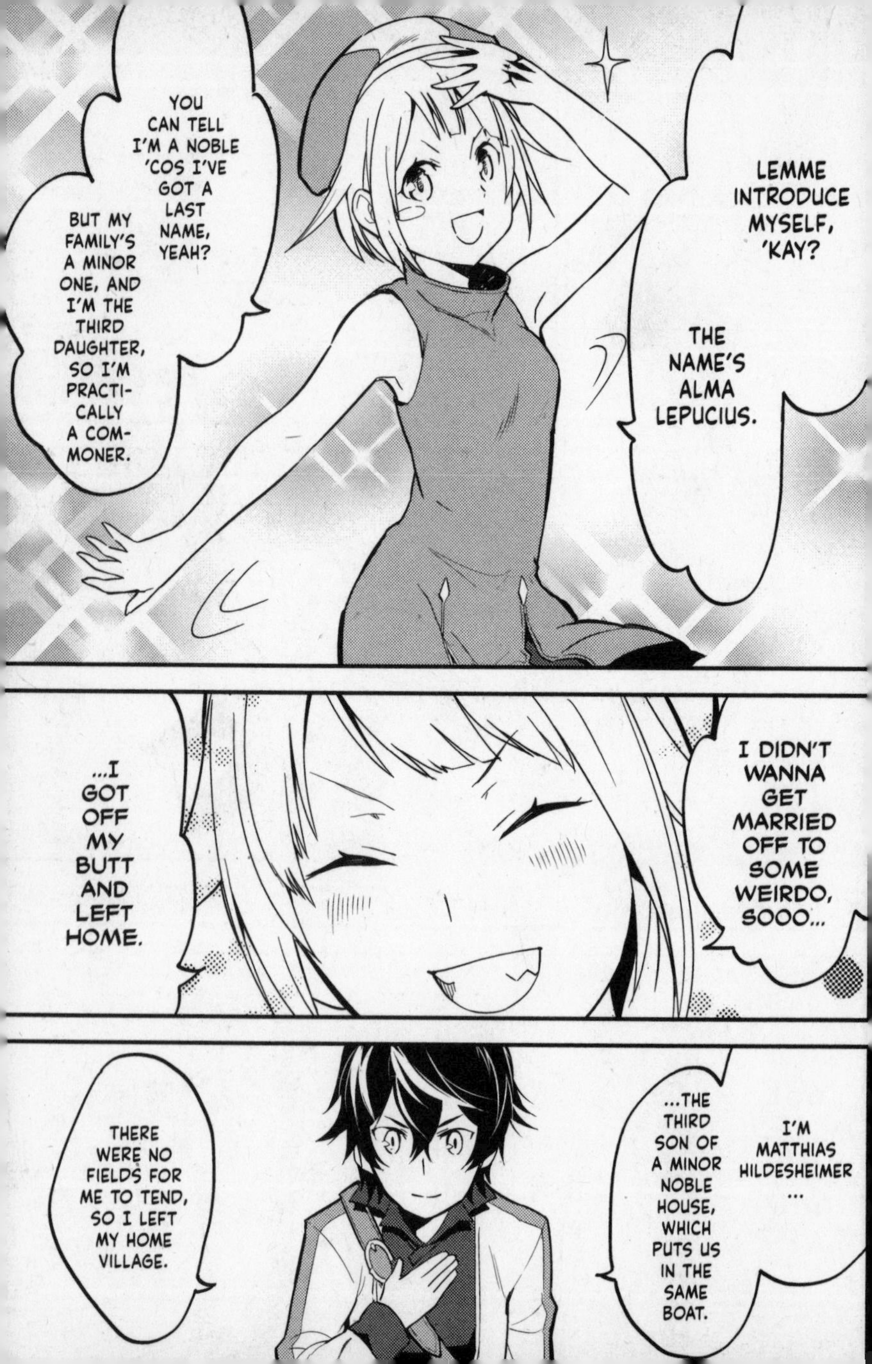

LEMME INTRODUCE MYSELF, 'KAY?
THE NAME'S ALMA LEPUCIUS.
YOU CAN TELL I'M A NOBLE 'COS I'VE GOT A LAST NAME, YEAH?
BUT MY FAMILY'S A MINOR ONE, AND I'M THE THIRD DAUGHTER, SO I'M PRACTICALLY A COMMONER.
I DIDN'T WANNA GET MARRIED OFF TO SOME WEIRDO, SOOO...
...I GOT OFF MY BUTT AND LEFT HOME.
I'M MATTHIAS HILDESHEIMER...
...THE THIRD SON OF A MINOR NOBLE HOUSE, WHICH PUTS US IN THE SAME BOAT.
THERE WERE NO FIELDS FOR ME TO TEND, SO I LEFT MY HOME VILLAGE.

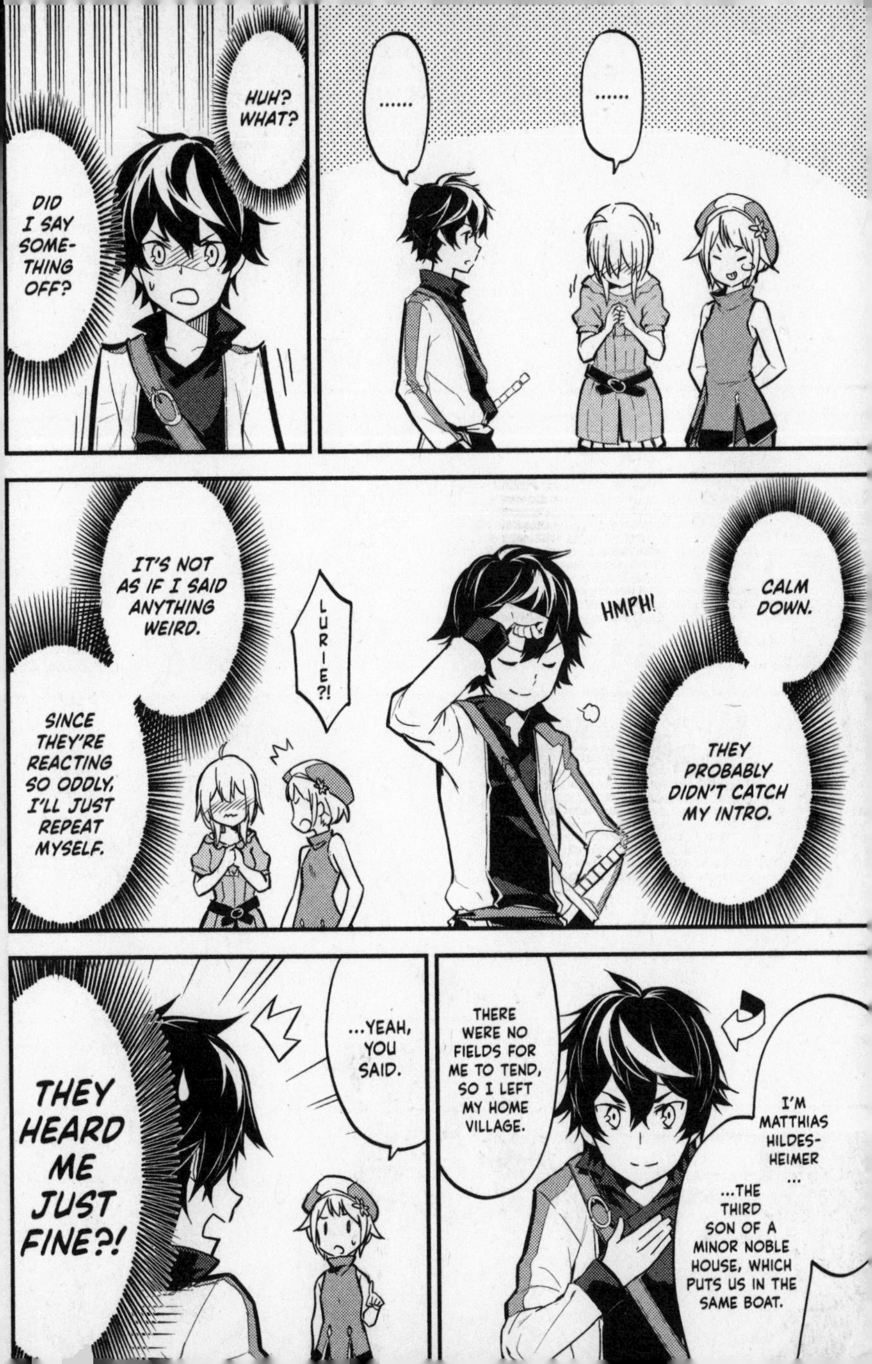
......
......
HUH? WHAT?
DID I SAY SOMETHING OFF?
CALM DOWN.
THEY PROBABLY DIDN'T CATCH MY INTRO.
HMPH!
LURIE?!
IT'S NOT AS IF I SAID ANYTHING WEIRD.
SINCE THEY'RE REACTING SO ODDLY, I'LL JUST REPEAT MYSELF.
I'M MATTHIAS HILDESHEIMER...
...THE THIRD SON OF A MINOR NOBLE HOUSE, WHICH PUTS US IN THE SAME BOAT.
THERE WERE NO FIELDS FOR ME TO TEND, SO I LEFT MY HOME VILLAGE.
...YEAH, YOU SAID.
THEY HEARD ME JUST FINE?!

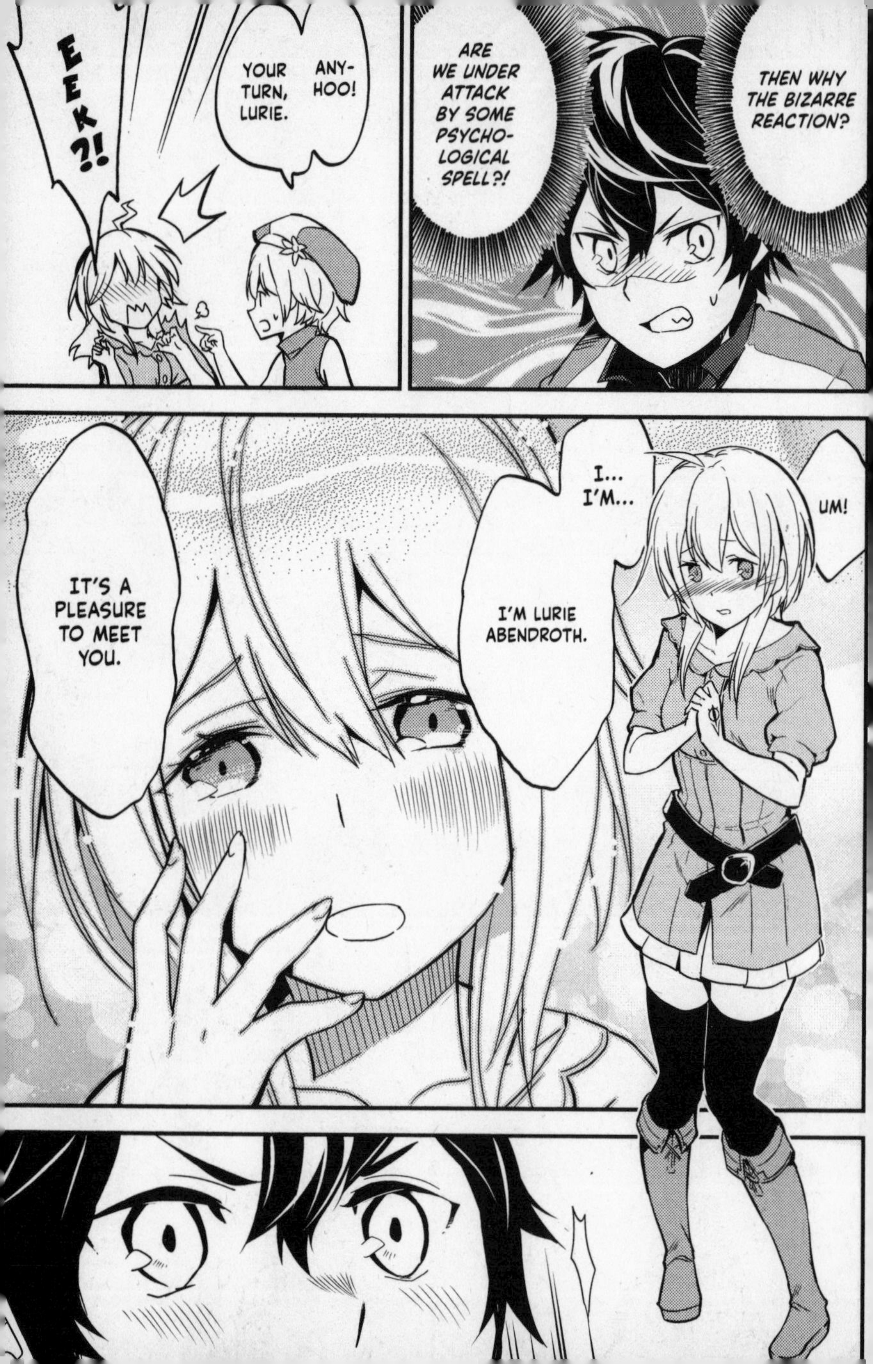
THEN WHY THE BIZARRE REACTION?
ARE WE UNDER ATTACK BY SOME PSYCHOLOGICAL SPELL?!
ANY-HOO! YOUR TURN, LURIE.
EEK?!
UM!
I... I'M...
I'M LURIE ABENDROTH.
IT'S A PLEASURE TO MEET YOU.

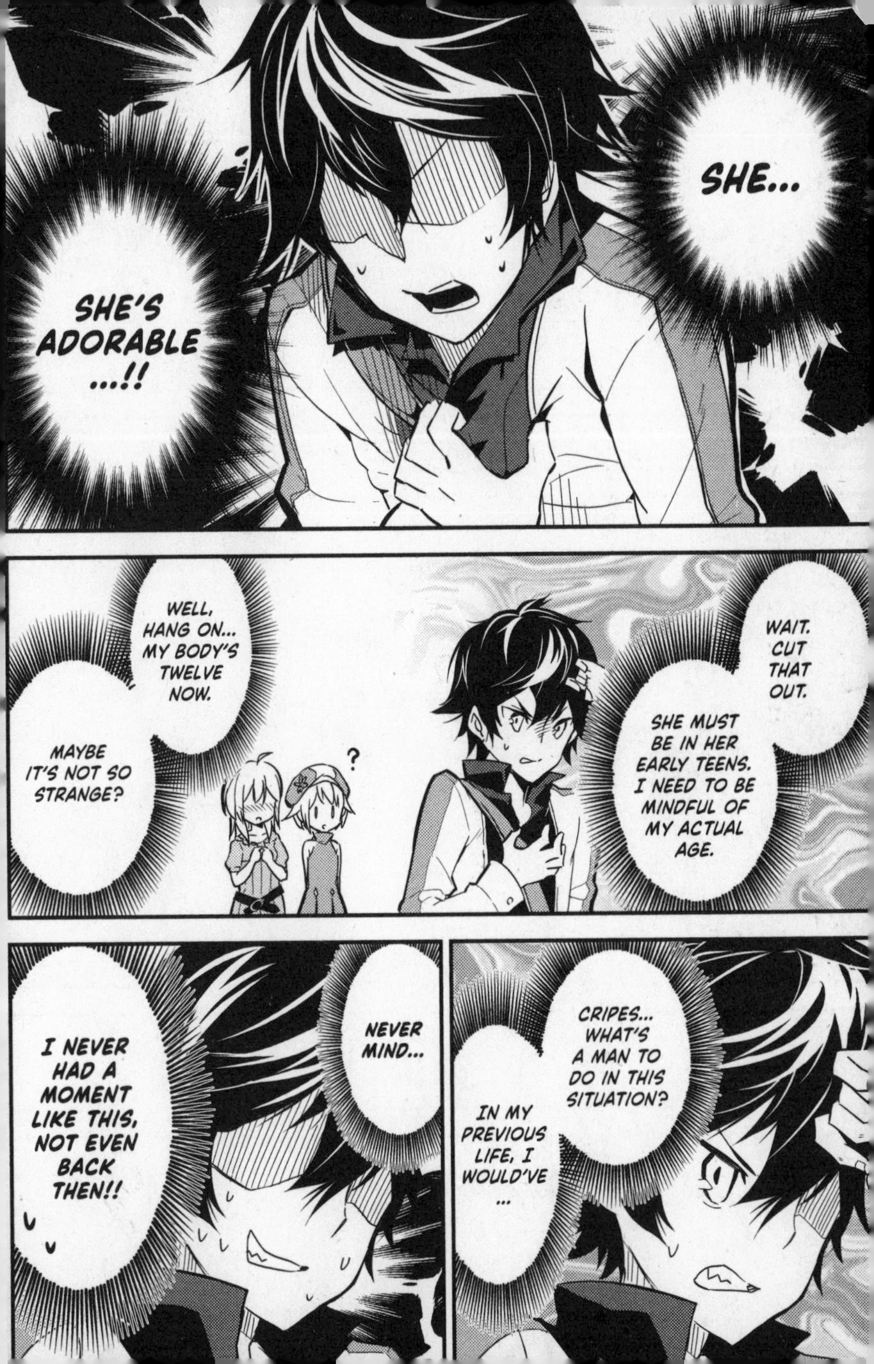
SHE...
SHE'S ADORABLE ...!!
WAIT. CUT THAT OUT.
SHE MUST BE IN HER EARLY TEENS. I NEED TO BE MINDFUL OF MY ACTUAL AGE.
?
WELL, HANG ON... MY BODY'S TWELVE NOW.
MAYBE IT'S NOT SO STRANGE?
CRIPES... WHAT'S A MAN TO DO IN THIS SITUATION?
IN MY PREVIOUS LIFE, I WOULD'VE ...
NEVER MIND...
I NEVER HAD A MOMENT LIKE THIS, NOT EVEN BACK THEN!!

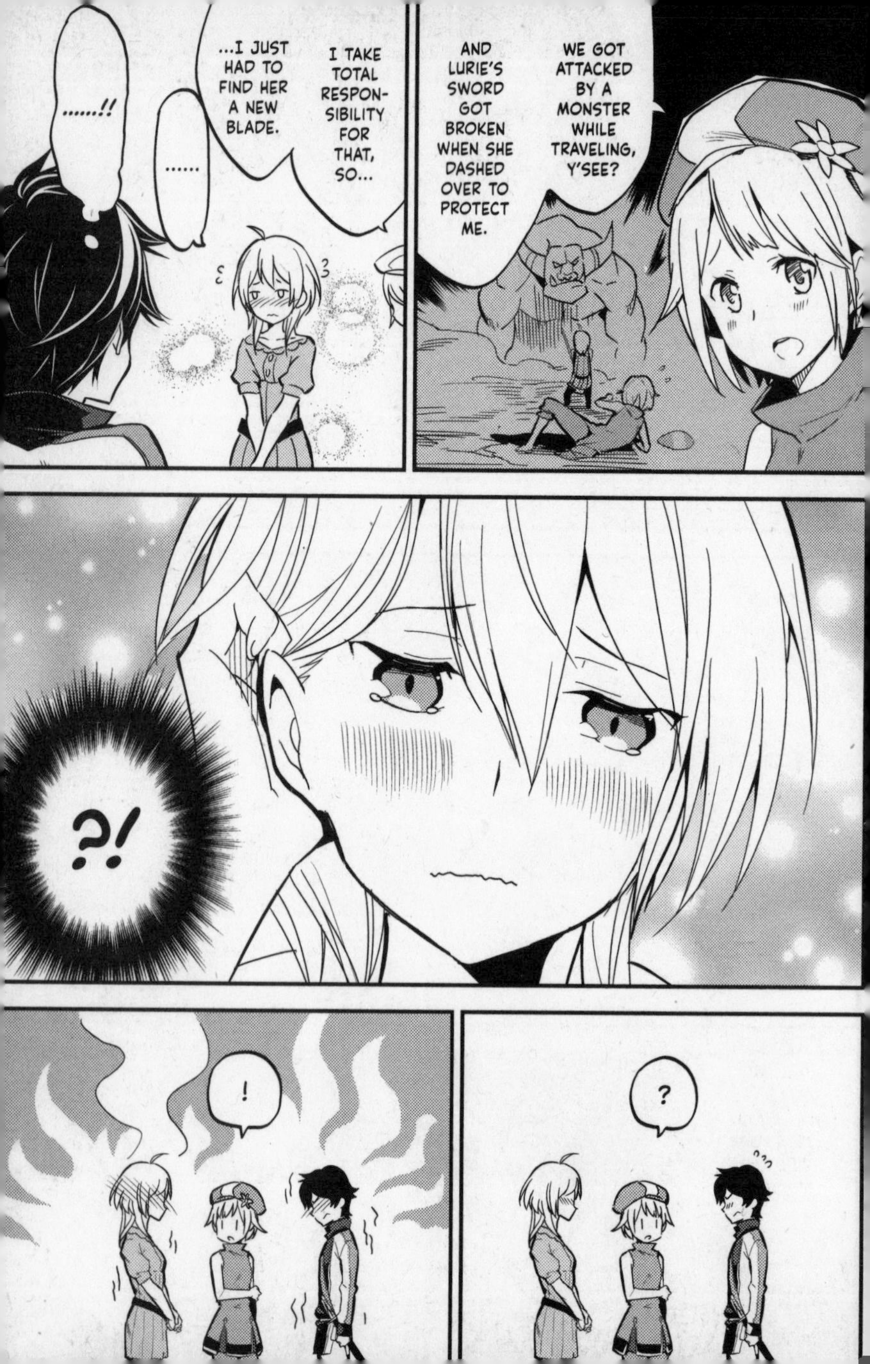
WE GOT ATTACKED BY A MONSTER WHILE TRAVELING, Y'SEE?
AND LURIE'S SWORD GOT BROKEN WHEN SHE DASHED OVER TO PROTECT ME.
I TAKE TOTAL RESPON-SIBILITY FOR THAT, SO...
...I JUST HAD TO FIND HER A NEW BLADE.
......
......!!
?!
?
!

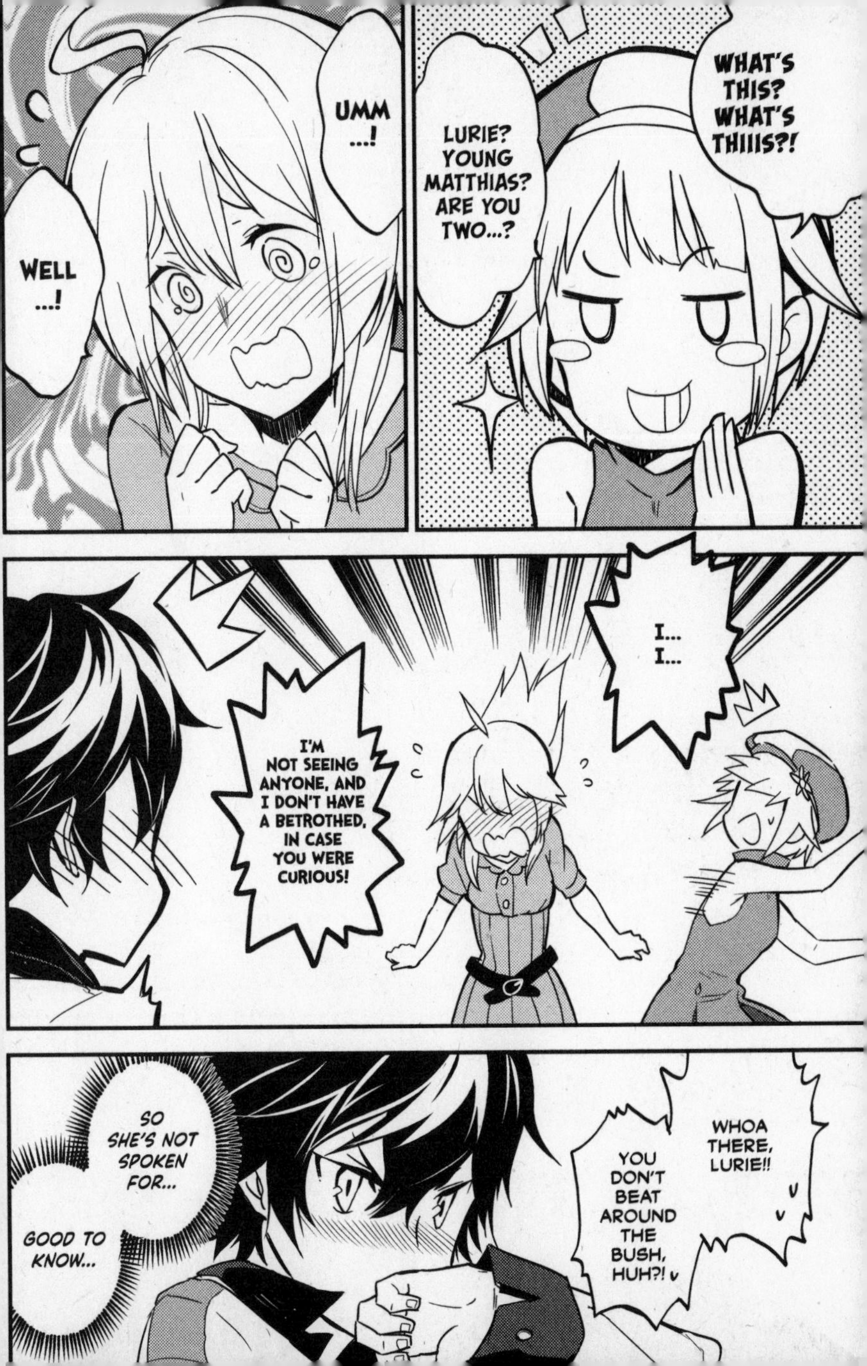
WHAT'S THIS? WHAT'S THIIIS?!
LURIE? YOUNG MATTHIAS? ARE YOU TWO...?
UMM ...!
WELL ...!
I... I...
I'M NOT SEEING ANYONE, AND I DON'T HAVE A BETROTHED, IN CASE YOU WERE CURIOUS!
WHOA THERE, LURIE!!
YOU DON'T BEAT AROUND THE BUSH, HUH?!
SO SHE'S NOT SPOKEN FOR...
GOOD TO KNOW...

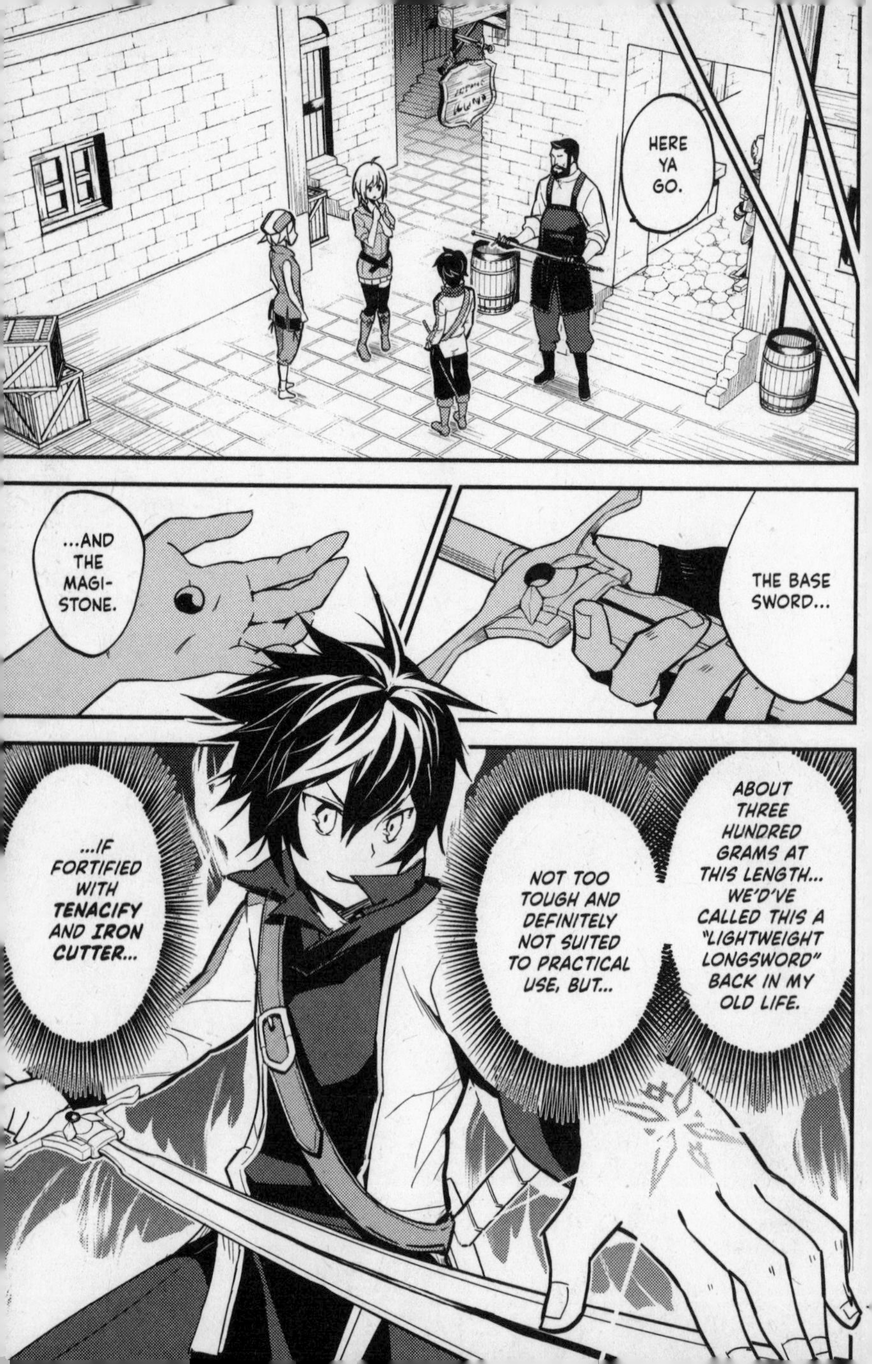
HERE YA GO.
THE BASE SWORD...
...AND THE MAGI-STONE.
ABOUT THREE HUNDRED GRAMS AT THIS LENGTH... WE'D'VE CALLED THIS A "LIGHTWEIGHT LONGSWORD" BACK IN MY OLD LIFE.
NOT TOO TOUGH AND DEFINITELY NOT SUITED TO PRACTICAL USE, BUT...
...IF FORTIFIED WITH TENACIFY AND IRON CUTTER...

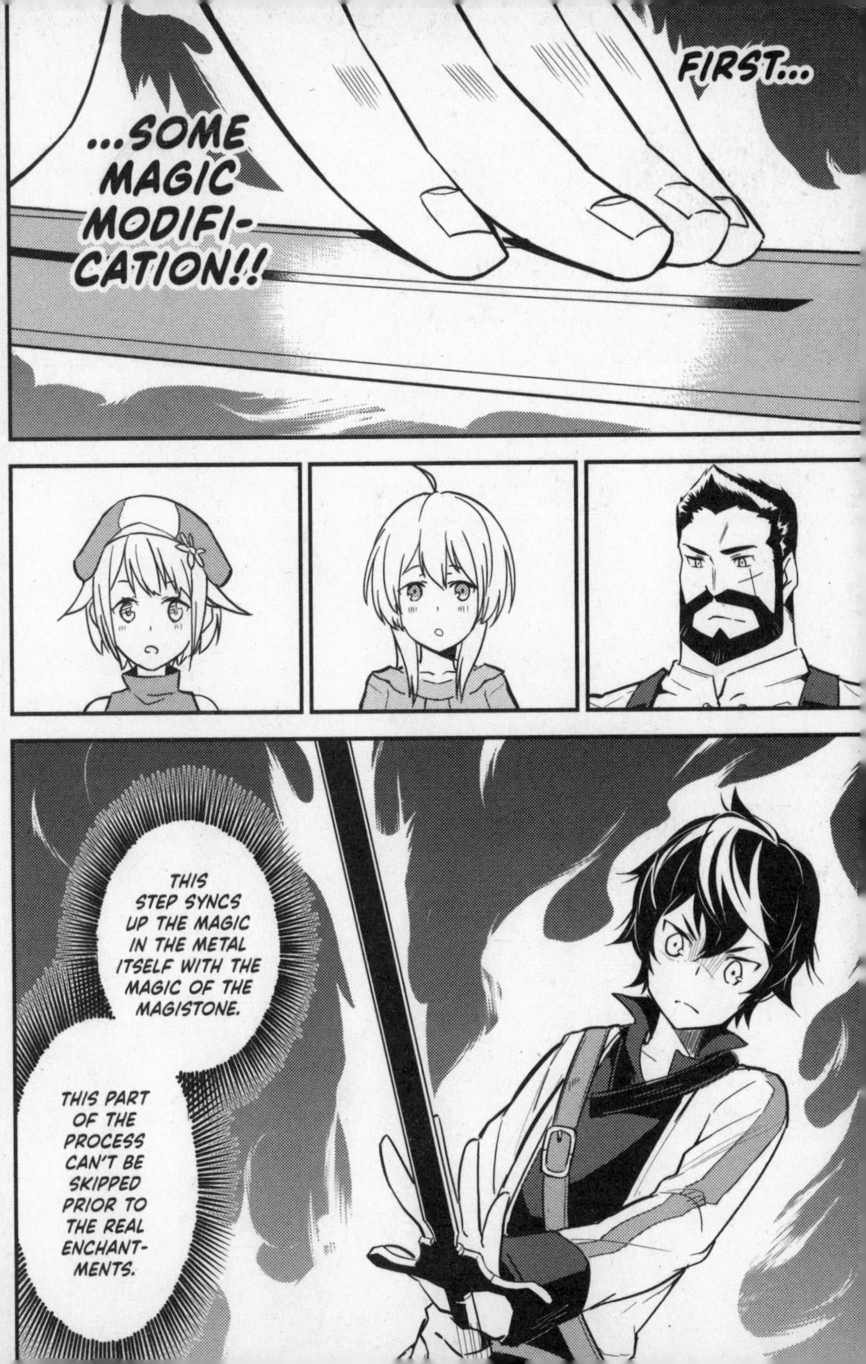
FIRST...
...SOME MAGIC MODIFI-CATION!!
THIS STEP SYNCS UP THE MAGIC IN THE METAL ITSELF WITH THE MAGIC OF THE MAGISTONE.
THIS PART OF THE PROCESS CAN'T BE SKIPPED PRIOR TO THE REAL ENCHANT-MENTS.

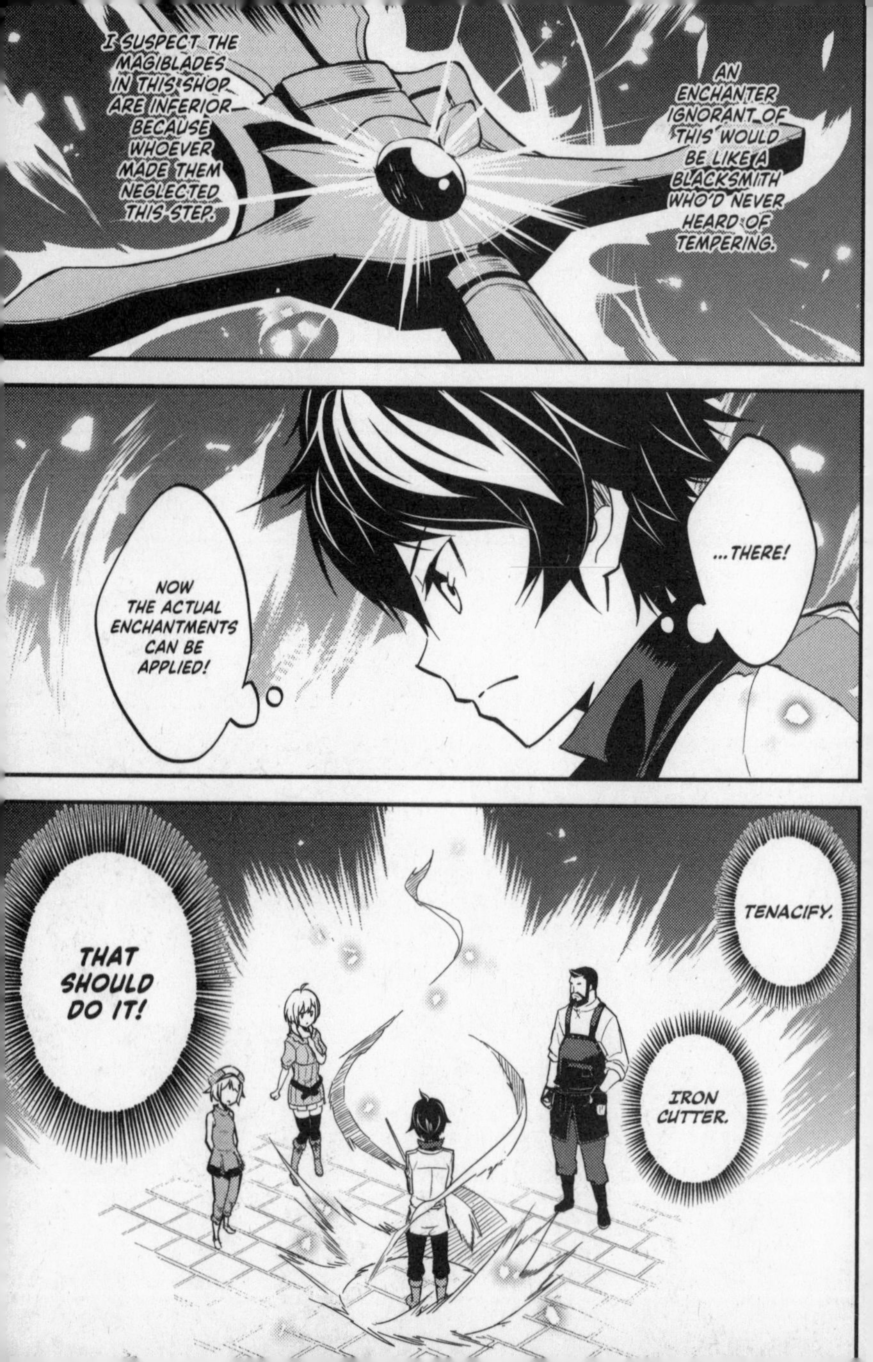
AN ENCHANTER IGNORANT OF THIS WOULD BE LIKE A BLACKSMITH WHO'D NEVER HEARD OF TEMPERING.
I SUSPECT THE MAGIBLADES IN THIS SHOP ARE INFERIOR BECAUSE WHOEVER MADE THEM NEGLECTED THIS STEP.
...THERE!
NOW THE ACTUAL ENCHANTMENTS CAN BE APPLIED!
TENACIFY.
IRON CUTTER.
THAT SHOULD DO IT!

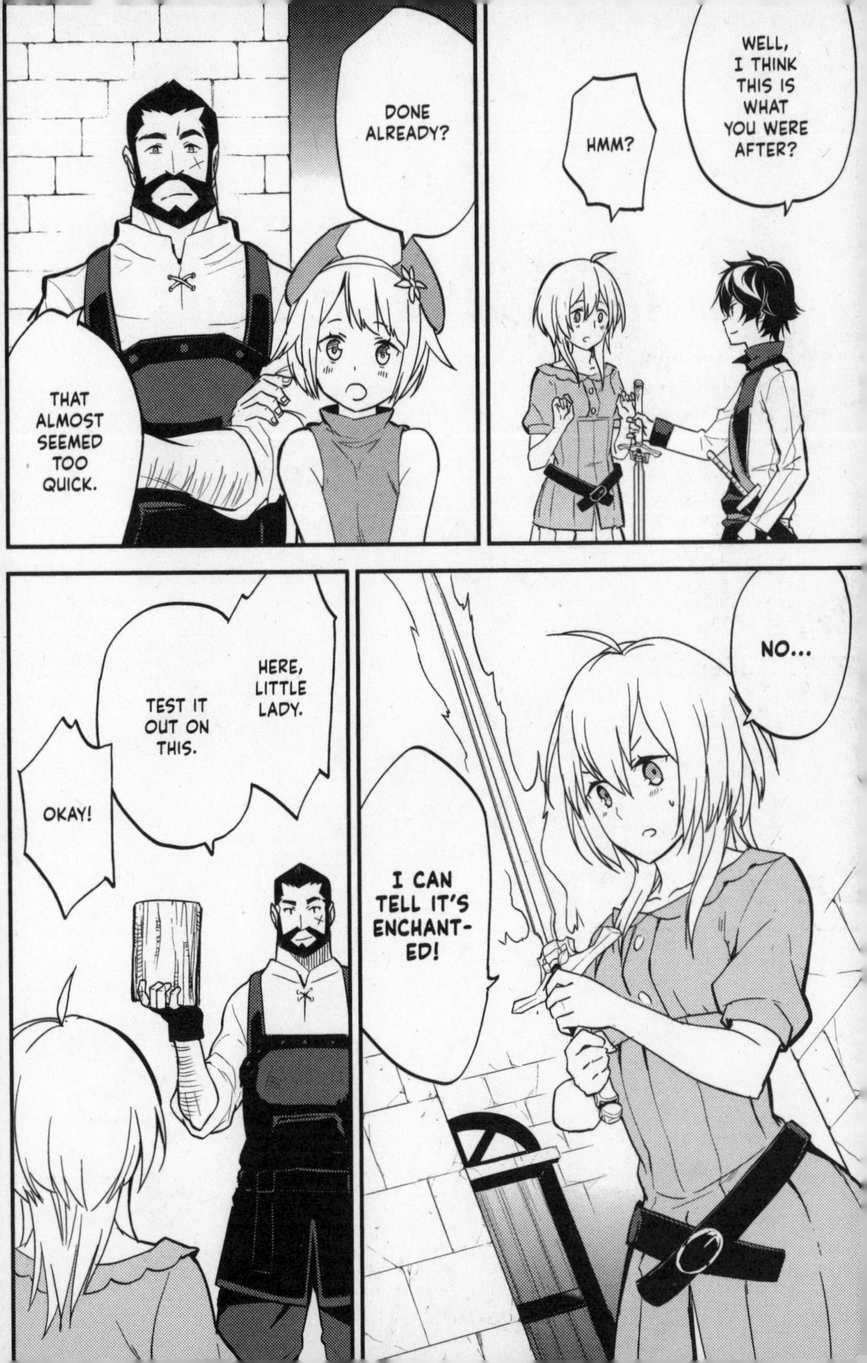
WELL, I THINK THIS IS WHAT YOU WERE AFTER?
HMM?
DONE ALREADY?
THAT ALMOST SEEMED TOO QUICK.
NO...
I CAN TELL IT'S ENCHANT-ED!
HERE, LITTLE LADY.
TEST IT OUT ON THIS.
OKAY!

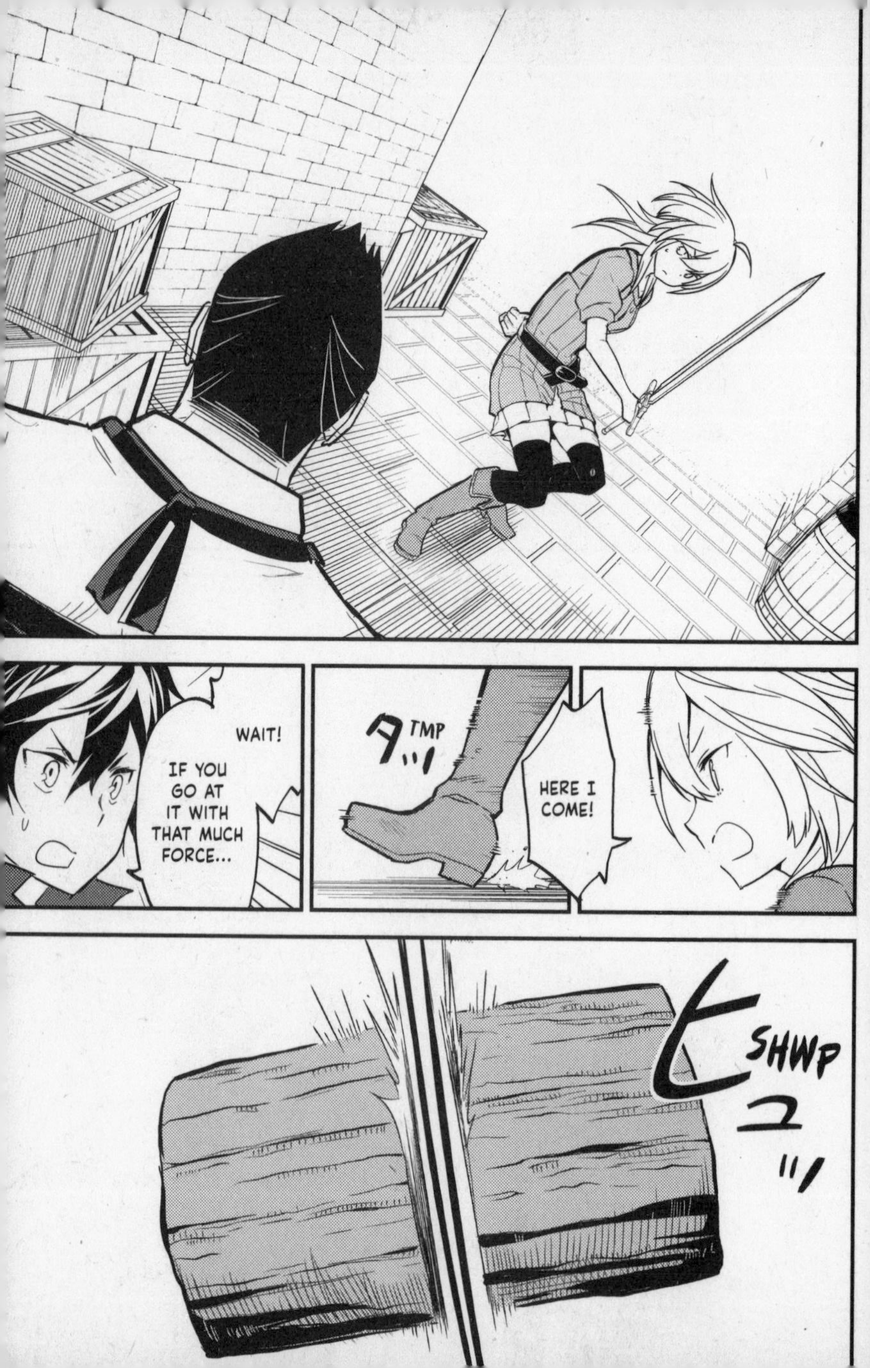
HERE I COME!
タッ
TMP
WAIT!
IF YOU GO AT IT WITH THAT MUCH FORCE...
ヒュッ
SHWP

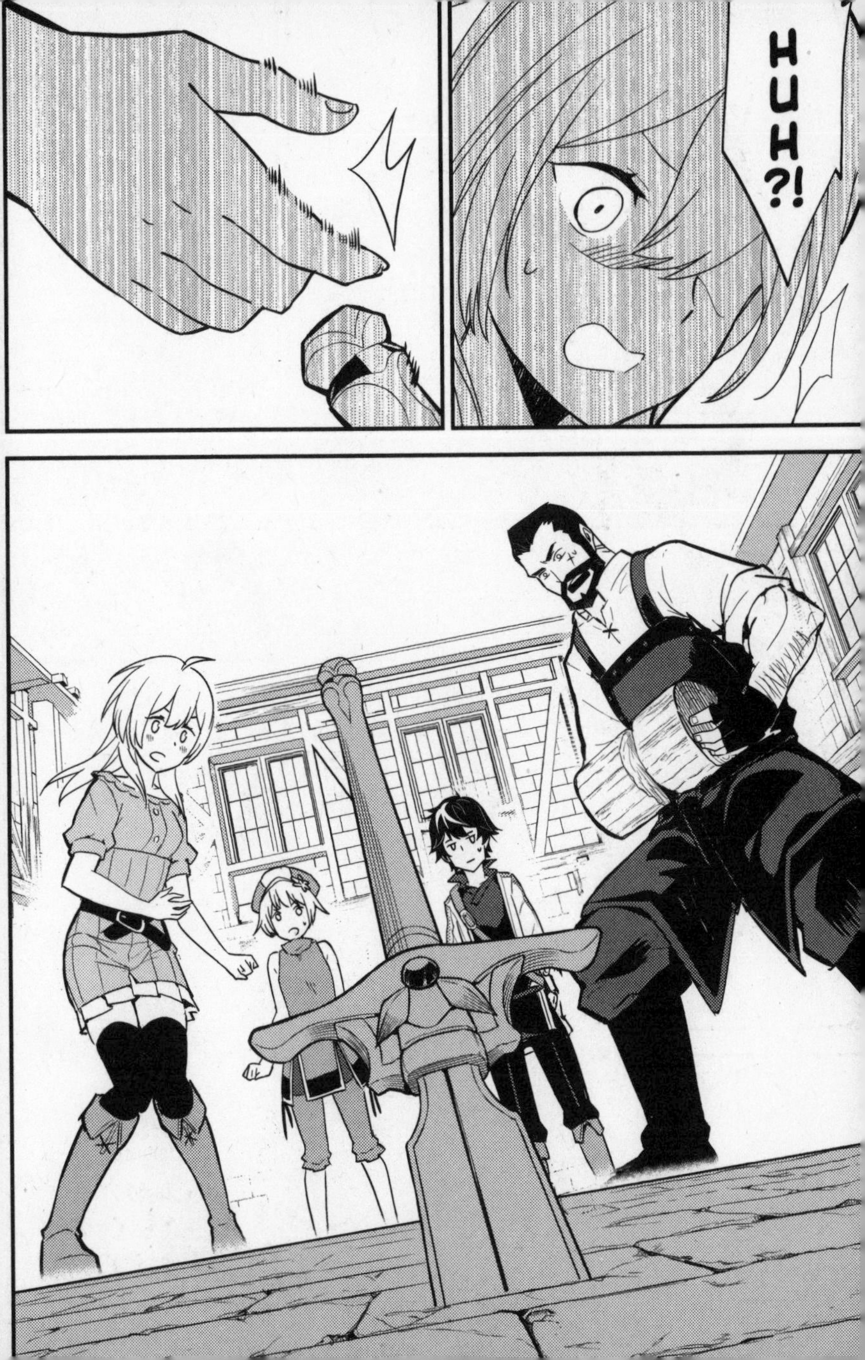
HUH?!

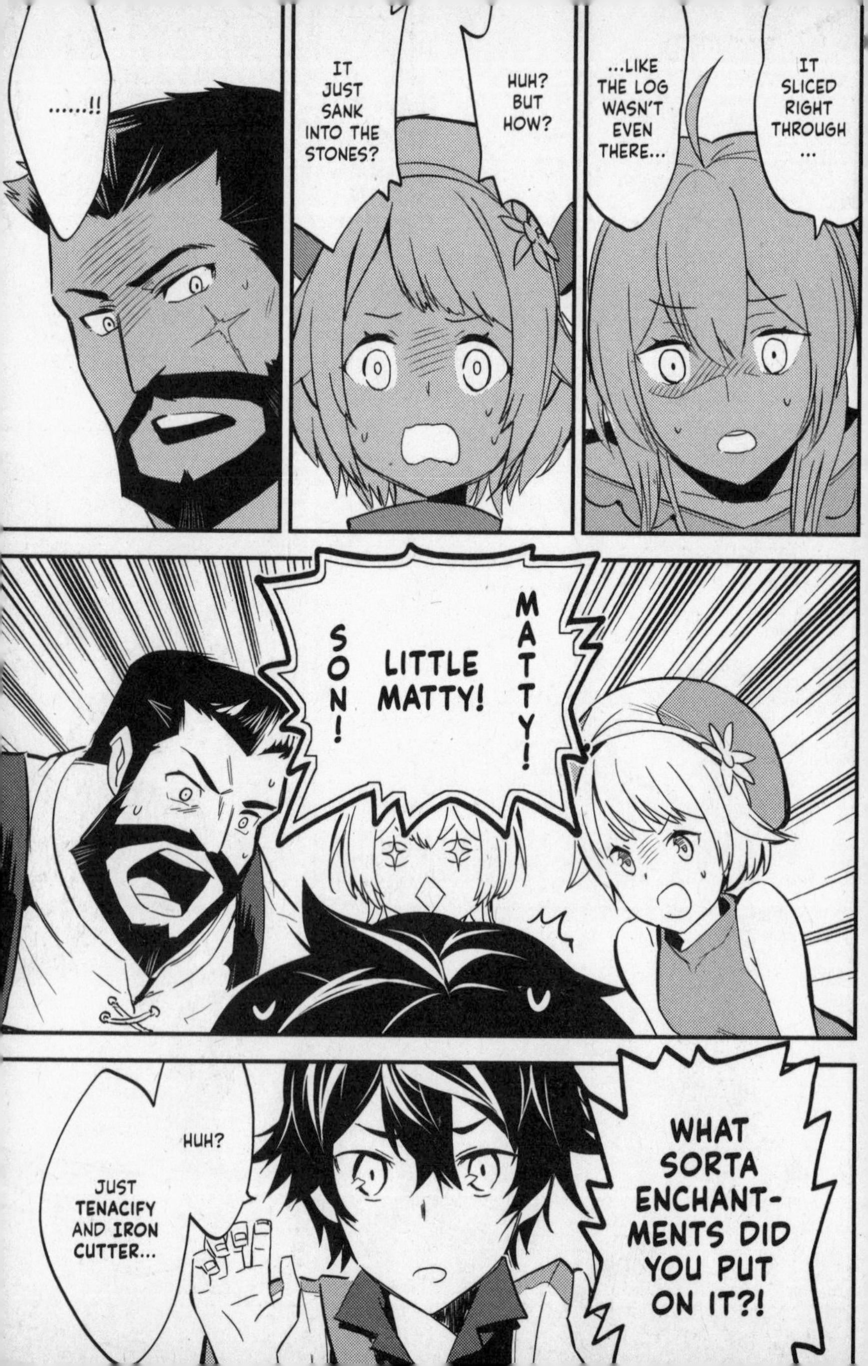
IT SLICED RIGHT THROUGH ...
...LIKE THE LOG WASN'T EVEN THERE...
HUH? BUT HOW?
IT JUST SANK INTO THE STONES?
......!!
MATTY!
LITTLE MATTY!
SON!
WHAT SORTA ENCHANTMENTS DID YOU PUT ON IT?!
HUH?
JUST TENACIFY AND IRON CUTTER...

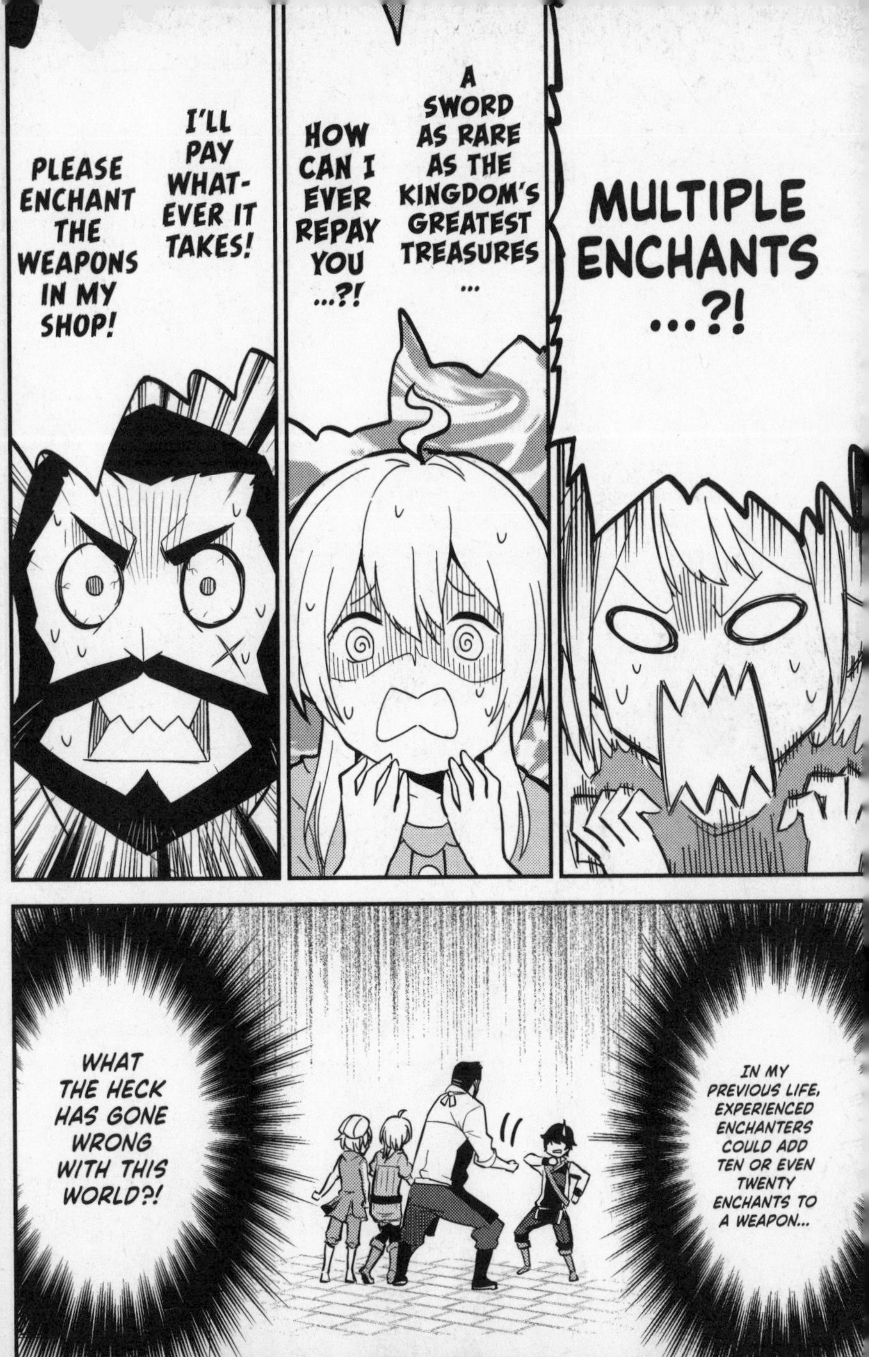
MULTIPLE ENCHANTS ...?!
A SWORD AS RARE AS THE KINGDOM'S GREATEST TREASURES ...
HOW CAN I EVER REPAY YOU ...?!
I'LL PAY WHAT-EVER IT TAKES!
PLEASE ENCHANT THE WEAPONS IN MY SHOP!
IN MY PREVIOUS LIFE, EXPERIENCED ENCHANTERS COULD ADD TEN OR EVEN TWENTY ENCHANTS TO A WEAPON...
WHAT THE HECK HAS GONE WRONG WITH THIS WORLD?!

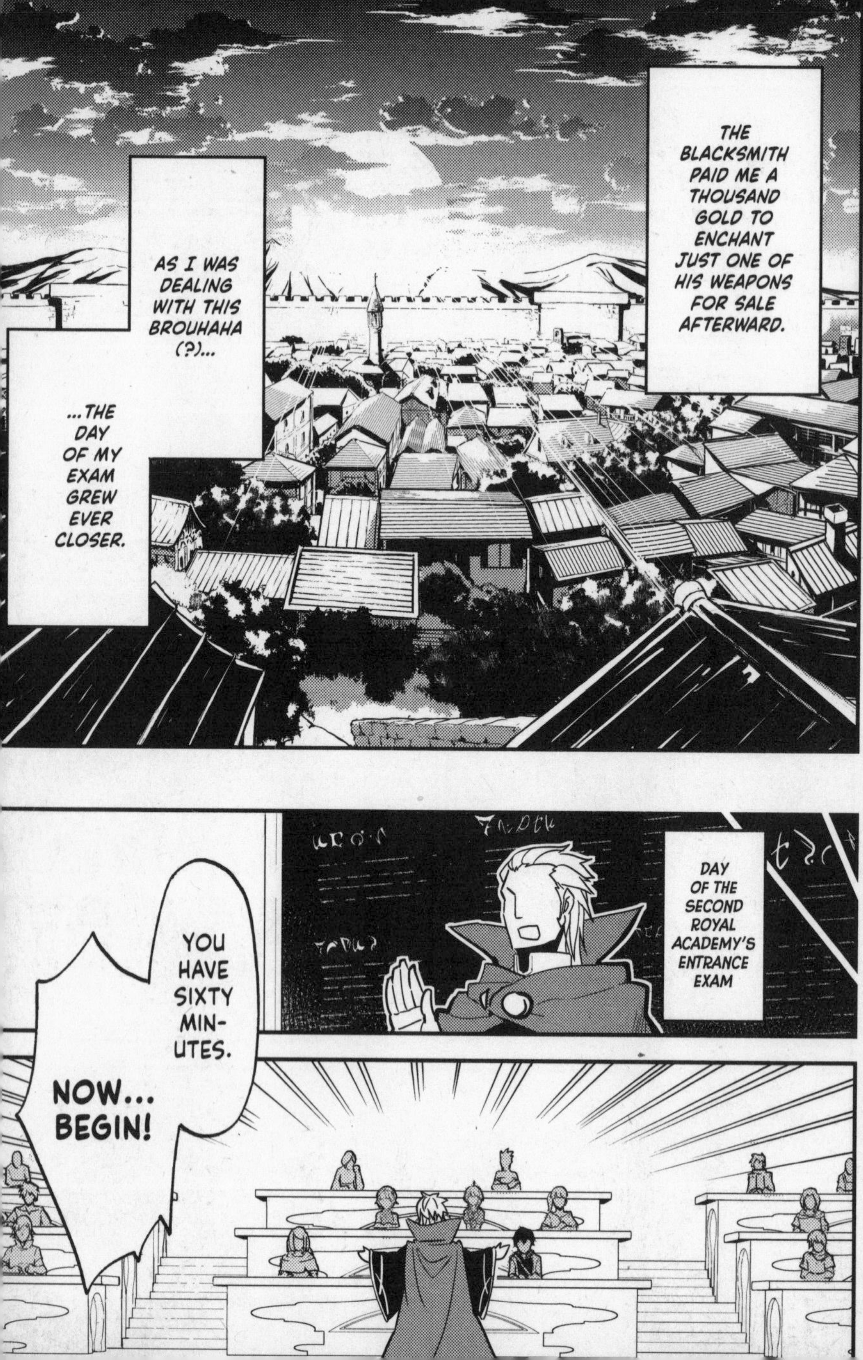
THE BLACKSMITH PAID ME A THOUSAND GOLD TO ENCHANT JUST ONE OF HIS WEAPONS FOR SALE AFTERWARD.
AS I WAS DEALING WITH THIS BROUHAHA (?)...
...THE DAY OF MY EXAM GREW EVER CLOSER.
DAY OF THE SECOND ROYAL ACADEMY'S ENTRANCE EXAM
YOU HAVE SIXTY MIN-UTES.
NOW... BEGIN!

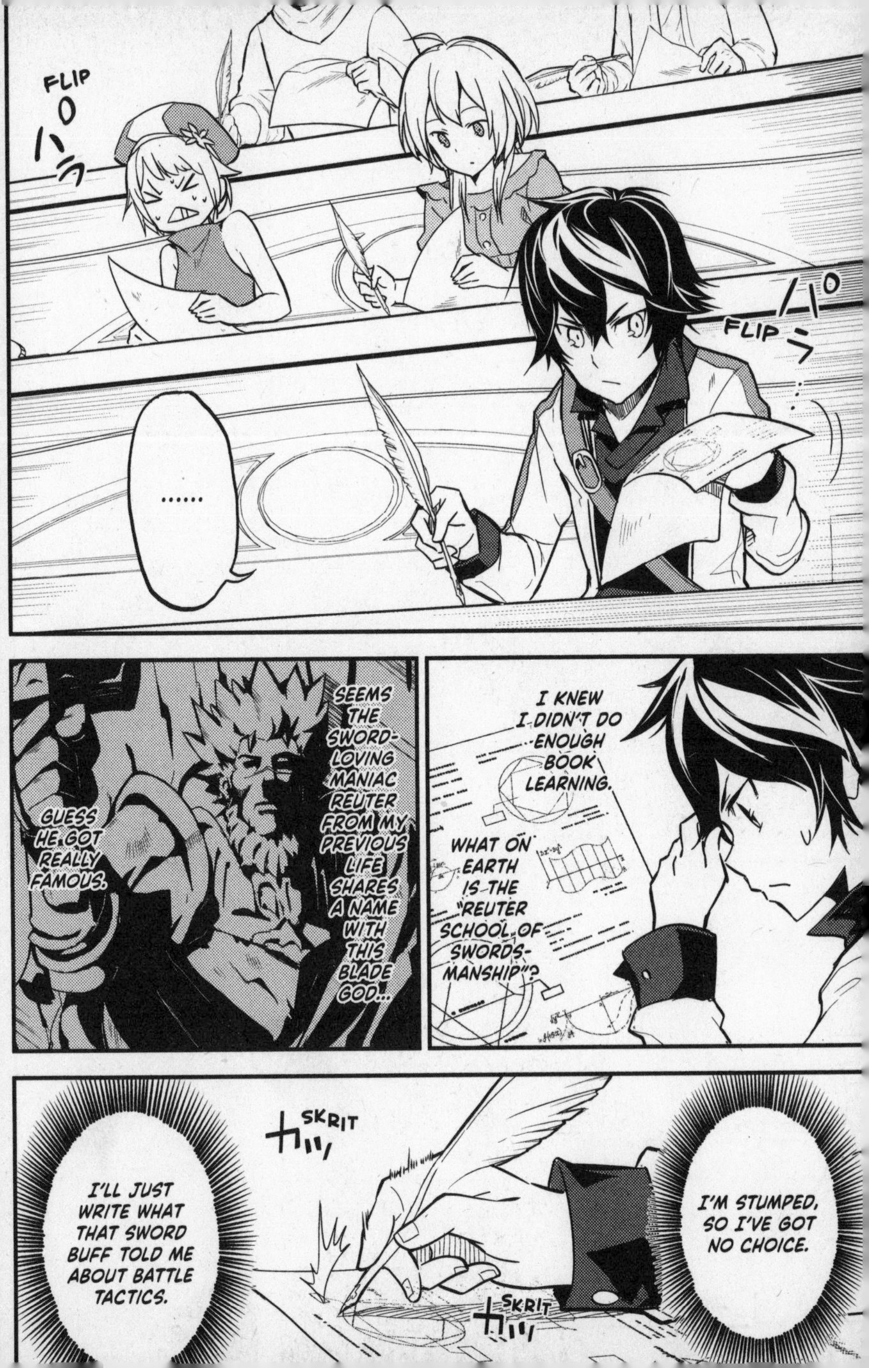
FLIP
ハラ
FLIP
パラ
......
I KNEW I DIDN'T DO ENOUGH BOOK LEARNING.
WHAT ON EARTH IS THE "REUTER SCHOOL OF SWORDS-MANSHIP"?
SEEMS THE SWORD-LOVING MANIAC REUTER FROM MY PREVIOUS LIFE SHARES A NAME WITH THIS BLADE GOD...
GUESS HE GOT REALLY FAMOUS.
I'M STUMPED, SO I'VE GOT NO CHOICE.
SKRIT
カリ
I'LL JUST WRITE WHAT THAT SWORD BUFF TOLD ME ABOUT BATTLE TACTICS.
SKRIT
カリ

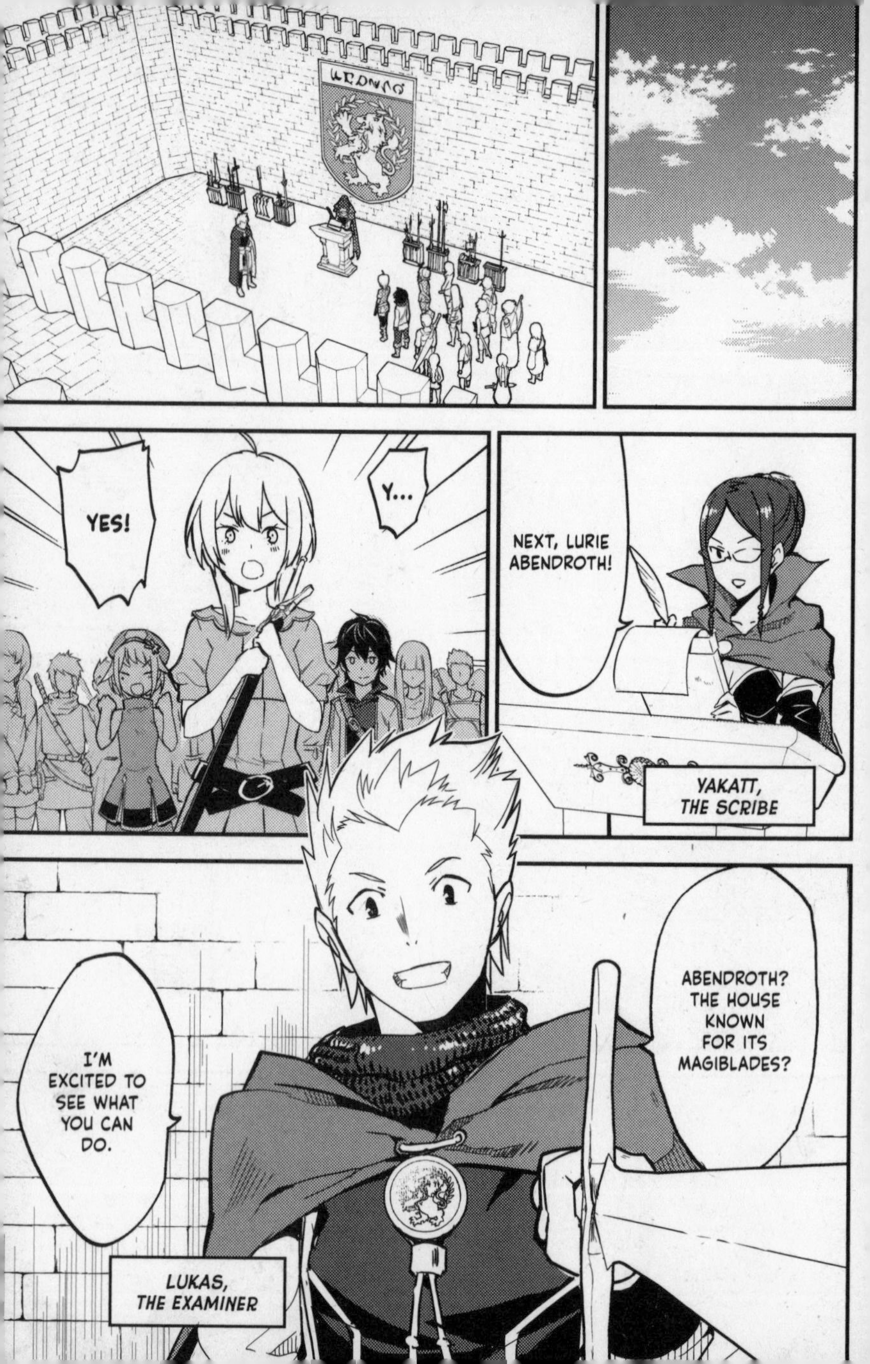
NEXT, LURIE ABENDROTH!
YAKATT, THE SCRIBE
Y...
YES!
ABENDROTH? THE HOUSE KNOWN FOR ITS MAGIBLADES?
I'M EXCITED TO SEE WHAT YOU CAN DO.
LUKAS, THE EXAMINER

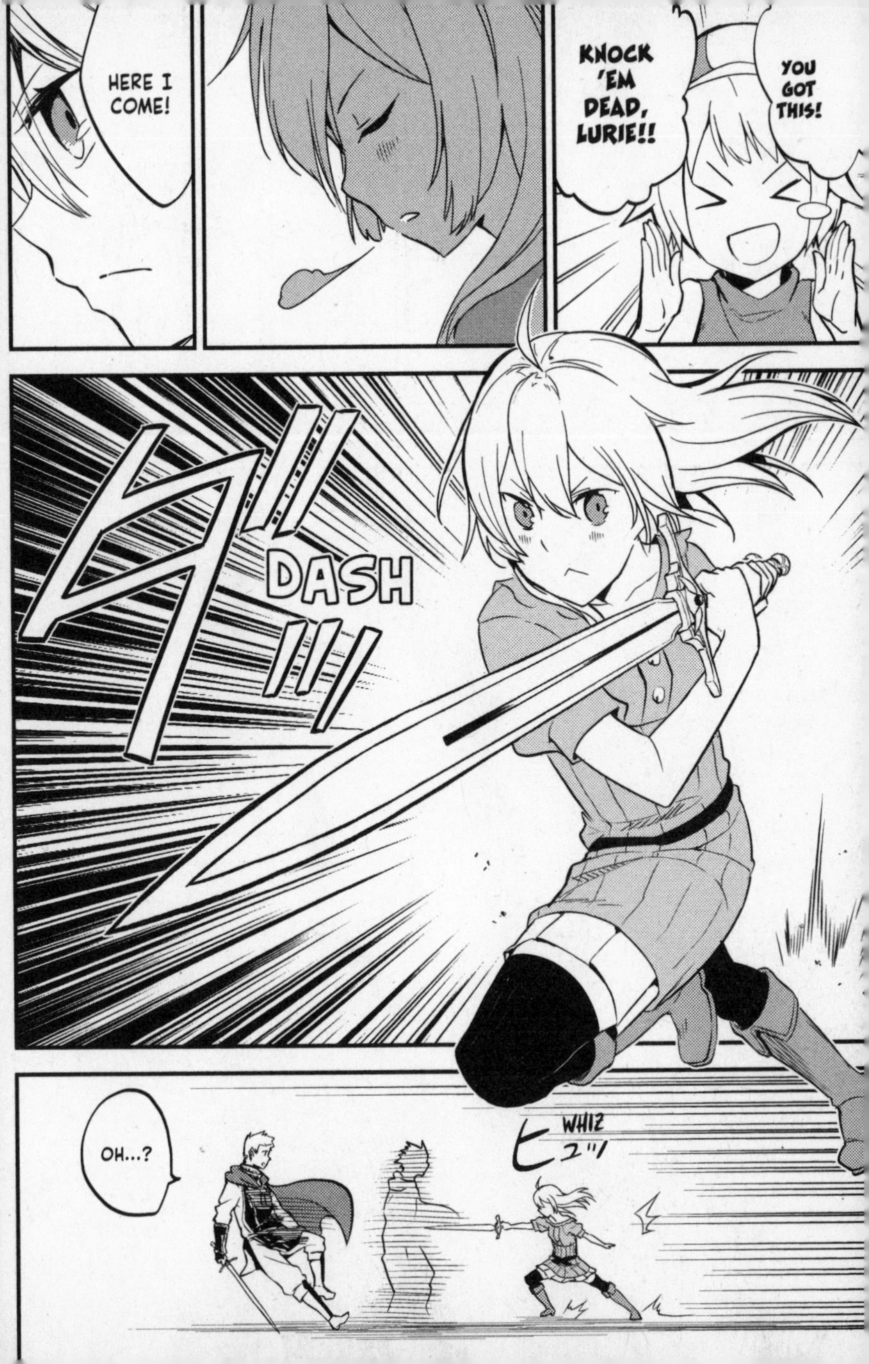
YOU GOT THIS!
KNOCK 'EM DEAD, LURIE!!
HERE I COME!
DASH
WHIZ
OH...?

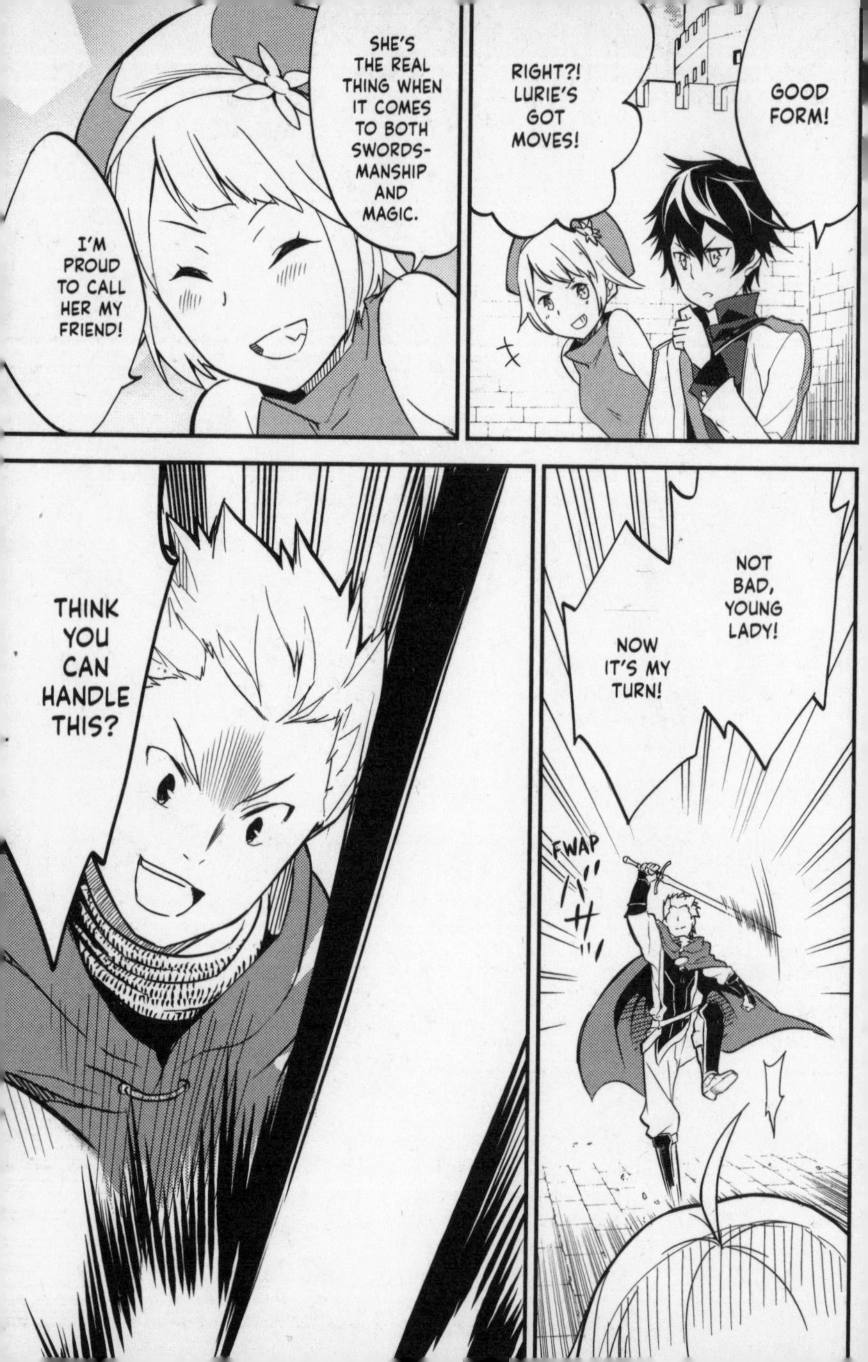
GOOD FORM!
RIGHT?! LURIE'S GOT MOVES!
SHE'S THE REAL THING WHEN IT COMES TO BOTH SWORDS-MANSHIP AND MAGIC.
I'M PROUD TO CALL HER MY FRIEND!
NOT BAD, YOUNG LADY!
NOW IT'S MY TURN!
FWAP
THINK YOU CAN HANDLE THIS?

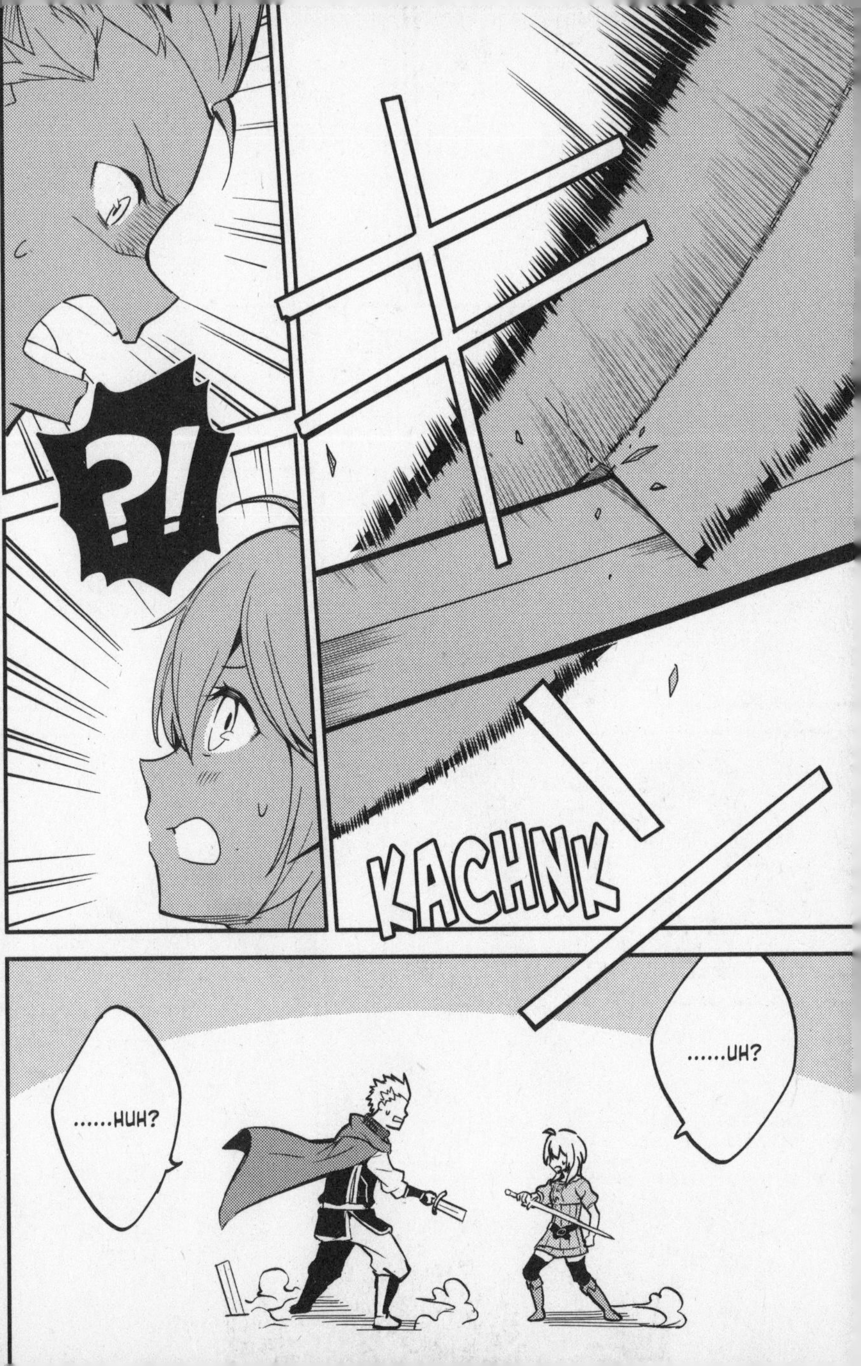
KACHNK
?!
......UH?
......HUH?

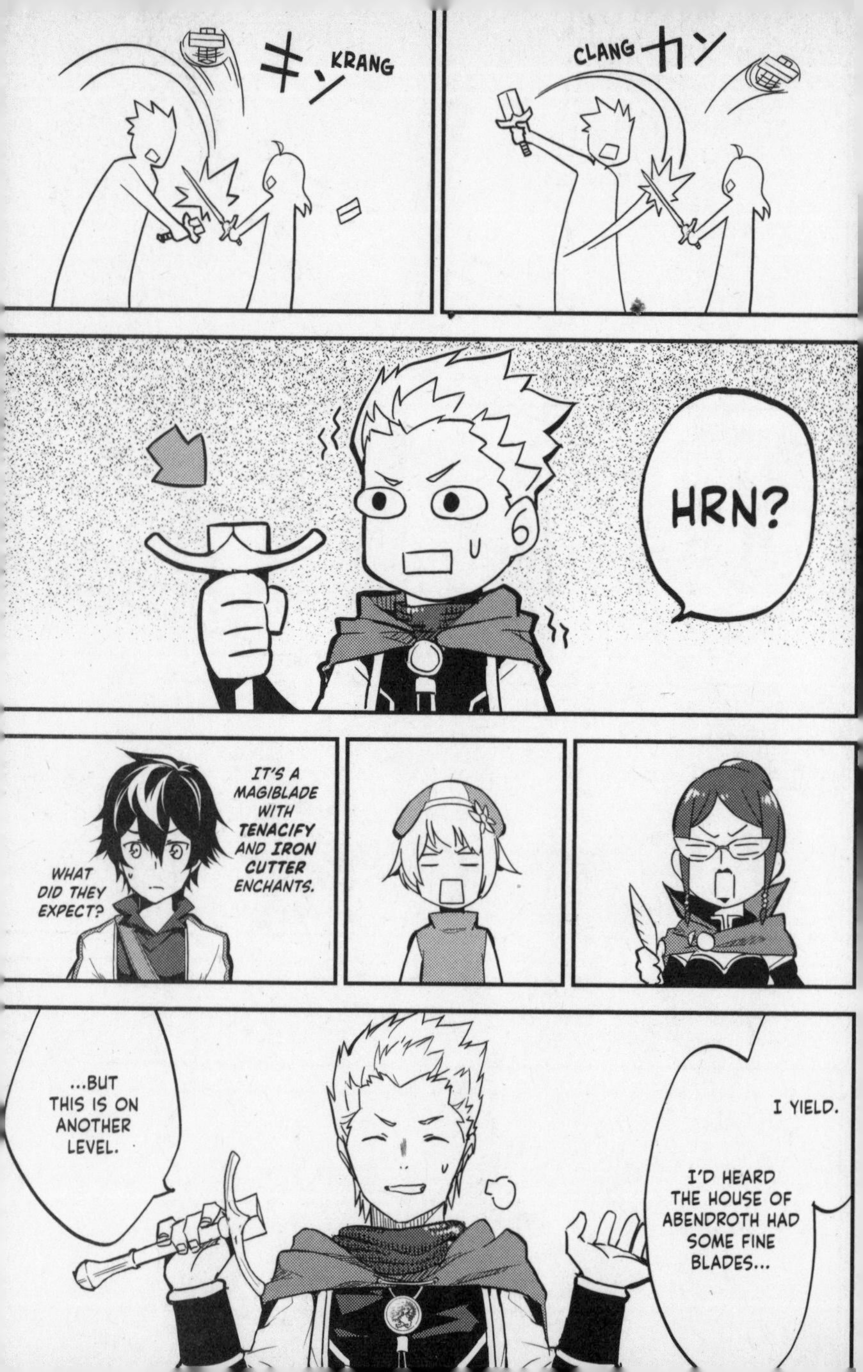
カン
CLANG
キン
KRANG
HRN?
IT'S A MAGIBLADE WITH TENACIFY AND IRON CUTTER ENCHANTS.
WHAT DID THEY EXPECT?
I YIELD.
I'D HEARD THE HOUSE OF ABENDROTH HAD SOME FINE BLADES...
...BUT THIS IS ON ANOTHER LEVEL.

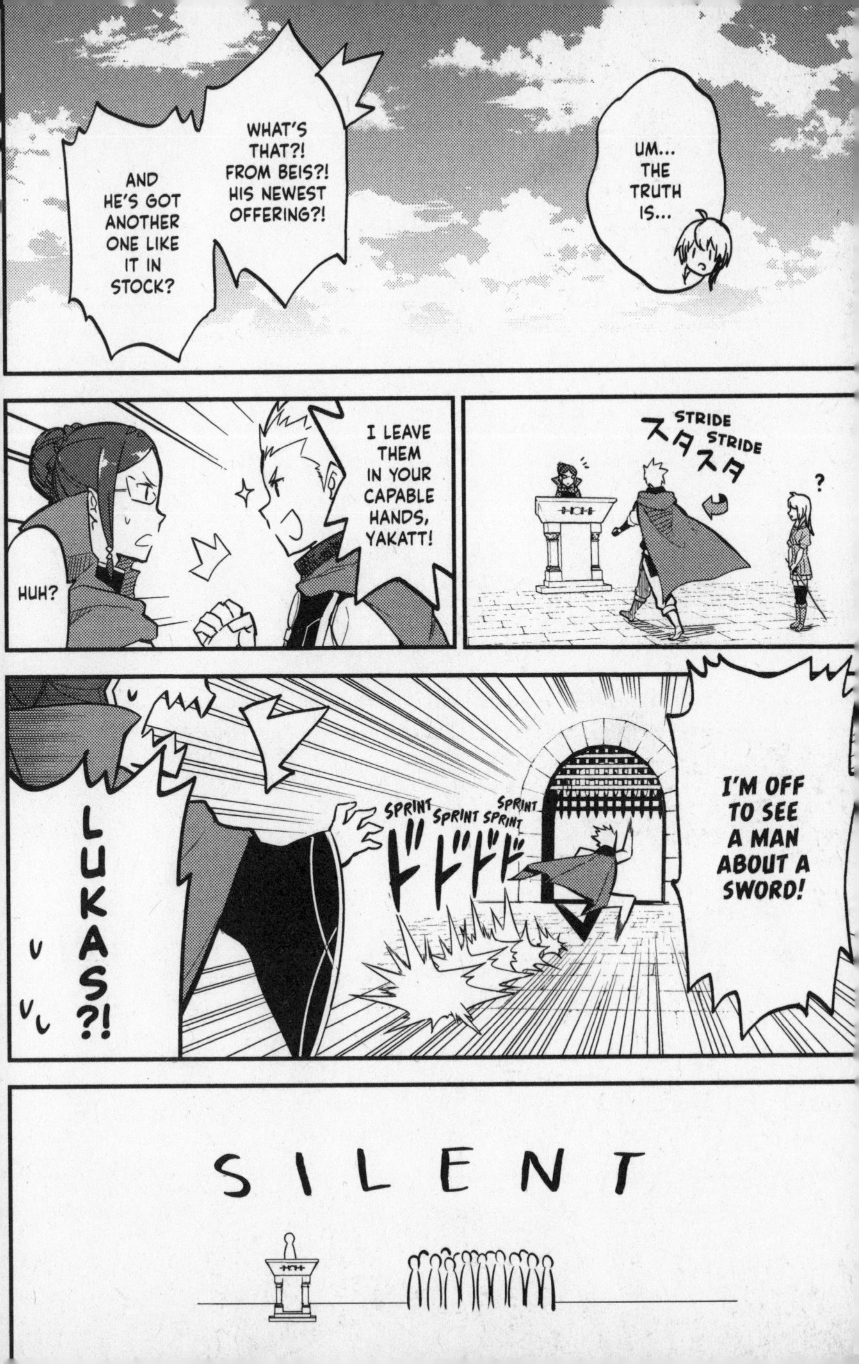
UM... THE TRUTH IS...
WHAT'S THAT?! FROM BEIS?! HIS NEWEST OFFERING?!
AND HE'S GOT ANOTHER ONE LIKE IT IN STOCK?
STRIDE STRIDE
スタスタ
?
I LEAVE THEM IN YOUR CAPABLE HANDS, YAKATT!
HUH?
I'M OFF TO SEE A MAN ABOUT A SWORD!
SPRINT SPRINT SPRINT SPRINT
ドドドド
LUKAS?!
SILENT

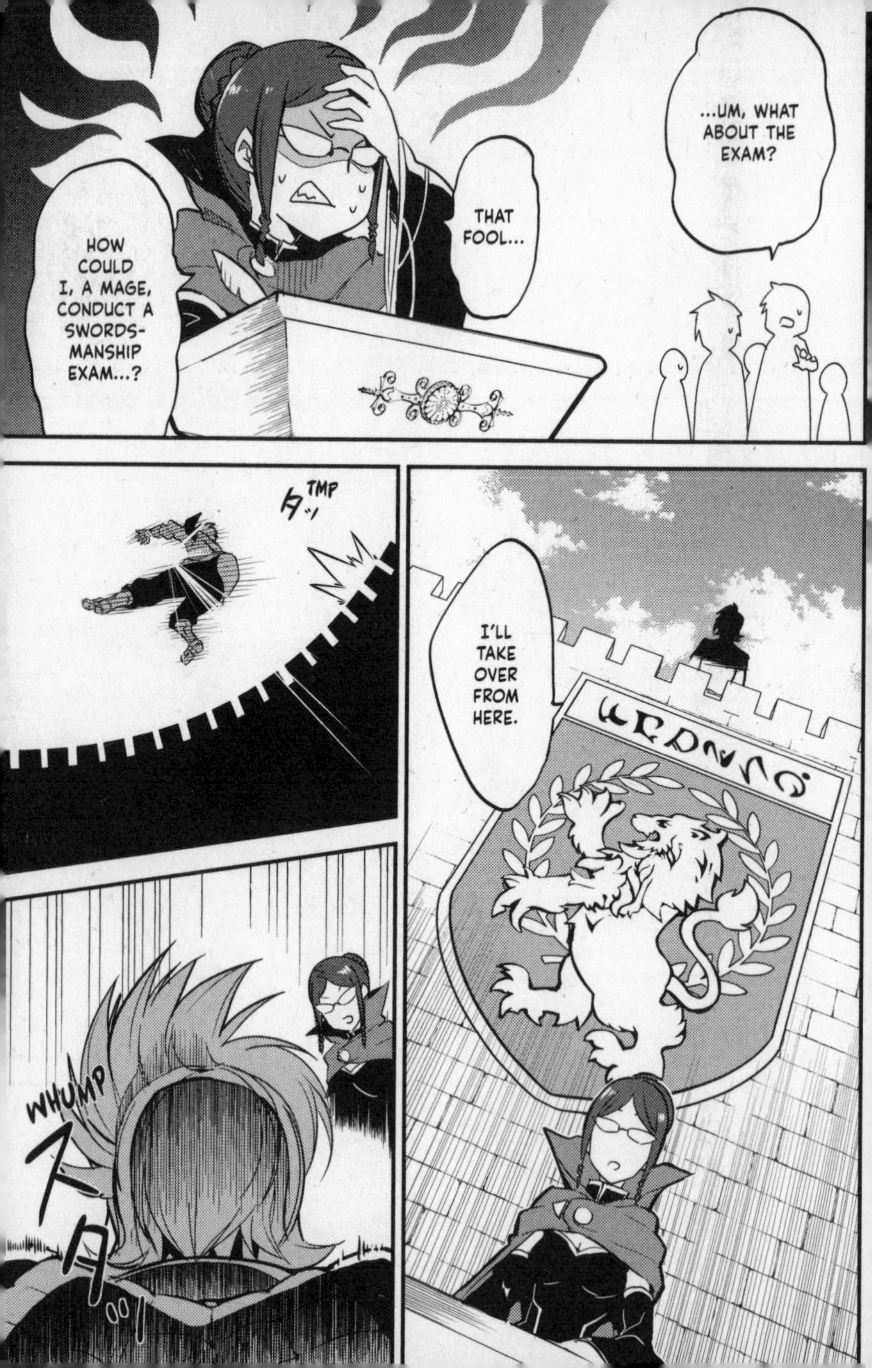
...UM, WHAT ABOUT THE EXAM?
THAT FOOL...
HOW COULD I, A MAGE, CONDUCT A SWORDS-MANSHIP EXAM...?
I'LL TAKE OVER FROM HERE.
TMP
WHUMP

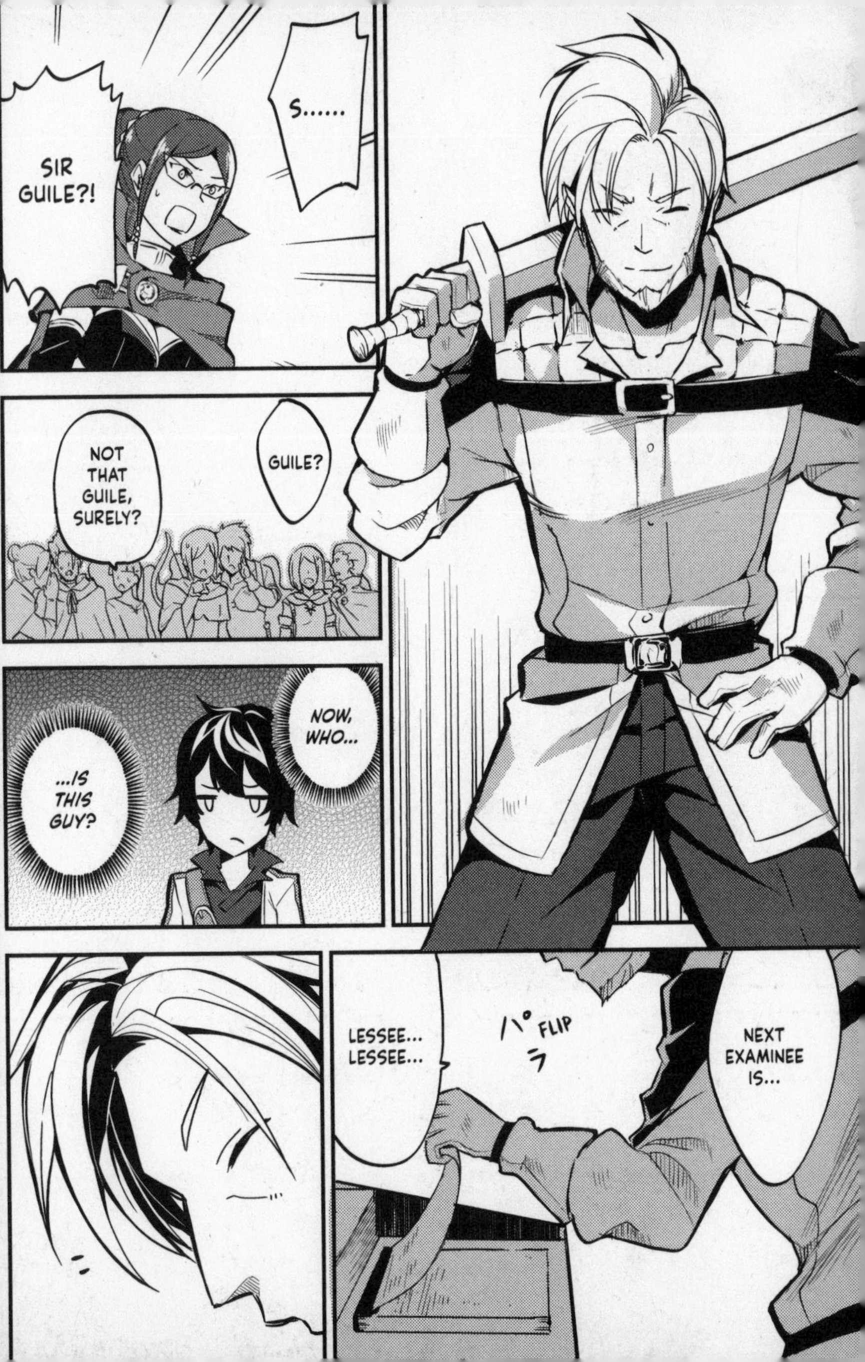
S......
SIR GUILE?!
GUILE?
NOT THAT GUILE, SURELY?
NOW, WHO...
...IS THIS GUY?
NEXT EXAMINEE IS...
パラ FLIP
LESSEE... LESSEE...

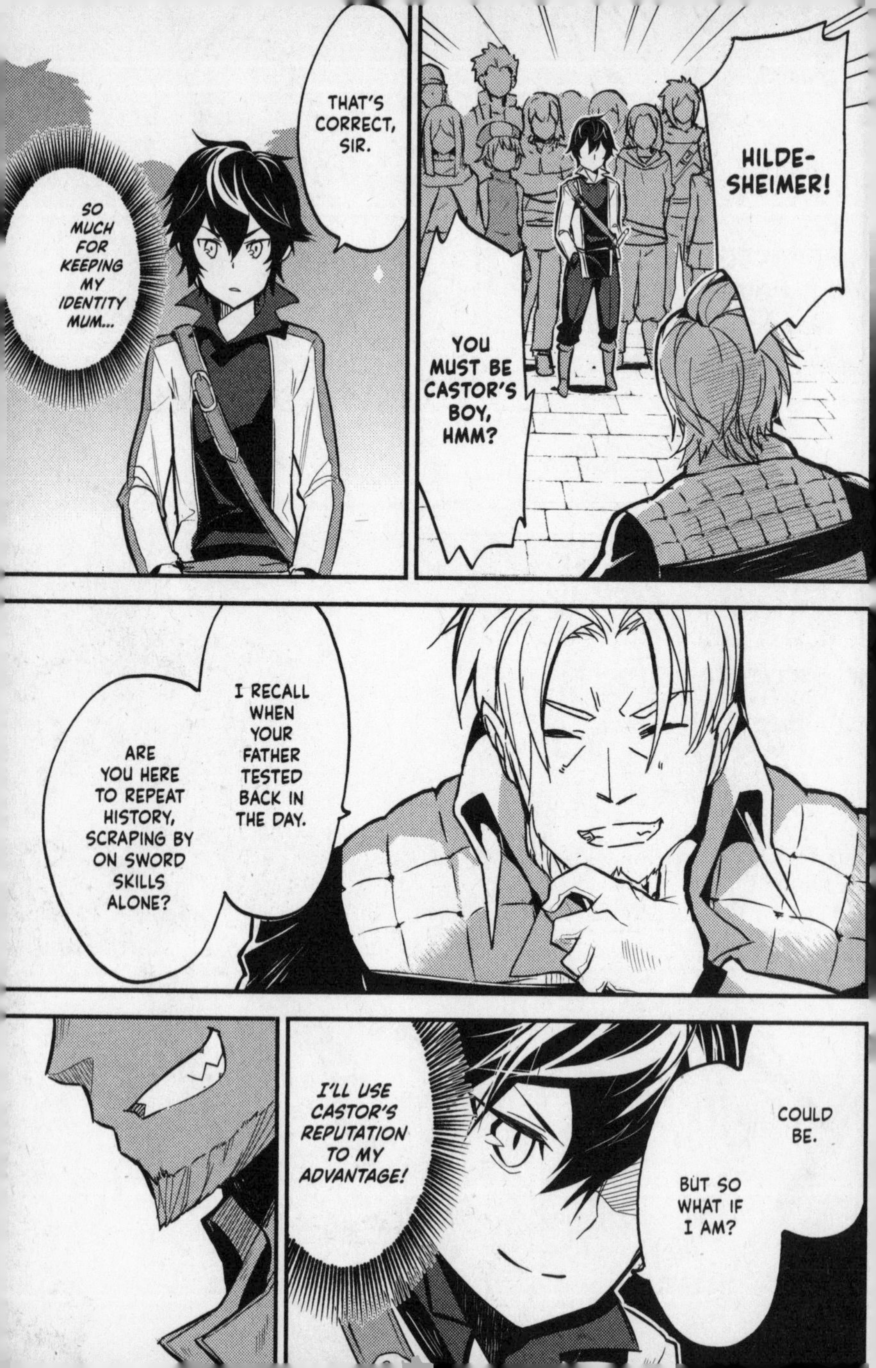
HILDE-SHEIMER!
YOU MUST BE CASTOR'S BOY, HMM?
THAT'S CORRECT, SIR.
SO MUCH FOR KEEPING MY IDENTITY MUM...
I RECALL WHEN YOUR FATHER TESTED BACK IN THE DAY.
ARE YOU HERE TO REPEAT HISTORY, SCRAPING BY ON SWORD SKILLS ALONE?
COULD BE.
BUT SO WHAT IF I AM?
I'LL USE CASTOR'S REPUTATION TO MY ADVANTAGE!

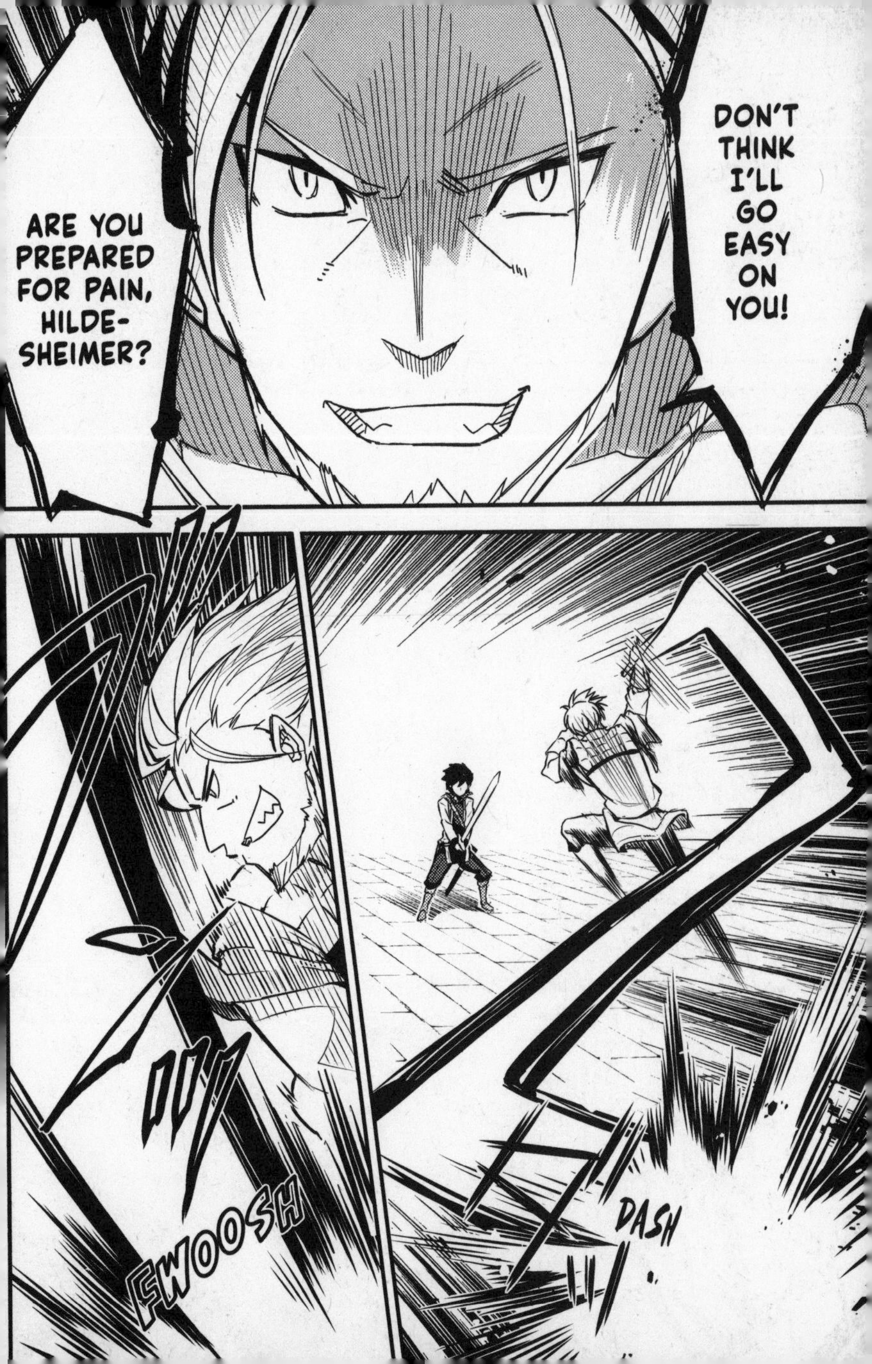
DON'T THINK I'LL GO EASY ON YOU!
ARE YOU PREPARED FOR PAIN, HILDE-SHEIMER?
DASH
FWOOSH

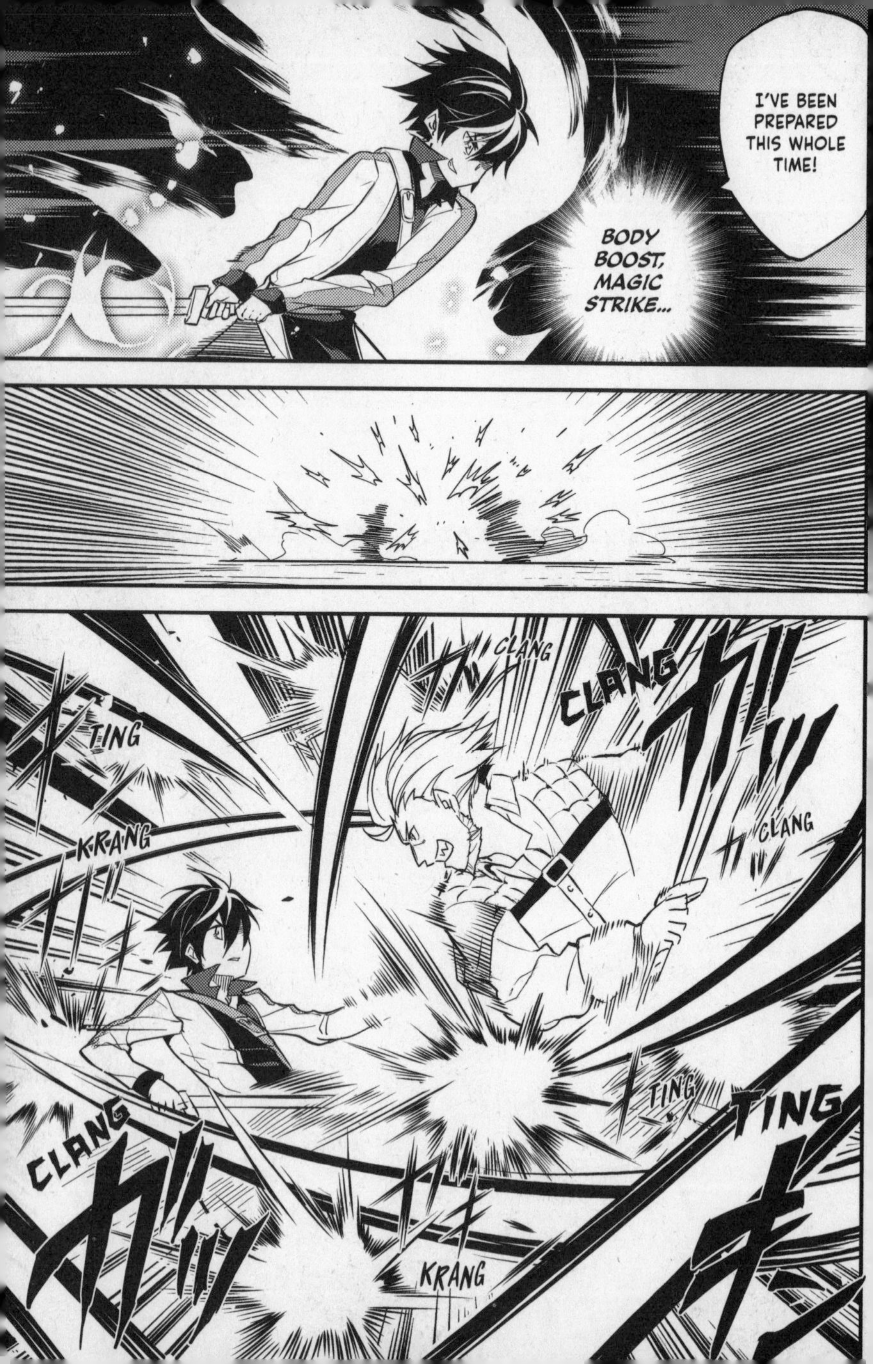
I'VE BEEN PREPARED THIS WHOLE TIME!
BODY BOOST, MAGIC STRIKE...
CLANG
CLANG
CLANG
TING
KRANG
TING
TING
CLANG
KRANG

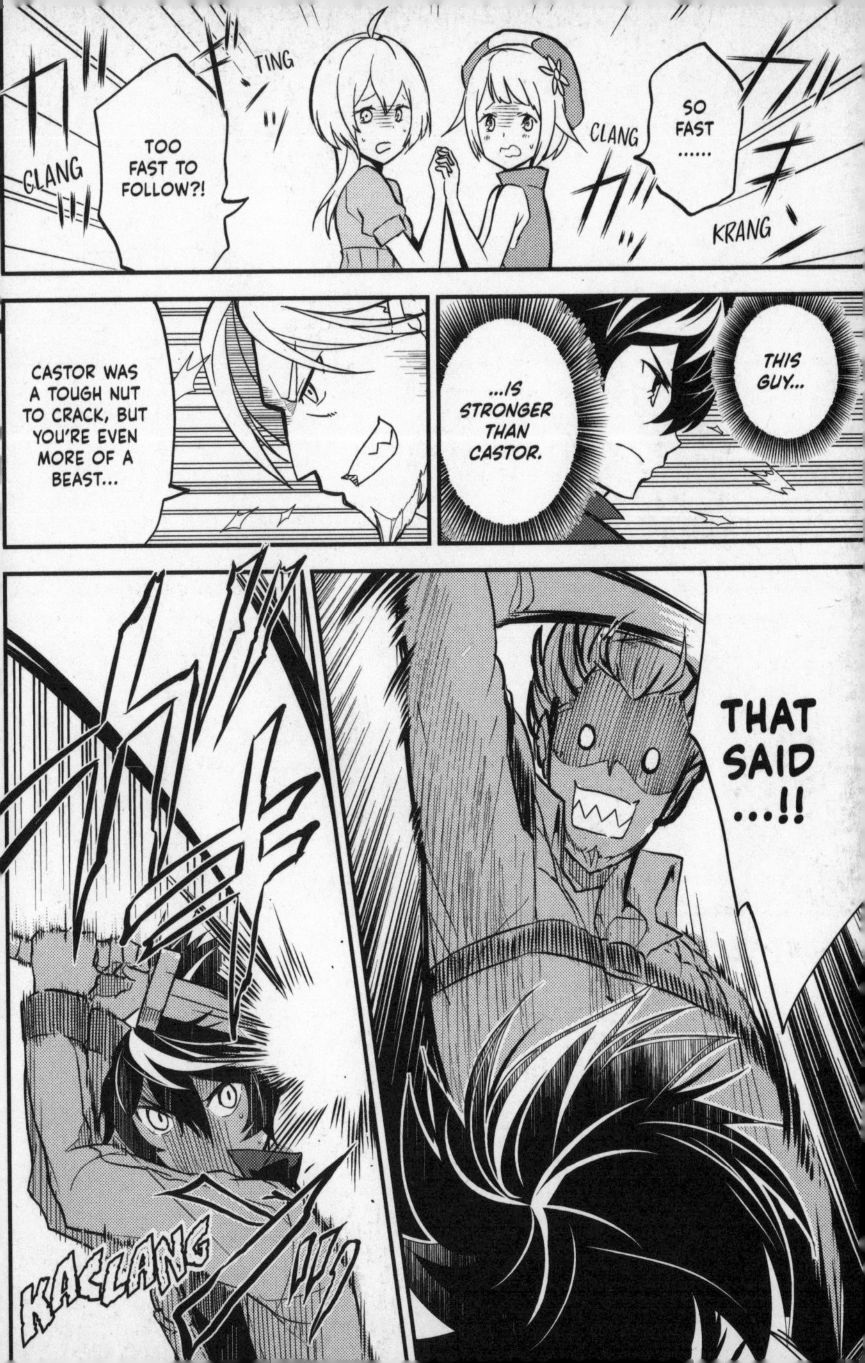
SO FAST ......
CLANG
KRANG
TING
TOO FAST TO FOLLOW?!
GLANG
THIS GUY...
...IS STRONGER THAN CASTOR.
CASTOR WAS A TOUGH NUT TO CRACK, BUT YOU'RE EVEN MORE OF A BEAST...
THAT SAID ...!!
KACLANG

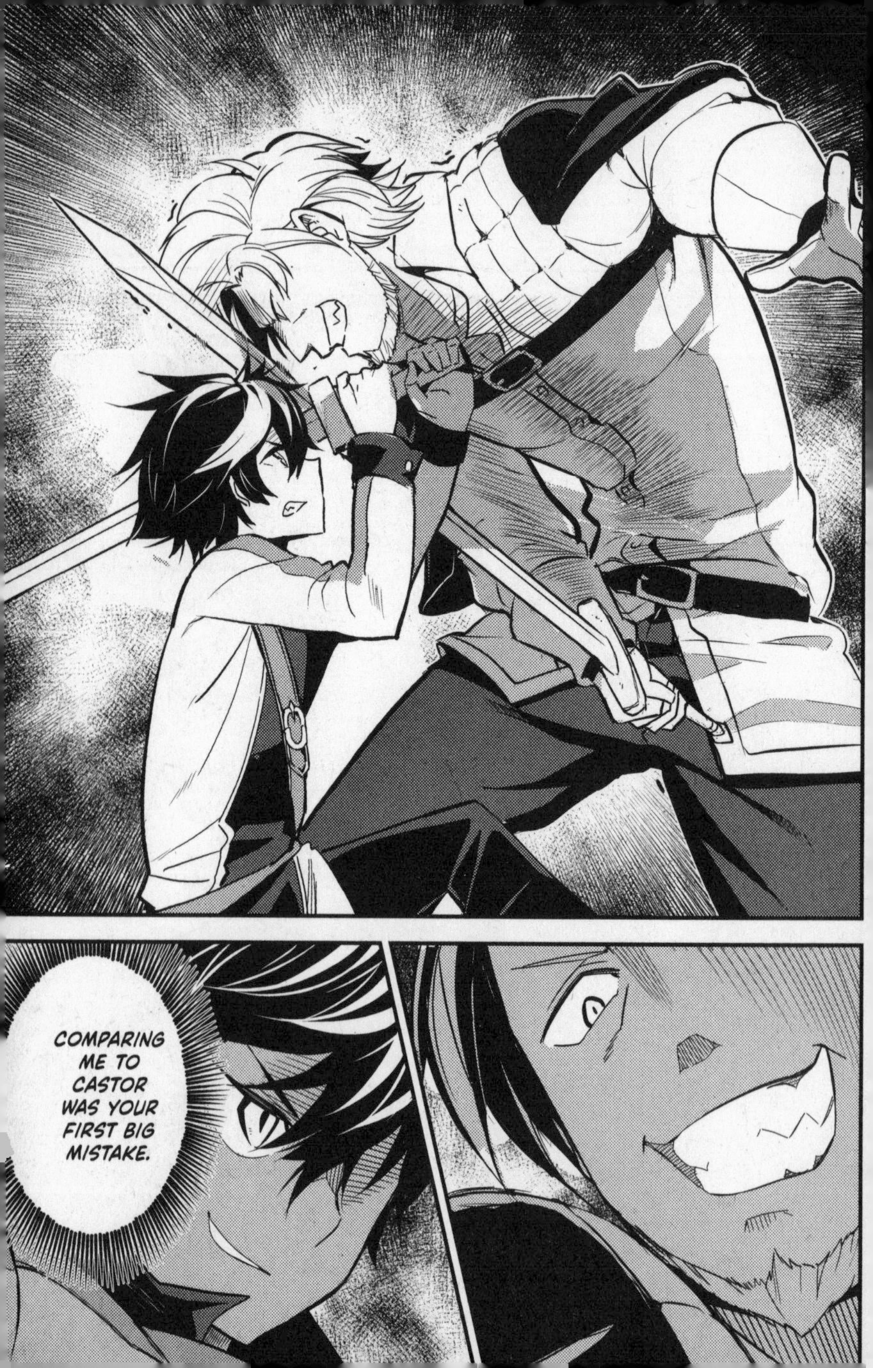
COMPARING ME TO CASTOR WAS YOUR FIRST BIG MISTAKE.

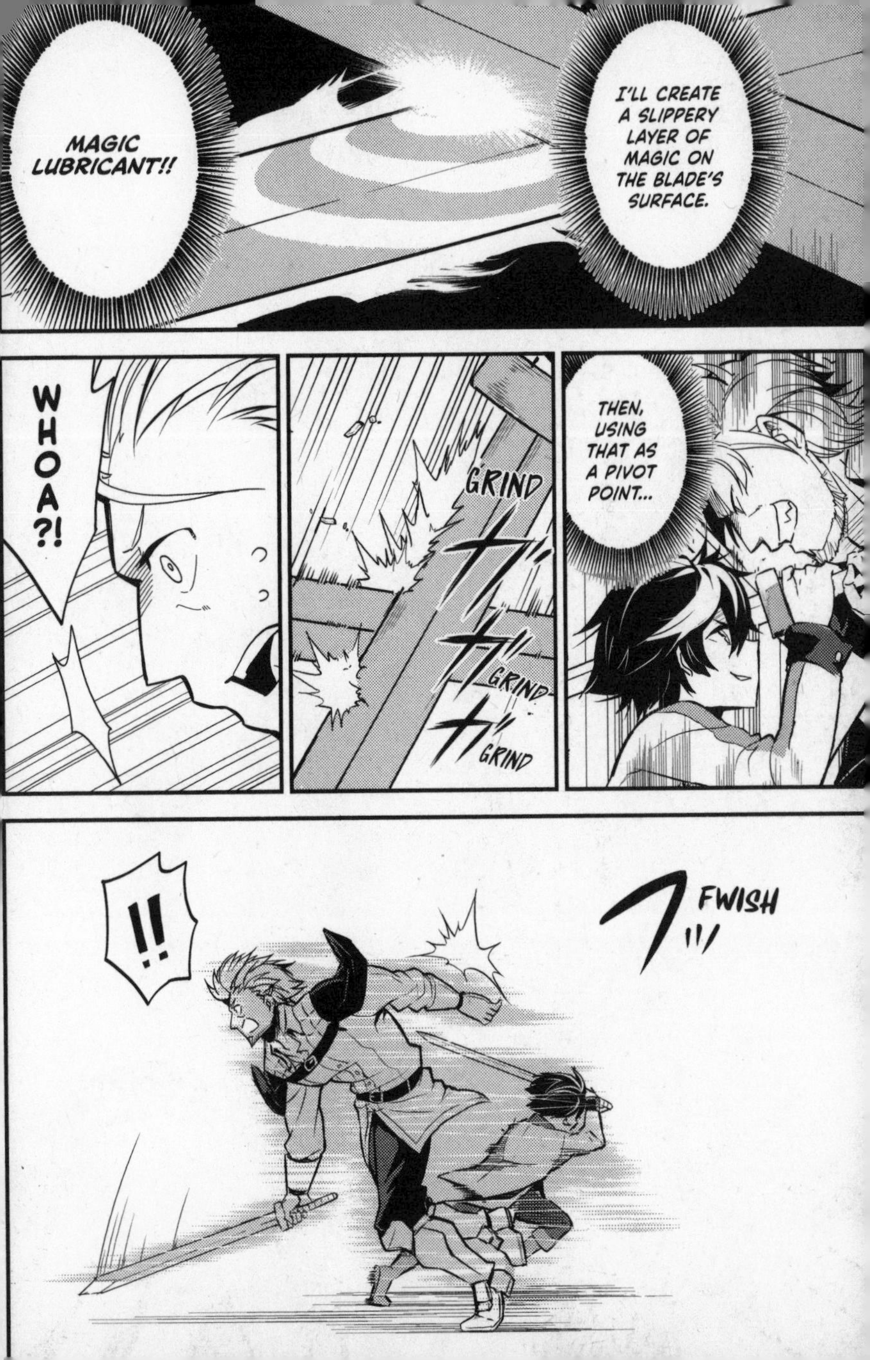
I'LL CREATE A SLIPPERY LAYER OF MAGIC ON THE BLADE'S SURFACE.
MAGIC LUBRICANT!!
THEN, USING THAT AS A PIVOT POINT...
GRIND
GRIND
GRIND
WHOA?!
FWISH
!!

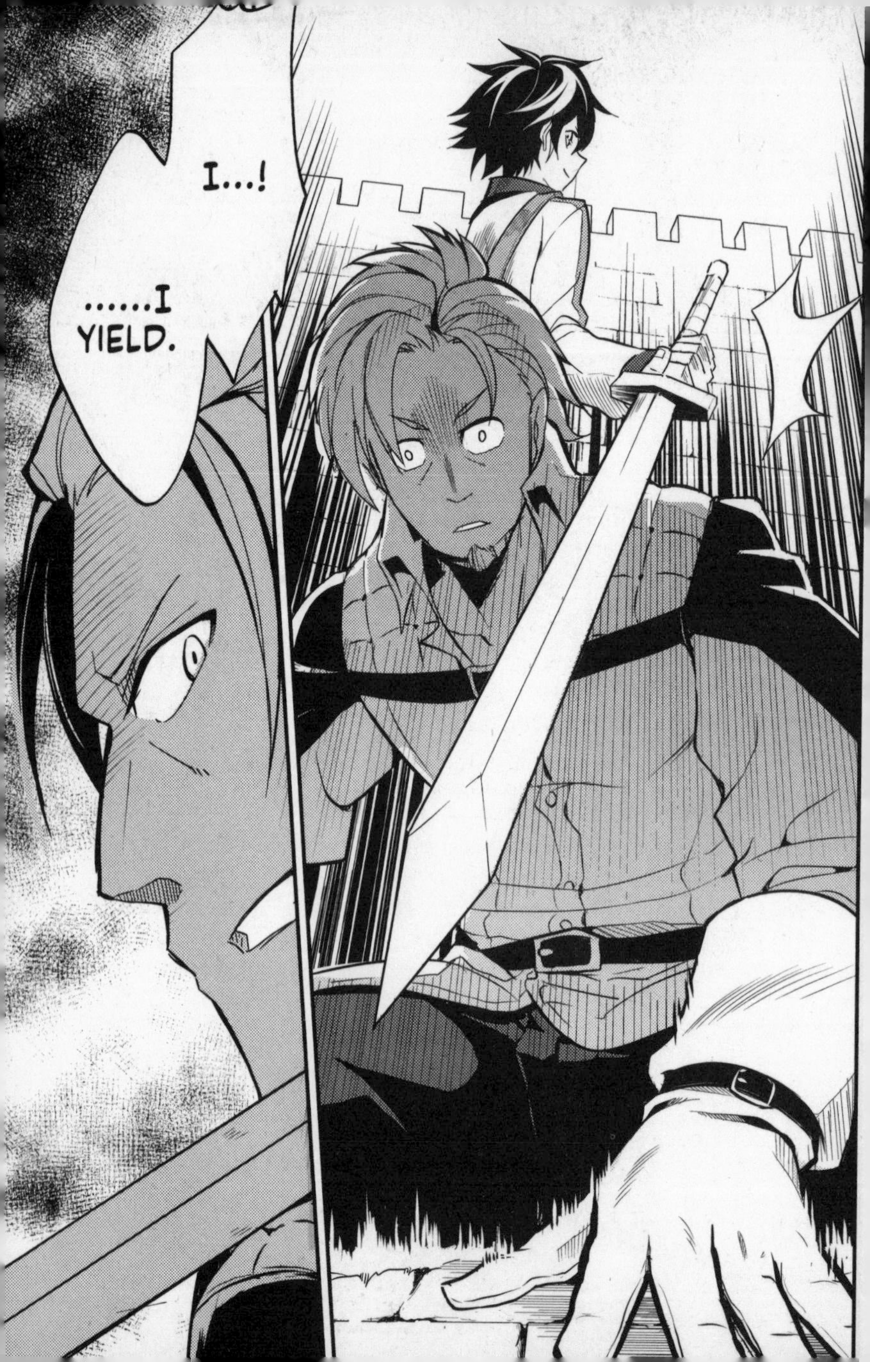
I...!
......I YIELD.

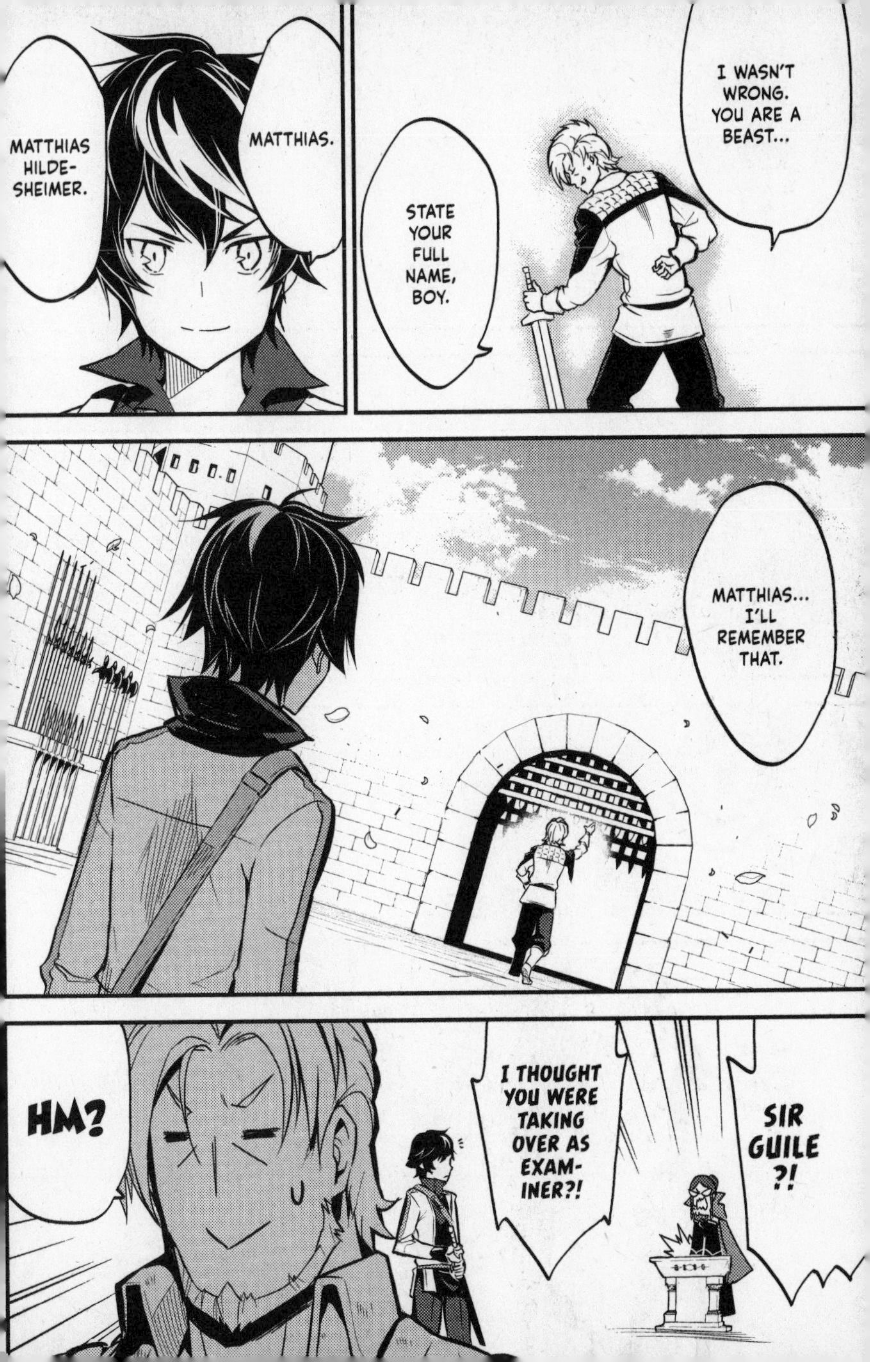
I WASN'T WRONG. YOU ARE A BEAST...
STATE YOUR FULL NAME, BOY.
MATTHIAS.
MATTHIAS HILDE-SHEIMER.
MATTHIAS... I'LL REMEMBER THAT.
SIR GUILE?!
I THOUGHT YOU WERE TAKING OVER AS EXAM-INER?!
HM?

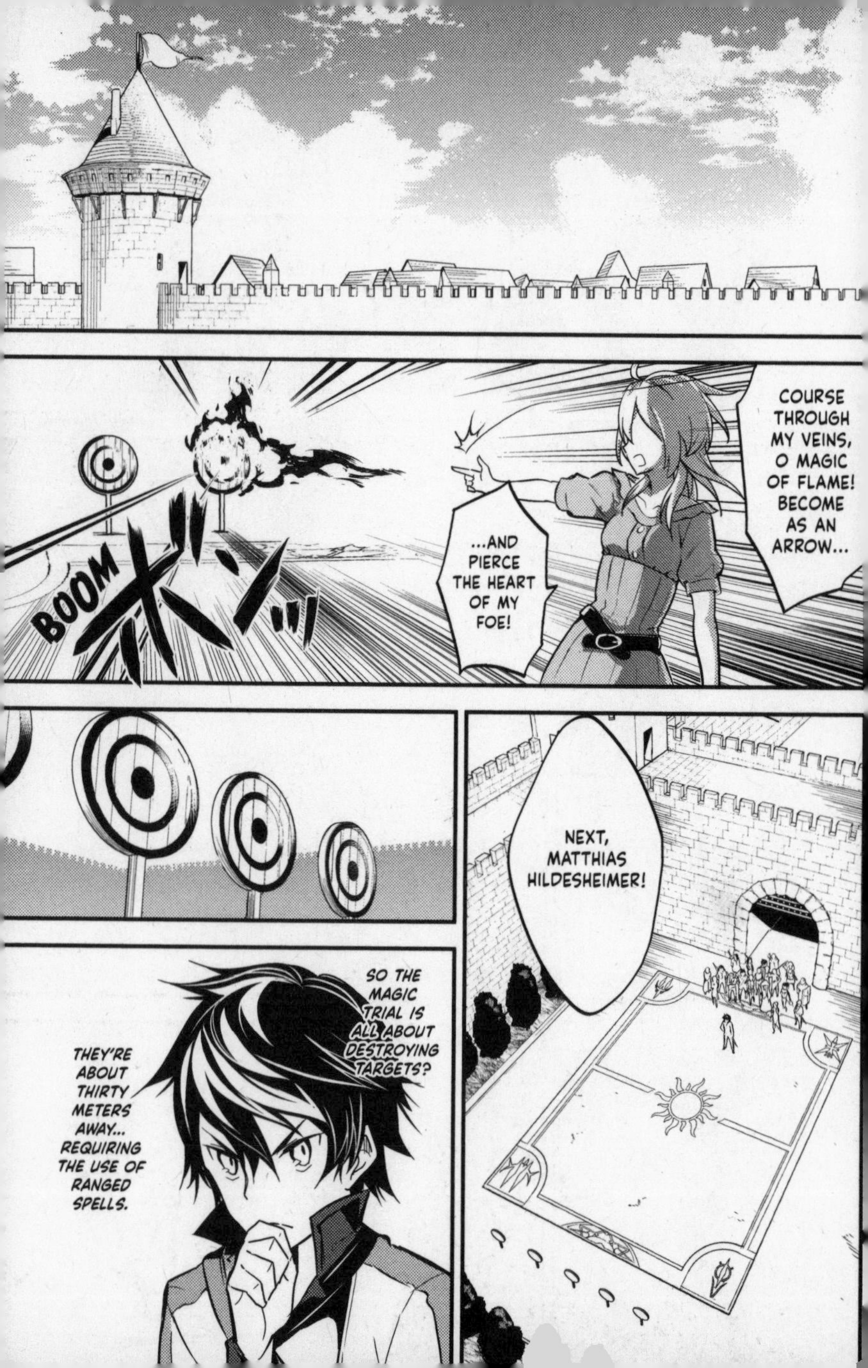
COURSE THROUGH MY VEINS, O MAGIC OF FLAME! BECOME AS AN ARROW...
...AND PIERCE THE HEART OF MY FOE!
BOOM
NEXT, MATTHIAS HILDESHEIMER!
SO THE MAGIC TRIAL IS ALL ABOUT DESTROYING TARGETS?
THEY'RE ABOUT THIRTY METERS AWAY... REQUIRING THE USE OF RANGED SPELLS.

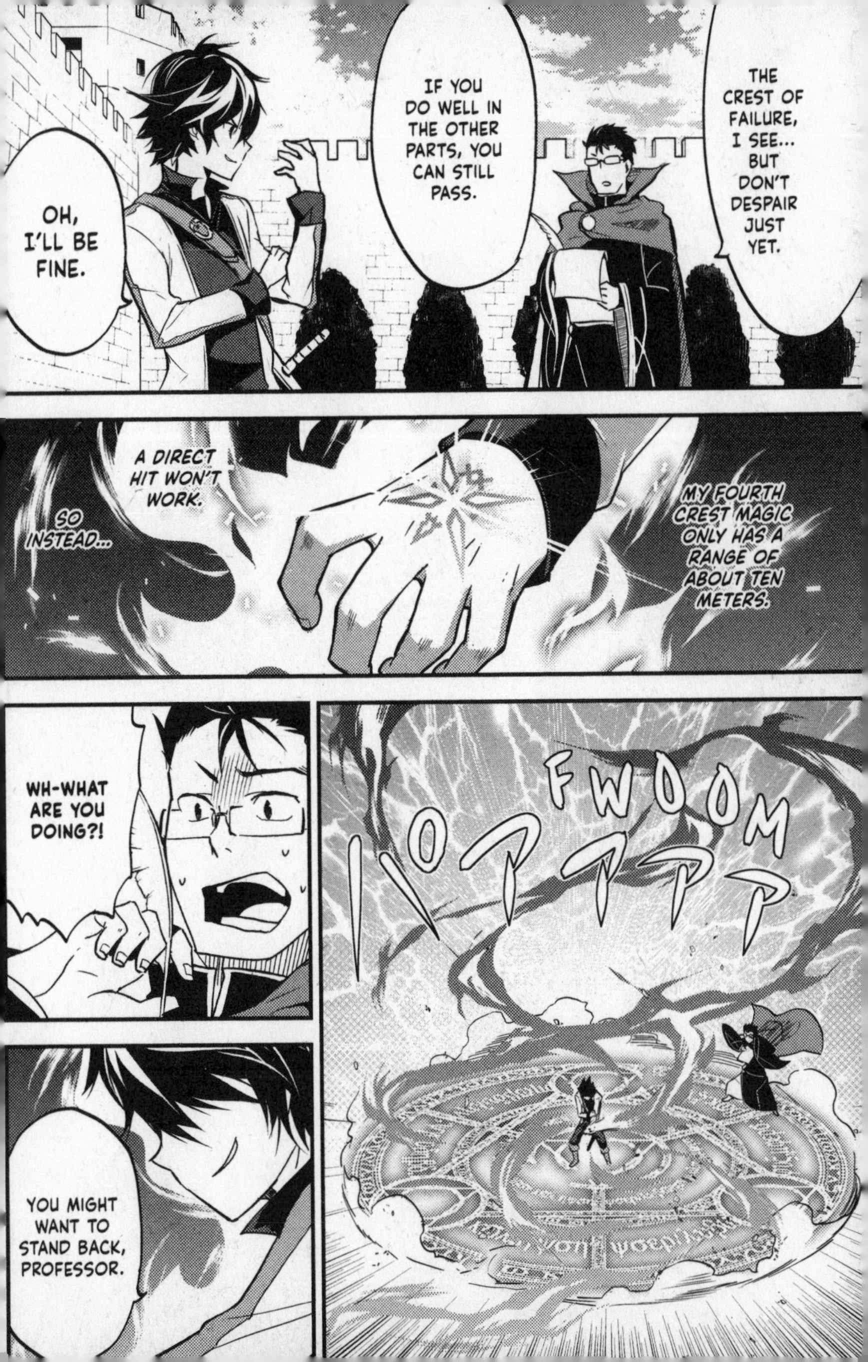
THE CREST OF FAILURE, I SEE... BUT DON'T DESPAIR JUST YET.
IF YOU DO WELL IN THE OTHER PARTS, YOU CAN STILL PASS.
OH, I'LL BE FINE.
MY FOURTH CREST MAGIC ONLY HAS A RANGE OF ABOUT TEN METERS.
A DIRECT HIT WON'T WORK.
SO INSTEAD...
FWOOM
WH-WHAT ARE YOU DOING?!
YOU MIGHT WANT TO STAND BACK, PROFESSOR.

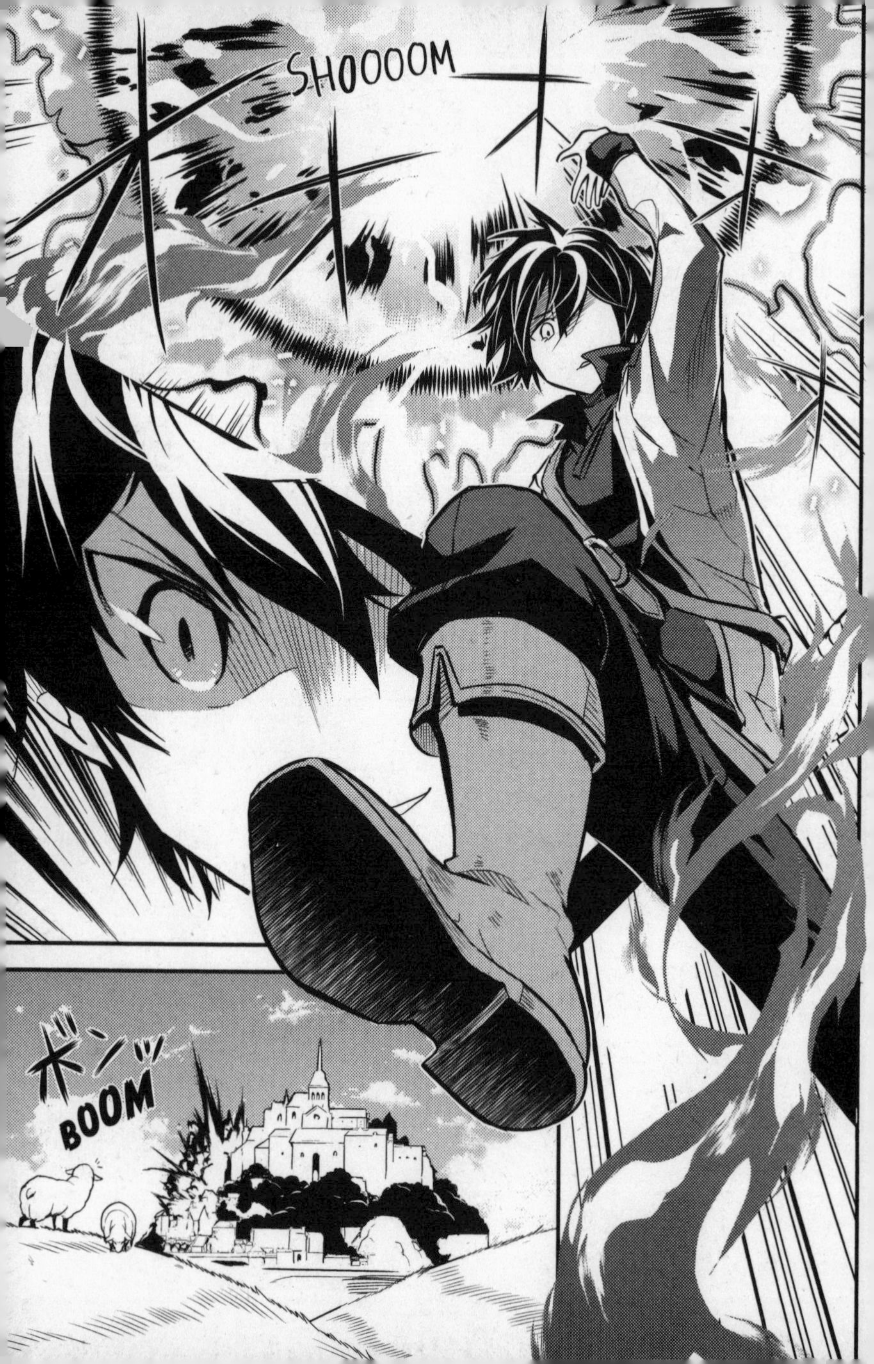
SHOOOOM
ボンッ
BOOM

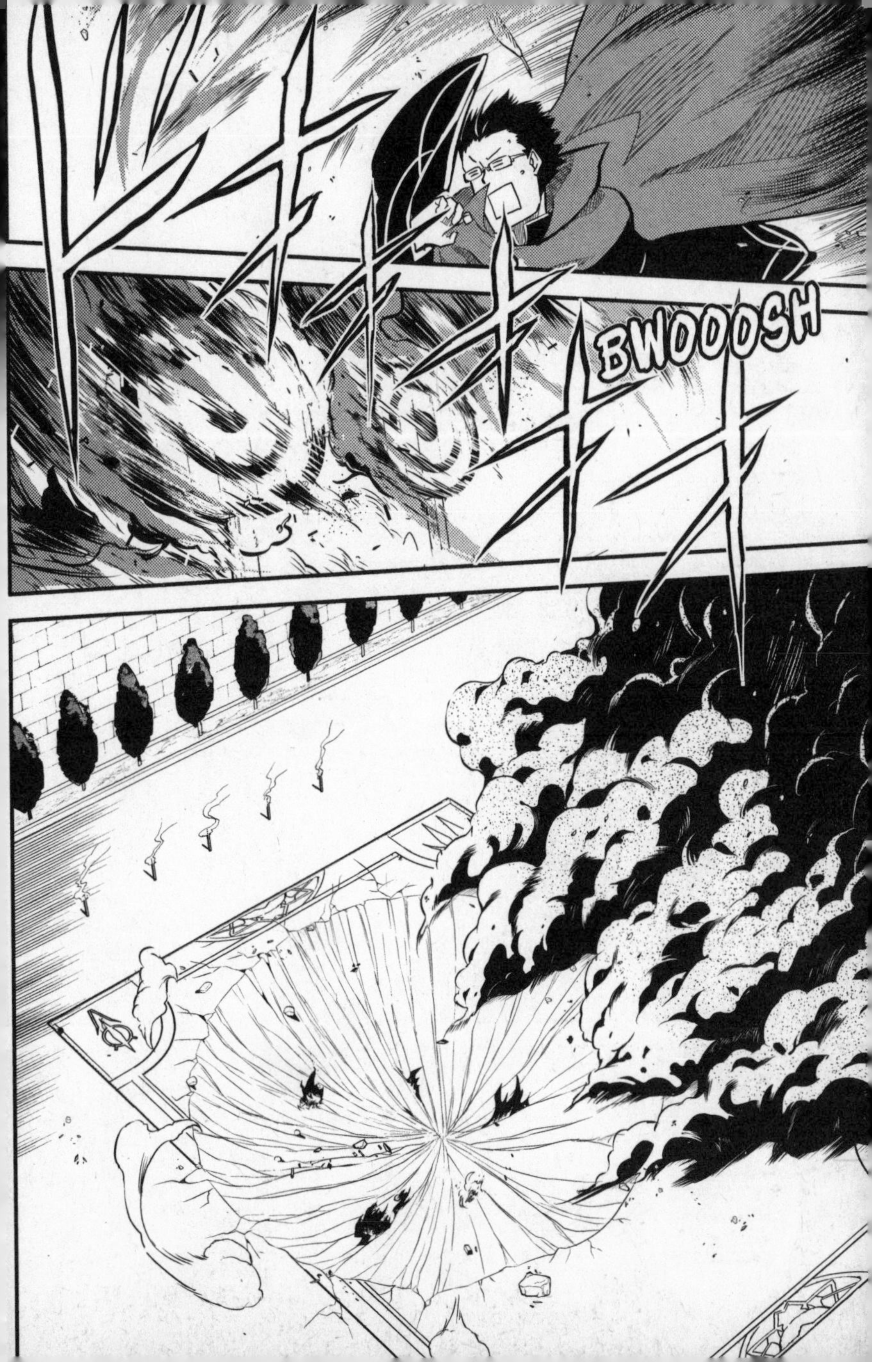
BWOOOSH

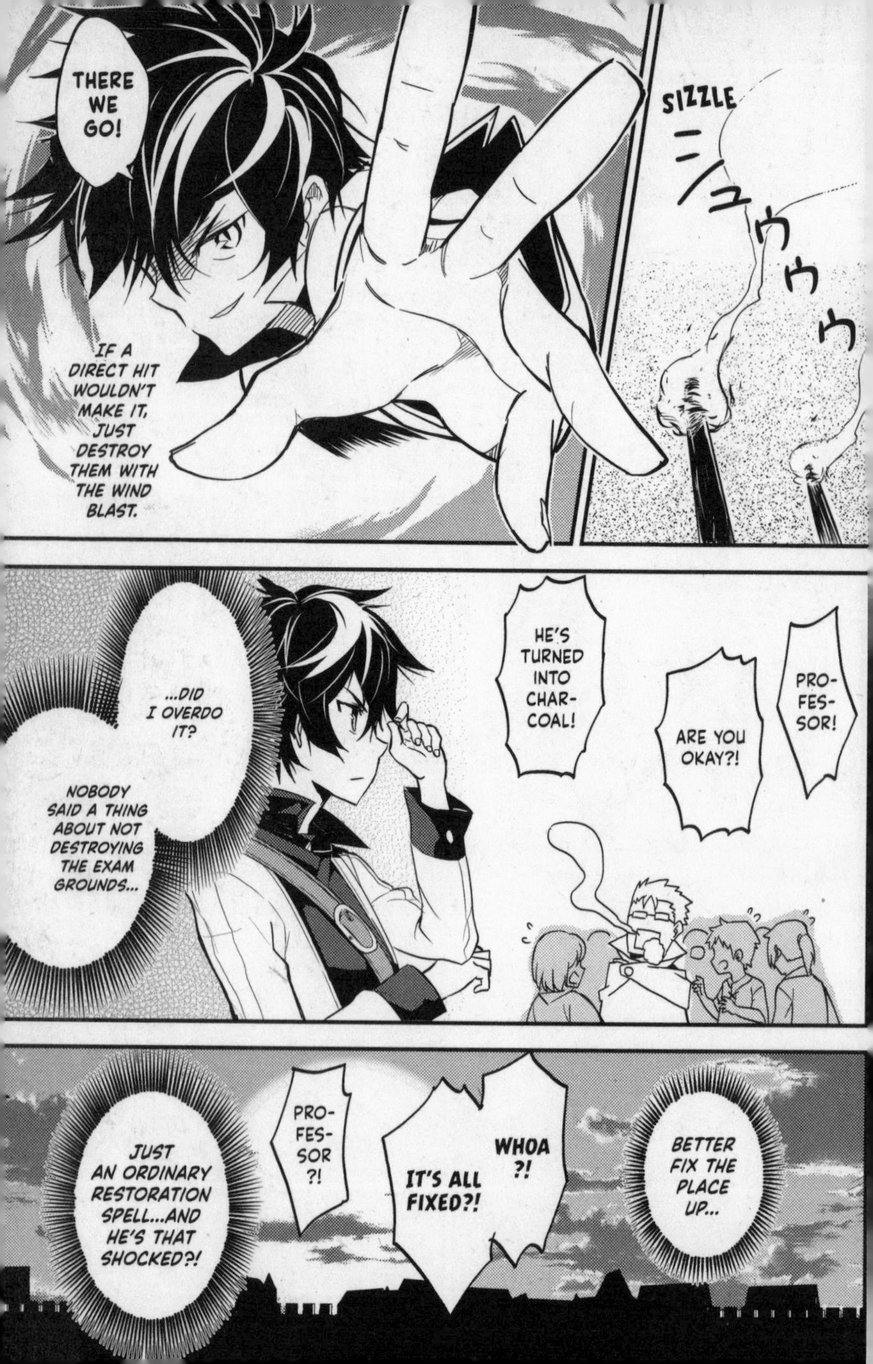
SIZZLE
シュウウウ
THERE WE GO!
IF A DIRECT HIT WOULDN'T MAKE IT, JUST DESTROY THEM WITH THE WIND BLAST.
PRO-FES-SOR!
ARE YOU OKAY?!
HE'S TURNED INTO CHAR-COAL!
...DID I OVERDO IT?
NOBODY SAID A THING ABOUT NOT DESTROYING THE EXAM GROUNDS...
BETTER FIX THE PLACE UP...
WHOA?!
IT'S ALL FIXED?!
PRO-FES-SOR?!
JUST AN ORDINARY RESTORATION SPELL...AND HE'S THAT SHOCKED?!

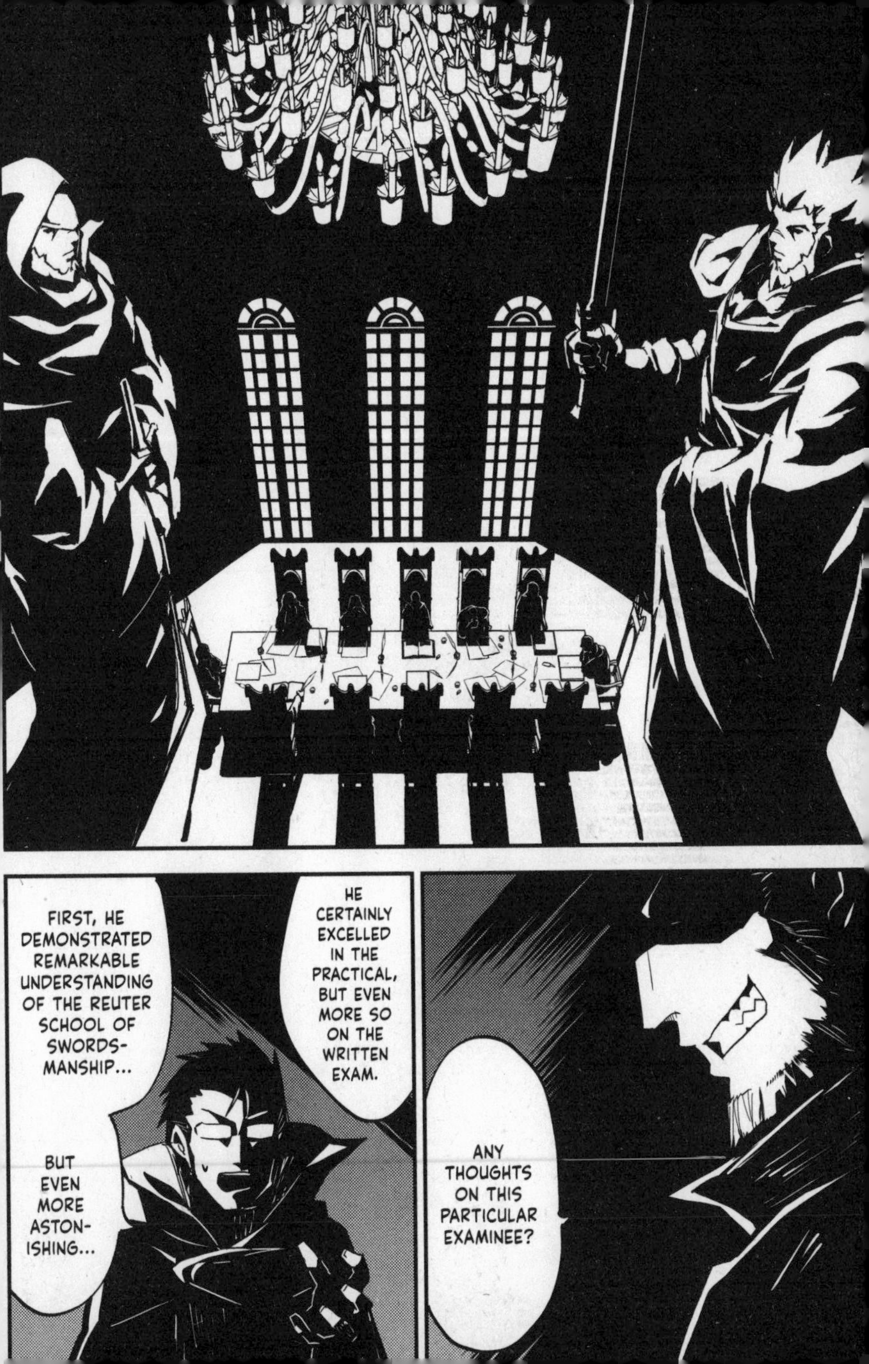
ANY THOUGHTS ON THIS PARTICULAR EXAMINEE?
HE CERTAINLY EXCELLED IN THE PRACTICAL, BUT EVEN MORE SO ON THE WRITTEN EXAM.
FIRST, HE DEMONSTRATED REMARKABLE UNDERSTANDING OF THE REUTER SCHOOL OF SWORDS-MANSHIP...
BUT EVEN MORE ASTON-ISHING...

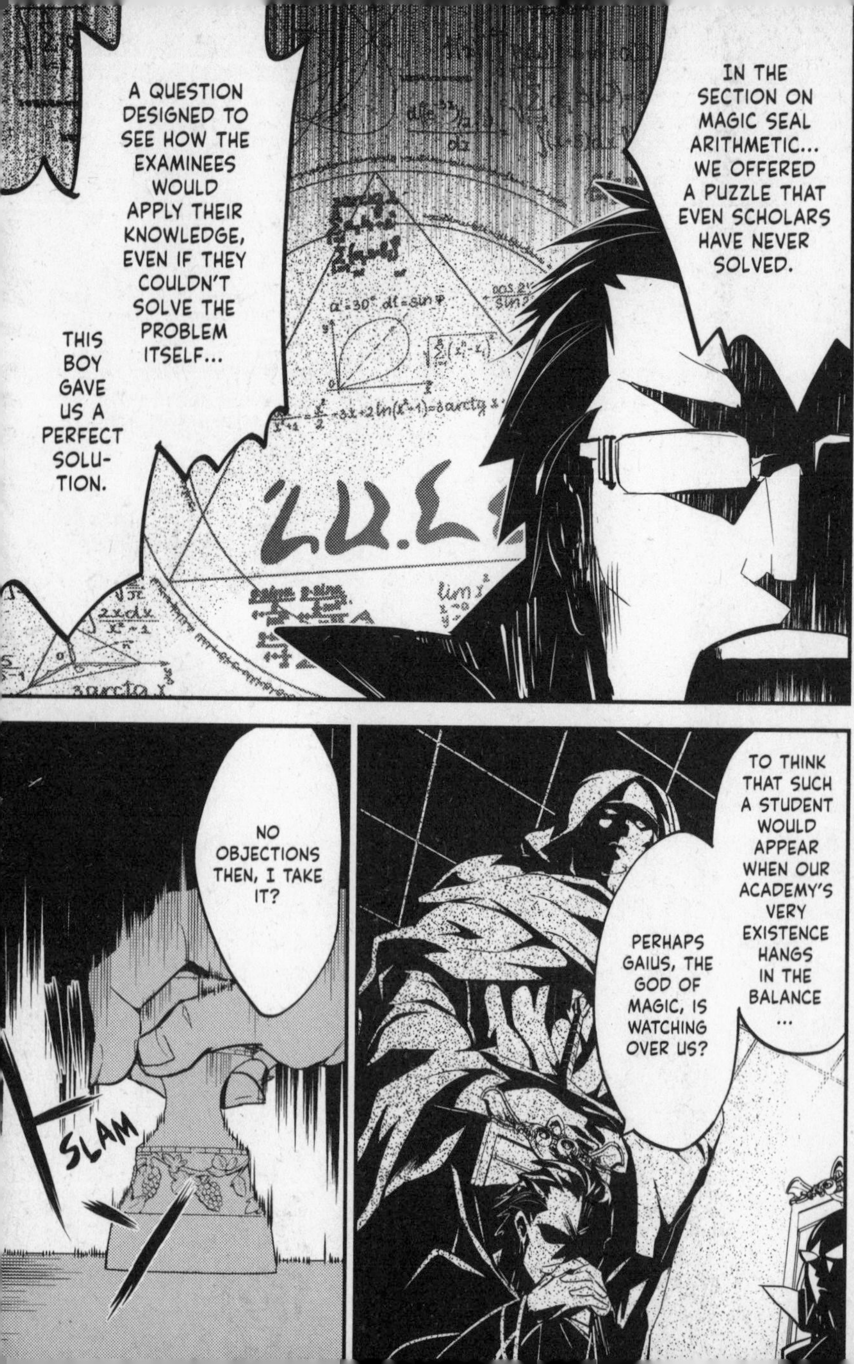
IN THE SECTION ON MAGIC SEAL ARITHMETIC... WE OFFERED A PUZZLE THAT EVEN SCHOLARS HAVE NEVER SOLVED.
A QUESTION DESIGNED TO SEE HOW THE EXAMINEES WOULD APPLY THEIR KNOWLEDGE, EVEN IF THEY COULDN'T SOLVE THE PROBLEM ITSELF...
THIS BOY GAVE US A PERFECT SOLU-TION.
TO THINK THAT SUCH A STUDENT WOULD APPEAR WHEN OUR ACADEMY'S VERY EXISTENCE HANGS IN THE BALANCE ...
PERHAPS GAIUS, THE GOD OF MAGIC, IS WATCHING OVER US?
NO OBJECTIONS THEN, I TAKE IT?
SLAM

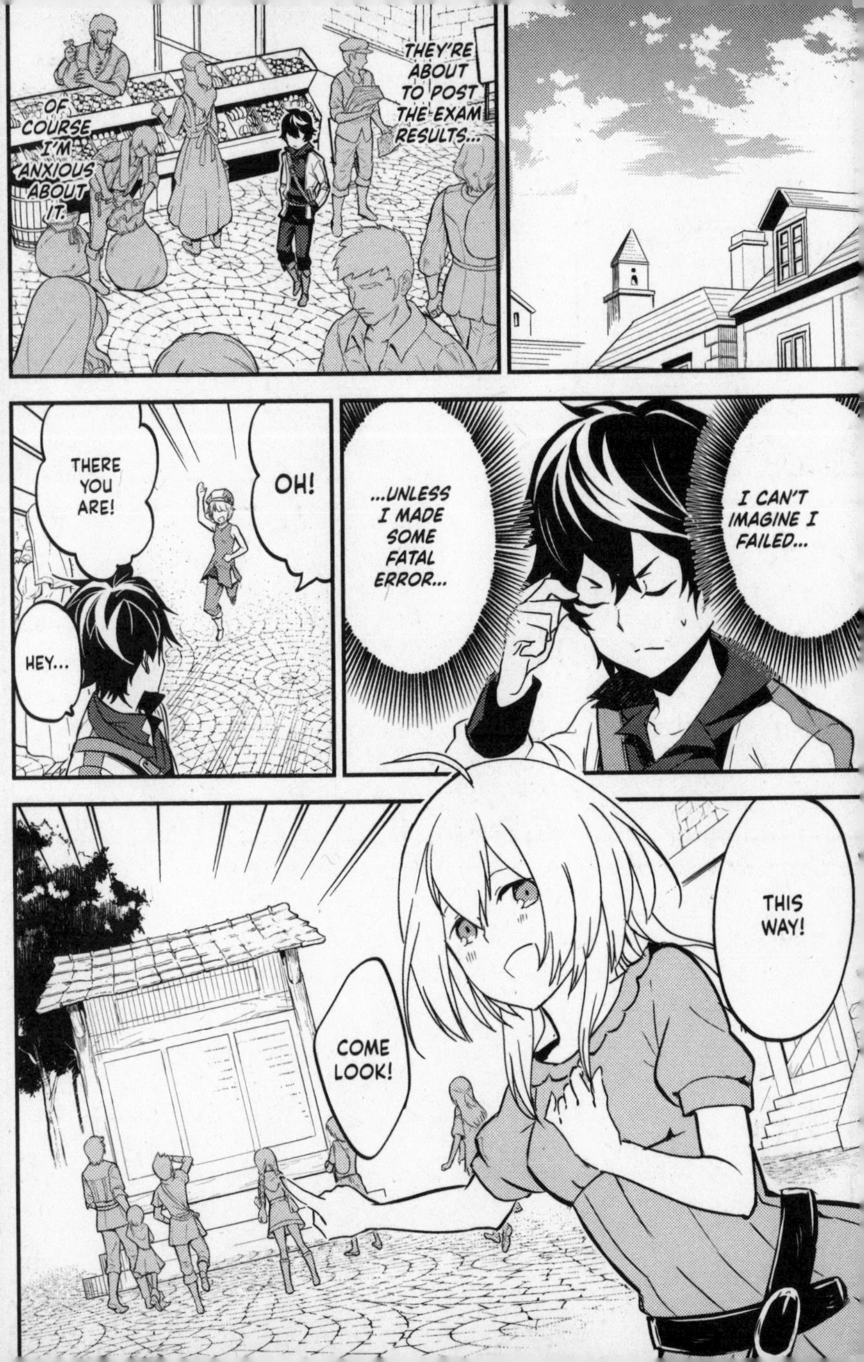
THEY'RE ABOUT TO POST THE EXAM RESULTS...
OF COURSE I'M ANXIOUS ABOUT IT.
I CAN'T IMAGINE I FAILED...
...UNLESS I MADE SOME FATAL ERROR...
OH!
THERE YOU ARE!
HEY...
THIS WAY!
COME LOOK!

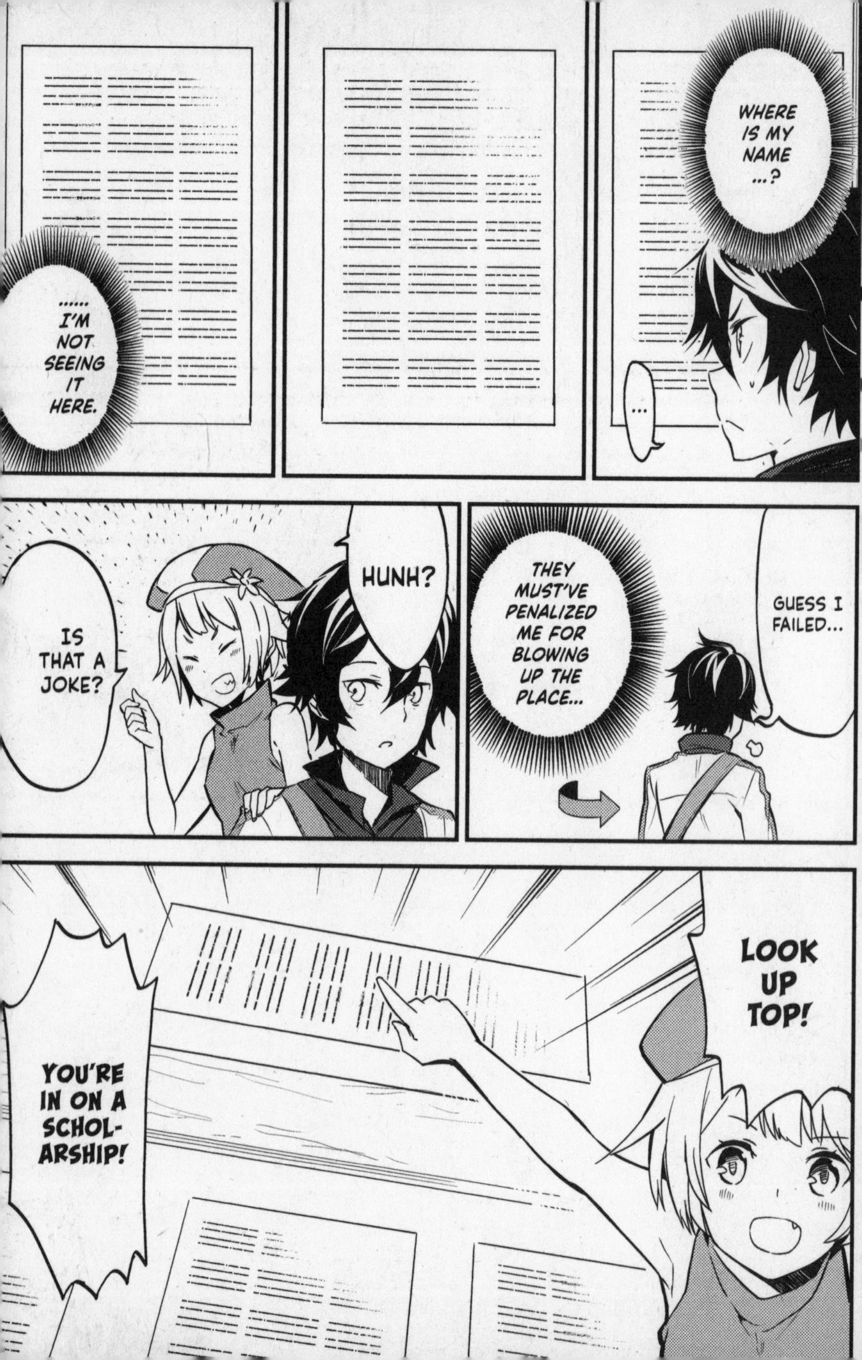
WHERE IS MY NAME ...?
...
...... I'M NOT SEEING IT HERE.
GUESS I FAILED...
THEY MUST'VE PENALIZED ME FOR BLOWING UP THE PLACE...
HUNH?
IS THAT A JOKE?
LOOK UP TOP!
YOU'RE IN ON A SCHOL-ARSHIP!

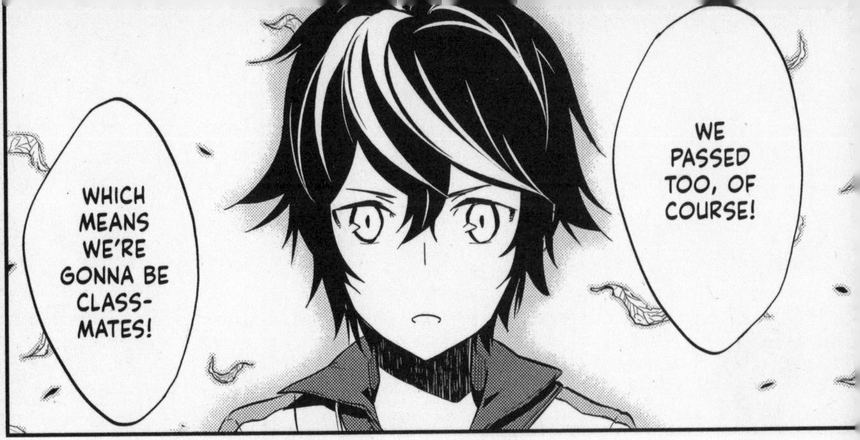
WE PASSED TOO, OF COURSE!
WHICH MEANS WE'RE GONNA BE CLASS-MATES!

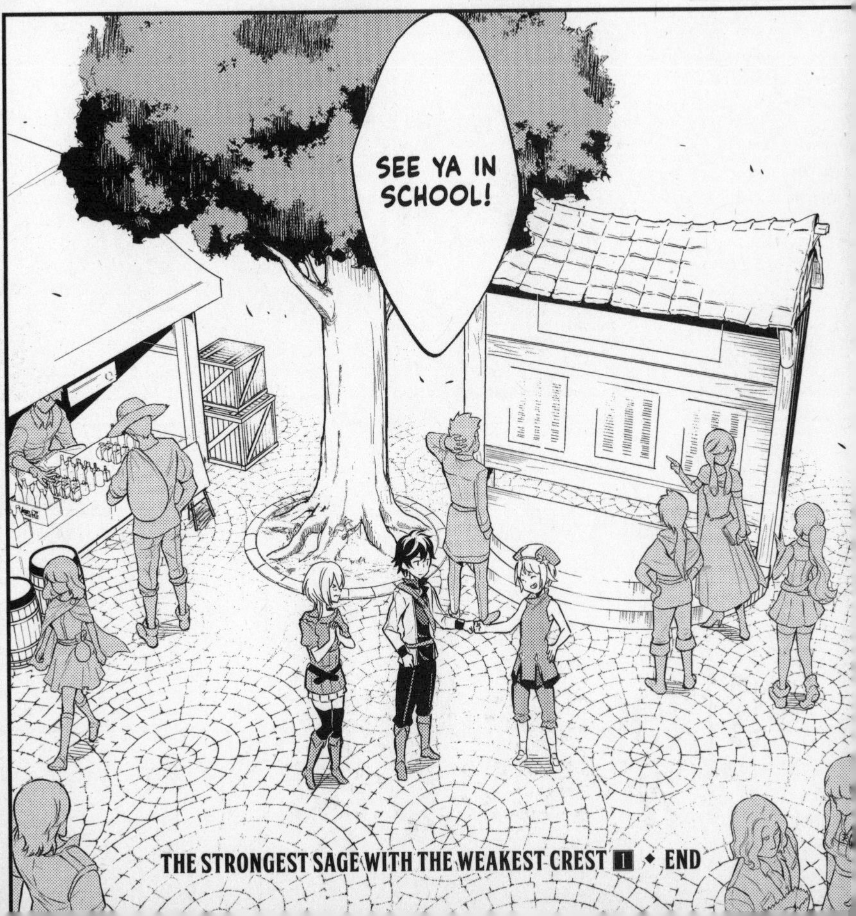
SEE YA IN SCHOOL!

THE STRONGEST SAGE WITH THE WEAKEST CREST 1 ◆ END

THE
STRONGEST SAGE
WITH THE WEAKEST CREST

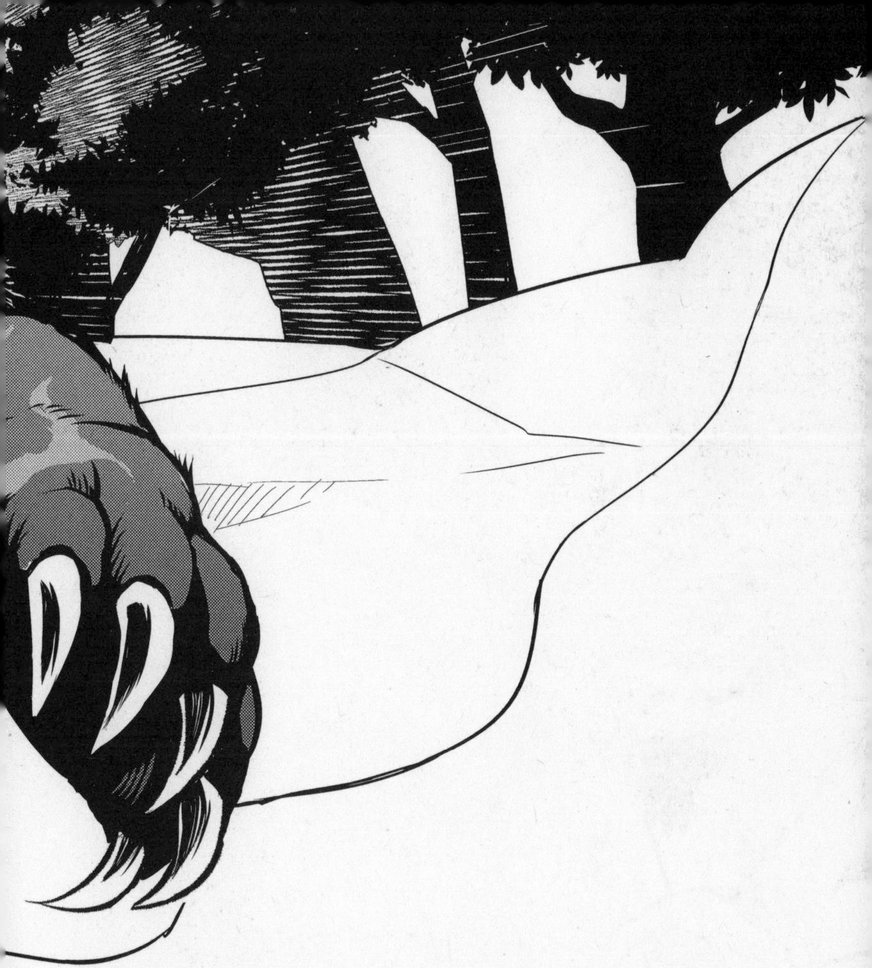

THE STRONGEST SAGE WITH THE WEAKEST CREST

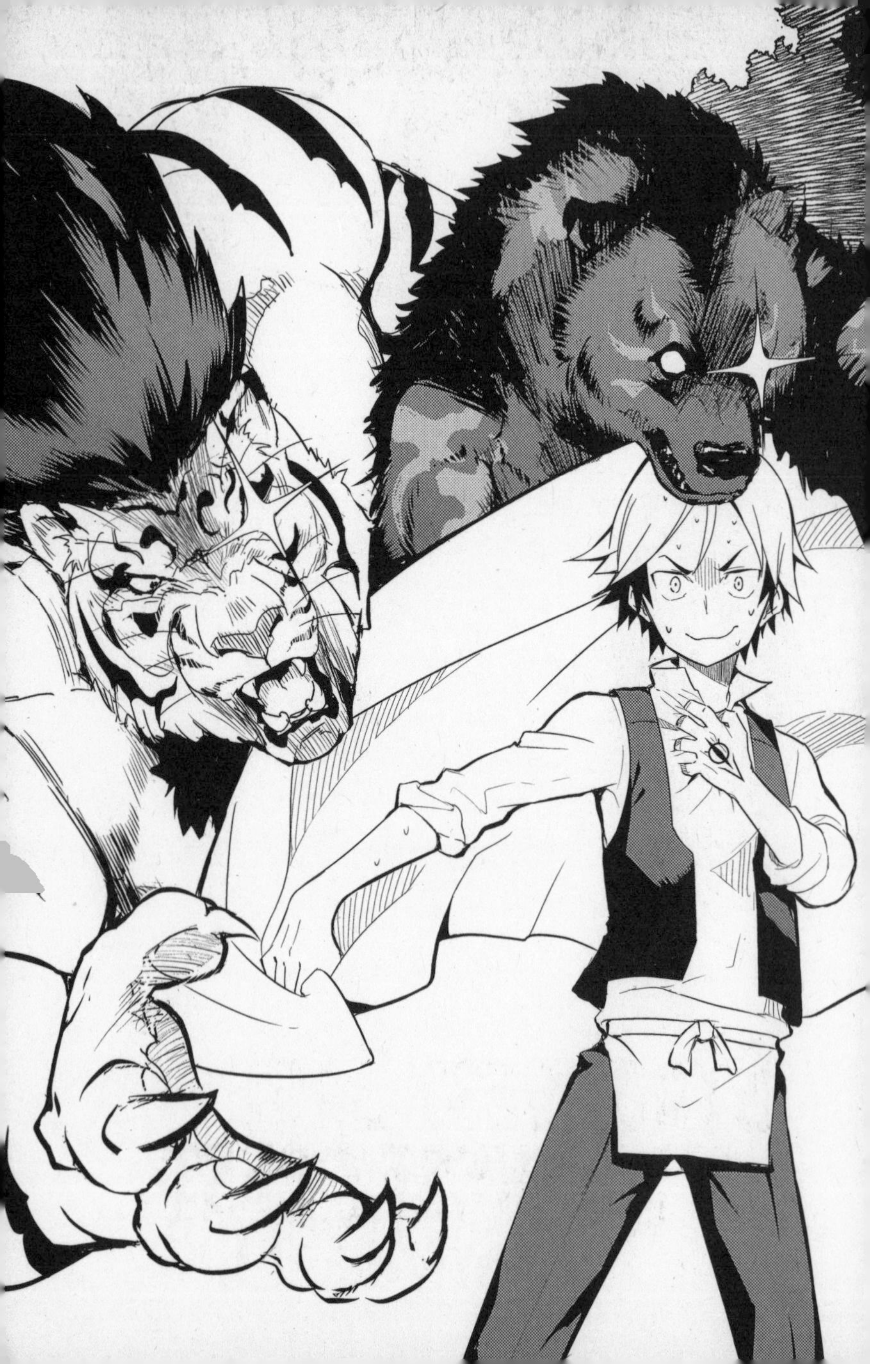

THE STRONGEST SAGE WITH THE WEAKEST CREST

To read a brand-new short story by Shinkoshoto, the author of *The Strongest Sage with the Weakest Crest*, please turn to the end of this book, where you'll find the story presented in left-to-right reading order!!

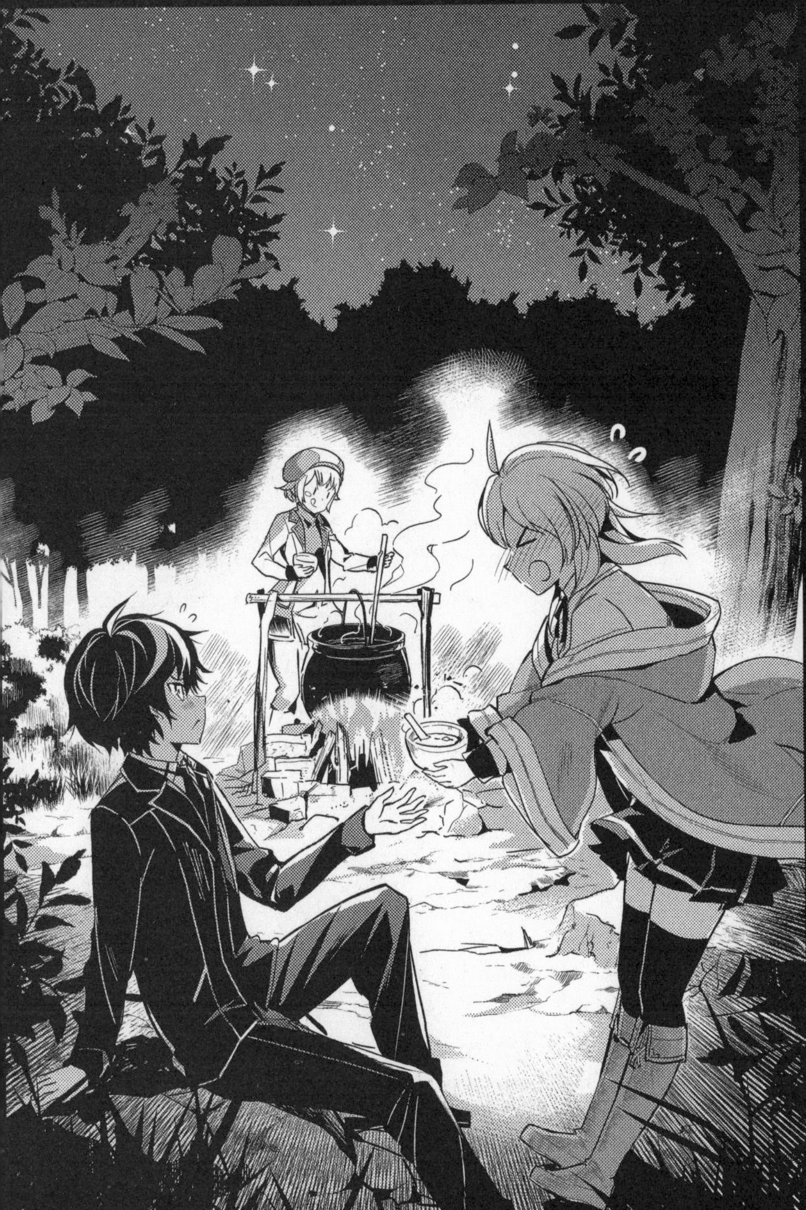

overdone it, but we weren't denied our acclaim, so...

All's well that ends well, I suppose.

The real hurdle came next.

"Your second trial: Culinary Training!" boomed the headmaster. "You'll take the locally sourced ingredients and materials you've hunted down here and turn them into something edible! But to conserve your magic power, use of spells is forbidden!"

Now this was worthwhile training, since feeding oneself with whatever happens to be on hand is an important element of surviving out in the wilds. But that special restriction hurt.

"No magic allowed, huh?" I muttered.

"Cooking's, uh, not exactly my forte," said Alma. "The last stew I attempted to make literally blew up in my face..."

I wouldn't call myself a bad cook, but the problem was, any cooking I'd ever done always relied on magic. Being asked to whip up a meal without spells was going to be something of a challenge.

On the other hand, I was impressed by Alma's claim; getting a watery stew to combust takes real talent.

"Please leave the cooking to me!" declared Lurie, who stepped forth and stood tall after seeing the despair on our faces. "That's right! I'm actually an excellent cook, and it's like Mother always said, 'A man's stomach is the quickest way to his...' Well, you know!"

"My stomach leads to what, exactly?" I asked.

I hadn't the faintest what she was talking about, but suffice it to say, Lurie's food was delicious.

Indeed, I was blessed with a talented pair of teammates.

THE END

"Um, you aren't joining us, Matty?" said Lurie.

"That sword of yours is more than enough! Here it comes!"

The Scarlet Wolf charged for Lurie.

"Hyaah!"

The magiblade cleaved through the wolf like a hot knife through butter, rending it cleanly in two. The weapon's leftover momentum sent Lurie pitching forward before she could stop herself.

"That one didn't put up much of a fight..." she ventured.

She still wasn't used to her new weapon, it seemed. While an ordinary sword would require that extra oomph and then some, simply connecting with the magiblade was enough to get the job done.

"Right through the bones and all, wow... That sword never fails to impress... But why'd you step back, Li'l Matty? You notice something we haven't?" asked Alma.

It definitely would've been faster for me to fell these monsters, but I had my reasons.

"The headmaster personally told me to avoid slaying."

"Trying to even the odds for the other parties? I guess they wouldn't stand a chance if you were going all-out, huh?" said Alma.

"I wasn't given a clear explanation," I said. "But he didn't say anything about you girls holding back, so we should still aim to win this thing!"

"Heck yeah!"

And sure enough, a few hours later...

"The winners: Team Matthias!"

It turned out our haul had ten times the value of that of the second place party. It still felt like we'd somehow

"But they're just as low-level as the ones everyone else is hunting. Getting surrounded could be dangerous, but I can use my Passive Detect to figure out where they all are. As long as we're picking them off one by one, those fights we can win."

I walked in the direction of the nearest beast, but its aura seemed to be above and off to the side.

"Uh, what's 'Passive Detect'?" queried Alma.

Does she really have no clue?

Passive Detect lets the caster search for magical auras and nail down their positions. It's one of the most fundamental spells around.

How were they planning to hunt without it?

While wondering, I used the spell to pinpoint our fellow academy trainees. Sure enough, their auras were all roving about, completely ignoring the actual locations of the creatures. They were utterly in the dark, hunting blindly.

Wow, seriously? I thought, lamenting the state of magic in this current era before offering an explanation.

"Passive Detect is a spell that tells you where monsters are based on their auras. We should come across one soon, in fact," I said, pointing to a spot ahead.

No sooner had I done so than a red canid leapt out at us—a Scarlet Wolf.

"Whoa, you were right on the money!" exclaimed Alma.

"It appears to be a Scarlet Wolf..." murmured Lurie.

"And it's coming our way."

Prepared to counter the monster, Lurie raised the magiblade I'd enchanted for her a few days ago, while Alma unsheathed her own sword. Seeing the two girls in battle-ready stances, I gave them some room.

"Great! One last warning. The far side of this forest is rife with danger, so be sure not to lose your way! Now let the training begin!"

Just as the speech ended, the students began to scamper.

"Over there! Let's hustle!"

"You remember the spot we're heading to, right? Move those legs!"

Apparently, the other parties had put together battle plans in advance, and they scattered in every direction without a moment's hesitation.

"Everyone sure is in a big hurry..." I said.

"Makes sense. I heard these woods weren't exactly crawling with monsters. If we drag our feet, we might come up empty-handed..." clarified Lurie.

"Seriously?!" said Alma. "In that case, we'd better get a move on too!"

It was true. I couldn't detect many bestial auras in the immediate area. But I had a better strategy that didn't involve competing for scarce resources.

"No need to rush," I said. "There's plenty of quarry over that way."

"That way? The way the headmaster told us not to go 'cos we'd get lost...?" asked Alma.

"Sure, he gave us that warning...but I don't see anyone stopping us, do you?"

With that, I made for the far end of the forest. I sensed a few of the professors shooting glances at me, but just as I suspected, none of them lifted a finger.

"You sure about this, Matty? I feel like they gave us that warning for a reason..." said Alma.

"It's true there are hordes of monsters this way," I said.